Martha Starr-McCluer

Issues in Pension Economics

A National Bureau
of Economic Research
Project Report

Issues in Pension Economics

Edited by Zvi Bodie, John B. Shoven, and David A. Wise

The University of Chicago Press

Chicago and London

Zvi Bodie is professor of finance at Boston University. John B. Shoven is professor of economics at Stanford University. David A. Wise is the John F. Stambaugh Professor of Political Economy at the John F. Kennedy School of Government, Harvard University.

The University of Chicago Press, Chicago 60637
The University of Chicago Press, Ltd., London

Library of Congress Cataloging in Publication Data

Issues in pension economics.

(A National Bureau of Economic Research project report)
 Bibliography: p.
 Includes indexes.
 1. Pension trusts—United States—Congresses.
2. Corporations—United States—Finance—Congresses.
3. Pensions—United States—Finance—Congresses.
I. Bodie, Zvi. II. Shoven, John B. III. Wise,
David A. IV. Series.
HD7105.45.U6I62 1987   331.25′2′0973   86-19346
ISBN 0-226-06284-8

Relation of the Directors to the
Work and Publications of the
National Bureau of Economic Research

1. The object of the National Bureau of Economic Research is to ascertain and to present to the public important economic facts and their interpretation in a scientific and impartial manner. The Board of Directors is charged with the responsibility of ensuring that the work of the National Bureau is carried on in strict conformity with this object.

2. The President of the National Bureau shall submit to the Board of Directors, or to its Executive Committee, for their formal adoption all specific proposals for research to be instituted.

3. No research report shall be published by the National Bureau until the President has sent each member of the Board a notice that a manuscript is recommended for publication and that in the President's opinion it is suitable for publication in accordance with the principles of the National Bureau. Such notification will include an abstract or summary of the manuscript's content and a response form for use by those Directors who desire a copy of the manuscript for review. Each manuscript shall contain a summary drawing attention to the nature and treatment of the problem studied, the character of the data and their utilization in the report, and the main conclusions reached.

4. For each manuscript so submitted, a special committee of the Directors (including Directors Emeriti) shall be appointed by majority agreement of the President and Vice Presidents (or by the Executive Committee in case of inability to decide on the part of the President and Vice Presidents), consisting of three Directors selected as nearly as may be one from each general division of the Board. The names of the special manuscript committee shall be stated to each Director when notice of the proposed publication is submitted to him. It shall be the duty of each member of the special manuscript committee to read the manuscript. If each member of the manuscript committee signifies his approval within thirty days of the transmittal of the manuscript, the report may be published. If at the end of that period any member of the manuscript committee withholds his approval, the President shall then notify each member of the Board, requesting approval or disapproval of publication, and thirty days additional shall be granted for this purpose. The manuscript shall then not be published unless at least a majority of the entire Board who shall have voted on the proposal within the time fixed for the receipt of votes shall have approved.

5. No manuscript may be published, though approved by each member of the special manuscript committee, until forty-five days have elapsed from the transmittal of the report in manuscript form. The interval is allowed for the receipt of any memorandum of dissent or reservation, together with a brief statement of his reasons, that any member may wish to express; and such memorandum of dissent or reservation shall be published with the manuscript if he so desires. Publication does not, however, imply that each member of the Board has read the manuscript, or that either members of the Board in general or the special committee have passed on its validity in every detail.

6. Publications of the National Bureau issued for informational purposes concerning the work of the Bureau and its staff, or issued to inform the public of activities of Bureau staff, and volumes issued as a result of various conferences involving the National Bureau shall contain a specific disclaimer noting that such publication has not passed through the normal review procedures required in this resolution. The Executive Committee of the Board is charged with review of all such publications from time to time to ensure that they do not take on the character of formal research reports of the National Bureau, requiring formal Board approval.

7. Unless otherwise determined by the Board or exempted by the terms of paragraph 6, a copy of this resolution shall be printed in each National Bureau publication.

(Resolution adopted October 25, 1926, as revised through September 30, 1974)

Contents

Acknowledgments

This volume consists of papers presented at a conference held at the Hotel del Coronado, San Diego, California, 13–14 April 1984, and is part of the National Bureau of Economic Research ongoing project on the economics of the United States pension system. The work reported here was sponsored by the United States Department of Health and Human Services. Earlier work on the project was supported by the following organizations: American Telephone and Telegraph Company, The Boeing Company, E. I. du Pont de Nemours and Company, Exxon Corporation, Ford Motor Company, IBM Corporation, the Lilly Endowment, The Procter and Gamble Fund, and the Sarah Scaife Foundation, Inc. The authors are grateful to Karen Prindle for guiding them and this volume through the editorial process.

Any opinions expressed in this volume are those of the respective authors and do not necessarily reflect the views of the National Bureau of Economic Research or any of the sponsoring organizations.

1   Introduction

Zvi Bodie, John B. Shoven, and David A. Wise

1.1   Introduction

For the past three decades the rapid growth of pension plans has been one of the most significant institutional influences in United States labor and financial markets. Furthermore, the past growth trend seems likely to continue into the future indefinitely. In order to study the economic effects of this development, the NBER embarked on a major research project which began in 1980.

This book represents the third in a series of four conference volumes reporting the findings of that study. The first volume, *Financial Aspects of the United States Pension System* (1983), included analysis of the financial soundness of the private pension system, the rights and obligations of plan sponsors and beneficiaries, the impact of inflation and cost-of-living adjustments of pension benefits, and the financial status of the elderly. The second volume, *Pensions, Labor, and Individual Choice* (1985), dealt with the incentive effects of pension plans and the labor market and distributional impacts of social security. The present volume covers a broader range of pension issues than the previous two, and makes use of new and richer data sources that have subsequently become available. The papers were originally presented at a conference held in San Diego, California, on April 13–14, 1984. We have included the discussants' comments for each paper.

In this introduction we intend to give the reader an overview of the issues discussed and the findings reported in the papers. We have grouped

Zvi Bodie is professor of finance, Boston University, and research associate, National Bureau of Economic Research. John B. Shoven is professor of economics, Stanford University, and research associate, National Bureau of Economic Research. David A. Wise is the John F. Stambaugh Professor of Political Economy, John F. Kennedy School of Government, Harvard University, and research associate, National Bureau of Economic Research.

the papers into four parts: (1) Pensions and Corporate Finance; (2) Pensions and Retirement Income Adequacy; (3) Pensions and Savings Behavior; and (4) Pensions and the Labor Market.

1.2 Pensions and Corporate Finance

There is a presumption on the part of the public and their elected representatives that pension plans sponsored by private corporations should be managed exclusively in the best interests of the beneficiaries of those plans. This presumption has always been the cornerstone of public policy toward pensions in the United States and was codified by Congress in the Employee Retirement Income Security Act of 1974 (ERISA). It is also the rationale for the tax-exempt status conferred on pension funds by Congress and for the provision of pension insurance through the Pension Benefit Guaranty Corporation (PBGC).

There is a justifiable concern that the use of pension fund assets for corporate purposes might violate the primary purpose of insuring retirement income adequacy for employees. Recently, such topics as corporations' right to terminate overfunded plans and retrieve surplus assets, the contribution of corporate securities and leaseholds to pension funds in lieu of cash, and the burden of unfunded liabilities on the PBGC have, therefore, become matters of intense debate and public scrutiny.

There is, of course, no necessary conflict between the interests of a corporation's shareholders and the interests of its employees in the pension plans sponsored by the corporation. Indeed, in the case of defined contribution pension plans (i.e., those in which the sponsor discharges his obligation by making contributions to the fund in the employee's name) the employer simply acts as a steward for the pension assets, which are held in trust for the employees. Such plans are not covered by PBGC insurance, but for defined benefit plans (i.e., those in which the employer is obliged to pay a retirement benefit determined according to a formula based on the employee's years of service and earnings history) the situation is more complex. In a defined benefit plan the employee has a claim on the employer equal in value to the present value of his or her vested accrued benefits under the plan's benefit formula. The plan's assets, in effect, serve as collateral for this claim.

In a number of papers, some of which were included in the first NBER pension volume in this project (Bodie and Shoven 1983), NBER researchers have explored the theoretical consequences of corporate pension policy under the assumption that management acts exclusively in the best interests of shareholders with regard to funding its pension plan and managing the pension assets. From this perspective, defined benefit liabilities are just one more set of fixed financial liabilities of the firm. Pension assets, while collateral for these liabilities, are really just assets of the firm in that the surplus/deficit belongs to the firm's shareholders.

This view explicitly ignores the interests of the beneficiaries, in part because their defined benefits are insured by the PBGC anyway. From the corporate financial perspective, then, the beneficiaries are protected by the government, and the corporate pension decisions become what amounts to a game between the corporation and various government agencies and interests, a game that can be thought of as an integral part of corporate financial policy.

The tax effects are the first, and for most companies the most important, part of this game. Because firms can effectively earn a pretax rate of return on any assets held in the pension fund and pass these returns through to shareholders much as if the pension fund were an Individual Retirement Account (IRA) or Keogh plan, the comparative advantage of a pension fund lies in its ability to be invested in the most heavily taxed assets.

Presumably this means that pension funds should be invested entirely in taxable bonds, as opposed to common stock, real estate, or other assets that are in effect taxed at lower marginal tax rates for most shareholders. Furthermore, the corporation should fund its pension plan to the maximum extent allowed by the Internal Revenue Service so as to maximize the value of this tax shelter to shareholders. The tax effects of pensions should therefore induce corporations to follow extreme policies—fully funded (indeed overfunded) pension plans with the pension assets invested entirely in taxable bonds.

A second effect results from government insurance of the firm's pension liabilities. Briefly, the PBGC's insurance of pension benefits gives the firm a put option—it can shed its pension liabilities by giving the PBGC the assets in the pension plan plus 30% of the market value of its net worth. As with any option, the value of this put increases with the risk of the underlying asset. Thus, as long as the PBGC neither regulates pension fund risk nor accelerates its own claim at the first sign of financial distress, the firm has an incentive to undermine the PBGC's claim. It can do so and maximize the value of its put option by funding its pension plan only to the minimum permissible extent and investing the pension assets in the riskiest possible securities. These policies are, of course, exactly opposite those suggested by the tax effects described above.

Combining these two effects, the tax effect and the PBGC put, the firm can be viewed as facing a trade-off. By overfunding and investing in bonds it maximizes tax benefits, but by underfunding and investing in risky assets it maximizes the value of the pension put. This trade-off does not produce a set of unique interior optimal policies, but rather implies that each firm should be following one of two very different extreme policies. If the firm is profitable and relatively safe, the pension put will probably have negligible value. Hence the firm should fully fund its pension plan and invest entirely in the most heavily taxed securities. On the other hand, if the firm is both unprofitable and risky, the tax shelter may be superfluous, and the pension put may be quite valuable. In order to maximize its value, the firm should underfund its plan to the greatest extent possible and invest entirely in the riskiest securities.

A third effect has emphasized the pension fund's usefulness as a source of corporate liquidity or as a store of temporarily excess corporate funds. The view that firms will maintain some financial slack has a long informal history based on the notion that they do not wish to be caught having to rely on external financing at "unfavorable" times.

Such slack could be kept in the form of either liquid assets and unused debt capacity or pension assets. The latter is advantageous from a tax standpoint, but liquid assets and unused debt capacity are presumably substantially more accessible, particularly in the short run. While firms have increasingly attempted to tap their excess pension assets in recent years, the legality and regulatory status of these attempts has yet to be clearly defined. One might, therefore, expect firms to trade tax benefits against accessibility in deciding how much of their financial slack to keep in the pension fund. The stronger are a firm's earnings and the greater its need for tax shelter, the greater will be its tendency to build financial slack in the form of additional pension assets, and vice versa.

Together, these different aspects of corporate pensions (the tax shelter, the PBGC put, and the accessibility of financial slack) form a corporate financial perspective on pension policy, which can be contrasted with the more traditional perspective which views the pension plan as entirely separate from the corporation's other assets and liabilities and managed strictly in the interests of the covered employees. Is the corporate financial perspective supported or confirmed by the data we have on corporate pension funding and asset allocation?

Previous attempts to test the theory empirically have been hampered by lack of appropriate data. In particular, information was lacking on the discount rate used by firms in computing the present value of their pension liabilities. Reported pension liabilities are very sensitive to this discount rate. The higher the rate, the lower the reported liability. Thus, different firms having the same funding status in reality might appear to have very different pension liabilities simply because they choose different discount rates.

The empirical research reported in the paper, "Funding and Asset Allocation in Corporate Pension Plans: An Empirical Investigation," by Zvi Bodie, Jay O. Light, Randall Mørck, and Robert A. Taggart, Jr., which uses a new data set containing this variable, indicates that the discount rate chosen by a firm is systematically related to its financial condition and therefore, unless all firms' liabilities are adjusted to a uniform rate, the true cross-sectional relationship between financial condition and funding status is obscured. In particular it shows that less profitable firms tend to choose higher discount rates and thus to report lower pension liabilities.

The empirical results on funding and asset allocation lend some support to the corporate financial perspective. First, there is a significant positive relationship between firm profitability and the degree of pension funding. Second, there is also some evidence that firms facing higher risk and lower tax liabilities are less inclined to fund their pension plans fully. Third, a significant fraction of firms invest their pension assets entirely in fixed income securities, and the proportion of assets allocated to fixed income securities is positively related to the level of funding. The results also indicate that the traditional and corporate financial perspectives on pension decisions are far from mutually exclusive. Across firms, the asset allocation findings suggest that the corporate financial perspective may be more appropriate in describing small pension plans, while larger plans appear to take on some of the characteristics of the traditional perspective. Moreover, even within the same firm, different plans may be more appropriately viewed from one perspective or the other depending on their level of PBGC insurance coverage.

The rules of the game regarding PBGC insurance of corporate defined benefit plans may be changing, however. Both the rate structure and the rules for voluntary termination of underfunded plans are being examined by Congress. The possibility of a graduated premium rate schedule based on risk is being considered, as is the elimination of voluntary terminations of underfunded plans.

The paper in this volume by Alan J. Marcus, "Corporate Pension Policy and the Value of PBGC Insurance," develops an analytical model which can give quantitative consideration to these issues. As noted before, PBGC insurance can be viewed as a put option provided by the government to the firm's shareholders. Marcus applies modern options pricing methodology to derive the value of this put under two scenarios. The first allows for voluntary termination of an underfunded plan, which is still legal under current statutes. In practice, however, virtually all terminations of underfunded pension plans occur as a by-product of corporate bankruptcy, and there is good reason to believe that the law will be changed to eliminate the voluntary termination of underfunded plans altogether. In the second scenario Marcus examines the effect of such a prohibition.

Under each scenario Marcus presents empirical estimates of the "fair market value" of the insurance provided by the PBGC for a sample of Fortune 100 firms. The results indicate that the magnitudes of the put values can differ substantially from the common measure, which is accrued benefits less the sum of fund assets plus 30% of firm net worth. Taking these estimated values as the measure of the PBGC's liability, a small number of firms appear to account for the bulk of these liabilities. Presumably, a risk-related premium structure based on the computed put values would result in drastic differences from the current structure of a flat amount per covered employee regardless of the firm's or its pension plan's financial status.

Prohibiting voluntary termination of underfunded plans drastically reduces the calculated value of the PBGC put. But, probably the main contribution of Marcus's paper is that it offers a starting point for devising a fair, operational risk-related premium structure for PBGC insurance.

In the final paper in the area of pensions and corporate finance, "How Does the Market Value Unfunded Pension Liabilities?" Jeremy I. Bulow, Randall Mørck, and Lawrence Summers confirm earlier analyses by Feldstein and others suggesting that the stock market valuation of firms reasonably accurately reflects their pension funding status. Their new contribution is in the methodology and broader data set they employ. Instead of using a straight cross-section test, they use a combination of time series and cross section.

1.3   Pensions and Retirement Income Adequacy

The two papers in this section deal with the role of pensions in providing an adequate and secure retirement income.

In the first, "Concepts and Measures of Earnings Replacement during Retirement," Michael J. Boskin and John B. Shoven present an examination of some of the issues surrounding the measurement of the well-being of the elderly relative to their previous standard of living, or so-called replacement rates. Among the issues they raise are the treatment of taxes, expenses of raising children, health and health care costs, income uncertainty, and uncertainty about the date of death. They actually adjust their data for three of these.

Taxes are adjusted to reflect the special provisions of the tax code affecting the elderly. For example, until 1984 social security benefits have been completely tax free, and even now such benefits are tax preferred relative to earnings in the working years. The elderly also have extra personal exemptions. Next a correction is made for family size. During the working life, typically there are children to care for, while in retirement there are only one or two individuals who do not need as much money as they did before. The third adjustment deals with uncertainty of income, and the argument is as follows. When a person is young there is substantial uncertainty surrounding the value of his future earnings, whereas by the time of retirement, social security benefits in particular are relatively certain. Boskin and Shoven, therefore, adjust the value of social security benefits to reflect their lower risk.

The paper then computes two measures of replacement adjusted in these three ways. The first is social security benefits relative to pre-retirement earnings and the second includes other sources of income including private pensions in the numerator.

The results in general indicate that fully adjusted replacement rates are very high for most people. They suggest that, for many of the elderly, earnings are virtually fully replaced by social security alone; for many more, social security replaces a large fraction of earnings; and total post-retirement income usually exceeds pre-retirement earnings.

In their paper, "Pension Plan Integration as Insurance against Social Security Risk," Robert C. Merton, Zvi Bodie, and Alan J. Marcus focus on a hitherto unexplored aspect of the integration of pension plans with social security. The manifest purposes of integrating an employer-provided pension plan with social security are (1) to insure adequate retirement income for all covered employees, and (2) to insure equity in retirement income defined as total replacement rates that are equal for all employees regardless of salary level. The focus of the authors' paper is on an equally important consequence of integration: the alteration of the risk-bearing relationships between employees, employers, and the government vis-à-vis social security benefits. The main alteration is that the employer, in effect, insures his covered employees against adverse changes in their social security (retirement) benefits. Using the option-pricing methodology of modern contingent claims analysis, the authors develop a formal model to explore the quantitative aspects of this change.

While the focus of the analysis is on full integration, the authors explicitly deal with various degrees of partial integration as is currently practiced. The authors analyze the effects of a switch from a nonintegrated to an equivalent-cost integrated plan when private benefits are fixed in nominal terms and when they are indexed. They also consider the effects of ad hoc post-retirement benefit increases and the incentive effects on worker mobility of the adoption of integrated plans.

The most important finding is that for a common type of integrated plan (i.e., an offset plan) covered employees at the high end of the earnings spectrum in effect are selling part of their rights to social security to the plan sponsor. They are, therefore, trading a claim against the social security system for a claim against the firm. At the low end of the earnings spectrum employees are maintaining much more of their claim to social security and obtaining insurance from the firm only against drastic reductions in the starting level of benefits.

1.4   Pensions and Savings Behavior

How do pensions, including social security, affect saving? This is a question which has received much attention from economists in the last few years, probably because pensions and social security have become such large economic institutions at the same time that the U.S. saving rate was perceived to be grossly inadequate. In the literature on the effect of social security on saving, Martin S. Feldstein's paper (1974) is seminal. In that study, Feldstein investigated how social security affects aggregate consumption, saving, and the nation's capital stock. His analysis emphasized the unfunded (pay-as-you-go) nature of the system. That is, he recognized that there is no social wealth or capital stock corresponding to the apparent wealth that individuals accumulate (the right to a future stream of retirement income). In his analysis, Feldstein found that the private rate of saving would be doubled if social security did not exist. The "false" wealth substituted for real capital accumulation dollar for dollar.

Two papers in this volume address a related issue and another reason why social security may reduce private saving. "Uncertain Lifetimes, Pensions, and Individual Saving," by R. Glenn Hubbard, and "Annuity Markets, Savings, and the Capital Stock," by Laurence J. Kotlikoff, John B. Shoven, and Avia Spivak, examine the effect of annuity markets (that is, the availability of longevity insurance) on saving. Both papers examine the consumption and saving behavior of risk-averse individuals facing uncertainty about the length of their life. In the absence of longevity insurance, people save in a precautionary way to provide for the possibility of living a long life. This is accomplished by reduced consumption and, on average, results in sizable unintended bequests. If annuity markets are perfected (and, importantly, social security benefits are paid out in an inflation-adjusted annuity form), both saving and bequests are reduced. The Kotlikoff, Shoven, and Spivak paper estimates that the introduction of a fully funded actuarially fair retirement annuity program would reduce the steady-state rate of saving and capital stock from 35% to 60%. Clearly, both papers are stylized simulations, but they do indicate that the annuity form of the payout of social security (given the substantial inperfections of private annuity markets) may depress saving as much as its unfunded pay-as-you-go nature.

The Kotlikoff, Shoven, and Spivak paper and the Hubbard paper differ in their modeling of the counterfactual non–social security state of the world. Hubbard has each family facing its longevity uncertainty alone with the resultant unintended bequests given to the children. Kotlikoff, Shoven, and Spivak, on the other hand, argue that substantial insurance-type risk pooling can be achieved within the family itself, and therefore model the non–social security state as one wherein family members pool longevity risks. In general, the existence of this inter-family contract would reduce the effect of the governmet or the private sector introducing actuarially fair annuity measures. The Kotlikoff, Shoven, and Spivak paper also examines the equilibrium distribution of wealth in their model, where everyone has the same earnings profile. A nondegenerate but discontinuous wealth distribution results from the model with an individual's wealth depending on the sequence of life spans of his ancestors.

The paper "Dissaving after Retirement: Testing the Pure Life Cycle Hypothesis," by B. Douglas Bernheim, involves a more empircal examination of saving and dissaving after retirement. The first question investigated is simply whether the elderly dissave or save during retirement. Bernheim provides new answers to this question looking at both bequeathable wealth and total wealth (that is, including the value of retirement annuities). The data set is the Retirement History Survey, so he is able to follow households longitudinally.

The advantage of this approach is that it does not require the strong assumption necessary to address the question with cross-sectional data. He finds some dissaving during retirement, particularly among single individuals and early retirees.

Bernheim investigates whether the observed patterns of saving and dissaving are consistent with the testable hypothesis following from the pure life cycle theory. He discovers that the empirical findings, in general, reject the implications of that model.

1.5 Pensions and the Labor Market

The two papers in this section employ data on characteristics of actual defined benefit plans to infer the incentive effects of these plans on labor market behavior and the implications of the plans for different demographic groups.

In their paper, "The Incentive Effects of Private Pension Plans," Laurence J. Kotlikoff and David A. Wise find that there is a strikingly wide variation in the incentive effects of pension plans. Typical plan designs provide a strong incentive for retirement at the plan's normal retirement age, and several plan types provide a strong incentive to retire at the age of early retirement.

For example, many plans have both early and normal retirement at age 55. For these plans, the average decline in the rate of pension accrual at age 55 is equivalent to about 30% of salary. If a person under these plans continued to work to age 65, pension accrual would be negative and equivalent to approximately 30% of earnings. Thus, between the ages of 54 and 65, the fall in the rate of pension accrual is approximately equivalent to a 60% salary reduction. The more common plans, with early retirement at age 55 and normal retirement at age 65, call, on average, for increasing rates of pension benefit accrual up to age 55 with a decline thereafter. However, the decline in accrual rates between the ages of 55 and 65 is not nearly as dramatic as the decline ascribed to plans that have both early and normal retirement at age 55. Under the more common plans, at age 65 pension wealth declines substantially.

Only under plans with both early and normal retirement at age 65 does pension wealth continue to increase until age 65. But even under plans with these provisions, the rate of pension accrual after age 65 drops precipitously. In this case, the averge loss in pension wealth from working an additional year would be approximately equivalent to 40% of salary. In short, typical plans provide a strong incentive to work up to the age of early retirement, then an incentive to leave the labor force that gets stronger every year until the age of normal retirement, when the incentive increases dramatically.

Even among plans with the same early and normal retirement ages, there is a wide range in plan provisions. While the typical plan may provide positive pension accrual rates at some age—say 62—the accrual rate may be substantially negative for some plans. But even a small proportion of plans that provide a strong incentive to retire at a given age could have a substantial effect on aggregate labor force participation rates.

For some employees, vesting could be a very important determinant of labor force participation. The accrual rate at the age of vesting can range from as low as 2% of wage earnings to as high as 100%, depending on the plan type and the age of initial employment. Given normal and early retirement ages, there is little difference in plan accrual profiles by industry or by occupation. Differences in pension benefits by industry depend more on the type of plan than on variations among plans with the same basic provision. Because women typically live longer than men, accrued pension benefits at any age are higher for women than for men, about 13% on average at age 65, for example. The authors conclude that the rapid increase in pension plan coverage over the past two or three decades may well have contributed substantially to the reduction in labor force participation of older workers during this period. The plans may also have an important effect on labor mobility.

In their paper, "Pension Inequality," Edward P. Lazear and Sherwin Rosen focus on how the size of a pension tends to vary with the sex and race of the individual, conditional on the individual's having a pension. Using data from the May 1979 Current Population Survey, they first try to determine the average tenure, age, and salary of the typical retiree by sex and race. They then use the 1980 Bankers Trust *Corporate Pension Plan Study* to derive data on pension plan characteristics. Their computations suggest that pension plans may exacerbate black-white compensation inequality while reducing male-female compensation inequality. Even though females are less likely than males to work in jobs entitling them to pensions, females who are eligible for pensions do receive relatively generous ones. The average pension that the typical retiring female receives is well below that of the typical male retiree, but the difference is not as pronounced as male-female differences in salary.

References

Bodie, Zvi, and Shoven, John B., eds. 1983. *Financial aspects of the United States pension system.* Chicago: University of Chicago Press.

Feldstein, Martin S. 1974. Social security, induced retirement, and aggregate capital accumulation. Journal of Political Economy 82 (October): 905–26.

Wise, David A., ed. 1985. *Pensions, labor, and individual choice.* Chicago: University of Chicago Press.

I   Pensions and Corporate Finance

2 Funding and Asset Allocation in Corporate Pension Plans: An Empirical Investigation

Zvi Bodie, Jay O. Light, Randall Mørck, and Robert A. Taggart, Jr.

2.1 Introduction

Financial aspects of corporate pension funds have increasingly attracted the attention of corporate managers, government officials, and academics. For example, practitioners have been debating such topics as corporations' right to terminate overfunded plans and retrieve surplus assets (Hawthorne 1983; Louis 1983; Smith 1983), the contribution of corporate securities and leaseholds to pension funds in lieu of cash (Webman 1983), and the burden of unfunded liabilities on the Pension Benefit Guaranty Corporation (PBGC) (Colvin 1982; Munnell 1982). Among academics, interest has centered on the tax and incentive aspects of corporate pensions. Models of optimal capital structure have yielded new implications for plan funding and investment (Black 1980; Tepper 1981), while advances in option pricing theory have illuminated the perverse incentives created by PBGC insurance (Sharpe 1976; Treynor 1977).

As yet, however, there has been relatively little empirical work done on corporate pension funding and asset allocation. Studies by Friedman (1983) and Westerfield and Marshall (1983) have produced interesting findings, but many details remain to be filled in before a clear picture

Zvi Bodie is professor of finance, Boston University, and research associate, National Bureau of Economic Research. Jay O. Light is professor of business administration, Harvard University, and research associate, National Bureau of Economic Research. Randall Mørck is assistant professor of finance, Boston University, and consultant, National Bureau of Economic Research. Robert A. Taggart, Jr., is professor of finance, Boston University, and research associate, National Bureau of Economic Research.

We are grateful to Roger Ibbotson, Krishna Palepu, and Myron Scholes for helpful suggestions on an earlier draft. Funding from the United States Department of Health and Human Services is gratefully acknowledged.

of these decisions can emerge. Our purpose in this study is to add to the stock of empirical knowledge and to pay particular attention to the ability of current theory to explain our findings.

In section 2.2 we outline two different perspectives on corporate pension decisions, the traditional perspective and the corporate financial perspective, the latter of which includes the recent theoretical work on corporate pensions mentioned above. In section 2.3, we review the small body of previous empirical evidence. In section 2.4, we discuss a significant empirical problem, namely, that firms have considerable latitude in reporting their pension liabilities and may thus obscure the true cross-sectional relationship between funding status and financial condition.

In section 2.5 we discuss our data sources and present our results. We find that there is indeed a significant inverse relationship between firms' profitability and the discount rates they choose to report their pension liabilities. In view of this we adjust all reported pension liabilities to a common discount rate assumption. We then find a significant positive relationship between firm profitability and the degree of pension funding, as is consistent with the corporate financial perspective. We also find some evidence that firms facing higher risk and lower tax liabilities are less inclined to fully fund their pension plans. On the asset allocation question, we find that the distribution of plan assets invested in bonds is bimodal, but that it does not tend to cluster around extreme portfolio configurations to the extent predicted by the corporate financial perspective. We also find that the percentage of plan assets invested in bonds is negatively related to both total size of plan and the proportion of unfunded liabilities. The latter relationship shows up particularly among the riskiest firms, and is consistent with the corporate financial perspective on pension decisions.

2.2   Alternative Perspectives on Pension Funds

2.2.1   The Traditional Perspective

Defined benefit pension funds are segregated pools of capital that collateralize the future liabilities explicit (and perhaps implicit) in defined benefit plans. Viewed from what we shall call the "traditional perspective," pension funds are entirely separate from the corporation and its shareholders and should be managed without regard to either corporate financial policy or the interests of the corporation and its shareholders.

From this perspective, funding decisions should be based solely upon the expected future stream of employee pension liabilities, irrespective of corporate financial condition and/or policy. Likewise, asset allocation decisions within the fund should be made solely in the best interests of the beneficiaries. Unfortunately, it is quite unclear what asset allocation policy would be best for beneficiaries. For example, if the defined benefit liabilities were really fixed such that beneficiaries would not not and could not share in any surplus of pension assets over liabilities, then the beneficiaries would want a well-funded plan to be invested in the least risky assets, presumably fixed income securities. If, on the other hand, the beneficiaries were able to participate in the ownership of such a surplus, as Miller and Scholes (1981) and Bulow and Scholes (1983) have argued, then the optimal asset allocation would be much less clear and, in principle, could include virtually any mix of stocks and bonds.

2.2.2   The Corporate Financial Perspective

In recent years, academic theorists have built an alternative perspective from which pension decisions are viewed as an integral part of overall corporate financial policy. From this perspective, defined benefit liabilities are just one more set of fixed financial liabilities of the firm. Pension assets, while collateral for these liabilities, are really just assets of the firm in that the surplus/deficit belongs to the firm's shareholders. This integrated perspective is then concerned with how to manage the firm's extended balance sheet, including both its normal assets and liabilities and its pension assets and liabilities, in the best interests of the shareholders. This view explicitly ignores the interests of the beneficiaries, in part because their defined benefits are insured by the PBGC anyway. From the corporate financial perspective, then, the beneficiaries are protected by the government, and the corporate pension decisions become what amount to a game between the corporation and various government agencies and interests, a game that can be and should be thought of as an integral part of corporate financial policy.

The tax effects are the first, and for most companies the most important, part of this game. In closely related papers, Black (1980) and Tepper (1981) argued that the unique feature of pension funds from this integrated perspective is their role as a tax shelter. Because firms can effectively earn a pre-tax rate of return on any assets held in the pension fund and pass these returns through to shareholders much as if the pension fund were an IRA or Keogh plan, the comparative advantage of a pension fund lies in its ability to be invested in the most heavily taxed assets.

Presumably this means that pension funds should be invested entirely in taxable bonds, as opposed to common stock, real estate, or other assets that are in effect taxed at lower marginal tax rates for most shareholders. Black and Tepper further point out that if (and, by the way, only if) the pension fund is invested in more heavily taxed assets such as bonds, the corporation should fund its pension plan to the maximum extent allowed by the IRS so as to maximize the value of this tax shelter to shareholders. The tax effects of pensions should therefore induce corporations to follow extreme policies. Fully funded or overfunded pension plans should place their assets entirely in taxable bonds.

A second effect, which we label the "pension put" effect, is associated with the work of Sharpe (1976) and Treynor (1977). Briefly, the PBGC's insurance of pension benefits gives the firm a put option—it can shed its pension liabilities by giving the PBGC the assets in the pension plan plus 30% of the market value of its net worth. As with any option, the value of this put increases with the risk of the underlying asset. Thus, as long as the PBGC neither regulates pension fund risk nor accelerates its own claim at the first sign of financial distress, the firm has an incentive to undermine the PBGC's claim. It can do so and maximize the value of its put option by funding its pension plan only to the minimum permissible extent and investing the pension assets in the riskiest possible securities. These are, of course, the exact opposite policies from those suggested by the tax effects described above.

It is possible to combine these two effects, the tax effect and the PBGC put, in a joint model, as discussed by Harrison and Sharpe (1983), Bulow (1983), Chen (1983), and Westerfield and Marshall (1983). Thus the firm can be viewed as facing a trade-off—by overfunding and investing in bonds it maximizes tax benefits, but by underfunding and investing in risky assets it maximizes the value of the pension put. However, it can be shown that this trade-off does not produce a set of unique interior optimal policies, but rather implies that each firm should be following one of two very different extreme policies. If the firm is profitable and relatively safe, the pension put will probably have negligible value. Hence the firm should fully fund its pension plan and invest entirely in the most heavily taxed securities. On the other hand, if the firm is both unprofitable and risky, the tax shelter may be superfluous, and the pension put may be quite valuable. In order to maximize its value, the firm should underfund its plan to the greatest extent possible and invest entirely in the riskiest securities.

A third effect, which we label the "financial slack" effect, has emphasized the pension fund's usefulness as a source of corporate liquidity or as a store of temporarily excess corporate funds. The view that firms will maintain some financial slack has a long informal history based on the notion that they do not wish to be caught having to rely on external financing at "unfavorable" times. A more formal version of this idea has recently been developed by Myers and Majluf (1983), who posit that a firm's managers are likely to have better information about its prospects than outside investors. In that event, there is an adverse selection problem, since managers have an incentive to issue more stock when they believe that it is overpriced, and consequently, investors will react negatively to news of a stock issue. Managers therefore maintain some financial slack in order to avoid the necessity of a stock issue.

Such slack could be kept in the form of either liquid assets and unused debt capacity or pension assets. The latter is advantageous from a tax standpoint, but liquid assets and unused debt capacity are presumably substantially more accessible, particularly in the short run. While firms have increasingly attempted to tap their excess pension assets in recent years (Hawthorne 1983; Louis 1983; Smith 1983), the legality and regulatory status of these attempts has yet to be clearly defined. One might therefore expect firms to trade tax benefits against accessibility in deciding how much of their financial slack to keep in the pension fund. As Tepper (1983) has shown, this can, in principle at least, lead to an interior optimum with partial funding. The stronger are a firm's earnings and the greater its need for tax shelter, the greater will be its tendency to build financial slack in the form of additional pension assets, and vice versa.

Together, these different aspects of corporate pensions (the tax shelter, the PBGC put, and the accessibility of financial slack) form what we shall call a corporate financial perspective on pension policy.

2.2.3   Distinguishing among the Perspectives

The two perspectives discussed above are not, of course, mutually exclusive theories or prescriptions for pension fund policies. The traditional perspective emphasizes the separate and segregated role of pension funds and their relationship to the beneficiaries' interests. The corporate financial perspective emphasizes instead the integral role of pension decisions in overall corporate financial policy and its relationship to the shareholders' interests. Clearly, both sets of interests could be determinants of actual corporate pension decisions.

In addition, it is difficult to develop meaningful empirical tests that would distinguish clearly between the two different perspectives. We can, however, make some generalizations in that regard. Suppose, for example, that our cross-sectional tests reveal that companies' pension funding seems to be importantly determined by variables describing the companies' past and present financial condition and/or their tax-paying status. We would interpret this as evidence that funding was being determined in part by the corporate financial perspective, particularly if a stronger financial condition and tax-paying status appeared to be associated with greater funding. If, on the other hand, the degree of funding seemed to be independent of corporate financial condition (or if weaker financial companies actually funded more), we would interpret this as evidence that funding was being determined by the interests of beneficiaries, as in the traditional perspective on pension decisions.

Distinguishing between the two perspectives on the basis of empirical tests of asset allocation is more difficult, particularly because it is not at all clear what asset allocation policy or sets of policies would be consistent with our traditional perspective. Roughly speaking, if the observed frequency distribution of asset allocation across firms is quite bimodal with most firms at one extreme or another, we would interpret this as evidence that the corporate financial perspective is driving asset allocation decisions. In addition, if risky firms with underfunded plans tend to invest in stocks and safe firms with overfunded plans in bonds, we would interpret this as evidence that the corporate financial perspective was influencing asset allocation decisions. We will discuss these alternative interpretations in more detail in section 2.5.

2.3 Existing Evidence

Before proceeding to our own empirical work, it is useful to review the small body of evidence on corporate pensions that currently exists. Friedman (1983) has conducted the most extensive empirical study to date, using IRS Form 5500 data for a broad sample of firms for the year 1977. This source provides data on pension funding and pension asset allocation for the firms in the sample, and Friedman supplemented it with finanical data from the Standard and Poor's Compustat tape.

One of the primary questions that Friedman addressed was whether corporate pension plans can be viewed as an integral part of the overall corporate financing decision. In the terminology of section 2.2 above, he looked for evidence that the corporate financial perspective is an appropriate one from which to view pension decisions. Accordingly, he estimated a number of relationships of the following form: on the left-hand side of the equation appeared some aspect of the pension decision such as unfunded liabilities or the proportion of pension assets invested in bonds; on the right-hand side appeared some measure of conventional financing, such as ordinary balance sheet liabilities, plus one other control variable. Among the control variables used were a number of measures of firm profitability, risk, and tax-paying status.

Friedman concluded that pension decisions are indeed related to other aspects of the corporate financing decision. He found that unfunded pension liabilities and the proportion of pension assets invested in bonds are both positively related to ordinary balance sheet liabilities. He also found that a reverse relationship holds, with balance sheet leverage depending positively on unfunded pension liabilities, regardless of the control variable used.

Such interrelationships would be predicted by the corporate financial perspective. From that perspective, the channels through which pension fund decisions affect firm value are also conditioned by the overall financing decision. Balance sheet leverage affects the firm's tax-paying status, the risk borne by both the PBGC and the firm's employees, and the firm's available borrowing power. Hence the pension and capital structure decisions are tied to the same set of underlying factors. Viewed from the corporate financial perspective, the results that we report below, therefore, concerning the linkages between pension decisions and the firm's tax-paying status, profitability, and risk, should be thought of as reduced-form relationships from a larger system.

While there is some evidence of the related nature of pension and other financing decisions in Friedman's results, the picture becomes clouded when we attempt to identify different effects. The positive relationship between unfunded pension liabilities and ordinary debt, for example, suggests that whatever financial risk firms assume through their pension funds is magnified by their financing decisions. This could be interpreted as an indication that firms with unfunded pension liabilities try to maximize the value of the pension put through balance sheet leverage. However, Friedman's asset allocation results appear to contradict this conclusion. There, greater balance sheet leverage seems to be offset by more conservative investment of pension assets.

The picture that emerges from Friedman's control variables is also clouded. Higher risk, as measured by earnings variability, is associated with pension investment strategies that are more heavily weighted toward bonds. This is consistent with the relationship between leverage and pension asset allocation and could be interpreted as evidence that pension portfolios are managed to protect the beneficiaries, as predicted by the traditional perspective. However, Friedman also found a positive relationship between firm profitability and unfunded pension liabilities, which is hard to reconcile with the traditional perspective. In addition, he could find no relationship between firms' tax-paying status and either their funding or pension investment decisions. Overall, then, Friedman's results do not strongly favor one perspective to the exclusion of the other and indeed convey the feeling that corporate pension decisions are not well understood.

The only other extensive empirical work on the subject that we are aware of is by Westerfield and Marshall (1983). Using quarterly SEC data for approximately 400 corporations over the period from 1972 through 1977, they studied pension asset allocation. They could not attribute any significant change in asset allocation to passage of the Employee Retirement Income Security Act (ERISA) in September of 1974, nor could they find a significant link between the asset mix and the variability of the PBGC's claim on the firm. They did find that the proportion of pension assets invested in stock was positively related

To measure the levels of pension funding for these firms, we first took reported pension liabilities and adjusted them to a common discount rate to correct for any systematic tendencies toward over- or underreporting. We chose 10% for our common rate, since this was approximately the rate used by the PBGC around this time to value the liabilities of terminated plans (Munnell 1982). In the absence of detailed information on the time profile of different firms' pension liabilities, we made the adjustment simply by multiplying each firm's reported liabilities by the ratio of the assumed discount rate to 10%. We used two measures of pension liabilities, adjusting both in the same manner. These were the present value of vested pension benefits and total accrued (that is, vested plus unvested) benefits. We then divided total pension assets (reported in the FASB 36 filings) by each of these liability measures to arrive at two measures of the level of pension funding.

The FASB 36 data did not include a breakdown of pension assets by security type. We were able to obtain asset allocation data from Greenwich Research Associates for a sample of firms, 369 of which overlapped with our FASB 36 sample. As our measure of asset allocation we used the proportion of total pension assets invested in fixed income securities, which include cash and short-term investments, bonds, guaranteed investment contracts, and insured pension plans.[2] We also obtained Greenwich data on the proportion of pension plan participants already retired for each firm. Under the traditional perspective, the allocation of pension assets might be affected by demographic characteristics of the participant pool, and we wished to test this possibility.

The second type of variable for which we needed data was firm profitability. We chose to measure this as 1980 inflation-adjusted return on net assets, or inflation-adjusted operating profits divided by the replacement cost of the firm's assets. These inflation-adjusted data for 1980 were available from FASB Statement 33 filings, but only for 508 of the 939 firms in our original sample.

The choice of this profitability measure was dictated primarily by two considerations. First, if we interpret our equations as reduced-form equations from a larger system, it is appropriate to consider the profitability measure that is driving the full system. Presumably the overall financial structure decision is affected by real profitability rather than some profitability concept that is subject to inflationary distortions. In addition, the reduced-form notion suggests that operating profit, which does not already reflect the firm's leverage choice, is the most appropriate profitability measure.[3] Second, the financial slack effect would seem to depend on a real profitability measure. Inflationary distortions, such as those stemming from inventory profits or understated depreciation, do not truly add to the firm's capacity to build financial slack. While the inflation-adjusted data have these advantages, however, one cost should also be noted. Ideally, several years worth of data might be used to smooth out short-run profitability fluctuations that may have little impact on the firm's decisions. Unfortunately the FASB 33 data are not available for years prior to 1979.

The third type of data we needed was measures of tax-paying status. The chief difficulty here is that taxes reported on firms' financial statements may differ markedly from the taxes they actually pay. However, only the reported figures are available, since the IRS does not disclose actual payments on a disaggregated basis. We decided to try two, admittedly imperfect, measures.

The first of these is the firm's tax loss carry-forward (divided by inflation-adjusted assets as a scaling factor). This variable is reported on the Standard and Poor's Compustat tape for 502 of the firms in our original sample, and it reflects their actual ability to make use of additional tax shields. The larger is the size of the carry-forward, the less likely is the firm to be in a tax-paying position in the immediate future, and hence the less valuable is the tax advantage from pension funding.

A second measure of tax-paying status is the firm's total reported taxes minus the change in deferred taxes over the previous year (again, scaled by inflation-adjusted assets).[4] Substracting the change in deferred tax liabilities provides an approximate adjustment for such practices as using straight-line depreciation for reporting purposes and accelerated depreciation for tax purposes. The data needed to construct this measure were also available on the Compustat tape, this time for 490 of the firms in our original sample.

The fourth variable that we needed to measure was risk. The same argument could be made here that we are really estimating a reduced-form relationship and that we are thus interested in an exogenous, or operating risk, measure. However, the value of the pension put option depends on the firm's total risk, including financial as well as operating risk and unsystematic as well as systematic risk. Since we were particularly interested in trying to isolate any pension put effect that might exist, we chose as our primary risk measure the firm's 1980 Standard and Poor's bond rating. This reflects an assessment of risk based on a composite of historical data and future expectations. Data were collected for 457 of our firms, and the ratings were coded from 1 to 10, with lower numbers representing lower ratings and presumably greater risk.

Since risk is a notoriously difficult concept to measure we also tried three other risk variables. The first of these is the firm's unlevered beta, which reflects the systematic risk of its assets. Levered beta estimates were collected for 439 of our firms from data provided by Merrill Lynch, and these were then adjusted for firms' market value debt/equity ratios.[5] The value of common stock was obtained from stock market data, while the market value of preferred stock was estimated by capitalizing each firm's preferred dividends for 1980 at the Standard and Poor's preferred dividend yield. The market value of debt was estimated using the current Baa bond rate.[6] An alternative measure of operating risk can be based on total, rather than systematic, variability. For this, we used a standard deviation of detrended return on net assets over a 10-year period. Since we did not have inflation-adjusted data for such a lengthy period, it was necessary to use book figures from the Compustat tape to measure this variable. In addition, the requirement of 10 consecutive years of data reduced the available subsample for this variable to 221 firms. Our final risk measure, which reflects financial as well as operating risk, is the standard deviation of monthly returns on the firm's stock, computed over the period of January 1979–December 1980. Data were available from the Center for Research in Security Prices for 506 of our firms.

The names and definitions of all of these variables are listed in table 2.1. We also show some summary statistics for the different variables to indicate the range of values represented in our sample. We turn now to our estimation.

Table 2.1   Summary Characteristics of the Data

Variable	Mean	Standard Deviation	Minimum Value	Maximum Value	Sample Size for this Variable
PA/TPL	1.480	.431	.554	2.956	908
PA/VPL	1.687	.601	.578	6.230	908
R	.071	.012	.040	.130	908
FI	.536	.239	0.0	1.0	369
PRET	.173	.095	0.0	.500	297
RONA	.069	.063	−.293	.402	492
CFWD/A	.003	.020	0.0	.280	502
T/A	.050	.058	−.154	.603	490
BETAU	.953	.444	−.068	4.260	439
SDRONA	.032	.021	.004	.148	234
BRAT	7.797	1.311	1.0	10.0	457
SDMR	.140	.066	.034	.469	506

NOTE: PA = Reported pension assets; TPL = Total pension liabilities, adjusted to common 10% discount rate; VPL = Vested pension liabilities, adjusted to common 10% discount rate; R = Discount rate assumed by firm in reporting pension liabilities; FI = Fraction of pension assets invested in fixed income securities; PRET = Percentage of pension plan participants who have already retired; A = Nonpension corporate assets, valued at replacement cost; RONA = Inflation-adjusted return on net assets (inflation-adjusted operating earnings divided by A); CFWD = End-of-year magnitude of tax loss carry-forwards; T = Reported total taxes minus the change during 1980 in deferred tax liabilities; BETAU = Unlevered beta; SDRONA = Standard deviation around trend of book return on net assets; BRAT = Standard & Poor's Bond Rating (10 = AAA, 1 = D); SDMR = Standard deviation of market return on firm's stock.

2.5.2   The Assumed Discount Rate

The first hypothesis we tested concerns the relationship between firm profitability and the discount rate chosen for reporting pension liabilities. A simple regression of the assumed discount rate against inflation-adjusted return on net assets, as reported in table 2.2, indicates a strong negative correlation between the two variables. That is, more profitable firms tend to choose lower discount rates and thus, in relative terms, to overstate their pension liabilities. This result suggests that it may be important to adjust reported liabilities to a common basis if the true relationships between pension funding and other variables are to be uncovered.

We also tested the constancy of the relationship between R and RONA. In particular, as the value of the put to the PBGC increases, one might expect firms to increase their assumed values of R at an even faster rate in order to conceal the PBGC's true exposure. To examine this possibility, we created a dummy variable, PBGC, which takes on a value of one if the pension put is "in the money" and zero otherwise. The pension put is deemed to be in the money if a firm's unfunded vested pension liabilities, calculated at reported discount rates, exceed 30% of the firm's market value of equity. The results of this experiment are also reported in table 2.2. The dummy variable has a significant coefficient, and the effect is in the hypothesized direction:

Table 2.2   **Assumed Discount Rate Regressions**

Independent Variables	Dependent Variable	
	R	R
CONSTANT	0.07	0.07
	(.0007)[a]	(.0007)
	$t = 100.0$	$t = 100.0$
RONA	−0.025	−0.017
	(.007)	(.007)
	$t = -3.6$	$t = -2.4$
PBGC[b]		0.017
		(.006)
		$t = 2.8$
R^2	.02	.05
No. of observations	515	515

[a]Standard errors and t-statistics in these and other regressions have been corrected for heteroscedasticity using White's (1980) procedure.

[b]PBGC = 1 if vested pension liabilities, valued at reported discount rate, exceed 30% of market value of firm's equity; 0 otherwise.

companies that have the PBGC in the riskiest position tend to increase their assumed discount rates by even greater amounts than other firms.

2.5.3 Pension Funding

Next, we investigated the relationship between pension funding (calculated on a uniform basis) and profitability, tax-paying status, and risk. As a preliminary step, we computed the simple correlation coefficients reported in table 2.3. The limitations of this measure are well known. However, it does allow us to examine relationships between the variables using as much of our sample as possible, in contrast to the regression analysis, in which data requirements forced considerable cuts in sample size.

One of the stronger results in the table is the positive correlation between funding and RONA. This is consistent with the corporate financial perspective under which pension decisions are related to firm profitability. Also of note is the strong negative correlation between funding and the percentage of plan participants retired. As mentioned in section 2.4.1, we collected data on this variable with an eye toward

Table 2.3   **Simple Correlations between Funding and Explanatory Variables**

	$\dfrac{\text{PA}}{\text{VPL}}$ (Vested Funding)	RONA (Profit-ability)	PRET (% Retired)	$\dfrac{\text{CFWD}}{\text{A}}$ (Carry-forwards)	$\dfrac{\text{T}}{\text{A}}$ (Taxes Paid)	BRAT (Bond Rating)
$\dfrac{\text{PA}}{\text{TPL}}$	.868 $\Pi = .0001$ $N = 908$	.203 $\Pi = .0001$ $N = 492$	−.238 $\Pi = .0001$ $N = 297$	−.104 $\Pi = .020$ $N = 502$	.197 $\Pi = .0001$ $N = 490$	.123 $\Pi = .009$ $N = 457$
$\dfrac{\text{PA}}{\text{VPL}}$		.192 $\Pi = .0001$ $N = 492$	−.331 $\Pi = .0001$ $N = 297$	−.096 $\Pi = .032$ $N = 502$	.184 $\Pi = .0001$ $N = 490$	.090 $\Pi = .056$ $N = 457$
RONA			−.359 $\Pi = .0001$ $N = 195$	−.123 $\Pi = .006$ $N = 492$	.693 $\Pi = .0001$ $N = 458$	.173 $\Pi = .007$ $N = 240$
PRET				.019 $\Pi = .792$ $N = 199$	−.180 $\Pi = .013$ $N = 191$	.085 $\Pi = .251$ $N = 183$
$\dfrac{\text{CFWD}}{\text{A}}$					−.076 $\Pi = .101$ $N = 467$	−.151 $\Pi = .018$ $N = 247$
$\dfrac{\text{T}}{\text{A}}$						.296 $\Pi = .0001$ $N = 243$

NOTE: Π = Probability of finding a sample correlation greater than that reported under the null hypotheses that the true correlation is zero. N = Number of observations used in computing this correlation.

its possible influence on asset allocation, and thus its strong correlation with pension funding came as a surprise. We believe, as will be discussed in further detail below, that this variable is serving as a proxy for the firm's long-run profitability.

Pension funding also appears to be strongly related to tax-paying status, particularly the T/A variable. The results for both CFWD/A and T/A are in the directions predicted by the tax and financial slack effects: that is, heavier tax burdens are associated with higher funding levels.

Finally, the bond rating variable is positively correlated with funding, which is consistent with the pension put effect. Riskier firms, as indicated by lower bond ratings, tend to exhibit lower funding levels. Correlations among the different risk measures are shown in table 2.4, and in general all four measures tend in the same direction (low values of BRAT denote higher risk, and thus BRAT should be negatively correlated with the alternative measures). The relation between bond rating and unlevered beta, however, is quite weak.

With an eye toward multicollinearity problems in the regression analysis, it is also worth noting in table 2.3 the correlations among the explanatory variables. As might be expected, RONA is related to both bond rating and the measures of tax-paying status, while bond rating and tax-paying status are in turn related to one another. These relationships suggest that it may be difficult to separate the different effects on funding.

We next regressed the level of pension funding against profitability, tax-paying status, and risk. The results when funding is measured as pension assets over vested pension liabilities are reported in table 2.5.

Table 2.4   **Correlation Matrix of Risk Measures**

	BETAU (Unlevered Beta)	SDRONA (S. D. Book Return)	SDMR (S.D. Mkt. Return)
BRAT (bond rating)	$-.048$ $\Pi = .477$ $N = 224$	$-.347$ $\Pi = .0001$ $N = 260$	$-.254$ $\Pi = .003$ $N = 140$
BETAU		.176 $\Pi = .0006$ $N = 382$	.198 $\Pi = .003$ $N = 224$
SDRONA			.266 $\Pi = .0001$ $N = 206$

NOTE: Π = Probability of finding a sample correlation greater than that reported under the null hypotheses that the true correlation is zero. N = Number of observations used in computing this correlation.

Table 2.5   **Pension Funding Regressions**

Independent Variables	Equation			
	(1)	(2)	(3)	(4)
Constant	1.279	1.352	1.282	1.304
	(0.160)	(0.068)	(0.172)	(0.065)
	$t = 8.0$	$t = 19.8$	$t = 7.5$	$t = 20.1$
RONA (profitability)	1.704	1.739	1.323	1.714
	(0.481)	(0.348)	(0.554)	(0.523)
	$t = 3.5$	$t = 5.0$	$t = 2.4$	$t = 3.3$
$\dfrac{CFWD}{A}$ (carry-forwards)	−0.504	−1.635		
	(0.514)	(0.938)		
	$t = -1.0$	$t = -1.7$		
$\dfrac{T}{A}$ (taxes paid)			1.177	0.370
			(0.767)	(0.662)
			$t = 1.5$	$t = 0.6$
BRAT (bond rating)	0.020		0.016	
	(0.020)		(0.022)	
	$t = 1.0$		$t = 0.7$	
BETAU (unlevered beta)		0.097		0.100
		(0.064)		(0.064)
		$t = 1.5$		$t = 1.6$
R^2	.04	.07	.05	.08
No. of observations	240	360	226	338

NOTE: Dependent variable = PA/VPL (vested funding). Numbers in parentheses are standard errors, calculated according to White (1980).

We obtained very similar results when funding was measured in terms of total accrued liabilities, and these results are not reported. Both measures of tax-paying status are used in table 2.5, and risk is measured in terms of both bond rating and unlevered beta. The results using SDRONA and SDMR were qualitatively similar and are not reported.

The strongest effect that emerges in table 2.5 is that of profitability. Inflation-adjusted return on net assets has a uniformly positive and significant association with the level of pension funding. This is consistent with the corporate financial perspective on pension decisions, and the direction of the effect is simultaneously consistent with the tax, pension put, and financial slack effects.

This finding is also in contrast to Friedman's (1983) results, which showed a negative relationship between profitability and funding. As discussed in section 2.3, Friedman used a different data source, a different year, reported instead of uniformly calculated measures of pension liabilities and a different specification, so it is difficult to attribute the difference in results to any one factor. We did, however, run the same regressions using reported pension liabilities to calculate our funding measures, and we found that the positive relationship persisted between funding and profitability.[7]

The tax effect in table 2.5 is consistently in the direction predicted by both the tax arbitrage and financial slack theories, but its statistical significance is generally much lower than that of the profitability effect. Whether tax-paying status is measured in terms of carry-forwards or reported tax payments adjusted for the change in deferred tax liabilities, an increase in the tax burden is associated with an increase in funding. In view of the correlations between profitability and tax-paying status reported in table 2.3, it is not surprising that the tax effect is difficult to distinguish.

Finally, the effect of risk in table 2.5 is neither consistent across equations nor very significant statistically. When risk is measured by bond rating, greater risk is associated with less funding, consistent with the pension put effect. When risk is measured by unlevered beta, on the other hand, higher risk is associated with higher funding levels. Since neither of these effects is statistically significant, no clear picture emerges of the true influence of risk on pension funding.

Perhaps, however, it is unreasonable to expect the pension put and tax effects to leave strong traces across the entire sample of firms. As pointed out in section 2.2.2, for example, the influence of risk on the value of the pension put might be expected to appear strongly only for the riskiest firms. To examine this possibility, we split our sample and performed the same regression for those firms whose bond rating was below average relative to the sample as a whole. This regression, using T/A as the tax variable, is reported in the first column of table 2.6. Lower bond ratings (higher risk) are still associated with lower funding levels, this time in a more significant fashion. To the extent that there is an identifiable pension put effect, it appears to be very nonlinear, as theory would suggest. The fact that the explanatory power of the equation increases substantially relative to the full sample regression also indicates that the effects we are seeking to identify do not fall along a single straight line for a broad cross-section of firms.[8]

In the same vein, we split our sample by values of T/A to see if the tax effect would make a stronger showing among firms facing the heaviest tax burdens. Results from the same regression performed over those firms having above-average values of T/A are reported in the second column of table 2.6. For this subsample, the estimated coefficient of T/A is quite large and more statistically significant than those reported in table 2.5.

Table 2.6   **Pension Funding Regressions for Subsamples**

Independent Variables	Subsample: Firms with Below-Average Bond Rating	Subsample: Firms with Above-Average T/A
Constant	0.684	1.049
	(0.347)	(0.291)
	$t = 2.0$	$t = 3.6$
RONA	1.221	0.359
(profitability)	(0.684)	(1.004)
	$t = 1.8$	$t = 0.4$
$\dfrac{T}{A}$	1.792	2.925
(taxes paid)	(1.277)	(1.367)
	$t = 1.4$	$t = 2.1$
BRAT	0.122	0.031
(bond rating)	(0.061)	(0.032)
	$t = 2.0$	$t = 1.0$
R^2	.09	.07
No. of observations	74	81

NOTE: Dependent variable = PA/VPL (vested funding). Numbers in parentheses are standard errors calculated according to White (1980).

Looking at tables 2.5 and 2.6 together, the profitability variable appears to be doing most of the work in the full sample regression. The tax and risk variable have relatively insignificant effects. However, when the sample is split into pieces, these latter effects show up more strongly among firms that deviate from the average. The pension put effect appears to have some plausibility for the high-risk subsample, while the tax effect is more pronounced for the high tax-paying subsample. In addition, the effect of profitability is attenuated in these subsamples. It may be that profitability is simply a proxy for some combination of tax and risk effects that best explains variations in funding for the sample as a whole. At the edges of the sample, however, where the tax and risk effects become separated, the explanatory power of profitability declines, and the tax and risk effects are more readily identifiable.

The suspicion that our RONA measure of profitability may be acting as a proxy for other variables receives further support when we add PRET, the percentage of plan participants retired, to our list of explanatory variables. The results of this experiment (performed over the largest sample of firms for which data on all the variables was available) are reported in table 2.7. Comparing these results with equation (3) in table 2.5, we see that the estimated coefficients of T/A and BRAT remain very similar in size and significance. However, in the presence of PRET, the effect of RONA virtually disappears. At the same time the explanatory power of the equation triples (although the sample size is cut in half).

Taken together, then, the smaller-sample results of tables 2.6 and 2.7 convey the strong impression that RONA is a very noisy measure of firms' financial condition. In addition, the results in table 2.7 raise the question of how PRET's apparently strong effect should be interpreted. Our feeling is that this variable is a measure of firm or industry life cycle and hence of long-run financial condition. Firms with the highest ratios of retired to active workers are most likely to be in a phase of maturity or even decline. They are likely to exhibit slower growth and lower profitability than other firms, and thus the finding that higher values of PRET are associated with lower levels of pension funding is consistent with the corporate financial perspective.[9]

The results thus far suggest that the corporate financial perspective is a plausible one from which to view pension funding decisions. A

Table 2.7   **Percentage of Plan Participants Retired as a Determinant of Pension Funding**

Independent Variables	Dependent Variable: PA/VPL (Vested Funding)
Constant	1.685
	(0.334)
	$t = 5.0$
RONA (profitability)	0.016
	(0.893)
	$t = 0.02$
PRET (% retired)	-1.980
	(0.626)
	$t = -3.2$
$\dfrac{T}{A}$ (taxes paid)	1.190
	(1.030)
	$t = 1.2$
BRAT (bond rating)	0.018
	(0.036)
	$t = 0.5$
R^2	.17
No. of observations	108

NOTE: Numbers in parentheses are standard errors calculated according to White (1980).

potential weakness of the tests conducted, however, is that pension variables have been measured on a firmwide basis, whereas many firms administer more than one plan. It is possible that different perspectives should be applied in analyzing the funding levels of different pension plans within the same firm.

For example, one of the rationales offered in section 2.2 for the corporate financial perspective was that promised benefits are insured by the PBGC and thus firms need not feel constrained to adopt funding levels that the beneficiaries would prefer in the absence of insurance. In fact, however, the extent of the insurance coverage is limited.[10] Different pension plans within the same firm, then, might be funded differently depending on the degrees of insurance coverage for their respective participants. Plans for hourly workers, who are more likely to have complete insurance coverage, might be managed from a corporate financial perspective. On the other hand, plans for salaried workers, who are more likely to have promised benefits in excess of insurance limits, might be managed from the traditional perspective.

To perform a rough examination of this possibility, we obtained funding data on over 10,000 different pension plans (each with more than 100 participants) from the IRS Form 5500 for 1980.[11] For each plan, we had data on pension assets, the present value of vested benefits, and the discount rate assumption, so we were able to compute vested funding (PA/VPL), where total pension liabilities have been adjusted to a 10% discount rate as in the company-wide data above. Unfortunately, it was not possible to determine with complete accuracy whether a given plan was for hourly workers, salaried workers, or both. Rather, the plans had been grouped into four mutually exclusive categories, corresponding to the formula used in calculating benefits. The first of these is the fixed benefit plans which pay a fixed percentage of final compensation. The second is the unit benefit plans which pay some percentage of final compensation times years of service. The third category is the flat benefit plans, which simply pay a stated dollar amount, while the fourth category consists of all other plans.

A simple test for differences in funding behavior is an analysis of variance, which tests for differences in mean funding across the four categories. This test is reported in the form of a dummy variable regression in table 2.8. The F-statistic value overwhelmingly rejects the hypothesis that there are no significant differences in funding across plan types. In addition, flat benefit plans appear to be significantly less funded than other types of plans. While not all hourly workers' plans are flat benefit plans, it is our understanding that flat benefit plans have hourly workers as their predominant participants. Thus there is some evidence that plans for workers whose benefits are more likely to be fully insured also tend to be less well funded on the average. This in turn suggests that whether the traditional or the corporate financial

Table 2.8   **Differences in Funding by Plan Type**

Independent Variables	Estimated Coefficient (Standard Error)
Constant	1.793
	(0.045)
	$t = 39.8$
FIXED[a]	0.106
	(0.053)
	$t = 2.0$
UNIT	0.025
	(0.046)
	$t = 0.5$
FLAT	−0.335
	(0.055)
	$t = -6.1$
R^2	.012
F	40.83
No. of observations	10,124

NOTE: Dependent variable = PA/VPL (vested funding).

[a]FIXED = 1 if fixed benefit plan, 0 otherwise; UNIT = 1 if unit benefit plan, 0 otherwise; FLAT = 1 if flat benefit plan, 0 otherwise.

perspective is a more accurate description of pension decisions may vary by type of plan. Further investigation of this issue would be worthwhile if a more accurate breakdown of plans by type of participant could be obtained.

2.5.4   Pension Asset Allocation

Finally, we investigated the asset allocation among our sample of corporate pension funds and its dependence upon various characteristics of the firm and the pension plan.

Figure 2.1 shows the frequency distribution for our asset allocation variable, the percentage of pension fund assets invested in fixed income securities (FI), for all 539 firms for which data was available. Recall that the corporate financial perspective on asset allocation implies that pension funds should be invested at either one of two extremes. In particular, because the vast majority of the plans in this sample are considerably overfunded, this perspective implies that most funds should be invested entirely in fixed income securities (because these securities are presumably more heavily taxed).

The data in figure 2.1 show that the distribution of asset allocation across firms is, in fact, bimodal. On the one hand, these data do hint that firms divide into two groups, much as the corporate financial per-

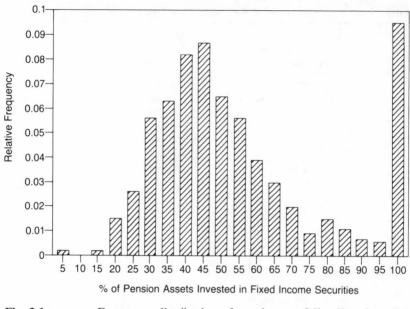

Fig. 2.1   Frequency distribution of pension portfolio allocation, 539 firms. (Source: Greenwich Research Associates data.)

spective suggests they should. And 10% do invest entirely in fixed income, the extreme allocation that should be chosen by most firms.[12] Unfortunately, however, the remaining 90% hold decidedly mixed portfolios with a mode of 45% of their pension assets invested in fixed income securities. These interior or nonextremal asset allocations cannot be explained by the corporate financial perspective on pension fund decisions.

To glean some insight into the possible determinants of asset allocation, we computed the correlation coefficients reported in table 2.9. To simplify and condense the presentation of our results in this section, we will report using only one measure of funding, the ratio of assets to vested liabilities (PA/VPL); one measure of risk, the bond rating (BRAT); and one measure of tax status (T/A).[13] While, again, the problems with simple correlation coefficients are well known, the values in table 2.9 are interesting. Surprisingly, the asset allocation does not depend upon the tax variable (T/A). Nor does it depend upon the percentage of pension plan members who are retired (PRET), our proxy for the demographics of the plan members and thus the shape of the future pension liability stream. Equally surprising, the asset allocation does depend upon the dollar value of vested liabilities, our proxy for the *size* of the company's pension plan and fund.[14] Also, the asset allocation appears to depend upon the degree of funding (PA/VPL).

Table 2.9   **Simple Correlations between Asset Allocation (FI) and Explanatory Variables**

	PA/VPL (Vested Funding)	T/A (Taxes Paid)	BRAT (Bond Rating)	VPL (Vested Liabilities)	PRET (% Retired)
FI (% invested in fixed income)	.139 Π = .007 N = 369	− .025 Π = .700 N = 243	− .107 Π = .119 N = 215	− .136 Π = .009 N = 369	− .082 Π = .160 N = 292
PA/VPL		.184 Π = .0001 N = 490	.090 Π = .056 N = 457	− .096 Π = .004 N = 908	− .331 Π = .0001 N = 297
T/A			.296 Π = .0001 N = 243	− .108 Π = .017 N = 490	− .180 Π = .013 N = 191
BRAT				.162 Π = .0005 N = 457	.085 Π = .251 N = 183
VPL					.091 Π = .118 N = 297

NOTE: Π = Probability of finding a sample correlation greater than that reported under the null hypotheses that the true population correlation is zero. N = Number of observations used.

While at first glance the dependence upon size is surprising, we believe it can be explained by an important difference between the implicit character of large and small pension plans. Other studies, particularly Clark et al. (1983) and Greenwich Research Associates (1983), have shown that large defined benefit pension plans have given frequent and sizable post-retirement benefit increases to their participants. It appears that large corporations tend to treat the "defined benefits" of their pension plans as contractually stipulated minimums or floors for the benefits paid to retirees, but they voluntarily and regularly increase benefits beyond these floors. To some extent this may reflect their efforts to award real dollar as opposed to nominal dollar benefits to their retired employees. To some extent it may reflect an attitude of sharing the surplus of pension assets (over liabilities) with retired employees, as if their plans were more like defined contribution plans. In any case, though, the pension benefits of large corporations are clearly not fixed in practice in the nominal dollar terms that the legal language of most pension contracts would imply.

The smaller pension plans associated with smaller companies, in contrast, have only given very infrequent post-retirement benefit increases, and many of them have never given any increase. For example, in a typical year in the mid-1970s fewer than 10% of the retirees of small pension plans received post-retirement increases, whereas more than three-quarters of the retirees of large plans received such increases (Clark el al. 1983). Apparently, small firms treat their pension claims much more as fixed nominal dollar liabilities of the corporation, as the corporate financial perspective on pensions assumes. We believe that this may well explain why small companies tend to invest a larger percentage of their pension funds in fixed income assets.

Perhaps more important, the corporate financial perspective on pension funds would suggest that asset allocation should be related to funding and risk. For that small fraction of companies where the value of the PBGC put is appreciable, the plans should hold a larger fraction of their assets in stocks; otherwise they should invest in bonds. Companies with low bond ratings that are underfunded might thus be expected to hold more stocks and less bonds, and vice versa.

Table 2.10 reports some of the regression results which attempt to explain asset allocation as a function of these different variables. In equation (1) with two explanatory variables, funding has a statistically significant effect in the hypothesized direction. That is, underfunded companies do indeed hold fewer bonds. Surprisingly, though, when bond rating is introduced as an independent variable in equations (2)

Table 2.10   **Asset Allocation Regressions** (Full Sample)

Independent Variables	Equation		
	(1)	(2)	(3)
Constant	.440	.556	.539
	(.041)	(.101)	(.100)
	$t = 10.7$	$t = 5.5$	$t = 5.4$
VPL	-3.58×10^{-5}		-2.25×10^{-5}
(vested	(2.01×10^{-5})		(1.49×10^{-5})
liabilities)	$t = -1.8$		$t = -1.5$
PA/VPL	.064	.054	.051
(vested funding)	(.025)	(.035)	(.0351)
	$t = 2.6$	$t = 1.5$	$t = 1.5$
BRAT		$-.0187$	$-.0151$
(bond rating)		(.0117)	(.0119)
		$t = -1.6$	$t = -1.3$
R^2	.04	.02	.04
No. of observations	369	215	215

NOTE: Dependent variable = FI (% invested in fixed income). Numbers in parentheses are standard errors calculated according to White (1980).

and (3), it enters with a negative sign. Riskier companies hold fewer bonds and more stocks, the opposite of what we might expect if companies were exploiting the PBGC put. This is the same dependence that Friedman (1983) found, a "risk-offsetting effect" between the asset mix of the pension fund and the risk of the company.

Table 2.11 reports the results of a similar regression for that subsample of 30 higher-risk firms whose bond ratings were BB+ or lower. For this group of companies the PBGC put effect and its dependence upon funding might be more clearly observed. As the coefficients and R^2 demonstrate, funding (PA/VPL) is an even more important determinant of asset allocation within this subsample, as we would expect.[15] The measures of statistical significance for both size and funding have an adjusted t-ratio of just about 2.

Table 2.12 presents an alternative look at this same data. Confirming the results of table 2.11, among all higher-risk firms the underfunded plans hold riskier portfolios (fewer bonds and more stocks). Furthermore, among all underfunded plans, the higher-risk firms own riskier portfolios. In our entire sample there were actually only three firms that were credible candidates for having a valuable PBGC put in that they had both underfunded pension plans and a bond rating less than BBB−. Interestingly, these firms tended to hold rather risky portfolios, just as the corporate financial perspective suggests they should.

The significance of these data are questionable, however, for both the obvious reason that three is not an overwhelming sample size and because of the subsequent history of these three firms. Upon looking

Table 2.11	**Asset Allocation Regressions for a Sample of Thirty Higher-Risk Firms with Bond Ratings of BB+ or Lower**	
	Independent Variables	Estimated Coefficient (Standard Error)
	Intercept	.272 (.188) $t = 1.4$
	VPL (vested liabilities)	-1.74×10^{-5} ($.89 \times 10^{-5}$) $t = -2.0$
	PA/VPL	.214 (.114) $t = 1.9$
	R^2	.14
	No. of observations	30

NOTE: Dependent Variable = FI (% invested in fixed income).

Table 2.12   **Average Percentage of Plan Assets Invested in Fixed Income Securities for Different Regions of Funding and Bond Rating**

	Funding	
	Overfunded (PA/TPL > 1.0)	Underfunded (PA/TPL < 1.0)
Bond rating:		
BBB− or above	.48	.50
	$N = 172$	$N = 13$
BB+ or below	.61	.34
	$N = 27$	$N = 3$

closely at these firms, we discovered that two of the three firms have subsequently switched their pension asset mixes to virtually 100% bonds using a bond dedication framework. Moreover, they did so in circumstances in which the probabilities of financial distress were clearly increasing not decreasing. Their subsequent asset mix decisions, then, were quite inconsistent with attempting to exploit the value of the PBGC put.

To summarize the empirical findings on asset allocation, there is an interesting dependence upon size which we believe can be explained by the quite different ways in which large and small firms seem to regard their employees' "defined benefits." In addition, underfunded plans tend to hold more equities and less fixed income securities. Finally, we found some very sketchy evidence that the extreme subset of companies with both lower ratings and unfunded pension plans tend to hold more of their pension assets in equities, exactly what the corporate financial perspective on pension decisions would suggest. The subsequent history of these firms, however, makes us reluctant to conclude we have found solid evidence of such behavior.

2.6 Conclusion

When we look at our results in their entirety, we believe that we have found several pieces of evidence supporting the corporate financial perspective on pension fund decisions. There appears to be a real sense, then, in which corporations manage their pension funds as an integral part of overall financial policy.

First, the reporting of pension fund liabilities is systematically linked to company profitability through the choice of a discount rate. More profitable firms tend to choose lower discount rates and thus to report greater pension liabilities. Second, the level of pension funding is positively related to companies' long-run profitability. This may be a combined reflection of tax, risk, and financial slack effects. Third, a significant fraction of firms invest their pension assets entirely in fixed income securities, and the proportion of assets allocated to fixed income securities is positively related to the level of funding.

However, the individual effects comprising the corporate financial perspective are more elusive. In our full sample of firms, the tax effect and the pension put effect do not leave strong traces. Rather, these effects are more clearly discernible only at the edges of our sample: a significant positive relationship between tax-paying status and funding shows up among firms with the heaviest tax burdens; a negative relationship between risk and funding shows up among the riskiest firms; and there is sketchy evidence of a tendency for the firms with the most valuable PBGC puts to invest their pension funds in riskier assets.

Our results also indicate that the traditional and corporate financial perspectives on pension decisions are far from mutually exclusive. Across firms, our asset allocation findings suggest that the corporate financial perspective may be more appropriate in describing small pension plans, while larger plans appear to take on some of the characteristics of the traditional perspective. Moreover, even within the same firm, different plans may be more appropriately viewed from one perspective or the other depending on their level of PBGC insurance coverage.

Clearly, the present study represents only an initial attempt to gain a working empirical knowledge of corporate pension funds. As more years of data become available, it would be desirable to check the robustness of our results across different periods and to examine the determinants of changes in pension funding and asset allocation over time. On the theoretical front, it is apparent that much remains to be understood about the underlying labor contracts of which pension plans are a part. A better understanding of the differences in these contracts across firms of different size or across categories of employees within the same firm may shed considerable further light on corporate pension decisions.

Notes

1. Friedman (1983) discussed the potential difficulties resulting from the discount rate choice, but he did not have the data to make any adjustments.

2. The measure of pension assets in the denominator of this fraction is not the same as the figure for total pension assets in the FASB 36 filings. In measuring asset allocation we deleted "real estate investments" and "miscellaneous assets," because it was not clear whether these were more like fixed income investments or more like common stock. The real estate category, for example, could include real property but could also include mortgages. We also deleted investments in the sponsoring company's stock, since these might be related to factors other than the desired risk and return position of the pension portfolio. The denominator of our asset allocation variable, then, is fixed income securities (as defined in the text) plus investments in the stock of other companies.

3. Unfortunately, our earnings measure is not entirely purged of leverage effects. Our measure is equal to inflation-adjusted, after-tax net income plus interest payments. Without further data, we were unable to adjust taxes to the levels that would have been paid in the absence of any debt.

4. This measure of tax-paying status has been used by Zimmerman (in press).

5. The adjustment we used was to multiply levered betas by the ratio of preferred plus common stock to debt plus preferred plus common stock. This adjustment treats preferred stock as equity. We did not include corporate taxes in our adjustment, as would be consistent with a Miller (1977) model of capital structure equilibrium.

6. More specifically, short-term liabilities (net of financial assets) were taken at book value. The market value of long-term debt was estimated from the book value by assuming a 10% average coupon rate and a 10-year average maturity. Estimated debt service payments were then discounted at the current Baa rate. This is similar to the procedure followed in Feldstein and Mørck (1983).

7. In view of the relationship between profitability and assumed discount rates reported in table 2.2, it might have been argued that we induced a correlation between funding and RONA through our adjustment to a common discount rate. The fact that the same correlation persists in the unadjusted data provides evidence against this argument.

8. Even further sample splitting may be justified. When we confined our sample to firms whose bond ratings were lower than BBB− (that is, lower than investment grade), we obtained an R^2 of .22 for a regression using PA/VPL as a dependent variable over a subsample of 32 firms. The estimated coefficient of BRAT in this regression was 0.110 with a t-statistic of 2.5.

9. PRET could of course be subject to alternative interpretations. One possibility is that firms with greater proportions of retired workers simply have less flexibility to alter their actuarial assumptions and thus fewer possibilities for effectively overfunding their pension plans. Since this interpretation implicitly rests on the notion that firms are managing their financial slack, it too is consistent with the corporate financial perspective. There may be other possible interpretations of PRET as well, but it is difficult to see how the findings in table 2.7 could be said to favor the traditional perspective over the corporate financial perspective. Although the traditional perspective might predict that demographic characteristics of the participant pool are important to firms' pension decisions, it is not clear under that view why greater proportions of retired workers should be associated with lower funding levels.

10. As of 1982, vested pension benefits were guaranteed by the PBGC up to a maximum of $16,568 per year.

11. We thank David Kennell of ICF, Inc., for his help in obtaining these data.

12. We did investigate the character of the firms that invested entirely in fixed income. They tended to be somewhat smaller, somewhat safer (as mea-

sured by their unlevered betas), and somewhat better funded, but they were not extraordinarily different from the full sample of firms on any of these dimensions. "Insured funds" accounted for 13.7% of their fixed income assets, as opposed to 9.2% of the fixed income assets in the full sample.

13. Other versions of these same basic variables were tested and yielded quite similar results, though often with less statistical significance.

14. Other potential proxies for size (for example, the dollar value of pension assets) produce the same results, confirming that *size* really is the important thing being captured by this variable.

15. There is an alternative explanation for this dependence upon funding. Conversations with corporate financial officers in the field suggest that at least some of them may believe that underfunded plans should "reach" for greater expected returns, while overfunded plans, in contrast, should minimize risks and focus on preserving their capital. Indeed, several pension consulting firms recommend such policies explicitly as part of their overall asset allocation service. In more formal terms, such behavior would be consistent with a preference or utility function for net pension wealth (assets minus liabilities) that is unusually sharply bent around zero, a behavior analogous to some observations of individual behavior in other quite different decision-making contexts.

References

Black, Fischer. 1980. The tax consequences of long-run pension policy. *Financial Analysts Journal* 36:25–31.

Bulow, Jeremy I. 1983. Pension funding and investment policy. Paper presented at the American Finance Association Annual Meetings, San Francisco.

Bulow, Jeremy I., and Scholes, Myron. 1983. Who owns the assets in a defined benefit pension plan? In *Financial aspects of the United States pension system,* ed. Zvi Bodie and John Shoven. Chicago: University of Chicago Press.

Chen, Andrew H. 1983. Taxes, insurance and corporate pension policy. Paper presented at the Johnson Symposium on Taxes and Finance, University of Wisconsin—Madison.

Clark, Robert L.; Allen, Steven G.; and Sumner, Daniel A. 1983. Inflation and pension benefits. Final report for the Department of Labor Contract no. J-9-P-1-0074.

Colvin, Geoffrey. 1982. How sick companies are endangering the pension system. *Fortune* 106:72–78.

Feldstein, Martin, and Mørck, Randall. 1983. Pension funding decisions, interest rate assumptions, and share prices. In *Financial aspects of the United States pension system,* ed. Zvi Bodie and John Shoven. Chicago: University of Chicago Press.

Friedman, Benjamin M. 1983. Pension funding, pension asset allocation, and corporation finance: Evidence from individual company data. In *Financial aspects of the United States pension system,* ed. Zvi Bodie and John Shoven. Chicago: University of Chicago Press.

Greenwich Research Associates. 1983. Large corporate pensions: 1983.

Harrison, Michael J., and Sharpe, William F. 1983. Optimal funding and asset allocation rules for defined benefit pension plans. In *Financial aspects of the United States pension system,* ed. Zvi Bodie and John Shoven. Chicago: University of Chicago Press.

Hawthorne, Fran. 1983. Raiding the corporate pension fund. *Institutional Investor* 17:101–13.

Louis, Arthur M. 1983. Tapping the riches in corporate pension plans. *Fortune* 108:129–34.

Miller, Merton H. 1977. Debt and taxes. *Journal of Finance* 32:261–75.

Miller, Merton H., and Scholes, Myron S. 1981. Pension funding and corporate valuation. Unpublished paper. University of Chicago.

Munnell, Alicia H. 1982. Guaranteeing private pension benefits: A potentially expensive business. *New England Economic Review:* 24–47.

Myers, Stewart C., and Majluf, Nicholas S. 1983. Corporate financing and investment decisions when firms have information that investors do not have. Unpublished paper. Sloan School of Management, M.I.T.

Sharpe, William F. 1976. Corporate pension funding policy. *Journal of Financial Economics* 3:183–93.

Smith, Randall. 1983. Firms increasingly tap their pension assets to use excess funds. *Wall Street Journal* 202:1.

Tepper, Irwin, 1981. Taxation and corporate pension policy. *Journal of Finance* 36:1–13.

———. 1983. Pension funding strategies and the management of corporate capital. Paper presented at the American Finance Association Annual Meetings, San Francisco.

Treynor, Jack. 1977. The principles of corporate pension finance. *Journal of Finance* 32:627–38.

Webman, Nancy. 1983. Funds play a growing role as corporate financing aid. *Pensions and Investment Age* 11:3.

Westerfield, Randolph, and Marshall, William. 1983. Pension plan funding decisions and corporate shareholder value: A new model and some empirical results. Unpublished paper. University of Pennsylvania.

White, Halbert. 1980. A heteroskedasticity-consistent covariance matrix estimator and a direct test for heteroskedasticity. *Econometrica* 48:817–38.

Zimmerman, Jerold L. In press. Taxes and firm size. *Journal of Accounting and Economics.*

Comment   André F. Perold

This empirical work is aimed at uncovering relationships among on-balance-sheet corporate financial characteristics and off-balance-sheet levels of pension funding and asset mix. The study differs somewhat from a closely related earlier paper by Friedman (1983) in that it is more clearly focused (e.g., by the choice of regression variables) on interpreting the data in the light of extant pension theory. The results involving pension funding are also more credible than Friedman's since the pension liability data were taken from filings of FASB Statement 36 instead of Form 5500. (FASB 36 imposes a uniform reporting standard up to the choice of discount rate, which is also reported.)

André F. Perold is associate professor of finance, Harvard Business School.

I will comment first on certain problems associated with adjusting the reported liabilities to a common discount rate, and then critically examine some of the paper's findings. Before doing so, let me say that I am generally in agreement with the authors' interpretation of the data, with the obvious caveat that the findings of any such cross-sectional study fixed in time (1980) should be treated with caution.

2.C.1   Adjusting reported pension liabilities to a common discount rate

Bodie et al. adjusted the pension liabilities to a common discount rate of 10% (the then-prevailing rate used by the PBGC) by multiplying the reported pension liability by a factor of $R/10\%$ where R is the reported discount rate.[1] This is an approximation and assumes that the accrued liability stream is a constant perpetuity. Since we do not live forever, and since currently employed beneficiaries only begin to receive benefits at some later date (i.e., retirement), the age distribution of the plan beneficiaries will be the single most important source of error in this approximation. If we let the percentage retired (called PRET in the paper) be a proxy for the age distribution, then the following simple model will illustrate the relationship of the exact adjustment to the above approximation.

Suppose that existing retirees are all paid \$1 n years from now and that current employees will receive \$1 m years from now, $m > n$. If R is the reported discount rate, the reported liability will be

$$L(R, \text{PRET}) = \frac{\text{PRET}}{(1 + R)^n} + \frac{(1 - \text{PRET})}{(1 + R)^m}$$

The exact[2] adjustment factor for a common rate of 10% is thus $L(10,\text{PRET}) \div L(R,\text{PRET})$. The following table gives values for the exact factor when $n = 10$, and $m = 40$, for the range of values of R and PRET encountered in the data.

R (Reported discount rate)	PRET (% retired)				Approximate factor $R/10\%$
	0%	10%	25%	50%	
4%	.11	.23	.35	.46	.40
7%	.33	.53	.64	.71	.70
10%	1.00	1.00	1.00	1.00	1.00
13%	2.93	1.61	1.42	1.35	1.30

Notice that for any given reported rate R less than 10%, there is a positive relationship between the exact adjustment factor and PRET. For reported rates in excess of the common rate (10%), there is a *negative* relationship. This will clearly be true more generally.

2.C.2   Implications for the study

One of the main regression results of the study is a strong negative relationship between funding and PRET. Since by far the majority of the firms reported discount rates below 10%, this means that this relationship would have been even more strongly negative had the exact adjustment factors been used. This analysis therefore strengthens that particular result.

However, if the assumed common discount rate is lower, for example, the average reported rate of 7%, then this regression result will quite possibly be significantly weakened, at the very least for the firms reporting discount rates above 7%.

This then leads to the question, what is the correct common discount rate? Feldstein and Mørck (1983) used the prevailing Baa rate on the assumption that the accrued liabilities are a fixed nominal cash flow stream. However, they also gave evidence that investors use something closer to the average reported rate to value pension liabilities. This is consistent with a view that accrued liabilities are partially inflation indexed, perhaps because of some implicit contract in which the firm shares inflation risk with the beneficiaries. While Bulow (1982) casts doubt on why such an implicit contract should exist in the first place, it cannot be ruled out in an empirical study of this nature.

2.C.3   The findings of the paper

There is one aspect of the data that is particularly troublesome to me, and that is the fact that only about 10% of the firms have underfunded pension plans. For example, with funding as the dependent variable, what does it mean to have a positive coefficient on bond rating, as predicted by the corporate financial perspective, in such a sample when the R^2 in addition is only in the range .04–.09? Because so many plans are overfunded, I see this as weak evidence for the financial slack effect, but not the pension put effect. Moreover, the discussion of the data in table 2.12 by Bodie et al. makes it difficult to make *any* case for the pension put effect.

Alternatively, it could be that corporations manage their pension plans with a different view of the true nature of their pension liabilities. If an average rate of 7% is the more appropriate one at which to discount the liabilities, then about half the plans will be underfunded, and there may then be some evidence for the pension put effect. It is then difficult to reinterpret the regressions in the paper, however, in view of my earlier comments on possible sources of error in the discount rate adjustment factor.

As to the strong relationship between asset mix and size (VPL), I would be much happier if the independent variable had been log (VPL) since Friedman's data clearly shows a big asymmetry in the distribution of pension plan assets. The largest pension plans are therefore outlying observations, and the regressions in tables 2.10 and 2.11 could just be telling us that a few of the very large pension plans have a higher proportion invested in stocks.

2.C.4 Conclusion

This paper shows that corporate pension plans are in part managed from an integrated corporate financial perspective. In my view it gives strong evidence of the tax effect, weaker evidence for the financial slack effect, and little if any evidence for the pension put effect. It also points out very clearly that we still have a lot explaining to do. I would like to see an analysis that more carefully takes into account the discount rate adjustment factor, since the effects could potentially alter the nature of the findings of the paper.

Overall, this is an important and thought-provoking study that will affect future work in this area both empirically and theoretically.

Notes

1. This is the approach as taken by Feldstein and Mørck (1983).
2. That is, exact for this model.

References

Bulow, Jeremy I. 1982. What are corporate pension liabilities? *Quarterly Journal of Economics* 97 (August): 435–52.

Feldstein, Martin and Randall Mørck. 1983. Pension Funding Decisions, Interest Rate Assumptions and Share Prices. In *Financial Aspects of the United States Pension System,* ed. Z. Bodie and J. Shoven. Chicago: University of Chicago Press.

Friedman, Benjamin M. 1983. Pension Funding, Pension Asset Allocation and Corporation Finance: Evidence from Individual Company Data. In *Financial Aspects of the United States Pension System,* ed. Z. Bodie and J. Shoven. Chicago: University of Chicago Press.

3   Corporate Pension Policy and the Value of PBGC Insurance

Alan J. Marcus

Title IV of the Employee Retirement Income Security Act of 1974 established the Pension Benefit Guarantee Corporation to insure the benefits of participants of defined benefit pension plans. The PBGC now insures the pension benefits of more than 28 million employees in single-employer plans and provides less extensive coverage to participants in multi-employer plans. Firms initially were charged a premium of $1.00 per year per employee for this coverage. This premium structure was meant to be temporary, until the data required to establish actuarially balanced plans became available. In 1980, the PBGC raised the premiums to $2.60 per employee per year. In 1982 the PBGC requested a further increase in the premium rate to $6.00, and warned that even this increase might be insufficient to cover prospective PBGC liabilities if several currently precarious large firms fail to regain financial stability (*Wall Street Journal* 1982). This latest request has led to renewed interest in PBGC pricing policy and the assessment of PBGC liabilities. Although the Multiemployer Pension Plan Amendment Act of 1980 directed the PBGC to study the possibility of a graduated premium rate schedule based on risk, such recommendations have yet to be made, and the current proposals for rate changes are still independent of risk.

One approach to valuing PBGC liabilities is provided by the options pricing framework. The formal correspondence between put options

Alan J. Marcus is associate professor of finance, Boston University School of Management, and faculty research fellow, National Bureau of Economic Research.

The research reported here is part of the NBER program in pensions, funded by the U.S. Department of Health and Human Services. Any opinions expressed are those of the author and not of the NBER or of the USDHHS. I am grateful to Zvi Bodie and Bob McDonald for many helpful discussions.

and term insurance policies has long been noted, and the option pricing methodology has been used to value insurance plans in other contexts (Mayers and Smith 1977; Merton 1977; Sosin 1980; Marcus and Shaked 1984). In fact, several authors (Sharpe 1976; Treynor 1977; da Motta 1979; Langetieg et al. 1982) already have used option pricing methodology to study the valuation of PBGC insurance. The provisions of ERISA allow firms to transfer their pension liabilities to the PBGC in return for pension fund assets plus 30% of the market value of the firm's net worth. Thus, viewing PBGC insurance as a put option, the pension liabilities play the role of the exercise price while the fund assets plus 30% of net worth play the role of the underlying asset or stock price.[1]

However, while the analogy between put options and the option to terminate a pension plan appears straightforward, the correspondence between the two is not at all clear with respect to the effective time to maturity of the pension put. Taken literally, ERISA rules seem to imply that a firm may terminate an underfunded plan, transfer its net liability to the PBGC, and reestablish a new insured plan. Under this reading of the law, firms would immediately terminate any plan that became underfunded by more than 30% of net worth. The option would have instantaneous maturity and be indefinitely renewable.

In practice, however, virtually all terminations of underfunded pension plans occur as a by-product of corporate bankruptcy. The lack of voluntary terminations suggests that there may be hidden costs to termination. Bulow (1982) suggests that voluntary termination might lead to unfavorable government treatment in other matters.[2] Other observers (e.g., Munnell 1982) cite damaged labor relations as an implicit cost of termination. This seems less convincing, however, since the firm may replace the terminated plan with another plan of equal value, in which case both employees and employers can gain at the expense of the PBGC. More explicit costs of termination might arise from legal entanglements. In one widely cited case, the PBGC brought suit to block the voluntary termination and reorganization of the underfunded pension plan of AlloyTek. The two sides ultimately settled out of court in 1981, with the PBGC assuming the underfunded plan and AlloyTek agreeing not to establish a new defined benefit plan. Instead, the firm was allowed to establish a defined contribution plan for its employees by buying Individual Retirement Accounts (IRAs) for them (Munell 1982).

Most authors have chosen to avoid the ambiguity regarding termination provisions. Treynor (1977) analyzes pension finance using a one-period model, in which the fund automatically terminates at the end of the period. Sharpe (1976) also uses a one-period model, which effectively transforms the termination put into a European option. In a similar vein, da Motta (1979) assumes an arbitrary finite maturity date. His model allows firms to drop out of the PBGC insurance program at interim moments when pension funding payments come due, but the firm cannot exercise the PBGC put until an exogenously given maturity date (p. 93). Harrison and Sharpe (1982) also study a multiperiod model in which the PBGC insurance is exercised only at the end of the last period. Bulow (1981, 1983), Bulow and Scholes (1982), and Bulow et al. (1982) generally pass over the issue of termination date per se, and focus instead on contingent liabilities at termination, whenever that may be. Finally, Langetieg et al. (1982) consider PBGC insurance in a general multiperiod contingent claims framework, but examine only the qualitative properties of the insurance, and do not derive a valuation formula for the insurance.

While these models offer several important insights, the issue of the implicit termination date remains problematic. It is clear that any estimates of the value of PBGC liabilities will be sensitive to the conditions that set off a plan termination. The sensitivity of the qualitative conclusions of these models to the imposition of an exogenous termination date remains an open question.

This paper presents two models of the pension insurance program that also use the contingent claims methodology but that do not impose an exogenous maturity date on PBGC insurance. The value of PBGC insurance is derived for two scenarios. In the first, the possibility of corporate bankruptcy is ruled out, and the pension plan is terminated only when that action is value maximizing for the firm. This scenario is motivated by the opportunity for profitable termination which ERISA seems to offer firms. The point of departure for this model is the AlloyTek case, the resolution of which indicates that a firm can terminate an underfunded pension plan with minimum explicit cost once, but only once.[3] A one-time-only termination provision makes the pension put formally identical to an infinite maturity American option, which expires only upon exercise. The cost of termination is the opportunity cost of not being able to terminate in the future for possible greater benefits. The termination decision becomes an optimal timing problem in which the option is exercised only if it is sufficiently in the money. Such a model potentially can explain the existence of underfunded plans which have not yet terminated without resorting to unspecified implicit costs of termination. Given the ability of a firm to replace the terminated defined benefit plan with a defined contribution plan, it is not clear that those costs would be significant for most firms.

The first model yields an upper-bound estimate of the value of PBGC insurance because the plan is terminated only when that action is optimal for the firm. In contrast, the second model should provide a lower bound on the value of the PBGC insurance. In this model, a pension plan terminates only at the occurrence of corporate bankruptcy. The motivation for this approach is twofold: First, it is consistent with the empirical fact that virtually no underfunded-but-solvent firms exercise the pension put. Second, it is consistent with proposals for pension insurance reform that would disallow termination of underfunded plans by solvent firms. The value derived for this scenario should represent a lower bound on the true value of the insurance, since it rules out the possibility for firms to choose a value-maximizing termination rule. The true value of PBGC insurance should lie between the valuation bounds generated by these two models.

The models employed in this paper allow for an analysis and valuation of pension insurance in a model in which plan termination is determined endogenously. The models also offer a framework for studying corporate pension funding and investment policy. The implications of these models confirm and extend those of Bulow (1981) and Harrison and Sharpe (1982), who analyzed pension funding strategies for plans with a given maturity date.

The next section presents a model of pension insurance. The valuation of PBGC liabilities is derived for each scenario, risk-rated pension insurance premium structures are considered, and optimal corporate financial policy is examined. It is shown that a fund can be significantly underfunded before a firm would find termination to be a profitable strategy. It also is shown that even under a bankruptcy-only termination rule, PBGC liabilities can be extremely large and quite sensitive to the pension funding policy of the firm.

Section 3.2 presents empirical estimates of the value of PBGC insurance for a sample of Fortune 100 firms. The results of this section indicate that the pension put has significant value for several firms, and that the true value of PBGC liabilities can differ substantially from the common measure of such liabilities, which is accrued benefits less the sum of fund assets plus 30% of firm net worth. Section 3.3 concludes.

3.1   A Model of Pension Insurance

3.1.1   Valuation of PBGC Pension Liabilities: Voluntary Termination

For simplicity, I will assume that all accrued benefits are vested and fully insured by the PBGC. In fact, guaranteed benefits typically account for between 90% and 95% of vested benefits, while approximately 80% of accrued benefits are vested (Amoroso 1983). This simplification is necessary to derive analytic solutions below; it should not affect the qualitative properties of the solution.

Following Bulow, let A denote the value of accrued benefits, F denote the value of assets in the pension fund, and $.3E$ denote the firm liability beyond assets in the pension fund (i.e., 30% of net worth). F and E are measured as market values, while A is the present value of accrued benefits calculated by discounting at the riskless nominal interest rate. The benefits represent an obligation which will be paid with certainty, either by the firm or by the PBGC.

At a termination, if the plan is sufficiently funded ($F + .3E \geq A$), the firm gains F and transfers assets of value A to the PBGC. Otherwise, the firm is liable only up to the amount $F + .3E$. The net proceeds to the firm at termination therefore equal[4]

(1) $$F - \min(A, F + .3E)$$

or equivalently,

(2) $$F - A + \max[A - (F + .3E), 0].$$

Expression (2) highlights the nature of the firm's put option. Its net pension liability is $F - A$; however, at the termination date it can transfer its liability of A to the PBGC in return for only $F + .3E$.

There is no explicit maturity date associated with the insurance plan. In this sense, it is isomorphic to an American put option with infinite maturity and exercise price A. Just as the put can be exercised only once, the firm can voluntarily terminate just one defined benefit plan. Thereafter, it may offer its employees only defined contribution plans. These plans are akin to mutual funds in that they neither require nor receive PBGC insurance. Part of the firm's problem will be to choose a rule for voluntary termination that, in conjunction with its other policies, maximizes firm value.

To solve for the value of the pension insurance it first is necessary to specify the dynamics for accrued liabilities and the assets backing the plan. These will differ from conventional specifications because of the effects of firm contributions to the pension fund and the effects of new retirees and deaths on the dynamics for A.

For convenience, use S to denote the sum $F + .3E$. I will assume that S follows the diffusion process

(3) $$dS = (C_S + \alpha_S)S dt + \sigma_S S dz_S$$

where α_S is a standard drift term attributable to the normal rate of return on the pension fund assets, F, and the firm equity, E, and where C_S is the rate (as a fraction of S) of firm contributions into the pension fund *net* of payments to retirees.[5] Solutions are presented below in which C_S is a function of the funding status of the plan; it need not be constant. If firm funding for accruing benefits exceeds payouts from the pension fund for current retirees, C_S will be positive. In a steady state with no uncertainty, a constant interest rate, and a constant number of retirees, the present value of accrued benefits would be constant

$< K^* < 1$ so that the put will be exercised only for $S < A$, that is, if fund assets plus 30% of net worth fall below accrued benefits. Parameters that result in nonnegative values for ϵ would imply that the option would never be exercised.[7]

Equations (6) and (7) generalize the formula for the perpetual American put option presented in Merton (1973). In the special case that A is nonstochastic, that $C_S = 0$ and $C_A = -r$ (which offsets the growth in A due to the time value of money and thereby causes the dollar value of the "exercise price," A, to be constant), ϵ equals $-2r/\sigma^2$ and (6) reduces to Merton's equation (52).

Comparative Statics for the Closed Form Solution

Although the closed form solution places an unrealistic restriction on the firm's pension-funding policy, it offers the opportunity to examine analytically some properties of the valuation equation. More realistic specifications of funding policy are considered in later sections. It is possible to show analytically for the special case presented in equation (6) that the value of the termination option increases with C_A and decreases with C_S. Conversely, the ratio of S/A at which it is optimal to terminate falls with C_A and increases with C_S. The intuition for these results is straightforward: when the gap between the growth rates of accrued benefits and the assets backing those benefits ($S = F + .3E$) increases, the expected profits from a future exercise of the put option increase and the value of waiting to exercise correspondingly increases. These results are illustrated in table 3.1, in which optimal ratios for pension termination, $K^* = (S/A)^*$, and the values of the pension put, $P(A,S)$, are presented for various combinations of C_A and C_S and for a variance rate of .05.[8] Recall that the certainty equivalent drifts in A and S are $r + C_A$ and $r + C_S$, respectively. Therefore the parameters presented in table 3.1 correspond to combinations of sustained growth rates in the value of the assets and liabilities of the fund ranging from $-.08$ to $+.06$.

The values of PBGC obligations presented in the second panel of table 3.1 are calculated assuming that $A = S = 1.0$. Therefore, these entries may be interpreted as the value of the pension insurance as a fraction of accrued benefits when the pension put is exactly at the money, that is, when the total assets backing the pension fund obligations equal the present value of those obligations. Remember, however, that this condition does not correspond to full funding of the pension fund, since S includes the contingent liability of the firm of .3E. Of course, equation (6) could be used to generate actuarially fair values of the insurance for any initial values of A and S.

The table demonstrates that the value of the termination put can be substantial. As a base case, the zero drift configuration of C_A and C_S

Table 3.1   **Termination Ratios and Option Values** ($\sigma^2 = .05$, $S_0/A_0 = 1$)

	Optimal Exercise Ratio, $K = (S/A)^*$							
$r + C_A$:	$-.08$	$-.06$	$-.04$	$-.02$	0	.02	.04	.06
$r + C_S$								
$-.08$	.69	.64	.58	.52	.44	.36	.28	.19
$-.06$	.72	.68	.62	.55	.48	.40	.31	.21
$-.04$	.75	.71	.66	.59	.52	.43	.34	.23
$-.02$	.78	.74	.69	.64	.56	.48	.38	.26
0	.80	.77	.73	.68	.61	.52	.42	.30
.02	.82	.79	.76	.72	.66	.58	.47	.37
.04	.83	.82	.79	.75	.70	.63	.53	.39
.06	.85	.84	.81	.78	.74	.68	.59	.46

	Put Value							
$r + C_A$:	$-.08$	$-.06$	$-.04$	$-.02$	0	.02	.04	.06
$r + C_S$								
$-.08$	.136	.162	.196	.238	.290	.356	.440	.549
$-.06$	.120	.144	.174	.214	.264	.328	.412	.523
$-.04$	.106	.126	.153	.189	.236	.298	.381	.494
$-.02$	.093	.110	.134	.165	.208	.266	.347	.461
0	.082	.097	.116	.143	.180	.233	.310	.423
.02	.073	.085	.101	.123	.154	.200	.270	.379
.04	.065	.075	.088	.106	.131	.169	.230	.330
.06	.058	.066	.077	.091	.111	.142	.191	.277

gives a pension put value of 18% of the value of accrued liabilities. Therefore even fully funded plans (where funding includes the firm's contingent liability of $.3E$) can pose significant risk to the PBGC. When $r + C_S$ is negative (i.e., when pension assets are being depleted because of payments to retirees) or when $r + C_A$ is positive, pension insurance values increase dramatically.

It is interesting to note that when $C_A = C_S = 0$, $\epsilon = 0$, and the pension put will never be terminated. In this case, the "exercise price," A, is growing at an expected rate equal to its cost of capital; therefore, in contrast to the standard put option, waiting to exercise does not impose a time-value-of-money cost.

The table also can be used to examine the effects of equal changes in C_S and C_A. Reading down the diagonals from top left to bottom right demonstrates that the optimal voluntary termination ratio decreases for larger (algebraic) values of these growth rates. The value of the pension put correspondingly increases. These results derive from the effect of scale on the termination decision. If a pension fund is increasing in size (large positive C_A, C_S), then the dollar gain from a termination for any given *ratio* of S/A is larger. If the fund is growing, it pays to wait to terminate, and the ratio S/A must be smaller to induce early termination. Thus, one should expect termination decisions to be more frequent in declining industries in which pension funds are shrinking. These results can be verified analytically: Equal (algebraic) increases in C_A and C_S always increase the value of $P(A,S)$ and lower the termination ratio, K^*.

Corporate Pension Funding Policy

Bulow (1981) and Harrison and Sharpe (1982) examine pension funding policy in a model with taxes and with an exogenous termination date. They conclude that a firm should fund its plan either to the maximum or the minimum level permitted. This razor's edge characteristic is also a property of the voluntary termination model.

To confirm this point, compute the first and second derivatives of $P(A,S)$ with respect to pension funding, S:

$$(8) \qquad P_S = \epsilon(1 - K)S^{\epsilon-1}A^{1-\epsilon}K^{-\epsilon}$$
$$= -LK/(S/A)]^{1-\epsilon}$$

$$(9) \qquad P_{SS} = \epsilon(\epsilon - 1)(1 - K)A^{1-\epsilon}S^{\epsilon-2}K^{-\epsilon} > 0,$$

where the final form of equation (8) is obtained by substituting for ϵ from (7). From (8), for any nonterminated plan (i.e., $K < S/A$), we have that $0 > P_S > -1$, so that each dollar contributed reduces the insurance value by less than \$1.00, and by (9), each successive dollar contributed reduces the insurance value by progressively smaller amounts. In contrast, the marginal tax shield arising from contributions to the pension fund is independent of the level of current funding (Black 1980; Tepper 1981). Therefore, the firm will always be forced to a corner solution: At any interior point, if \$1.00 of extra funding results in an incremental tax shield that exceeds the marginal decrease in the value of pension insurance, then so must the next dollar contribution, and so on. Conversely, if marginally decreased funding is optimal in the interior, then so must be further decreases until some statutory limit is reached. See figure 3.1.

Discretionary Funding: Voluntary Termination

The analytic solution studied in sections 3.1.1.1 and 3.1.1.2 imposes passive behavior on the firm in that pension funding always equals a fixed fraction of current assets, S. In fact, one would expect firms to adjust funding as financial circumstances change. Figure 3.2 presents numerical solutions for PBGC insurance values for three behavioral assumptions.[9] Suppose that firm funding behavior can be described by the following specification:

$$(10) \qquad C_S = c_0 + c_1[\ln(A/S)].$$

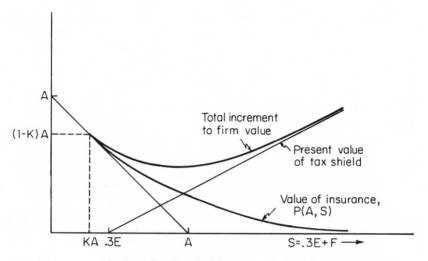

Fig. 3.1   Optimal funding decision

NOTE: The pension plan is terminated when $S/A \leq K$, or at $S = KA$. At termination, the obligation of the PBGC equals $A - S = (1 - K)A$. Before termination, the insurance is worth $P(A,S)$. The tangency at $S = KA$ is the termination point.

The present value of tax savings from pension funding increases with funding, or, holding E fixed, with S. The present value of tax savings is proportional to the level of funding. The total increment to firm value is maximized at either the minimum or maximum permitted funding levels.

For $c_1 = 0$, funding is independent of the current status of the pension plan; this is the passive rule. For $c_1 < 0$, the firm follows an exploitative strategy: if the plan becomes underfunded ($A > S$), then C_S falls, contributions to the plan are reduced, and the value of the pension insurance is increased. Conversely, if the plan is overfunded, then PGBC insurance is less valuable, and funding increases to exploit the tax benefit of further contributions. This specification thus induces the value-maximizing, extreme funding behavior discussed in section 3.1.1.2. Finally, for $c_1 > 0$, the firm follows what might be called socially responsible behavior. Its contribution rate increases when the plan is underfunded and falls when overfunded.

Figure 3.2 presents numerical solutions to equation (5) using parameters $c_0 = -r$ and $c_1 = -.1, 0,$ and $.1$. The figure demonstrates that the value of pension insurance (as a fraction of accrued liabilities) is most variable for the exploitative strategy. For underfunded plans, the value of the insurance is greatest for $c_1 = -.1$, and lowest for $c_1 = .1$. (The values of the pension insurance for $c_1 = .1$ and $c_1 = 0$ are equal for $S/A < .5$, since the pension plan would be terminated at that

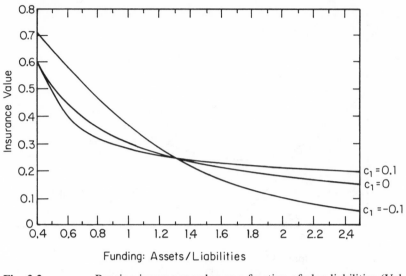

Fig. 3.2   Pension-insurance value as a fraction of plan liabilities (Voluntary-termination scenario)

point for either value of c_1.) Conversely, for overfunded plans, the insurance value is lowest for $c_1 = -.1$.

3.1.2 PBGC Liabilities with Termination Only at Bankruptcy

If the pension plan terminates only when the firm bankrupts, the special put option conveyed by the current pension insurance system is lost. Instead, at bankruptcy, the PBGC simply assumes the pension fund.

The value of the PBGC liability will depend in general upon the exact conditions that set off a bankruptcy. I will assume that bankruptcy is declared when the value of the firm, V, falls below the present value of the debt obligations of the firm, where that value is computed under the assumption that the obligations will be fully met. (This notion of debt, rather than market value, is the appropriate one because limited liability assures that the market value of debt can never exceed V.) Although this definition of bankruptcy is at odds with the technical definition that a firm fails to meet a coupon or principal payment, it still seems a useful way to model bankruptcy for the present purpose. Firms in practice have several overlapping debt issues outstanding with associated sinking fund covenants that would make the modeling of bankruptcy in a legal context exceedingly complex and firm specific. Economic insolvency offers a more straightforward approach.

Denote by D the present value of debt obligations computed by discounting at the riskless-in-terms-of-default interest rate and let $v = V/D$. Then insolvency occurs at the first occurrence of $v \leq 1$. At that moment, the PBGC inherits a net liability of $A - F$, where F denotes the value of the funds in the pension plan. The PBGC's claim to 30% of firm net worth is irrelevant in this instance, since at bankruptcy, when $V \leq D$, equity has no value.

To derive the value of the PBGC insurance, we proceed as before. The dynamics for debt, pension funds, and firm value are taken to be the diffusion processes

$$dD = \alpha_D D dt + \sigma_D D dz_D$$
$$dF = (\alpha_F + C_F) F dt + \sigma_F F dz_F$$
$$dV = \alpha_V V dt + \sigma_V V dz_V,$$

where C_F denotes the rate of contributions to the pension fund as a fraction of F. In a nonstochastic steady state with a constant interest rate, C_F would equal $-r$. All fund earnings would be withdrawn to help pay benefits to current retirees so that total fund assets would remain unchanged over time. The covariances between the instantaneous rates of return on the variables will be denoted by σ_{DF}, σ_{DV}, and so on.

Letting $P(v,F,A)$ be the value of the PBGC liabilities, one can show that P must satisfy the p.d.e.

(11)
$$\frac{1}{2} (P_{vv} \sigma_v^2 v^2 + P_{FF} \sigma_F^2 F^2 + P_{AA} \sigma_A^2 A^2) + P_{vF} \sigma_{vF} vF + P_{vA} \sigma_{vA} vA$$
$$+ P_{FA} \sigma_{FA} FA + P_v rv + P_F (C_F + r)F + P_A (C_A + r)A - rP = 0$$

subject to the boundary conditions
  a) $P = A - F$ when $v = 1$
  b) the limit of P as v approaches infinity is zero
  c) the limit of P as A and F approach zero is zero.

These boundary conditions embody the assumption that if a firm with an overfunded plan goes bankrupt, then the PBGC simply inherits the plan together with its surplus. Given this rule, the present value of the PBGC's net liability can be negative. This assumption is likely to be irrelevant in practice, however, since it is highly improbable that a firm with discretionary funding would ever reach bankruptcy with an overfunded pension plan.

For the special case in which C_F and C_A are constant, the solution to this equation is

(12) $$P = Av^{-\phi} - Fv^{-\theta},$$

where

$$\theta = \frac{K}{M} + \left[\left(\frac{K}{M} \right)^2 - \frac{2C_F}{M} \right]^{\frac{1}{2}}$$

$$\phi = \frac{L}{M} + \left[\left(\frac{L}{M} \right)^2 - \frac{2C_A}{M} \right]^{\frac{1}{2}}$$

$$K = -\frac{1}{2} \sigma_V^2 + \frac{1}{2} \sigma_D^2 - \sigma_{DF} + \sigma_{VF}$$

$$L = -\frac{1}{2} \sigma_V^2 + \frac{1}{2} \sigma_D^2 - \sigma_{DA} + \sigma_{VA}$$

$$M = \sigma_V^2 + \sigma_D^2 - 2\sigma_{DV} = \sigma_v^2,$$

and where the solution is valid for parameters which result in positive values for θ and ϕ.[10]

Optimal corporate pension funding policy in the bankruptcy-only model resembles that in the voluntary termination model. The partial derivative of $P(v,F,A)$ with respect to the funding level, F, is simply $-v^{-\theta}$, which is independent of F. Thus, we again obtain a razor's edge property: If v is sufficiently large, then the tax benefits of additional funding will dominate the transfer of wealth to the PBGC and the firm will fund to the statutory limit. Otherwise, minimal funding will be value maximizing.

Discretionary Funding: Bankruptcy-Only Termination

Bodie et al. (1986) have found some tendency for pension funding policy to vary positively with firm profitability and negatively with the firm's tax-paying status. These results are consistent with the trade-off between the tax and pension-insurance considerations investigated in this paper. In order to explore the implications of discretionary funding policy in the bankruptcy-only termination model, consider the following specification for funding behavior:

(13) $$C_F = c_0 - c_1(D/V).$$

For $c_1 > 0$, funding declines with the firm's debt ratio (and associated probability of bankruptcy) to a minimum possible level of $c_0 - c_1$. Although debt ratios are not perfect measures of firm financial status, especially in interindustry comparisons, this specification does capture the stylized notion that as a firm approaches bankruptcy, its pension funding will decrease and in fact can become negative. Negative contributions are, strictly speaking, disallowed by ERISA. However, de facto negative funding is realized when the pension plan purchases equity or debt of the firm.

Figure 3.3 displays numerical solutions for the value of PBGC insurance as a function of the debt ratio, D/V, for a fully funded plan for three values of c_1.[11] We set c_0 at a level such that at $D/V = 0$, the ratio of plan assets to liabilities would increase at a rate of 2% per year. As D/V increases, the funding rate falls, and eventually the ratio of assets to liabilities will decrease over time.

For extreme values of the debt ratio, the present value of PBGC liabilities equals zero. Because the plan is fully funded, the PBGC faces no liability even if the firm bankrupts (i.e., $D/V = 1$). At the other extreme, as the debt ratio approaches zero, PBGC liabilities fall to zero because the probability of bankruptcy vanishes. For middle-range values of the debt ratio, however, PBGC liabilities can be quite large. If the firm reaches a debt ratio of .6, for example, there is a significant chance of bankruptcy, and until bankruptcy is reached, the firm will

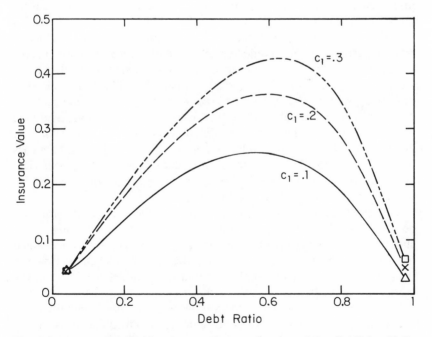

Fig. 3.3   Pension-insurance value as a fraction of plan liabilities (Fully funded plan, bankruptcy-only termination)

continue to drain the pension plan. In contrast, if the firm is fully funded when $D/V = .9$, bankruptcy might be imminent, but there is less time for the firm to extract funds from the plan. The PBGC's liability is correspondingly small.

Figure 3.3 shows that the PBGC's liability can be a significant fraction of vested benefits, even for fully funded plans. Using the conservative assumption that $c_1 = .1$, the value of pension insurance still can rise to more than 20% of benefits. Further, the disparity in insurance values between the $c_1 = .1$ and $c_1 = .3$ curves shows that the value of pension insurance can be quite sensitive to firm funding policy, even without the option for firms to voluntarily terminate plans. These results imply that the common practice of estimating PBGC liabilities as max(0, $A - S$) can be quite misleading. They also indicate that spinoff/terminations, which allow firms to recapture the surplus assets from a pension fund and leave the PBGC guaranteeing a fund with no cushion against adverse investment experience, can result in significant PBGC liabilities.

3.1.3   The General Case

A general treatment of PBGC insurance would allow for termination either at the first occurrence of a voluntary termination point or at the first occurrence of corporate bankruptcy. As a general rule, there is no closed-form solution for the value of PBGC pension insurance in this mixed case, even with passive funding policies. The difficulty arises from the effects of debt on the variance rate of the firm's equity. Geske (1979) has shown that the variance rate evolves stochastically in this situation. Because the assets backing pension benefits, S, include 30% of firm net worth, σ^2 in equation (6) could no longer be taken as a fixed parameter, and the solution for the value of the pension insurance consequently would need to be modified. This effect, together with the fact that termination can result from either of two conditions, appears to make a numerical solution technique necessary. Even the numerical approach presents difficulties, however, since the problem would involve four state variables: A, S, F, and v.

Notwithstanding these complications, the above solutions still can be of use in valuing PBGC liabilities. The voluntary termination model should provide an upper bound on the value of pension insurance, since the termination rule is chosen to maximize the value of the insurance. In contrast, the termination-only-at-bankruptcy model provides a lower bound on the value of the insurance.

In practice, underfunded plans are associated with financially troubled firms. The models provide some clues to why troubled firms should tend to maintain underfunded plans. One possibility is that such firms have low marginal tax rates due to loss carry-forward provisions, and therefore derive less tax benefit from pension funding. Another explanation is that underfunding the pension plan represents a source of financing cheaper than that available in outside credit markets. This advantage will be greatest for firms with the highest borrowing rates. Finally, if bankruptcy causes the firm to forfeit the pension assets to the PBGC, overfunding of the plan would create a potential bankruptcy cost to which troubled firms would be more sensitive. This effect was made explicit in section 3.1.2, in which it was shown that firms with large values of D/V will find that minimal funding is value maximizing.

3.1.4 Risk-Rated Premiums

The valuation equations derived in sections 3.1.1 and 3.1.2 provide the present value of PBGC liabilities under different scenarios. They do not, however, provide explicit means to calculate fair annual premium *rates* for pension insurance. Because fund termination dates are stochastic, the premium annuity that has an ex ante present value equal to the present value of PBGC obligations cannot be easily calculated. One approach that might provide a reasonable approximation to the fair premium rate would be first to calculate the expected value of the time to termination, and then to calculate the annuity appropriate to the present value of PBGC obligations using a horizon equal to the expected time until termination and an interest rate equal to that paid on the firm's outstanding debt.

A different approach would require ex post settling up. At the start of each period, the present value of PBGC obligations would be calculated. At period-end, that value would be recalculated, and the firm would pay (or be paid) the change in the value of PBGC liabilities. The advantage of this scheme is that it eliminates most of the moral hazard problems involved in prespecified rate structures. Any increase in risk would induce increased premiums. The firm would always pay a fair price for its pension-put option (or for its limited liability in the bankruptcy model) and would thus lose the ability and the incentive to underfund at the expense of the PBGC.

3.2 Empirical Estimates

Estimates of the value of PBGC insurance will be presented for both the voluntary and bankruptcy-only termination models. For each model, three scenarios are considered, corresponding to different plan-funding strategies. Values in the voluntary termination model are calculated for $c_0 = -r$ and for $c_1 = -.1$ (exploitative strategy), 0 (passive strategy), and .1 (socially responsible strategy). (See eq. [10].) Values in the bankruptcy-only termination model are calculated for coefficients on the debt ratio equal to .1, .2, and .3, and for $c_0 = -r + .02$. (See eq. [13].) The (real) interest rate in all of the calculations is set at .04.

3.2.1 Data

Pensions and Investment Age (July 11, 1983) reports pension fund statistics derived from the 1982 annual reports of the Fortune 100 companies. The survey includes pension fund assets, vested benefits, and the assumed interest rate used to derive the present value of vested benefits.

The survey expresses pension fund assets as market values. The market value of vested benefits can be approximated by multiplying the reported value of benefits by the ratio of the plan's assumed interest rate to the actual long-term market interest rate for 1982. This adjustment assumes that pension benefit payout streams have time paths similar to perpetuities. The average rate on 30-year United States government obligations in 1982 was 12.76%. The market value of equity is easily derived from stock market data at year-end 1982, and total firm value can be approximated as equity plus book value of long-term debt.

The remaining inputs required to estimate the value of PBGC insurance are the variance and covariance rates on underlying securities. Table 3.2 presents the values assigned to these variables. These values are meant to be reasonable guesses only. The low variance rates on A and D and high correlation between the two reflect their similar natures as nominal liabilities. The variance rates on firm value and pension

Table 3.2   **Assumptions Used to Compute Value of Insurance**

		Variance Rate (annual)
Fund liabilities	A	.01
Fund assets	F	.04
Assets + .3 equity	S	.04
Firm debt	D	.01
Firm value	V	.04

Correlation Matrix				
	A	F	S	D	V
A					
F	n				
S	.1	n			
D	.8	.1	n		
V	.1	.5	n	.2	

NOTE: n = correlation coefficient between these variables was not necessary for calculations.

fund assets compare to a historical value for the S&P 500 of approximately .05 annually. The variance rate for V is derived by unlevering the S&P 500 variance using a debt/value ratio of 1/3 and then by doubling that variance to account for the lack of diversification of a single stock relative to the index. The variance rate on fund assets is set slightly below that on the S&P 500: The fund is probably less well diversified than the index, but this effect is offset by debt held in the fund.

3.2.2   Results

Tables 3.3a and 3.3b present estimates of the value of PBGC insurance for 87 of the Fortune 100 firms. Thirteen observations were lost because of missing data. Table 3.3a presents results in which the present values of benefits are calculated using the 12.76% yield on 30-year T-bonds that prevailed during 1982, while table 3.3b uses a 10% interest rate. Columns 1 and 2 of the tables are the present value of vested benefits for each plan, and the level of overfunding of each plan, respectively. Columns 3–8 are the ratios of the value of PBGC insurance to vested benefits for the voluntary termination scenario and the bankruptcy-only scenario under the three assumptions for firm funding behavior. These ratios can be interpreted as the fraction of pension benefits that are financed (in present value terms) by the PBGC. The ratios thus give a measure of the PBGC subsidy per dollar of pension benefits.

The results in tables 3.3a and 3.3b are consolidated in tables 3.4 and 3.5. Table 3.4 presents summary statistics for the voluntary termination model. The table reveals that PBGC liabilities can be extremely sensitive to firm funding policy. At current funding levels, total liabilities for the exploitative strategy ($c_1 = -.1$) are less than one-third their value for the socially responsible strategy ($c_1 = .1$). This result reflects the overfunded status of most plans in 1982. At 1982 funding levels, the exploitative strategy entailed the largest contribution rate into the pension fund (in order to maximize tax benefits), and thus resulted in the smallest insurance values.

Although table 3.4 indicates that most firms derive little value from pension insurance, a small number of "problem firms" derive considerable value from the pension insurance. These tend to be the larger firms: the weighted averages of the insurance values are substantially greater than the means.

As expected, PBGC liabilities are extremely sensitive to the interest rate used in calculating vested benefits. Table 3.4 shows that the total insurance values for the 87 firms in the voluntary termination scenario are 1.4–2.0 times as large for a 10% interest rate as they are for the actual 1982 rate of 12.76%. The total value of PBGC liabilities for the 87 firms is extremely large, ranging from $6.7 billion to $20.6 billion

Table 3.3a   **PBGC Insurance Values** (Nominal interest rate = 12.76%)

Company	Vested Benefits	Over-Funding	Voluntary Termination Sensitivity to Funding −.10	0	.10	Bankruptcy-Only Sensitivity to Debt .10	.20	.30
			Insurance Value as a Fraction of Vested Benefits					
ALLIED	551.	259.	0.0687	0.1537	0.1898	0.1417	0.2717	0.3352
ALCOA	1053.	322.	0.0672	0.1501	0.1855	0.1763	0.2917	0.3481
AMER HESS	37.	70.	0.0	0.0292	0.1355	−.2307	0.0504	0.1958
AM BRANDS	239.	97.	0.0029	0.0824	0.1558	0.0991	0.1537	0.1734
AM CAN	655.	247.	0.1511	0.2032	0.2217	0.1352	0.2812	0.3622
AN-BUSCH	149.	165.	0.0001	0.0441	0.1273	0.0597	0.1698	0.2128
ARMCO	842.	328.	0.1218	0.1873	0.2118	0.1586	0.2815	0.3415
ASHLAND OIL	135.	205.	0.0027	0.0765	0.1446	−.2301	0.0375	0.1860
ARCO	878.	635.	0.0005	0.0569	0.1275	0.1047	0.2224	0.2732
BETH STEEL	2472.	−148.	0.3384	0.2878	0.2703	0.2699	0.3751	0.4387
BOEING	1140.	1261.	0.0171	0.1093	0.1651	0.0357	0.0738	0.0866
BORDEN	150.	92.	0.0028	0.0779	0.1473	0.1068	0.1910	0.2238
BURROUGHS	348.	223.	0.0181	0.1161	0.1754	0.1163	0.2283	0.2766
CATERPILLAR	1260.	733.	0.0508	0.1478	0.1931	0.1182	0.2580	0.3263
CHRYSLER	2277.	−329.	0.3380	0.2875	0.2700	0.3055	0.4013	0.4591
COASTAL	37.	71.	0.0006	0.0680	0.1523	−.9242	−.6312	−.4335
COCA-COLA	139.	96.	0.0	0.0253	0.1172	0.0423	0.0588	0.0644
COLG-PALMOL	211.	274.	0.0029	0.0827	0.1564	0.0351	0.1037	0.1274
CONS FOODS	61.	80.	0.0001	0.0463	0.1339	0.0398	0.1340	0.1681
CONTL GROUP	614.	304.	0.0684	0.1528	0.1887	0.1246	0.2700	0.3452
CONTROL DATA	120.	157.	0.0006	0.0621	0.1392	−.5791	−.3450	−.1871
CPC INTL	136.	17.	0.0006	0.0604	0.1352	0.0637	0.0841	0.0909
DEERE	569.	545.	0.0173	0.1110	0.1676	0.0721	0.2060	0.2637
DIGITAL EQ	22.	151.	0.0	0.0	0.0228	0.0420	0.0438	0.0443
DOW CHEM	655.	513.	0.0026	0.0737	0.1392	0.0754	0.2332	0.3103
DRESSER	326.	291.	0.0191	0.1225	0.1850	0.0735	0.1580	0.1894
DU PONT	3586.	4057.	0.0165	0.1054	0.1592	0.0024	0.1908	0.2829
EAST KODAK	1276.	1466.	0.0005	0.0596	0.1336	0.0440	0.0445	0.0446
EXXON	1939.	2306.	0.0006	0.0671	0.1504	0.0431	0.1159	0.1413
FIRESTONE	745.	256.	0.1199	0.1843	0.2084	0.1444	0.2240	0.2564
FORD	4420.	2800.	0.0969	0.1759	0.2073	0.1175	0.2384	0.2925
GEN DYNAMICS	569.	726.	0.0185	0.1187	0.1793	0.0440	0.0445	0.0446
GEN ELEC	4208.	4474.	0.0082	0.0962	0.1604	0.0412	0.0469	0.0488
GEN FOODS	397.	535.	0.0088	0.1041	0.1735	0.0350	0.1652	0.2171
GEN MILLS	221.	102.	0.0031	0.0866	0.1637	0.0681	0.1063	0.1193
GEN MOTORS	13195.	1237.	0.1808	0.2180	0.2307	0.1297	0.1762	0.1933
GEORGIA PAC	97.	122.	0.0	0.0157	0.0726	0.0043	0.1859	0.2705
GETTY OIL	232.	255.	0.0001	0.0378	0.1093	0.0599	0.1699	0.2128
GOODYEAR	983.	590.	0.0501	0.1459	0.1905	0.1189	0.2204	0.2629
WR GRACE	109.	240.	0.0001	0.0436	0.1259	−.2231	0.0600	0.1983
GREYHOUND	656.	326.	0.0913	0.1658	0.1953	0.1359	0.2381	0.2823
GULF OIL	1067.	856.	0.0188	0.1204	0.1818	0.0941	0.2083	0.2561
GULF&WEST	245.	132.	0.0176	0.1128	0.1704	0.0173	0.1899	0.2941
HEWLETT-PACK	230.	270.	0.0	0.0211	0.0976	0.0440	0.0445	0.0446

Table 3.3a   (continued)

Company	Vested Benefits	Over-Funding	Insurance Value as a Fraction of Vested Benefits					
			Voluntary Termination			Bankruptcy-Only		
			Sensitivity to Funding			Sensitivity to Debt		
			−.10	0	.10	.10	.20	.30
IC INDUS	174.	103.	0.0501	0.1456	0.1902	−.1592	0.0031	0.1126
IBM	2909.	5481.	0.0001	0.0465	0.1345	0.0354	0.0463	0.0499
INTL PAPER	401.	560.	0.0027	0.0754	0.1426	0.0203	0.1723	0.2359
ITT	1039.	625.	0.0330	0.1350	0.1883	0.1140	0.2556	0.3248
J&JOHNSON	146.	218.	0.0	0.0	0.0058	0.0439	0.0444	0.0446
KERR-MCGEE	41.	85.	0.0	0.0211	0.0977	−.1381	0.1076	0.2220
LITTON INDUS	290.	289.	0.0026	0.0741	0.1401	0.0399	0.0795	0.0928
LOCKHEED	1228.	1296.	0.0498	0.1448	0.1892	0.0394	0.2052	0.2824
LTV	1333.	115.	0.2572	0.2480	0.2443	0.1437	0.2543	0.3288
MCDERMOTT	311.	270.	0.0307	0.1253	0.1748	0.0810	0.2192	0.2810
MCDONNELL DO	949.	1052.	0.0309	0.1265	0.1764	0.0432	0.0451	0.0457
3M	330.	403.	0.0	0.0154	0.0713	0.0440	0.0445	0.0446
MOBIL	1315.	1643.	0.0029	0.0830	0.1568	0.0319	0.1856	0.2519
MONSANTO	803.	894.	0.0188	0.1205	0.1820	0.0590	0.1695	0.2126
MOTOROLA	43.	146.	0.0	0.0	0.0075	−.0421	0.0538	0.0861
NABISCO	261.	77.	0.0026	0.0743	0.1404	0.1198	0.1776	0.1991
PEPSICO	111.	172.	0.0	0.0173	0.0803	0.0223	0.1362	0.1786
PHILIP MORRI	195.	296.	0.0	0.0212	0.0983	−.0202	0.1661	0.2493
PHILLIPS PET	445.	648.	0.0006	0.0631	0.1414	0.0195	0.1648	0.2240
RALSTON PUR.	81.	191.	0.0001	0.0523	0.1513	−.1217	0.1080	0.2071
RJ REYNOLDS	391.	475.	0.0007	0.0719	0.1611	0.0334	0.0584	0.0668
ROCKWELL INT	1322.	1436.	0.0334	0.1364	0.1903	0.0468	0.2013	0.2703
SHELL OIL	715.	942.	0.0001	0.0374	0.1082	0.0440	0.0445	0.0446
SIGNAL COS.	388.	322.	0.0185	0.1187	0.1793	−.2992	−.1130	0.0126
SPERRY	424.	618.	0.0080	0.0938	0.1563	0.0265	0.1549	0.2050
STD OIL CAL	607.	584.	0.0001	0.0388	0.1121	0.0383	0.0549	0.0605
STD OIL IND	848.	585.	0.0006	0.0630	0.1411	0.0684	0.1225	0.1413
STD OIL OHIO	494.	516.	0.0001	0.0388	0.1120	0.0601	0.1999	0.2602
SUN CO	486.	524.	0.0028	0.0787	0.1488	−.0885	0.1320	0.2543
TEXACO	541.	632.	0.0007	0.0722	0.1618	0.0529	0.1547	0.1930
TEXAS INST	81.	258.	0.0	0.0238	0.1104	−.4265	−.0581	0.1220
TENNECO	374.	322.	0.0005	0.0580	0.1299	0.0416	0.0482	0.0503
TRW	586.	550.	0.0179	0.1149	0.1735	−.3646	−.1672	−.0340
UNION CARB	945.	787.	0.0173	0.1107	0.1672	0.0420	0.0714	0.0813
UNION OIL CA	325.	389.	0.0006	0.0701	0.1571	0.0299	0.1924	0.2650
UNION PACIFI	107.	112.	0.0	0.0222	0.1030	0.0643	0.1655	0.2043
UNITED BRAND	136.	79.	0.1249	0.1922	0.2173	−.5156	−.4857	−.4623
US STEEL	5003.	2236.	0.1451	0.1951	0.2129	0.0581	0.0876	0.0976
UNITED TECH	1205.	1650.	0.0180	0.1153	0.1742	−.6196	−.3786	−.2161
WARNER COMM	26.	38.	0.0	0.0	0.0074	0.0088	0.1667	0.2328
WESTINGHOUSE	1832.	883.	0.0684	0.1529	0.1889	0.0627	0.0980	0.1099
WEYERHAEUSER	296.	175.	0.0006	0.0676	0.1514	0.0542	0.0878	0.0991
XEROX	557.	386.	0.0077	0.0908	0.1513	0.1090	0.2246	0.2744

Table 3.3b   **PBGC Insurance Values** (Nominal interest rate = 10%)

			Insurance Value as a Fraction of Vested Benefits					
			Voluntary Termination			Bankruptcy-Only		
	Vested	Over-	Sensitivity to Funding			Sensitivity to Debt		
Company	Benefits	Funding	−.10	0	.10	.10	.20	.30
ALLIED	703.	107.	0.1480	0.1991	0.2173	0.2087	0.3105	0.3603
ALCOA	1344.	31.	0.1446	0.1945	0.2122	0.2358	0.3262	0.3705
AMER HESS	47.	60.	0.0	0.0229	0.1062	−.0715	0.1488	0.2627
AM BRANDS	306.	30.	0.0081	0.0957	0.1595	0.1190	0.1618	0.1772
AM CAN	836.	66.	0.2294	0.2350	0.2363	0.2301	0.3445	0.4080
AN-BUSCH	190.	124.	0.0007	0.0711	0.1594	0.1030	0.1893	0.2229
ARMCO	1074.	96.	0.2027	0.2236	0.2302	0.2219	0.3182	0.3653
ASHLAND OIL	172.	168.	0.0191	0.1224	0.1849	−.0562	0.1536	0.2699
ARCO	1121.	392.	0.0026	0.0742	0.1402	0.1562	0.2484	0.2882
BETH STEEL	3154.	−830.	0.4387	0.3387	0.3049	0.3553	0.4378	0.4876
BOEING	1455.	946.	0.0487	0.1418	0.1852	0.0487	0.0786	0.0886
BORDEN	192.	50.	0.0077	0.0905	0.1509	0.1399	0.2059	0.2316
BURROUGHS	445.	126.	0.0518	0.1507	0.1968	0.1652	0.2530	0.2908
CATERPILLAR	1608.	385.	0.0943	0.1712	0.2017	0.1902	0.2998	0.3534
CHRYSLER	2906.	−958.	0.4383	0.3384	0.3046	0.3832	0.4582	0.5036
COASTAL	48.	60.	0.0031	0.0887	0.1676	−.5534	−.3237	−.1688
COCA-COLA	178.	57.	0.0	0.0198	0.0918	0.0479	0.0609	0.0652
COLG-PALMOL	269.	216.	0.0082	0.0961	0.1601	0.0592	0.1130	0.1315
CONS FOODS	78.	63.	0.0001	0.0363	0.1049	0.0745	0.1482	0.1750
CONTL GROUP	783.	135.	0.1472	0.1979	0.2160	0.2069	0.3208	0.3798
CONTROL DATA	154.	123.	0.0029	0.0810	0.1531	−.2828	−.0994	0.0243
CPC INTL	174.	−21.	0.0028	0.0787	0.1487	0.0707	0.0866	0.0920
DEERE	726.	388.	0.0495	0.1440	0.1881	0.1306	0.2355	0.2807
DIGITAL EQ	28.	145.	0.0	0.0	0.0179	0.0426	0.0440	0.0444
DOW CHEM	835.	333.	0.0184	0.1179	0.1781	0.1567	0.2804	0.3408
DRESSER	416.	201.	0.0308	0.1258	0.1755	0.1053	0.1714	0.1960
DU PONT	4576.	3067.	0.0470	0.1368	0.1787	0.0995	0.2472	0.3193
EAST KODAK	1628.	1114.	0.0028	0.0778	0.1469	0.0442	0.0445	0.0447
EXXON	2474.	1771.	0.0031	0.0875	0.1654	0.0690	0.1261	0.1460
FIRESTONE	951.	50.	0.1995	0.2201	0.2266	0.1771	0.2394	0.2648
FORD	5640.	1580.	0.1808	0.2180	0.2306	0.1726	0.2674	0.3097
GEN DYNAMICS	726.	569.	0.0298	0.1219	0.1700	0.0441	0.0445	0.0447
GEN ELEC	5370.	3312.	0.0333	0.1362	0.1900	0.0432	0.0476	0.0491
GEN FOODS	507.	425.	0.0176	0.1125	0.1699	0.0872	0.1893	0.2299
GEN MILLS	282.	41.	0.0085	0.1006	0.1677	0.0813	0.1113	0.1215
GEN MOTORS	16837.	−2405.	0.2545	0.2454	0.2417	0.1470	0.1834	0.1968
GEORGIA PAC	124.	95.	0.0001	0.0431	0.1245	0.0916	0.2340	0.3002
GETTY OIL	295.	192.	0.0006	0.0611	0.1368	0.1031	0.1894	0.2230
GOODYEAR	1254.	319.	0.0930	0.1689	0.1990	0.1618	0.2414	0.2747
WR GRACE	139.	210.	0.0006	0.0704	0.1577	−.0772	0.1446	0.2530
GREYHOUND	837.	145.	0.1704	0.2054	0.2174	0.1806	0.2607	0.2953
GULF OIL	1362.	561.	0.0302	0.1236	0.1724	0.1423	0.2319	0.2693
GULF&WEST	312.	65.	0.0503	0.1464	0.1912	0.1573	0.2926	0.3743
HEWLETT-PACK	294.	206.	0.0	0.0165	0.0765	0.0442	0.0445	0.0447

Table 3.3b   (continued)

			Insurance Value as a Fraction of Vested Benefits					
			Voluntary Termination			Bankruptcy-Only		
Company	Vested Benefits	Over-Funding	Sensitivity to Funding			Sensitivity to Debt		
			−.10	0	.10	.10	.20	.30
IC INDUS	222.	55.	0.0929	0.1686	0.1987	0.0462	0.1734	0.2592
IBM	3711.	4679.	0.0001	0.0365	0.1054	0.0391	0.0476	0.0505
INTL PAPER	511.	450.	0.0188	0.1208	0.1824	0.0845	0.2037	0.2535
ITT	1326.	338.	0.0735	0.1643	0.2030	0.1870	0.2979	0.3522
J&JOHNSON	187.	177.	0.0	0.0254	0.1179	0.0441	0.0445	0.0446
KERR-MCGEE	53.	73.	0.0	0.0165	0.0765	−.0200	0.1726	0.2622
LITTON INDUS	370.	209.	0.0185	0.1186	0.1792	0.0534	0.0845	0.0949
LOCKHEED	1567.	957.	0.0924	0.1677	0.1976	0.1191	0.2491	0.3096
LTV	1701.	−253.	0.3862	0.3121	0.2868	0.2836	0.3702	0.4287
MCDERMOTT	397.	184.	0.0682	0.1525	0.1884	0.1440	0.2523	0.3008
MCDONNELL DO	1211.	790.	0.0688	0.1539	0.1901	0.0438	0.0453	0.0458
3M	421.	312.	0.0001	0.0423	0.1222	0.0441	0.0445	0.0447
MOBIL	1678.	1280.	0.0082	0.0964	0.1606	0.0991	0.2196	0.2715
MONSANTO	1024.	673.	0.0303	0.1237	0.1726	0.1024	0.1890	0.2228
MOTOROLA	55.	134.	0.0	0.0	0.0059	−.0092	0.0660	0.0913
NABISCO	333.	5.	0.0186	0.1189	0.1796	0.1415	0.1868	0.2037
PEPSICO	141.	142.	0.0001	0.0476	0.1376	0.0651	0.1544	0.1876
PHILIP MORRI	249.	242.	0.0	0.0166	0.0770	0.0647	0.2107	0.2759
PHILLIPS PET	568.	525.	0.0029	0.0823	0.1555	0.0791	0.1931	0.2395
RALSTON PUR.	103.	169.	0.0001	0.0410	0.1185	−.0213	0.1587	0.2364
RJ REYNOLDS	499.	367.	0.0005	0.0563	0.1263	0.0418	0.0615	0.0680
ROCKWELL INT	1686.	1072.	0.0743	0.1660	0.2051	0.1172	0.2383	0.2924
SHELL OIL	912.	745.	0.0006	0.0605	0.1355	0.0441	0.0445	0.0446
SIGNAL COS.	495.	215.	0.0298	0.1219	0.1701	−.0635	0.0824	0.1809
SPERRY	542.	500.	0.0325	0.1327	0.1852	0.0770	0.1776	0.2168
STD OIL CAL	774.	417.	0.0006	0.0626	0.1403	0.0440	0.0570	0.0613
STD OIL IND	1082.	351.	0.0029	0.0821	0.1552	0.0875	0.1300	0.1447
STD OIL OHIO	630.	380.	0.0006	0.0626	0.1403	0.1212	0.2307	0.2780
SUN CO	620.	390.	0.0078	0.0914	0.1524	0.0547	0.2276	0.3234
TEXACO	690.	483.	0.0005	0.0566	0.1268	0.0917	0.1714	0.2014
TEXAS INST	104.	235.	0.0	0.0187	0.0865	−.2367	0.0521	0.1932
TENNECO	477.	219.	0.0027	0.0756	0.1429	0.0438	0.0490	0.0507
TRW	747.	389.	0.0512	0.1491	0.1947	−.1148	0.0399	0.1443
UNION CARB	1206.	526.	0.0494	0.1436	0.1876	0.0520	0.0751	0.0828
UNION OIL CA	415.	299.	0.0005	0.0549	0.1231	0.1040	0.2313	0.2882
UNION PACIFI	136.	83.	0.0	0.0174	0.0807	0.1034	0.1827	0.2131
UNITED BRAND	174.	41.	0.2080	0.2294	0.2362	−.1929	−.1694	−.1511
US STEEL	6384.	855.	0.2618	0.2525	0.2487	0.0682	0.0914	0.0992
UNITED TECH	1538.	1317.	0.0514	0.1496	0.1954	−.3146	−.1258	0.0016
WARNER COMM	33.	31.	0.0	0.0	0.0058	0.0755	0.1993	0.2511
WESTINGHOUSE	2338.	377.	0.1473	0.1981	0.2162	0.0748	0.1025	0.1118
WEYERHAEUSER	377.	94.	0.0031	0.0881	0.1665	0.0657	0.0920	0.1009
XEROX	711.	232.	0.0314	0.1285	0.1792	0.1595	0.2501	0.2891

Table 3.4   **Insurance Value Summary Statistics (Voluntary Termination Model)**

Insurance Value as a Fraction of Vested Benefits	$C_1 = -.1$		$C_1 = 0$		$C_1 = .1$	
	$r = .1276$	$r = .10$	$r = .1276$	$r = .10$	$r = .1276$	$r = .10$
A. Frequency Distribution						
0–.01	51	42	4	3	3	2
.01–.025	13	6	8	7	1	1
.025–.05	5	12	10	7	0	0
.05–.075	7	8	17	10	2	0
.075–.10	2	4	11	14	4	6
.10 –.15	4	4	22	22	26	19
.15 –.25	2	6	13	20	49	56
.25+	3	5	2	4	2	3
B. Summary Statistics						
Maximum value	.338	.439	.288	.389	.270	.305
Mean value	.033	.058	.095	.117	.153	.166
Median value	.003	.018	.082	.118	.156	.170
Weighted average[a]	.084	.134	.145	.175	.187	.204
Total value ($ billion)	6.7	13.6	11.5	17.7	14.8	20.6

[a]Weights = value of vested benefits.

for the different cases considered in the table 3.4. These values compare with PBGC reserves for insured future benefits of only $1.14 billion (PBGC *Annual Report,* fiscal year 1982). Therefore, if the option to terminate voluntarily is to be taken seriously, the PBGC reserve calculations are wildly optimistic. Keep in mind that the total insurance values presented in tables 3.4 and 3.5 are summed only over the 87 firms in the sample. The PBGC liabilities for all insured firms must be significantly greater.

The insurance values for individual firms also differ from the traditional measure of underfunding $(A - F - .3E)$ by wide margins, and highlight the pitfalls of ignoring the option component of pension insurance in assessing PBGC liabilities. In fact, even ignoring the firm's contingent liability of $.3E,$ the total underfunding of all the underfunded plans in the sample is only $0.48 billion for benefits calculated using a 12.76% interest rate and $4.47 billion using a 10% rate. These values are small fractions of the values derived from the voluntary termination model.

Table 3.5 presents summary statistics for the bankruptcy-only termination model. These results are similar to those presented in table 3.4. The same sensitivity to the interest rate and even greater sensitivity to the firm's funding behavior is evidenced. Interestingly, the values

Table 3.5   **Insurance Value Summary Statistics (Bankruptcy-Only Termination Model)**

Insurance Value as a Fraction of Vested Benefits	$C_1 = .10$		$C_1 = .20$		$C_1 = .30$	
	$r = .1276$	$r = .10$	$r = .1276$	$r = .10$	$r = .1276$	$r = .10$
A. Frequency Distribution						
−.6–0	16	13	7	4	5	2
0–.1	51	39	26	24	22	22
.1–.2	18	27	31	26	17	14
.2–.3	1	6	21	25	32	31
.3–.4	1	2	1	6	9	14
.4–.5	0	0	1	2	2	3
.5+	0	0	0	0	0	1
B Summary Statistics						
Maximum value	.306	.383	.401	.452	.459	.504
Mean value	.003	.073	.115	.161	.169	.203
Median value	.044	.079	.155	.173	.199	.223
Weighted average[a]	.070	.119	.155	.186	.196	.217
Total value ($ billion)	5.6	12.0	12.3	18.8	15.5	22.0

[a]Weights = value of vested benefits.

for total dollar liabilities of the PBGC are quite similar in the two models, despite the disparities in assumed funding behavior and plan-termination conditions.

The value of PBGC insurance for some firms in the bankruptcy-only model is negative. This reflects the two assumptions that (1) the PBGC would inherit the surplus of an overfunded plan if the firm were to bankrupt and that (2) there is a limit on the rate at which the firm can drain funds from the plan as bankruptcy approaches. (See eq. [13].) The firms with negative PBGC liabilities tend to be extremely over-funded. A nonlinear version of equation (13) that allowed plan dis-funding to increase without bound as D/V neared 1.0 would eliminate the negative values. However, it is not clear that the latter assumption is superior to the one embodied in (13). The ability of insurance values to be negative makes the distribution of values in table 3.5 more symmetric than in table 3.4. The mean, median, and weighted average of pension insurance values are all of similar magnitudes.

3.3 Conclusion

This paper derives the value of PBGC pension insurance liabilities under two scenarios of interest. The first allows for voluntary plan termination, which appears to be legal under current statutes. The second is a termination-only-at-bankruptcy rule that has been suggested as a reform to current law. Optimal pension fund financing decisions are examined; extreme pension funding policies are shown to be optimal in both settings. This result corroborates and generalizes those of earlier authors. Finally, empirical estimates of PBGC liabilities are derived. These show that a small number of funds account for a large fraction of total prospective PBGC liabilities, and that those total liabilities far exceed current reserves for plan termination.

The empirical results support several conclusions. First, the ability of firms to voluntarily terminate pension plans is a potentially important option, the value of which can be substantially underestimated by the simple measure $\max(0, A - S)$. Second, even without the ability to terminate, discretionary pension-funding policy can lead to equally large PBGC liabilities. Even fully funded plans can impose contingent liabilities with present value more than 25% of vested benefits. This result implies that so-called spinoff/terminations, which effectively allow firms to recapture the surplus assets in a pension plan, impose significant costs on the PBGC, in the sense that the present value of PBGC liabilities increases substantially as surplus assets are siphoned out of funds. Moreover, these liabilities are extremely sensitive to small changes in ongoing funding policy. These results again call into question the common practice of measuring PBGC liabilities as $\max(0, A - S)$. Finally, the estimates of PBGC liabilities support the view that the PBGC's reserves for future terminations are far below the present value of its contingent liabilities.

Notes

1. A put option gives its owner the right to sell to the issuer of the option share of stock at a prespecified price (the exercise price) regardless of the actual price of the stock. Thus, if the stock price, S, falls below the exercise price, X, exercise of the option yields a profit of $X - S$. Similarly, PBGC insurance gives firms the right to "sell" the assets of the plan plus 30% of net worth to the PBGC at a "price" equal to the present value of pension liabilities. The gain to the firm equals the pension liabilities it transfers to the PBGC less the assets the PBGC acquires.

2. Bulow cites Chrysler as an example of a firm for which the potential costs of a termination could be large if it affected the government's willingness to participate in a bail-out scheme for the company. Such extreme examples are probably rare, however.

3. A related issue pertains to so-called spinoff/terminations that allow firms with overfunded plans to recover the surplus assets and then continue to offer a defined benefit plan with a reduced level of funding. This option obviously affects the value of PBGC insurance since firms should be expected to recapture

periodically the surplus assets that otherwise would offer a cushion against adverse investment experience. However, this option may soon be eliminated. The Labor and Treasury Departments and the PBGC are all attempting to restrict such terminations (Chernoff 1983), and Congress is expected to consider restrictions on terminations during 1984 (Chernoff 1984).

4. If the fund is overfunded, eqq. (1) and (2) imply that the firm receives $F - A$. This might be unrealistic: Bulow and Scholes (1982) cite an example of a terminating fund in which the surplus was split between the firm and its employees. However, this issue is of limited relevance for this paper. The PBGC is unconcerned with termination of overfunded plans and presumably would not block the establishment of a new fund. Overfunded plans are not terminated in order to escape liabilities and so fall outside of the scope of this paper.

5. I will treat σ_S in eq. (3) as a constant. This treatment is appropriate when the firm has no debt outstanding other than its pension liabilities (Geske 1979). Thus, this specification is suitable for the voluntary termination model but would need to be modified for the more general case in which the firm can go bankrupt. I will assume that no dividends are paid out by the firm, and that all dividends received by the pension fund are reinvested in the fund, so that α_S may be equated with the expected rate of return on the assets backing the pension liabilities.

6. This condition does not necessarily imply that the firm's goal is to maximize the value of the pension option. It implies only that conditional on other decisions, the termination rule is option value maximizing. For example, in some situations, tax considerations may lead a firm to pursue pension funding policies that reduce the value of the pension put. Nevertheless, the termination rule must maximize the value of the put given that funding policy.

7. The insurance policy could have infinite value in this case. For example, for large C_A and $C_S = 0$, the option would provide a claim on a payoff that would be growing faster than the rate of interest. The value would be infinite although the option would never be exercised. Obviously, one would not observe values of (constant) C_A and C_S leading to these singular cases.

8. Using a variance rate for S of .05 (which approximates the historical variance of the S&P 500), a variance rate for A of .01 and a correlation coefficient of .1 yields $\sigma^2 = .05 + .01 - 2(.1)(.0005)^{1/2} = .055$. I rounded down to account for the fact that pension funds hold some debt in their portfolios. The entries in table 3.1 were not extremely sensitive to changes in σ.

9. For the numerical solutions a maximum time-to-termination of 75 years was assumed. Because the option is no longer of perpetual maturity, the term P_t must be added to the left-hand side of eqq. (5) and (11).

10. Negative values for θ or ϕ would indicate nonfinite values for the insurance.

11. The variance and covariance rates used to solve (11) are set forth in table 3.2 and discussed in section 3.2.1. A time horizon of 75 years was used in the solution. For values of parameters that allow closed form solutions, the numerical and analytic solutions differed by less than 1%.

References

Amoroso, Vincent. 1983. Termination insurance for single-employer pension plans: Costs and benefits. *Transactions, Society of Actuaries* 35:71–83.

Bodie, Zvi; Light, Jay; Mørck, Randall; and Taggart, Robert. 1986. Corporate pension funding behavior. In this volume.

Black, Fischer. 1980. The tax consequences of long-run pension policy. *Financial Analysts' Journal,* 21–28.

Bulow, Jeremy I. 1981. Pension funding and investment policy. Stanford University. Mimeographed.

———. 1982. What are corporate pension liabilities? *Quarterly Journal of Economics* 97:435–52.

Bulow, Jeremy I., and Scholes, Myron S. 1982. Who owns the assets in a defined benefit pension plan. NBER Working Paper no. 924.

Bulow, Jeremy I.; Scholes, Myron S.; and Menell, Peter. 1982. Economic implications of ERISA. NBER Working Paper no. 927.

Chernoff, Joel. 1983. Termination restrictions seen. *Pensions and Investment Age* (December 12, 1983), p. 1.

———. 1984. Senator targets termination issue. *Pensions and Investment Age* (February 20, 1984), p. 3.

Geske, Robert. 1979. Valuation of compound options. *Journal of Financial Economics* 7:63–81.

Harrison, J. Michael, and Sharpe, William F. 1982. Funding and asset allocation for defined-benefit pension plans. NBER Working Paper no. 935.

Langetieg, T. C.; Findlay, M. C.; and da Motta, L. F. J. 1982. Multiperiod pension plans and ERISA. *Journal of Financial and Quantitative Analysis* 17:603–31.

Marcus, Alan J., and Shaked, Israel. 1984. The valuation of FDIC deposit insurance using options-pricing estimates. *Journal of Money, Credit, and Banking* 16:446–60.

da Motta, Luiz F. J. 1979. Multiperiod contingent claim models with stochastic exercise prices: An application to pension fund liability insurance and valuation of firms. Doctoral dissertation. University of Southern California.

Mayers, David, and Smith, Clifford. 1977. Toward a theory of financial contracts: The insurance policy. University of Rochester. Mimeographed.

McDonald, Robert, and Siegal, Daniel. 1982. The value of waiting to invest. NBER Working Paper no. 1019.

Merton, Robert C. 1973. The theory of rational option pricing. *Bell Journal of Economics and Management Science* 4:141–83.

———. 1977. An analytic derivation of the cost of deposit insurance and loan guarantees. *Journal of Banking and Finance* 1:3–11.

Munnell, Alicia H. 1982. Guaranteeing private pension benefits: A potentially expensive business. *New England Economic Review,* 24–47.

Sharpe, William F. 1976. Corporate pension funding policy. *Journal of Financial Economics,* 183–93.

Sosin, Howard B. 1980. On the valuation of federal loan guarantees to corporations. *Journal of Finance* 35:1209–21.

Tepper, Irwin. 1981. Taxation and corporate pension policy. *Journal of Finance* 36:1–13.

Treynor, Jack L. 1977. The principles of corporate pension finance. *Journal of Finance* 32:627–38.

Wall Street Journal. 1982. Pension agency asks Congress to approve rise in premiums for one-employer plans. (May 20, 1982), p. 8.

Comment   William F. Sharpe

Milton Friedman has taught us not to question assumptions, but rather to consider the consistency of implications with the facts. This applies, however, to positive theories with testable implications. This paper has relatively few such implications. Instead, it attempts to estimate values that cannot be measured directly. Thus testing is difficult, if not impossible, and it is reasonable to examine the assumptions seriously.

The subject of the paper is, in effect, the value of the PBGC's liability under different assumptions about (1) the types of behavior allowed the firm, and (2) the type of behavior chosen by the firm within those constraints. The paper examines two major policies that the PBGC might choose and attempts to determine the resultant liabilities. The implications suggest that either of the two policies could be disastrous. It is not clear whether the current policy (whatever it may be) is better or worse.

The paper has the great advantage of dealing explicitly with the true multiperiod nature of this problem. Former models had finessed or ignored this aspect, and it is gratifying to see it taken into account. On the other hand, a multiperiod problem of this sort is very difficult, and many simplifying assumptions must be made.

Technically, the paper models the process as a diffusion. This allows analytic solutions in special cases, but it is important to note that the "interesting" cases require numeric solutions. Such cases are evaluated here with a finite-period model (using 75 periods) in which difference equations are used instead of differential equations.

One of the problems with this type of formulation is the difficulty of insuring that all relevant cash flows have been included. Prior to termination, the firm contributes money to the fund and pays retired benefits. At termination, the firm either recovers the amount overfunded or pays in the shortfall, up to 30% of its equity. After termination, the firm either is bankrupt (the second major case) or institutes a defined contribution plan. In the latter case, new accruals are paid, but previously accrued benefits are covered by the PBGC.

It is less than clear that maximizing the value of the put option, as defined here, is equivalent to maximizing the present value of the firm. The benefit payments are not included, nor are the values of the tax shields, which are lost after termination. The contribution includes 30% of the equity, which is not a cash flow. It is thus possible that the optimal termination decision for a firm wishing to maximize the present

William F. Sharpe is Timken Professor of Finance, Graduate School of Business, Stanford University.

value of cash flows might differ from that found here, and with it the implied value of the PBGC liability.

The tax aspect is important. In all probability, only the IRS has saved the PBGC. The tax advantage of overfunding has probably dominated the maximization of the put value for the vast majority of funds.

It is interesting to note that the value of the PBGC liability will be sensitive to the coefficient of adjustment of contributions to funding status (c_1 in this model). According to the author, total adjustment to full funding requires that c_1 equal infinity, since this is a continuous time model. Most actuarial methods lead to adjustments of 5%–10% per year. The procedure currently proposed by the Financial Accounting Standard Board (officially for reporting purposes, but widely believed to be likely to be used for funding as well) would increase this to 20% for a typical plan. It would be interesting to estimate the impact of such "socially responsible" behavior on the PBGC liability.

Another interesting issue concerns the correlation between the fund assets and the value of the accrued benefits. Since 30% of the firm's equity is included in the former, the correlation might be higher than the value (.1) used in the paper. Since the results depend significantly on the value of σ, and since it is clearly the standard deviation of $(A - S)$, the extent to which a fund's assets "hedge" its liabilities will greatly affect the value of the PBGC liability.

The similarity of the magnitudes of the liabilities in the two cases (voluntary termination and bankruptcy) should not be surprising. The firm approaching bankruptcy is allowed to shortchange or even raid the pension fund. This is, in effect, a form of voluntary termination. Presumably, the PBGC should have some control over such activities.

If numeric methods must be used to cover interesting cases, it may be worthwhile to consider an alternative to the procedures employed here. The state variables can be assumed to follow binomial jump processes. It is a simple matter to program complex decision rules in this type of regime and to insure that all relevant ingredients for valuation have been included. The mapping between continuous-time and discrete-time formulations is not unique, however. For example, one way to model the voluntary termination case would allow four states of the world in each discrete time period. Accrued benefits (A) could go to either of two states, as could the assets backing the liabilities (S). Since the two variables are not perfectly correlated, four states would result. To compute the present value of cash flows in this model, four state-contingent claim prices would be needed for each time period. To determine them, four marketed instruments would be required (to span the space). Here, however, we have only three (A, S, and the riskless asset). Other discrete-jump processes might be adopted, or the value of some fourth asset might be introduced.

While the paper is not primarily an exercise in positive economics, it does have an important testable implication. Like previous papers that assume value maximization by the firm, it obtains the "razor's edge" conclusion that firms will adopt corner (extreme) strategies concerning funding and asset allocation. Almost any model that uses complete-market (or "complete enough" market) assumptions is likely to obtain such results. The observation of few such situations indicates either (1) that the implicit contracts with the PBGC and the IRS are more constraining (and more complex) than usually assumed or (2) that firms use a maximand that involves a utility function. If the latter is the case, models such as this predicated on value maximization may be inappropriate.

In sum, the paper provides a major start on the very difficult task of building multiperiod models of implicit contracts between government agencies (the PBGC and the IRS) and firms with pension plans, when the latter can "game" against the former. Not surprisingly, there is more to be done.

4 How Does the Market Value Unfunded Pension Liabilities?

Jeremy I. Bulow, Randall Mørck, and
Lawrence Summers

The question of how the stock market values pension assets and liabilities is of central importance to corporate decision makers, financial economists, and economists concerned with level of national savings. If investors treat pension debt differently from other forms of debt in valuing firms, prudent value-maximizing managers should recognize these differences and adjust their pension funding policies accordingly. A convincing demonstration that market valuations failed to take account of pension assets or liabilities would either challenge prevailing theories of market efficiency and rational valuation or force a reexamination of conventional views about effective ownership of pension claims. Finally, if potential beneficiaries of pensions recognized the value of the pensions and adjusted their savings accordingly, but no comparable adjustment occurred because holders of pension liabilities did not recognize their liabilities, or were confident of their ability to shift them to some other source such as the PBGC, then pensions would reduce national savings. These effects might be quite significant. Contributions to private pensions represented 58% of personal savings in 1977.

A number of empirical studies including Oldfield (1977), Feldstein and Seligman (1981), Feldstein and Mørck (1983), and Gersovitz (1980) have attempted to study the market's valuation of pension liabilities using cross-sectional valuation models. Other analysts have taken the

Jeremy I. Bulow is associate professor of economics at the Graduate School of Business, Stanford University, and faculty research fellow, National Bureau of Economic Research. Randall Mørck is assistant professor of finance at the University of Alberta. Lawrence Summers is professor of economics, Harvard University, and research associate, National Bureau of Economic Research.

position that the overwhelming empirical evidence in support of the hypothesis of market efficiency makes studying the market valuation of pension assets and liabilities irrelevant. This position seems unwarranted. A great deal of controversy as reflected in Modigliani-Cohn (1979), Summers (1981), and French et al. (1983) focuses on the effects of inflation on firms' nominal assets and liabilities. Furthermore, if the supposition of rational valuation is accepted, studies of the market valuation effect of changes in pension liabilities offer an ideal methodology for examining the true ownership of pension claims.

In adding to the already fairly extensive empirical literature on the valuation of pension assets and liabilities, this paper makes two significant innovations. First, we report results using a "variable effect" event study methodology for studying the valuation of pension claims. This methodology is far superior to the traditional cross-sectional valuation model approach for examining the determinants of market valuations. Indeed, we suggest that identification is highly problematic using standard approaches. Second, following recent work by Bulow (1982), Lazear (1985), and others we recognize that pensions may be only one aspect of complicated contracts through which firms offer workers deferred compensation. If deferred compensation is an important aspect of the labor market, one would expect it to leave traces in the market valuations of otherwise equivalent firms with demographically different labor forces. We examine this issue using both the standard cross-section and the "variable effect" event study methodology. In addition to these innovations, the availability of a larger and more recent data set made it possible for us to replicate the estimates presented in earlier studies and examine their robustness.

The plan of the paper is as follows. Section 4.1 examines the theoretical relationships between pension assets and liabilities and the market valuation of firms. A number of possible reasons why unfunded pension liabilities may not reduce equity valuations dollar for dollar are considered. Section 4.2 presents evidence on the relationship between pension obligations and market valuations using standard cross-sectional techniques. Other forms of deferred compensation are also considered. Our doubts about cross-sectional methodologies are also discussed. Section 4.3 presents estimates of the effect of pension obligations on market valuation using the variable effect event study methodology. We argue that this methodology provides a superior basis for testing market valuation issues than does the standard approach. While the available evidence is weak, it does tend to corroborate standard theories regarding the economic effects of pension obligations. Finally, section 4.4 presents our conclusions and suggests directions for future research.

4.1 Valuing a Firm's Net Pension Wealth

A number of empirical studies have attempted to examine the extent to which market valuations of firm equity accurately reflect firms' pension positions. These studies have typically not discussed in any detail how rational investors should combine a firm's regular balance sheet and its pension position in valuing it. It turns out, however, that because of complexities engendered by the legal nature of the pension contract, the nature of the long-term implicit contracts between workers and firms, and the tax code, the valuation of pension assets and liabilities is quite a subtle issue. This section begins by sketching a naive benchmark model for evaluating firms' pension positions and then considers five qualifications to it. These qualifications provide the basis for much of the empirical discussion in the next two sections.

Perhaps the simplest model of a defined benefit plan is the "consolidated balance sheet" approach. In this approach, pension liabilities are defined on a "quit" basis—what workers would receive if they individually quit the firm today, or their vested benefits—and those obligations are treated like a general corporate liability. Pension assets are similarly treated as a general corporate asset, so any difference between pension assets and liabilities is part of net shareholder wealth. On this view unfunded pension liabilities should reduce firms' market value dollar for dollar.

4.1.1 ERISA's Effect on the Pension Obligation

The first qualification to this simple model is that it does not take into account the special legal nature of the pension liability. Prior to ERISA employees' pension benefits were nonrecourse claims against corporate pension assets. Because of the workers' nonrecourse claim we could think of the firm's net pension wealth as being an option on the fund's assets, F, with an exercise price equal to V, vested benefits. If we think of the firm and its employees as constantly negotiating over the levels of F and V so that either side always had the ability to force immediate exercise of the option, then the firm's net pension wealth would be max $(0, F - V)$ and workers' net pension wealth would be min(F, V).

With the passage of ERISA firms are liable for varying sums depending on the level of guaranteed benefits G (which in terminations in the first few years of PBGC existence averaged .85 of vested benefits), accrued benefits A (which because they include nonvested benefits slightly exceed vested benefits), the amount of money in the pension fund F, and the market value of the firm's equity E.

Following Bulow (1982) we can make a table of the firm's total pension obligations and unfunded liability as a function of these four variables (see unnumbered table below).

Note that in case 1, a severely underfunded plan, the firm's pension liability is less than the present value of workers' benefits. The difference is made up by the PBGC through its "insurance" program, and is often referred to as the "pension put."

Level of Funding	Pension Liability	Net Firm Liability
(1) $F + .3E < G$	$F + .3E$	$.3E$
(2) $G < F + .3E < G + .3E$	G	$G - F$
(3) $G < F < A$	F	0
(4) $A < F$	A	$F - A$ (overfunded)

An empirical implication of the valuation model implied in the table is that the firms with overfunded pensions (where $F > A$) are the residual claimants in their plans and should benefit from increases in F (through plan asset growth) and decreases in A (caused by interest rate increases that decrease the present value of accrued benefits). Again in the case where $G < F + .3E < G + .3E$ the firm is the residual claimant. However, in cases 1 and 3, for vastly underfunded plans and for those with $G < A < F$, the firm is not the residual claimant and should be unaffected by changes in pension asset and liability values. Of course, if we realistically assume that pension policy cannot be instantaneously revised, then the firm may be a partial gainer or loser from changes in pension asset and liability valuation. For example, following Sharpe (1976) one might view the firm as having a call option on the assets of the fund F at an exercise price A, so changes in F and A change the value of that option but not dollar for dollar with A-F. On average, though, we would expect firms with overfunded pension plans to have valuations that are more sensitive to pension asset and liability values than firms with less well funded plans. We test this hypothesis in the next two sections.

4.1.2 Implicit Contracting

A second qualification to the benchmark analysis of pension obligations is that one may be reluctant to take literally all the aspects of the employment contract. For example, firms often raise the benefits of already retired workers and workers may find their pension benefits much higher if they leave a firm just after qualifying for early retirement rather than just before. A literal view of individuals' pension wealth would say that increasing benefits to retired workers is a gift of the firm and that a worker accumulates a large amount of wealth the day he becomes eligible for early retirement. Neither assumption seems very satisfying.

Bulow and Scholes (1983) make the argument that in fact compensation is negotiated cross-sectionally between a firm and its employees, either explicitly through a union or implicitly. Workers bargain for part of the quasi rents earned by firms and have some leeway as to how to split those rents among themselves. Their model allows for the possibility that sometimes a worker will be paid much more than marginal product, such as when retirement benefits are raised or early retirement eligibility is attained. Their measure of worker compensation in a period is the salary, pension, and other benefits legally accrued during the period (the workers' extra compensation if they all left at the end of the period rather than at its beginning) plus any increment in the present value of the quasi rents that the workers expect to be able to negotiate with the firm. In particular, it is widely believed that workers benefit from their firm's reinvestment in their industry. Bulow and Scholes argue the reason is that even if such investment did not change the *marginal* product of the last worker employed in the firm, average product would be greater and the workers would be in a position as a group to negotiate greater compensation. Similarly, increases in pension assets may affect the workers' ability to bargain with their employers. A company with extra cash in its pension fund may find its workers are able to bargain for a better deal, implying that part of any gain on the pension portfolio will find its way to the workers.

The Bulow-Scholes model has the empirical implication that workers share in the gain or loss on the pension portfolio and, therefore, pension gains and losses should be only partially reflected in stock prices. It most clearly differs from the first qualification in its prediction of the treatment of changes in net pension assets for vastly overfunded plans ($F >> A$) where the first qualification would predict that all incremental gains would go to stockholders.

4.1.3   Pensions and Other Aspects of Compensation Arrangements

Third, it is extremely difficult to isolate pensions from the rest of the compensation contract. For example, a firm may have more generous severance arrangements for workers who leave before the early retirement date. If so, the extra pay for staying until early retirement is much less than implied by the pension plan because the gain in pension benefits is mitigated by a loss in severance pay. Other benefits such as health benefits and (in universities especially) college tuition may also be spread unevenly across an employee's career. Thus looking at pension wealth in isolation may be an error if pension wealth is correlated with other non-balance-sheet compensation.

Most important, pension contributions are less than 10% of salary for most firms and have been decreasing for the past 2 years. Clearly small percentage changes in salary can cancel much larger percentage changes in pensions.

The implication of all this is that we know little about how the pension obligation correlates with other elements of the compensation package. If there is a correlation between firms with large gross pension liabilities and firms with older workers, say, and older workers get overpaid regardless of the nature of the firm's pension plan, then a relation between large pension liabilities and low firm valuation may be due to the correlation of those liabilities with the age composition of the firm's labor force. In section 4.2 we make preliminary tests of whether steep wage/age profiles and older labor forces are correlated with firms' stock market value.

4.1.4   Tax Effects

The fourth issue which causes significant conceptual difficulty in valuing a firm's net claim on its pension fund is taxes. For simplicity we will confine our analysis here primarily to the case of an overfunded plan, making the assumption that the firm can use any excess assets to reduce future pension costs, and thus bear the entire risk of changes in pension asset and liability values. Therefore, we will be placing an upper bound on the value of an increment in pension assets to a firm.

We limit our discussions to three tax issues that have not received wide attention among pension researchers. The first is an explicit calculation of the value of being overfunded. The second is the implications of that calculation for changes in pension asset and liability valuation. The third is simply that overfunding a pension fund can serve many of the same purposes as a stock repurchase, with better tax implications. We use as an arbitrary benchmark a plan which is always funded at the level of accrued benefits. (Defined contribution plans are generally like this.) We compare such a plan with one where the plan is funded at some level $F(s)$ at time s where $F(s)$ may differ from the level of accrued benefits. Then it is easy to show that the tax advantage to having a defined benefit plan is equal to the present value of interest earned on pension assets in excess of pension liabilities, times the tax rate on pension contributions.

To illustrate this point we introduce the following notation:

Let r = pre-tax market interest rate

τ_1 = marginal tax rate of the firm

τ_2 = implicit tax rate the firm pays on investment income; that is, its after-tax discount rate is $r(1 - \tau_2)$

$F(s)$ = amount of money in pension fund at time s

$B(s)$ = benefits paid at time s.

We compare the tax benefits of beginning a plan at time t, making an initial contribution $F(t)$, and subsequently operating with funding at level $F(s)$ versus making an initial contribution of $A(t)$ and subsequently remaining fully funded at level $A(s)$.

With funding maintained at level $F(s)$ the present value of after-tax future pension contributions needed to supply a benefit stream $B(s)$ is

$$(1) \quad (1 - \tau_1)F(t) + (1 - \tau_1) \int_t^\infty [\dot{F}(s) + B(s) - rF(s)] \, e^{-r(1-\tau_2)(s-t)}ds$$

The present value of contributions to a plan that is always fully funded is

$$(2) \quad (1 - \tau_1)A(t) + (1 - \tau_1) \int_t^\infty [\dot{A}(s) + B(s) - rA(s)] \, e^{-r(1-\tau_2)(s-t)}ds$$

The tax saving from funding at level F is simply (2) minus (1) or

$$(3) \qquad \text{tax saving} = r\tau_2(1 - \tau_1) \int_t^\infty [F(s) - A(s)]e^{-r(1-\tau_2)(s-t)}ds$$

It should be clear that the way to maximize (3) is to set $F(s)$ as high as possible at each moment. In such a simple model, then, firms will always be up against their IRS funding limitation.

What is the implication for firm valuation of a shock to the value of $F(s)$ or $A(s)$? First, consider a rise in $F(s)$. With increased excess funding the firm would get larger tax benefits. It would amortize its "experience gain" on asset performance as slowly as possible. If amortization occurs over T years, annual pension contributions will drop by $r\Delta F/(1 - e^{-rT})$ where ΔF is the gain in the value of fund assets. The present value to the firm of its savings is

$$(4) \qquad \frac{\Delta F(1 - \tau_1)(1 - e^{-r(1-\tau_2)T})}{(1 - \tau_2)(1 - e^{-rT})}.$$

This formula is most understandable by considering some extreme cases. First, assume $\tau_2 = 0$: there is no tax paid on investment income earned outside the pension fund. Then there is no advantage to funding per se and an increase in F of one dollar will raise firm value by $1 - \tau_1$, the amount of money the firm would get if it were able to immediately withdraw the extra dollar from the plan. Second, consider the oft-considered case where $\tau_2 = \tau_1 = \tau$: the implicit tax rate on corporate nonpension investment income is the same as the corporate marginal rate of τ_1 (generally considered 46%). This view is consistent with that of Miller's (1977) model of corporate finance. Furthermore, assume that $T = \infty$; the increment in pension assets does not have to be amortized and the firm may be overfunded by an extra dollar forever. Then the increment in firm value is ΔF. Of this gain of ΔF, then, $\Delta F(1 - \tau)$ is created because the value of assets in the pension fund (which holds pre-tax assets) has risen by ΔF. Also, because those ΔF dollars will earn returns of $r\Delta F$ each year forever instead of $r(1 - \tau)\Delta F$ as nonpension assets would earn, there is an annual saving in pension costs of $r\tau\Delta F$ because of the tax-sheltered nature of the pension returns. The after-tax value of this saving is $r\tau\Delta F(1 - \tau)$. If we discount this saving at the after-tax rate of $r(1 - \tau)$, we find that the present value of the tax saving from being able to remain overfunded forever is

$$(5) \qquad \frac{r\tau\Delta F(1 - \tau)}{r(1 - \tau)} = \tau\Delta F.$$

If in fact we assume 15 years' amortization of excess funding, that $\tau_1 = \tau_2 = .46$, and that pre-tax interest rates are 10%, then (4) implies that a firm's value should rise by approximately 72 cents for each dollar its pension assets rise in value. There is an asymmetry on the loss side in that while excess assets will be defunded as slowly as possible asset shortfalls will be made up as quickly as allowed. Of course, if a funding deficiency could be made up instantly then the cost to a firm of a decline in the value of its pension assets would be 54 cents. Because of the asymmetry firms have a mitigated incentive to establish "dedicated" bond portfolios which preclude gains or losses on a fraction of their pension obligations.

Changes in the value of pension liabilities are a bit more complicated. The reason is that funding limitations are based on the book value of liabilities rather than market value. If interest rates rise, causing the value of liabilities to fall, in the short run the firm will be more overfunded than before. This overfunding will only be recognized for funding limitation purposes through the channel of the firm's pension assets earning a return greater than the plan's actuarial rate. As these greater returns are earned each year they must then be amortized as experienced gains. Thus changes in liability values will end up being effectively amortized more slowly than changes in asset values and a slightly higher coefficient would be expected in the sensitivity of firm value to changes in pension liabilities than to changes in pension assets.

Finally, we note the large amount of corporate stock and other assets held in private pension plans. Numerous firms hold pension assets in excess of the market value of firm equity. Because pension contributions are tax deductible, except for the fact that transfer of assets to a pension fund may involve a transfer of corporate wealth from stock-holders to employees, pension overfunding seems to dominate corporate share repurchases on two grounds. First is the deductibility of contributions, and second the fund can use money to hold a wider variety of assets than just the firm's own stock. As such, we might expect excess pension fund contributions to provide a signaling role much like that of dividends and repurchases. However, we leave this last point for future research.

4.1.5 Investor Rationality

A fifth reason that changes in firms' pension assets and liabilities may not be reflected dollar for dollar in stock prices is that the market may be inefficient in valuing pension liabilities. While this reason may seem implausible, concern over the effect of large pension contributions on reported earnings may be one of the reasons that managements often contribute much less to their pension funds than they are permitted by IRS regulations.

Other studies such as French et al. (1983) have indicated that it is difficult to find the effect of the change in the market value of conventional debt on stock prices. Pension debt, which does not appear on corporate balance sheets and has only recently appeared in any form in the footnotes, may thus be discounted by the market because of its complexity.

In this section we have discussed a number of reasons why a naive model of changes in a firm's net pension wealth being reflected dollar for dollar in stock market valuation may fail. In particular, we have discussed the details of ERISA, implicit contracting issues, the correlation between pension and nonpension compensation, tax effects, and investor rationality in valuing pension claims. In the subsequent sections of the paper we attempt to estimate what in fact is the relation between a firm's pension assets and liabilities and the market value of its equity.

4.2 Cross-sectional Valuation Models

The extent to which share prices reflect unfunded pension obligations is a key issue in considering the effect of private pensions on national savings. It has been argued (Feldstein 1978) that if unfunded pension liabilities are not fully reflected in stock prices, equity owners will save less and consume more than they would in a world where perceptions were correct. National savings might thus be reduced by the introduction of private pensions.

For this reason and because of intrinsic interest as an aspect of financial behavior, a series of pioneering papers including Oldfield (1977),

Gersovitz (1980), Feldstein and Seligman (1981), and Feldstein and Mørck (1983) have endeavored to explore this issue. These efforts have focused on listing variables likely to be determinants of a firm's market value. If an effect of unfunded pension liabilities on market value can be detected after these other likely factors are controlled for, the studies conclude that unfunded pension obligations influence share prices.

Feldstein and Mørck (1983), for example, model a firm's market value (V) per dollar of net assets (A) as depending on the firm's future earnings potential, its riskiness, its leverage, and (perhaps) its pension obligations.

(6) $$\frac{V}{A} = F \text{ (future earnings potential, risk, leverage, unfunded pension liability).}$$

As proxies for future earnings potential, they use the firm's current earnings (E), its historical growth rate in earnings (GROW), and its research and development spending (RD). They employ the firm's beta as a measure of risk, and the market value of its debt as a fraction of net assets as a leverage indicator. The firm's unfunded vested pension liability (UVPL) per dollar of net assets is used to measure its pension obligations. Thus Feldstein and Mørck ended up estimating

(7) $$\frac{V}{A} = \beta_0 + \beta_1\frac{E}{A} + \beta_2\text{GROW} + \beta_3\frac{RD}{A} + \beta_4\text{BETA} + \beta_5\frac{\text{DEBT}}{A} + \beta_6\frac{\text{UVPL}}{A} + \epsilon.$$

They found a coefficient of about minus one on unfunded vested pension liabilities, and concluded that an added dollar of net pension obligations depresses the firm's market value by about one dollar. Their study was plagued by fairly difficult data problems—primarily by the use of only very coarse inflation adjustments and by the very small size of their sample.

Preliminary to this study, we replicated the Feldstein/Mørck regressions using a much larger body of more recent data. Although their result could be reproduced, it was quite unstable. Seemingly innocuous changes in the sample made it come or go. The estimated coefficients on the proxies for future earnings potential—especially on GROW—were also disturbingly unstable.

In this section, we shall point out severe problems inherent in the cross-sectional valuation methodology used by these previous authors. We then suggest alternative, more satisfactory cross-sectional estimating equations. Estimation of these equations yields results consistent with Feldstein and Mørck's conclusion that pension liabilities are largely reflected in a firms' market valuation.

4.2.1 Problems with the Cross-sectional Valuation

The lack of robustness of the Feldstein-Mørck equations when replicated for a larger sample using more recent data calls into question the validity of the cross-sectional valuation methodology used by them and other authors. This inference is supported by the conflicting evidence found in previous cross-sectional valuation studies. Feldstein and Seligman (1981), for example, obtain results similar to those of Feldstein and Mørck, while Oldfield (1977) found no such relation.

It should not be surprising that such cross-sectional studies lead to conflicting inferences about the valuation of pension liabilities. It is not at all clear in what sense these equations can be said to identify structural parameters of any interest. Standard financial theory postulates that the value of a firm (V) may be expressed either as the sum of assets (A_i) and liabilities (L_j) or as the present value of future cash flows (CF_t) discounted at some rate s. These two alternatives may be written as

$$(8) \qquad V = \sum_{i=1}^{n} A_i - \sum_{j=1}^{m} L_j$$

$$(9) \qquad V = \sum_{t=1}^{\infty} \frac{CF_t}{(1 + \rho)^t}.$$

Note that neither of these equations includes an error term. The standard procedure in estimating a cross-sectional valuation equation seems to be to deflate both sides of (8) by an estimate of the replacement value of the firm's capital stock, insert proxies for whatever assets and liabilities are easily measured in the equation, and then try to adhere to the spirit of equation (9) in adding to the equation measures of earnings and earnings growth to cover for assets and liabilities which are hard to measure. Reasoning of this sort appears to guide the specification of Feldstein and Mørck and the earlier work of Tobin and Brainard (1977) upon which they rely.

It is difficult to know how to interpret the error term in such a mongrel equation. Presumably it reflects unmeasured assets or liabilities. But since the opportunity cost of purchasing these assets (incurring these liabilities) is not being able to purchase measured assets (not incurring measured liabilities), it is hard to believe that the error is orthogonal to the included balance sheet variables. Furthermore, since earnings depend on the assets and liabilities held by a firm, it is difficult to see how they could be orthogonal to the error term in the cross-section. As a consequence it seems very difficult to interpret the coefficients of equations such as those reported by the authors who have previously examined the market valuation of pension obligations. Since almost every right-hand-side variable in standard valuation equations is endogenous, adequate instruments do not seem to be available for estimating the parameters of the standard hedonic equation consistently. Given these problems, instability in the estimated coefficients is not surprising. Even if the parameters of standard hedonic market valuation equations could be estimated consistently, serious problems of interpretation would remain. The standard procedure for using these equations to answer questions about pension obligations involves focusing on the coefficient on the pension variables in the equation. For example, a coefficient of minus one on the UVPL variable was to be interpreted as meaning that if a firm gets an extra dollar in its pension fund, its value will rise by one dollar.

This conclusion is unwarranted. If the firm contributes a dollar to its pension fund, current earnings are reduced by one dollar. Taken literally the Feldstein-Mørck equation implies that this decrement would *reduce* market value by almost $2. The presence of the growth variable makes the situation even more complex. It is clear, however, that simply looking at the pension variable will not be satisfactory. A similar problem of inference holds with respect to the R&D and debt variables in hedonic valuation equations.

We conclude that the standard hedonic equation approach is not a useful instrument for studying the market valuation of pension liabilities. In the remainder of this section, we modify the standard cross-sectional approach by using only balance sheet variables to explain firm valuations. The next section uses an alternative variable effect event study methodology to study the questions at hand.

4.2.2   Modified Cross-Sectional Equations

In the remainder of this section we estimate equations relating to market valuation of firms only to items that can be thought of as elements in their balance sheet. This avoids the problems of interpretation discussed in the previous section, although the possibility of inconsistent parameter estimates remains. In particular the equation we estimate is of the form

$$(10) \quad \frac{V}{A} = \beta_0 + \beta_1 \frac{UVPL}{A} + \beta_2 \frac{DEBT}{A} + \beta_3 \frac{RD}{A} + \beta_4 \, BETA + \Sigma \gamma_i D_i,$$

where
V = market value of firm
A = replacement cost of firm
RD = research and development spending

BETA = beta
DEBT = market value of firm's debt
UVPL = unfunded vested pension liabilities
D_i = two-digit SIC industry code dummies.

Our data for 1980 and 1981 are constructed exactly as described by Feldstein and Mørck's (1984) numbers with a few exceptions which are explained below. The reader is referred to the earlier paper for a detailed account of the data. Following Meyers's (1983) comments, an unlevered rather than a standard BETA is used here. We also make use of inflation-adjusted figures that have become available recently. In this study we use inflation-adjusted asset figures from the Financial Accounting Standards Board's statement 33 (FASB 33). Our replacement cost number A is the inflation-adjusted value of property plan and equipment plus the inflation-adjusted value of inventories. Our pension numbers were taken from the Financial Accounting Standards Board's statement 36 (FASB 36). Pension liabilities are adjusted to reflect a common discount rate of 7%.

Dummies for two-digit industries are included in the equation to capture the notion that different types of physical capital are valued differently in the marketplace. The estimation results for 1979, 1980, and 1981 are shown in table 4.1. Like the Feldstein and Mørck conclusion the results for all 3 years suggest that firms' market values do reflect their pension obligations. In each case the parameter estimates imply that firms' market values are reduced more than dollar for dollar with unfunded pension liabilities, though the hypothesis $\beta_1 = -1$ can never be rejected.

Table 4.1   **Balance Sheet Approach to Measuring the Impact of Unfunded Vested Pension Liabilities on Firm Valuation** (Dependent variable: Market value over replacement cost V/A)

		1979	1980	1981
Unfunded vested liabilities	UVPL/A	-1.42	-1.54	-1.16
		(1.17)	(0.70)	(0.50)
Leverage	DEBT/A	1.06	-0.16	-0.32
		(0.31)	(0.33)	(0.21)
Research	RD/A	6.94	10.75	7.58
		(2.18)	(1.54)	(1.12)
Beta	BETA	0.18	0.08	0.06
		(0.15)	(0.13)	(0.04)
Constant	C	0.18	0.56	0.68
		(0.21)	(0.30)	(0.15)
Sample	N	70	266	256
R^2		0.48	0.39	.53

One possible objection to these questions is the "weak firm" problem raised by Meyers (1983) in his comments on the Feldstein-Mørck paper and confirmed by Bodie et al. (1984) as an important effect. Firms with low value assets will tend to have low market values and because of financial pressure will tend to underfund their pension funds. As a result a spurious negative association between firm value and unfunded pension liabilities may be observed. This is addressed in table 4.2 by using two different techniques.

First, in the equations in the left half of the table a variable RATING is included, reflecting the firm's Standard and Poor's bond rating, is added to the specification. The RATING variable takes values ranging from one for firms rated D to 10 for firms ranked AAA. It should be at least a partial control for weak firm effects.

Second, in the second half of the table UVPL is treated as an endogenous variable and is instrumented using the firm's total pension liabilities. The justification is that the total size of the firm's liabilities is independent of its funding policy, and so should be a satisfactory instrument. It obviously should also be correlated with the firm's level of unfunded liabilities and so should provide reasonably efficient estimates.

The results unambiguously and robustly point to a negative relationship between a firm's unfunded vested pension liabilities and its market value. Using either of our two procedures for controlling for weak firm effects, the absolute value of the UVPL coefficient actually

Table 4.2   **Balance Sheet Approach to Measuring the Impact of Unfunded Vested Pension Liabilities on Firm Valuation and the Weak Firm Problem** (Dependent variable: Market value over replacement cost V/A)

		1980	1981	1980	1981
Unfunded vested liabilities	UVPL/A	−1.92	−1.45	−3.15	−2.38
		(0.93)	(0.69)	(1.63)	(1.15)
Rating	RATING	0.05	0.04	—	—
		(0.06)	(0.04)	—	—
Leverage	DEBT/A	−0.06	−0.24	0.052	0.39
		(0.54)	(0.30)	(0.39)	(0.24)
Research	RD/A	10.66	7.43	12.27	8.15
		(1.84)	(1.37)	(1.76)	(1.22)
Beta	BETA	0.03	0.08	−0.10	0.05
		(0.20)	(0.05)	(0.15)	(0.04)
Constant	C	0.16	0.48	0.74	0.65
		(0.80)	(0.33)	(0.32)	(0.17)
Sample	N	153	147	256	257
R^2		0.45	0.46	0.41	0.52

increases. While the standard errors are large, we are able to find no evidence that weak firm problems account for these results, suggesting that the market penalizes firms with unfunded pension liabilities.

The discussion in the previous section suggested that the marginal effect of reduced pension liabilities may be different for underfunded than for overfunded plans. The analysis of section 4.1 implies that generally stockholders will gain more from a reduction in an already overfunded plan, because unfunded liabilities will be put in part to the PBGC and in part to employees. We address this issue by adding a variable PUT to the specification of equation (10). The variable PUT is defined as max (0, UVPL). Results are shown in table 4.3.

Unfortunately, the data do not appear to be powerful enough to reject any interesting hypothesis concerning this issue. In the more reliable 1980 and 1981 equations, there is very weak evidence that the availability of the pension put influences the marginal valuation of liabilities for troubled firms.

A final major issue suggested by the discussion in section 4.1 is the role of other deferred compensation arrangements which may be correlated with our included pension variables. Firms may have implicit contracts with their workers which require them to pay older workers in excess of their marginal products. If so, the capitalized value of these obligations represents a liability of the firm. This liability is of interest in its own right. In addition, it is likely to be correlated with pension liabilities.

Table 4.3   **Balance Sheet Approach to Measuring the Impact of Unfunded Vested Pension Liabilities on Firm Valuation and the PBGC Put**
(Dependent variable: Market value over replacement cost V/A)

		1979	1980	1981
Unfunded vested liabilities	UVPL/A	0.75	−2.63	−1.59
		(3.64)	(1.80)	(1.44)
PBGC Put Indicator	PUT	−2.65	1.43	0.61
		(4.21)	(2.16)	(1.44)
Leverage	DEBT/A	1.03	−0.16	−0.32
		(0.31)	(0.33)	(0.21)
Research	RD/A	7.02	10.65	7.49
		(2.20)	(1.55)	(1.14)
Beta	BETA	0.16	0.07	0.06
		(0.16)	(0.13)	(0.04)
Constant	C	0.23	0.55	0.66
		(0.23)	(0.30)	(0.16)
Sample	N	70	266	256
R^2		0.48	0.39	0.53

Unfortunately, there is no apparent way to construct an estimate of the firm's deferred compensation liability. As a crude approximation, we added three variables to equation (8): AGE, SLOPE, and AGE × SLOPE where AGE is an estimate of the average age of a firm's workforce, SLOPE is an estimate of the slope of its age-wage profile, and AGE × SLOPE should should enter the equation negatively. Firms with steep age-wage profiles and old workforces should have the largest deferred compensation liability. The other variables cannot be signed on an a priori basis.

Our estimates of AGE and SLOPE were obtained from a merge of the January and March 1978 Current Population Survey tapes. This collection of data included the ages, wages, tenures, and three-digit employer industry codes for over forty thousand individuals. Parameters of an age distribution and an age versus log(wage) profile were estimated for each three-digit industry code. These codes were matched to the SIC codes on the compustat tape. In general a three-digit CPS industry code corresponded to a three-digit or in a few cases a four-digit SIC code. Each firm in our sample was thus assigned a wage-age profile corresponding to its SIC industry code.

The results of estimating equation (10) with the additional variables AGE, SLOPE, and AGE × SLOPE are displayed in table 4.4. They are

Table 4.4   **Balance Sheet Approach to the Impact of Pensions and Labor Force Structure on Firm Valuation** (Dependent variable: Market value over replacement cost V/A)

		1980	1981
Mean age	AGE	0.05	−0.03
		(0.04)	(0.03)
Slope of age/wage profile	SLOPE	144.44	−67.88
		(67.09)	(62.52)
Age and slope interaction term	AGE × SLOPE	−3.78	1.66
		(1.74)	(1.62)
Unfunded vested liabilities	UVPL/A	−1.99	−1.81
		(0.90)	(0.61)
Leverage	DEBT/A	−0.39	−0.27
		(0.39)	(0.22)
Research	RD/A	11.06	7.90
		(1.87)	(1.25)
Beta	BETA	0.08	0.07
		(0.15)	(0.04)
Constant	C	−1.38	1.82
		(1.49)	(1.30)
Sample	N	233	234
R^2		0.40	0.55

disappointing. The 1980 estimates are consistent with the hypothesis advanced above. The age-slope interaction variable is both satistically and substantively significant. However, its sign is reversed with equal statistical significance in the 1981 equation. As a consequence, we cannot reach any judgment about the role of deferred compensation in affecting firm valuations. However, our results suggest that taking account of several deferred compensation liabilities does not alter the estimates of the influence of unfunded pension liabilities.

4.3   Interest Rate Changes and the Valuation of Pension Liabilities

This section uses an alternative methodology to circumvent some of the problems in the standard cross-sectional approach discussed in the preceding section. The essential insight underlying our tests may be illustrated as follows. Consider two otherwise equivalent firms, one of which has more pension liabilities than the other. Now suppose the nominal long-term interest rate rises unexpectedly. The firm with more pension liabilities should do relatively better than the firm with fewer liabilities because of the greater capital gain it experiences as the higher interest rate unexpectedly erodes the value of long-term obligations. By examining the response of firms with different pension obligations to interest rate changes, it should be possible to determine the extent to which the market values changes in the status of a firm's pension fund.

Because the approach taken here looks at the effect of an exogenous event, a change in the interest rate on the valuation of different firms, it does not depend on any assumption about how firms decide how much to fund their pension plan. Thus the variable effect event study method used here is not subject to the weak firm problem described in the previous section.

More formally our approach is as follows. We postulate that the return on firm i, in month t, can be expressed as

$$(11) \qquad \rho_{it} = \alpha_i + \beta_{it}\Delta R_t + u_{it},$$

where α_i is the normal required expected return on firm i and β_{it} reflects its sensitivity to interest rate news, here proxied by the change in the long-term interest rate, and u_{it} is a random error term. We initially specify that β_{it} depends on the firm's characteristics at time t according to

$$(12) \qquad \beta_{it} = \gamma_0 + \gamma_1\frac{\text{UVPL}_{it}}{V_{it}} + \gamma_2\frac{\text{LTD}}{V_{it}} + Z_{it}\gamma_4 + \epsilon_{it},$$

where UVPL represents unfunded vested pension liabilities. LTD represents long-term debt, Z refers to control variables discussed in more detail below, and V is the equity value of the firm. Combining equations (11) and (12) yields the cross-section time series equation which provides the basis for an empirical work:

$$(13) \qquad \rho_{it} = \alpha_i + \left[\gamma_0 + \gamma_1\frac{\text{UVPL}}{V_{it}} + \gamma_2\frac{\text{LTD}}{V_{it}} + Z_{it}\gamma_4\right]\Delta R_t$$
$$+ u_{it} + \Delta R_t\epsilon_{it}.$$

Equation (13) can be estimated, given cross-section time series data using ordinary least squares, to yield unbiased estimates of the parameters. However, the error term does not satisfy the requirements for consistency of the standard errors. In the results reported below we allow for the inclusion of firm and/or period effects in (13). This should make it possible to compute approximately accurate standard errors.

Our procedure is entirely consistent in spirit with the event study methodology that is widely used in financial economics. The approach involves looking at the response of securities prices to unexpected developments or "news" in an effort to gauge the effects of the variables being studied on firms' market value. Our "variable effect–event study methodology" represents an improvement over the techniques normally used in finance in two ways.

First, the events we look at are developments that are exogenous from the viewpoint of the firm. A standard event study approach to the problem of studying how the market values firms' pension liabilities would involve looking at how firms' market value responded to news about their pension funding decision. The difficulty is that firms' decisions are themselves responses to news or to privately held information. It is not really possible to sort out the effects of policy changes from the independent effects of their causes. Our indirect procedure of looking at the differential effects of interest rate changes on firms entirely avoids these problems. Second, our econometric procedure is superior to the grouping techniques normally used in event studies. One could, as many financial economists would, group as firms by pension funding status and then look at how different portfolios responded to news about interest rate developments. Such a procedure simply discards information about within-group differences in pension funding status and therefore is inefficient.

Before turning to a description of our data, it is useful to discuss the expected signs of the coefficient in (13) and possible biases arising from omitted variables. We expect γ_1 and γ_2 to be positive, reflecting the capital gains firms earn on their nominal liabilities as interest rates reduce the value of outstanding liabilities. The principal problem in estimating (13) is that some long-term nominal assets or liabilities which might be correlated with the included variables are excluded. These might include the value of depreciation in tax shields or of prospective lease obligations. If these variables have a systematic impact on firms' pension funding decisions, our results will be biased. However, we know of no previous arguments suggesting a role for these variables in pension funding decisions. They might, however, be related to the amount of long-term debt a firm decides to carry.

In estimating equation (13) we use data for the 36-month period from January 1979 to December 1981. We assume that pension assets and liabilities are constant within each year.[1] Data on pension assets and liabilities are drawn from a tape provided by the FASB. Liabilities are adjusted to current interest rates using the rule of thumb described in Feldstein and Mørck (1983). Essentially, this procedure involves multiplying reported liabilities by the ratio of the actuarially assumed interest rate to the actual market interest rate. This is done on a monthly basis. The market value of long-term debt is calculated from information available on the Compustat tape. It is assumed that all debt reported as long-term by Compustat has a 10-year maturity and a 10% coupon rate. This debt is then valued using the monthly BAA interest rate. Monthly stock returns are drawn from the CRSP tapes. To insure robustness, extreme values of the right-hand-side variables were eliminated from the sample. All necessary data were available for about 200 firms in 1979, about 470 firms in 1980, and about 400 firms in 1981, giving us a total of 12,715 observations in a 36-month sample period.

The results of estimating (13) omitting any Z variables are reported in table 4.5 for various specifications of the error term. In some cases

Table 4.5   **The Effect of Interest Rate Changes on Monthly Stock Returns Reflected through Pension Assets and Liabilities As Well As from Long Term Debt**

	Eq. (1)	Eq. (2)	Eq. (3)
Unfunded vested pension liabilities $\times \Delta R$	30.6 (10.4)	29.2 (10.4)	29.1 (9.10)
Long-term debt $\times \Delta R$	−8.05 (3.42)	−7.97 (3.43)	−3.41 (2.95)
ΔR	−13.0 (2.10)	13.2 (2.09)	86.1 (6.84)
Constant	0.012 (0.000707)		
Firm effects	No	Yes	No
Month effects	No	No	Yes
Sample	12,563	12,563	12,563
R^2	1.93%	1.97%	29.9%

α_i is treated as a constant, in others it is allowed to vary across firms, and in others to vary from month to month.

The results are broadly consistent with the hypothesis that the market values pension obligations rationally. In each case the unfunded liability variable is both substantively and statistically significant. The estimates in column 1, for example, imply that for a firm with unfunded liabilities equal to 10% of equity value, a 1% increase in the interest rate would raise market value by about 0.3%. While this is only about half the value that would be predicted by a naive model in which firms "owned" all unfunded liabilities and none of the other complicating factors discussed in the first section arose, it seems very reasonable, especially in light of tax considerations.

In all the equations the debt variable has the wrong sign, and it is highly statistically significant in equations (1) and (2). This finding confirms the results of French et al. (1983), who were unable to find any evidence in support of the nominal credit hypothesis. It also supports the Modigliani-Cohn inflation illusion hypothesis. These surprising results may alternatively be a consequence of our short sample period or of our failure to measure accurately all the firms' nominal assets and liabilities. In any event, they stand as a major puzzle. We recognize that it is implausible to assert, as our results seem to suggest, that market participants recognize the effects of increases in interest rates on pension debt but not on regular balance sheet debt. But we do not at this point have any resolution to offer.

Our results are somewhat less unsatisfactory for equation (3) where month dummies are included in the specification. The unfunded pension liabilities variable remains statistically significant in (3), although its substantive significance is much less than that suggested by equations (1) and (2). The debt variable, though it continues to have the wrong sign, becomes insignificant in equation (3).

4.3.1 Further Tests

A major problem with the cross-sectional valuation tests presented in the previous section was the "weak firm" problem. Firms with capital that cannot earn a high rate of return tend to find themselves in financial trouble and try to underfund their pension plans. A negative relationship between firm value and unfunded pension liabilities is observed but may well be spurious. Both low firm value and underfunding of the pension liability are consequences of the firm's ownership of the unprofitable assets. There is no reason to expect a similar problem here. Weak firms should not be differentially affected by changes in the nominal interest rate. However, as a further check we added a variable $\Delta R \cdot \text{RATING}$ to equation (2) in table 4.5, where RATING is a categorical variable which ranges from one for firms whose debt is rated D to 10 for firms whose debt is rated AAA. The estimated equation was

(14) $\rho_{it} = \alpha_i + \Delta R \cdot [25.7 \, (UVPL)$
                    (14.0)
                                        $- 22.6 \, (LTD) - 3.4 \, (RATING) + 20.3]$
                                        (6.2) (1.6) (14.2)

While the RATING interaction variable enters significantly, it does not have an important influence on the pension variable's coefficient, which rises slightly. The introduction of RATING has little effect on the anomalous debt coefficient.

A concern in previous pension research has been whether the market responds to pension liabilities as measured at market or actuarial interest rates. The equations reported so far in this section assume that liabilities are valued at market interest rates. To test this assumption we add an additional variable to equation (2) in table 4.5 equal to $\Delta R(PL^A - PL^M)$ where PL^M is the pension liability valued at market interest rates and PL^A is the pension liability valued at actuarial interest rates. If the market responds to actuarial interest rates rather than market rates, one would expect that this variable would have a positive sign. The estimated equation was

(15) $\rho_{it} = \alpha_i + \Delta R \, [13.6 \, (UVPL)$
                    (12.3)
                                $+ \quad 29.9(PL^A - PL^M) - 6.14 \, (LTD) - 12.5 \,].$
                                (12.7) (3.5) (2.1)

This equation provides very weak evidence that actuarial interest rates influence market valuations. It appears that firms that overstate their pension liabilities by more gain more when interest rates rise. These results are in accord with the results obtained in the preceding section using a different methodology. They do also support the claim of Feldstein and Mørck (1983) that market participants appear to use below-market interest rates in valuing pension liabilities.

The results in the previous section provided evidence that the pension put and the possibility of bankruptcy influenced the market's valuation of pension liabilities. This issue can be examined by investigating whether interest rate changes have smaller effects for firms with large relative pension liabilities. This issue can be examined by investigating whether interest rate changes have smaller effects for firms with large relative pension liabilities. We examine this issue by adding a variable $\Delta R \cdot$ PUT to our basic equation where PUT $= \max(0, \, UVPL)$. Our hypothesis is that the coefficient on this variable will be negative but smaller in absolute value than the coefficient on (UVPL). This reflects the attenuated impact of interest rate changes on badly underfunded firms discussed in section 4.1 The estimation result was

(16) $\rho_{it} = \alpha_i + \Delta R$ [33.7 $(PL - PA)$
                    (10.7)

                               $- 165$ (PUT) $- 6.9$ (LTD) $- 12.8$]
                                 (99)   (3.5)   (2.1).

Although the coefficient on the put variable is statistically insignificant because it cannot be estimated with any accuracy, its magnitude is consistent with our hypothesis. This evidence thus dovetails with the evidence in the preceding section on potential importance of the level of unfunded benefits.

A final issue to be considered is the relationship between a firm's pension arrangements and other parts of its compensation scheme. In the previous section we presented some crude tests of the idea that firms with steep age-earnings profiles and aging workforces were valued by the market as if they had a formal debt liability to their workforce. While the results were inconclusive, taking account of this liability did not have a large impact on the estimated effect of pension obligations on firms' market valuations.

It would be desirable to examine these questions using the methodology of this section. However, a serious problem presents itself. Any long-term implicit contract between workers and firms is likely to be formulated in real terms. The changes in interest rates which provide the basis for our tests largely reflect changing inflationary expectations. Separating out real interest rate changes in monthly data is probably not feasible. Hence we cannot in this section shed much light on the existence of non-pension-deferred compensation. On the possibility that interest rate changes over our 1979–81 sample period might reflect real interest rate variations, or that non-pension long-term contracts might be nominally denominated, we reestimated equation (13) with various wage growth and age structure variables included. In no case did they enter significantly or affect the magnitude of the pension coefficients. Therefore, no results are displayed here. We reluctantly conclude that this section's method cannot be used to examine the important deferred compensation issue.

4.4 Conclusions

The results in this paper confirm earlier analyses suggesting that the stock market valuation of firms reasonably accurately reflects their pension funding situations. This conclusion is reached using alternative methodological approaches and data from several different years and so is reasonably robust. In particular we demonstrate that it is not simply a consequence of weak firm effects. Our results also suggest that the availability of the termination and the pension put influences the market valuation of pension liabilities. Finally, we provide some evidence suggesting that market valuations of firms reflect implicit contractual liabilities to pay older workers amounts in excess of their marginal products. These contractual liabilities appear to be denominated in real rather than nominal terms.

Our results provide no support for the notion that investors ignore pension liabilities in valuing firms. As a consequence, they suggest that corporate managers will benefit if they fund their plans as fully as possible. Furthermore, they suggest that the private pension may not have a large effect on aggregate saving since both the asset and liability side of pension balance sheets influence private savings decisions.

Perhaps the most promising area suggested for future research is the market's valuation of implicit contractual liabilities to older workers. It would be desirable to extend the tests reported here in order to get an estimate of the value of this liability. If it were to be significant, strong evidence would be provided for incentive contracting models of the labor market.

Note

1. An alternative which we intend to explore would involve interpolating net assets and liabilities within years.

References

Bulow, J. 1982. What are corporate pension liabilities? *Quarterly Journal of Economics* 97:435–52.

Bulow, J., and Scholes, M. 1983. Who owns the assets in a defined-benefit pension plan? In *Financial Aspects of the United States Pension System*, ed. Zvi Bodie and John B. Shoven. Chicago: University of Chicago Press.

Bodie, Z.; Light, J.; Mørck, R.; and Taggart, R. 1984. Funding and asset allocation in corporate pension plans: An empirical investigation. In this volume.

Feldstein, M. 1978. Do private pensions increase national saving? *Journal of Public Economics* 10:277–93.

Feldstein, M. S., and Mørck, R. 1983. Pension funding decisions, interest rate assumptions, and share prices. In *Financial Aspects of the United States*

Pension System, ed. Zvi Bodie and John B. Shoven. Chicago: University of Chicago Press.

Feldstein, M.S., and Seligman, S. 1981. Pension funding, share prices and national savings. *Journal of Finance* 36:801–24.

French, K. R.; Ruback, R. S.; and Schwert, G. W. 1983. Effects of nominal contracting on stock returns. *Journal of Political Economy* 91:70–96.

Gersovitz, M. 1980. Economic consequences of unfunded vested pension benefits. NBER Working Paper no. 480.

Lazear, E. P. 1979. Why is there mandatory retirement? *Journal of Political Economy* 87:1261–64.

Lazear, E. 1985. Incentive effects of pensions. In *Pensions, Labor, and Individual Choice,* ed. D. Wise. Chicago: University of Chicago Press.

Miller, M. 1977. Debt and taxes. *Journal of Finance* 32:261–75.

Modigliani, F., and Cohn, R. A. 1979. Inflation, national valuation and the market. *Financial Analysts Journal* 35:24–44.

Meyers, S. C. 1983. Comment on Feldstein and Mørck. In *Financial aspects of the United States pension system,* ed. Zvi Bodie and John B. Shoven. Chicago: University of Chicago Press.

Oldfeld, G. S. 1977. Financial aspects of the private pension system. *Journal of Money, Credit and Banking* 9:48–93.

Sharpe, W. 1976. Corporate pension funding policy. *Journal of Financial Economics* 3:183–93.

Tobin, J., and Brainard, W. 1977. Asset markets and the cost of capital. In *Economic progress, private values and public policy: Essays in honor of William Fellner,* ed. R. Nelson and B. Balassa. Amsterdam: North-Holland.

Summers, L. H. 1981. Inflation and the valuation of corporate equities. NBER Working Paper no. 824.

Comment   Myron S. Scholes

4.C.1   Overview

Is the question of whether unfunded liabilities of pension funds reflected in stock prices an interesting question? We would expect that these liabilities would be reflected in stock prices. Several papers, however, address this question. Although we might disagree with their methodologies, these papers, on average, show that unfunded liabilities are reflected in stock prices. Most of the papers, including this paper by Bulow, Mørck, and Summers, produce coefficients with such large standard errors that it is impossible to judge how accurately the unfunded liabilities of pension funds are reflected in security prices.

It is interesting that the coefficients are in the right direction (for most years) given the difficulty of measuring unfunded liabilities. Not all firms disclose the duration of their liabilities. Simple adjustments

Myron S. Scholes is professor of economics at the Graduate School of Business, Stanford University.

such as dividing the stated interest rate by the then market interest rate could lead to large errors of measurement for many firms. Firms do not disclose their asset mix, the percentage of bonds in their pension fund. If the tax model were true, there is a differential impact on firm value depending on what proportion of the assets of the pension fund are invested in bonds. Moreover, Bulow et al. ignore changes in funding policy.

In most empirical tests in economics, it is difficult to test whether levels differ from equilibrium levels. As the authors note, it is necessary not only to value the liabilities and assets of the pension fund but also to model how investors value the entire firm. Although we can postulate a valuation model such as their model, it is not obvious that investors use their model to value shares. Most empirical success comes in the analysis of a change in policy. For example, how does a change in funding policy affect the value of shares? How does a change in the tax status of firms affect their share values? Is there a differential effect depending on the degree of unfunded liabilities? Is the change in status anticipated by market participants? These are examples of ways to discover whether the market adjusts to changes in variables affecting the pension plan. If there are price reactions to unanticipated changes in events affecting the liabilities of pension funds, we can argue then that the market does recognize the assets and liabilities of pension funds. With this approach, however, we cannot be sure that the market reflects these liabilities fully. For prices to fully reflect these liabilities requires that investors would expect to earn abnormal profits if these liabilities were not fully reflected in securities prices. It is obvious that if the liabilities were not incorporated in security prices, investors discovering such discrepancies could profit by trading in such stocks and informing other investors that they also could profit from acting on these discrepancies.

Bulow et al. do develop a new and important return test. They use changes in interest rates to test whether there is a differential effect on the value of shares of firms depending on the magnitude of unfunded pension liabilities. Unanticipated changes in interest rates should have a differential effect between firms with underfunded pension plans and those with overfunded pension plans.

In all of their empirical tests, Bulow et al. conduct joint tests. They test not only for the effects of changes in interest rates but also their model of valuation. If their model is misspecified, the effects of interest rates might be lost or the interest rate variable could proxy for other variables not included in the analysis. These problems make it difficult to make strong statements about the import of the work. For example, in their stock market required rate of return regression (eq. [15]), the authors ignore the market factor (or other pervasive market factors) as explanatory variables of security returns. These omissions affect the interpretations of the magnitude and significance of the coefficients.

4.C.2 Over Issues

As I mentioned previously, the concern that stockholders would not take account of pension liabilities appears to be of limited importance. The Bodie, Light, Mørck, and Taggart paper in this volume tests approximately the same issues as that of Bulow et al. but does it directly, not under the guise of testing the hypothesis whether the market recognizes whether a firm's pension fund is over- or underfunded. Bodie et al. test alternative models of pension funding. Moreover, if Bulow et al. can model the effects of pension liabilities, market participants, in their own interest, must be able to cause prices to reflect pension liabilities.

In Bulow's other papers, we are told that if pension plans are overfunded, the assets are those of the stockholders; if underfunded the assets are those of the beneficiaries, and the liabilities are overstated. This differential allocation of the assets results in a nonlinear relation between funding and asset ownership. In the modeling in the paper, it is assumed that there is a linear relation between funding and benefits (costs) of the plan. The market price of shares cannot reflect a quantity that does not belong to the stockholders.

The tax model in the paper is valid only if the pension fund is funded with bonds. If, as the authors state, the risk-adjusted returns on stock are less than the risk-adjusted returns on bonds (before tax), they have a badly misspecified model if firms differ on the proportion of bonds and stock held in the pension fund. The tax effect is trivial if the pension fund holds only stock. Bulow et al. do not explain why the firm holds other than bonds in pension account, or for that matter, why firms have unfunded pension plans.

The cross-sectional regressions are most likely misspecified. They cannot differentiate among the various models: the tax model; the rational market model with an implicit contract model; the irrational market model; the rational market model with employee-owned pension plans. Throwing more variables into the cross-sectional regression will not separate among these various models. The regression coefficient on the pension liability variable cannot be the same across all of the firms: it cannot be independent of a firm's particular choice of a pension policy model. It is possible, for example, that for some firms the tax model dominates while for other firms the rational market model with an employee-owned pension plan dominates. These firms are not part of the same model as the other firms in their sample. The work assumes that all firms have the same weighing on each of the possible models and differ only because of funding policy. Funding policy and choice of an operating policy (model) might be correlated. A cleaner test of whether the market accounts for pension liabilities is to study the effects of changes in stock prices as a result of changes in the funding and asset policies of pension funds.

I do not understand the economic proposition that if unfunded pension liabilities are not fully reflected in stock prices, equity owners will save less and consume more than in a world where perceptions were correct. Who consumes more? It would seem that the original stockholders would have consumed more, thereby reducing the capital stock. It cannot be a continuing problem. Overconsumption might have occurred many years prior to the test period. Only further unanticipated and unreflected changes in funding levels could cause additional aberrations in saving. In addition, if stockholders do not know, why should pension beneficiaries be more knowledgeable about the level of their savings? If they miscalculate in the same direction, they might increase their savings. On balance, it is difficult to predict the net effects of a failure to account for pension liabilities.

I did not understand the asset value regressions. Using only balance sheet variables tells us very little. The balance sheet algebra is an identity. This is an accounting model, not a regression model. There is no error in an accounting model.

4.C.3   Interest Rate Changes and Valuations of Pension Liabilities

In this section, the authors argue that changes in the rate of interest should have a greater effect on firms with greater unfunded pension liabilities. With unexpected increases in interest rates, the firm with greater liabilities should do relatively better than the firm with less underfunded liabilities because of the greater capital gain it experiences as higher interest rates erode the value of long-term pension obligations.

Everything else being equal, this is true. To run a cross-sectional regression, however, is inappropriate because everything else is not held equal. The responsiveness of the value of each of the firms given a change in interest rates is not the same for a given level of unfunded pension liabilities. To illustrate, consider a firm whose pension assets are invested in bonds such that the sensitivity of the value of its assets to changes in interest rates just matches the sensitivity of its pension liabilities. In this extreme case, the market value of the firm would not change with a change in interest rates. With differing amounts of matching of assets and liabilities, the regression coefficient will differ independent of the crucial underfunded pension fund variable that is used as the independent variable in the regression.

In selecting a single change in interest rates to capture change in value, Bulow et al. create another problem of misspecification. A mature firm with older employees has a liability of shorter duration than a firm with younger employees. Bulow et al. assume parallel shifts in the term structure. Since this is never true, the model must incorporate the effects of changes in the shape of the term structure and use the interest rate that most closely measures the change in interest rates for each particular firm. The debt variable in the model has similar problems. The reason the debt variable is not significant may have resulted from a mismatch of the interest rate and the duration of the debt. The problem might be more severe for debt because of greater dispersions of duration and risk levels than for pension liabilities.

In this discussion, I have concentrated on unanticipated changes in interest rates as affecting share value. Bulow et al. never distinguish between anticipated and unanticipated changes in interest rates in their tests of the model. If the stock market were to react negatively to an increase in interest rates, anticipations of changes in interest rates must already be incorporated in the price of the stock. This omission leads to an additional errors-in-variables problem.

The paper is silent on how V, the value of equity, was determined. The reason this is important is that there is a significant negative relation between the returns on stock and $1/V$. In deflating by V to reduce heteroscedasticity, Bulow et al. might induce the negative relation between returns and unfunded liabilities if small firms (in market value of their equity) have greater unfunded liabilities. Care must be taken in using this variable as a deflator. The relation might be none other than a noisy replication of the standard negative relation between returns and $1/V$.

4.C.4   Summary

It is hard from the analysis in the paper to agree or to disagree with its conclusions. I believe from other evidence that the market does take account of pension assets and pension liabilities. I am never told why investors would ignore pension liabilities in valuing firms. I am never told how the fact that investors ignore these liabilities affects a change in the price of their stock.

The more important discussion of the paper is the realization that there are two models of pension equilibrium. One model is called the "explicit contract model" (legal model); the other model is called the "implicit contract model." A firm can operate with either model; both models, however, cannot operate at the same time for the same employees in the firm. Until more evidence can separate when a firm is using one model or the other, it will not be possible to measure how completely the market reacts to underfunded liabilities. In the implicit contract model, the liabilities might exceed the measured liabilities (in the Bulow et al. model) by a large and variable amount depending on the particular firm.

I agree with Bulow et al. that more effort must be expended to separate the explicit contract equilibrium from the implicit contract equilibrium. That effort is crucial for determining the effects of pensions on savings. Implicit contracts imply that the savings rate is far greater than the measured savings rate as determined by the explicit contract value of pension liabilities.

References

Bulow, J., Mørck, R.; and Summers, L. 1985. How does the market value unfunded pension liabilities? In this volume.

Bodie, Z.; Light, J.; Mørck, R.; and Taggart, R. 1985. Funding and asset allocation in corporate pension plans: an empirical investigation. In this volume.

II   Pensions and Retirement Income Adequacy

5 Concepts and Measures of Earnings Replacement During Retirement

Michael J. Boskin and John B. Shoven

5.1 Introduction

The current generation of elderly retired persons is wealthier than any elderly generation that has preceded it. By some measures, it is quite well off relative to the current younger generation of workers. For a variety of reasons, however, we may be interested in comparing elderly retirees' standard of living to their standard of living during their own working years. This interest may stem from a desire to infer the private planning and foresight capabilities of persons prior to retirement; or to report the economic history of the entire life cycle of the cohort; or to evaluate the role of public policy in affecting the well-being of the elderly (for example, by providing social security benefits).

Any such comparison is fraught with conceptual and measurement difficulties. The concepts and measures one might employ to examine the economic well-being of the elderly relative to their own previous economic well-being certainly presume much about the structure of the economy, not to mention what makes people economically better or worse off. For example, most life cycles have age-specific opportunities and expenses, such as those involved with raising children. One's views about the extent to which capital markets are sufficiently

Michael J. Boskin is professor of economics, Stanford University, and research associate, National Bureau of Economic Research. John B. Shoven is professor of economics, Stanford University, and research associate, National Bureau of Economic Research.

This paper was prepared for the National Bureau of Economic Research Conference, "Pensions and Retirement in the United States," April 13–14, 1984, San Diego. We would like to thank Doug Puffert and Tim Wilson for their excellent research assistance and Alan Gustman for comments on the original draft. Funding for this research was provided by the Department of Health and Human Services in a grant to the National Bureau of Economic Research.

well developed to insure against all risks at actuarially fair rates certainly must color the time period over which well-being is measured and the method of valuing income streams at different dates from alternative sources with varying risk properties. Many other such issues arise, some of which will be discussed in more detail below.

Perhaps the most commonly used measure of relative well-being post- and pre-retirement is the so-called replacement rate. Replacement rates frequently are used in describing, and evaluating, the level of social security or private pension benefits. They are, simply, a ratio of *some* measure of post-retirement income to *some,* not necessarily similar, measure of pre-retirement income. Many private pensions report the ratio of the pension benefits to earnings in the year prior to retirement. A frequent measure for social security is the ratio of social security benefits to an average of the highest 3 of the 10 years prior to retirement. While such measures of relative well-being may be simplistic, and subsume much about absolute versus relative incomes, the value of leisure, income versus consumption, ability to draw down the principal from accumulated savings, and so on, they do tend to dominate public policy discussions. For example, recent proposals to alter the structure of social security benefits were often criticized because they would have reduced replacement rates, as usually measured, somewhat. Current replacement rates are due to fall slightly for low-income, and rise somewhat for high-income, families through time (see Hay/Huggins 1983). As we shall see, it is by no means evident that average replacement rates are "low," as the usual measures seem to imply, from the standpoint either of relative economic position of pre- and post-retirement or of apparent planning/foresight ability.

The purpose of this paper is to begin to examine some of the issues surrounding potential improvements in concepts and measures of replacement rates. We are aware that more elaborate information may be useful, but since much of the discussion undoubtedly will continue to take place in the context of replacement rates, we seek to point toward some improvements in their measurement. Some of these (potential) improvements have been suggested, explicitly or implicitly, in previous research. Section 5.2 presents a brief literature review focusing on concepts and measures of the economic well-being of the elderly and/or of comparisons of post- and pre-retirement incomes, consumption, wealth, and so on.

Section 5.3 highlights what we consider to be many of the major conceptual issues in measuring the well-being of the elderly relative to their previous standard of living. Among the issues raised are the treatment of taxes, expenses of raising children, health and health care costs, income uncertainty, and uncertainty about the date of death.

Section 5.4 presents our empirical results, a series of measures of replacement rates under alternative assumptions/definitions for various groups in the elderly population. These are estimated from the longitudinal Retirement History Survey combined with social security earnings records. The adjustments we tentatively propose as reasonable lead to a quite different perception about the "adequacy" of replacement rates, both for social security and for total income, than the traditional measures. Indeed, they suggest that earnings are virtually fully replaced for many of the elderly by social security alone; that for many more, social security replaces a large fraction of earnings; and that total post-retirement income usually exceeds pre-retirement income.

Section 5.5 discusses potential future research. Included are the need to go beyond averages to better understand the extent and causes of low replacement rates among those elderly not very well off and to analyze more fully the potential role by imperfections in annuities markets combined with rapidly increasing life expectancies for the elderly and difference between anticipated and unanticipated beneficiaries. This section also offers a brief summary and conclusion.

The appendix details the data and our use of them.

5.2 A Brief Literature Review

A variety of previous studies have attempted to explore questions that are similar or related to those we pose here. For example, Fox (1982) calculates social security, pension, and total income replacement rates for 1976 for various population groups based on the first few waves of the Retirement History Survey. While he makes several comparisons similar in spirit to some of our adjustments (before and after tax; relative to career average earnings; etc.), his results are comparable only to the earlier years we report. The continued growth of social security benefits, the additional benefits as spouses reach eligibility age, and several other factors render our results noncomparable. Even by 1976, however, he shows the importance such adjustments might make. However, his career average earnings are indexed by wage growth and therefore greatly overstate the average *absolute* real level of earnings; his career average replacement rates have a relative income component embedded in them.

Schultz et al. (1974) discuss alternative concepts and measures of replacement. They report various organizations' notions of appropriate measures of "full replacement." For example, the AAUP suggests comparing post-retirement benefits to the last few years of after-tax earnings prior to retirement, and that two-thirds is the appropriate replacement rate.

Various cost-of-living comparisons by the Bureau of Labor Statistics (1968) put the income required of a couple with husband aged 65–74 at 51% of that of a couple aged 35–54 with children 15 and 6 years of age. Henle (1972) adjusts for differences in expenses and taxes and gets 0.7 and 0.8 as estimates of "full" replacement for high- and low-wage workers, respectively.

Marilyn Moon (1977), using data from the Survey of Economic Opportunity of 1966–67, makes a variety of adjustments in the usual money income measure to get a more comprehensive measure of the "real income" of the elderly. Among her important adjustments are for in-kind transfers, the annuitized value of assets (following Hansen and Weisbrod's [1968] approach), and so on. These adjustments substantially increase the incomes of the elderly.

Boskin and Hurd (1985) establish that the cost of living for the elderly as a group, and also by various 5-year age cohorts, is quite close to that of the general population, once a rental equivalence substitution is made (as is now being done in the CPI) in the historical CPI figures. Thus, income measures will reflect real purchasing power.

The most extensive recent treatment of the real income of the elderly is by Hurd and Shoven (1982). They document the repaid absolute and relative gains made by the elderly in the 1970s and attribute much of it to the growth of real social security benefits.

Hammermesh (1982) attempts to estimate consumption and annuitizable income for a subsample of the Retirement History Survey. He reports for 1973 and 1975 that consumption exceeds annuitizable income and therefore argues savings are inadequate to maintain consumption. While direct examination of consumption is surely an important contribution, several reasons lead us to be dubious of these conclusions. First, as noted above, real benefits continued to increase in social security. More important, for many of these families, the value of the spouse's social security benefit would not be apparent until later on when he or she became eligible (it is not apparent how Hammermesh treated spouse's and widow's benefits). Also, at this stage of their lives, the elderly spend substantial amounts on health care, and (apparently) no adjustment is made for medicare. Most important, the estimated ratio of consumption spending reported in the Retirement History Survey to true consumption is about 0.6. The inclusion of nonsustainability is sensitive to any potential measurement error in the ratio.

Finally, Kotlikoff et al. (1982) come to a conclusion that is exactly opposite to that of Hammermesh, again examining early years of the Retirement History Survey. They attempt to estimate two polar cases: simulating perfect annuities markets, and no annuities markets. They calculate the ratio of the level consumption paths which could be purchased when young and old, respectively, based on the present expected value of lifetime resources and old age resources in the annuities case; and the constant levels which would be planned assuming no annuities but level consumption until age 88. They also examine the level of the annuity which could be purchased in 1969 versus 1971, to examine how the elderly manage their retirement resources. They conclude that no strong case can be made that savings are inadequate and that the ratios of old age to lifetime consumption streams as constructed cluster around one or slightly above one. Their results are not really comparable to ours, but are complementary in that they examine consumption possibilities before retirement *based on eventual realized* social security and pension "wealth"; we examine earnings before retirement, a likely upper bound on *actual* consumption. Since it is unclear that consumption plans before retirement could be based on expectation of the growth in social security benefits and coverage which eventually occurred, including the introduction of Medicare in 1965, an alternative interpretation to that of Kotlikoff et al. (1982) is possible. It may well be that these households did not expect these large windfalls and that their modest pre-retirement consumption levels were due less to careful retirement planning than to lower expected wealth.

In brief summary, other than documenting the rise in real social security benefits in recent years and the improved absolute and relative income of the elderly, there is little agreement on whether consumption can be maintained during retirement given current resources, or on the proper measurement of consumption, or on what income or consumption-based replacement rate is "appropriate."

5.3 Conceptual Issues

The primary purpose of this paper is to compare the standard of living of the elderly with their own standard of living in their earlier work years. This topic raises several research questions. First, is the observed pattern of consumption by age consistent with the perfect foresight life-cycle model, or is there evidence of suboptimal saving during work life resulting in inadequate provision for consumption during retirement? Second, is there evidence that the large and unexpected windfall gains from social security received by the Retirement History population (see Hurd and Shoven 1985) distorted the age profile of consumption for this group? Third, what is the distribution of standard of living in retirement relative to that before retirement? What are the figures for those with different earnings histories? Fourth, who in the population has low replacement rates? Who is at the bottom of the replacement rate distribution, particularly among the poor? We will not answer all of these questions, but they are our research agenda.

The problem we are addressing is not a simple one. There are both serious methodological and measurement issues. Should the replacement rate be defined in terms of consumption, income, or utility? While utility is closest to what we would like, it is the least measurable. Consumption is better than income, but again, consumption data are notoriously bad in panel surveys. This leads us to an income-based measure which can be adjusted in several ways to make it correspond more closely with our more ideal measures.

The literature on replacement rates has always had unity as the standard. Certainly for income-based measures, however, there is no particular appeal to unity, and the life-cycle model would predict a replacement rate below one. Take, for example, the simplest life-cycle model with a fixed lifetime D, fixed retirement age R, fixed labor earnings between age 0 and R, and a rate of time preference equal to the interest rate. If utility is time separable, if there is no bequest motive, and if $U'' < 0$, then the optimal age-consumption profile is flat, as shown in figure 5.1. The point for our purposes is that if we compare post-retirement income, r W(age), where r is the interest rate and W is accumulated wealth, with before-retirement earnings, we get a ratio far less than unity, highly dependent on the rate of return on accumulated wealth. For example, if the interest rate were zero, an income-

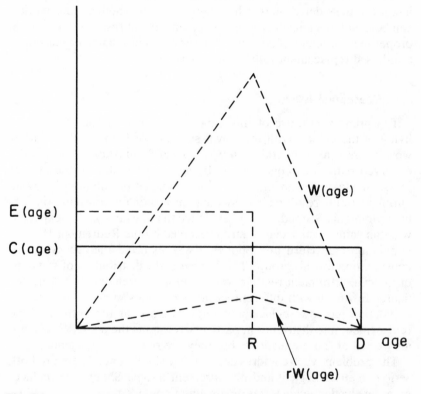

Fig. 5.1   Wealth (W), Earnings (E), Consumption (C), and Capital Income (rW) as a Function of Age for a Simple Life-cycle Model

based measure of replacement rates would be zero, while there would be full replacement of consumption. In fact, retirement income, in this example, must always be less than consumption (which must be less than pre-retirement earnings). If it were not, wealth would continue to accumulate and large bequests would be left. However, this cannot be optimal since we have assumed $U' > 0$ and zero bequest motive.

While capital income in retirement in figure 5.1 falls short of preretirement earnings, the remaining wealth at each retirement year is sufficient to finance a consumption annuity. If a tax-transfer version of social security is imposed on the above life-cycle model, it would lower after-tax earnings during the work life and raise income during retirement. Income-based measures of replacement rates would be higher, but the basic pattern would be similar and the magnitude would still be less than unity if social security benefits were fully anticipated and there were perfect capital markets.

The example above would change if we incorporate an uncertain date of death. With perfect annuity markets, the analysis would be identical to that of a certain death date at the life expectancy. However, with imperfect or no annuity markets, the pattern of planned consumption is more likely to decline with age. This is due to discounting at the sum of the pure rate of time preference plus the mortality hazard rate (which increases with age and which at least eventually exceeds the interest rate).

5.3.1   A Notation for Discussing Some Important Issues

We follow the usual convention of writing lifetime well-being as an additively separable utility function of instantaneous, or annual, utilities:

$$(1) \qquad\qquad W_\ell = \sum_{t=1}^{D} U_t(C_t, L_t, \mathbf{Z}_t)$$

where C_t, L_t, and $\mathbf{Z}_t$ are consumption of goods, leisure, and a vector of other variables at time t, and D is the (known) date of death. Clearly, additive separability is quite extreme in discussing lifetimes; for example, a minimum consumption of food, medical care, and so on, is necessary for survival. We merely use this as a way of discussing issues, not as an estimation device.

Further simplification divides the lifetime into two periods, working years (W) and retirement (R). Representative utility in each period is described by

$$(2) \qquad\qquad U_i = U_i(C_i, L_i, \mathbf{Z}_i), \qquad i = W, R.$$

Usually, W will be about twice (or more) as long as R. Let us, however, compare a typical or representative year in each period. We then need to evaluate

$$(3) \qquad \frac{U^R(C_R, L_R, \mathbf{Z}_R)}{U^W(C_W, L_W, \mathbf{Z}_W)}$$

Of course, in actuality, income, consumption, and other variables fluctuate during both the work life and the retirement period. Some of this fluctuation may represent errors in measurement and some imperfect capital markets and therefore imperfect opportunities for smoothing. Most important, opportunities for income generation are not constant during an individual's work life. These considerations regarding income and consumption variability imply that there is a large difference between career average consumption or income and the peaks of these flows. Our judgment is that retirement resources should be compared with career *average* resources as the base case, with other comparisons augmenting this information.

5.3.2 Some Conceptual Issues

The first difficulty in usual replacement rate calculations or comparisons of consumption streams is readily apparent: the failure to value leisure or nonmarket work time. Obviously, $L_R > L_W$ on average, as usually measured. The interpretation of this phenomenon is, however, quite complicated. For the "young" elderly without severe health problems, it is not reasonable to ignore the value of the extra nonmarket time available to them relative to working years. However, a variety of distortions, selection problems, and so on, make it difficult to argue that the market wage of "similar" persons continuing to work is the relevant shadow value of the leisure at the margin. Further, we suspect several institutional rigidities make it difficult for all those who wish to do so to move to part-time work (see Fuchs [1984], who notes a trend to shift to self-employment presumably as one vehicle for making hours more flexible). Blinder et al. (1980) note a decline in hourly earnings as the elderly change jobs. Presumably, valuing the marginal unit of extra leisure at the corresponding wage of those who work places a lower bound on the value of the first unit of leisure. But, as leisure (or household work or volunteer time) becomes "full-time," it is likely that its marginal value will fall. And the trend to earlier retirement (see Hurd and Boskin 1984) at a time of improved health of the elderly[1] surely indicates the voluntary nature of much of this "leisure."

At the other extreme, the "old" elderly may contain a substantial number of persons whose health would be seriously impaired if they continued to work. Others may suffer severe psychological problems from withdrawal from the labor force.

All of these issues, and more, make it difficult to value "leisure" for the elderly. We only note the problems here and return to the more usual measures.

The vector **Z** may include items such as age-specific expenses, for example, in raising children or on health care. This immediately raises additional issues. The direct utility function (3) may be rewritten in indirect form;

$$\frac{V^R(\mathbf{P}_R, I_R)}{V^W(P_W, I_W)},$$

where $\mathbf{P}_i$ is the vector of prices faced by the household in stage of life i, and I_i is income in i. Is gross income the appropriate measure to include in V^i? In addition to netting out taxes (and perhaps pension contributions and other retirement saving), what about "necessary" expenses? Suppose K represents spending on children. If expenditure on children is perfectly inelastic—a basic amount is necessary to "produce and raise" a standard child—there is no joint consumption and no special utility value of children early in life (children are a "durable good" providing [net] utility throughout one's life), then the appropriate income measure is $I - K$ and we should calculate

$$\frac{V^R(P_R, I_R)}{V^W[P_W(I_W - K)]}.$$

Even worse examples of ignoring expenditures on children exist. Suppose, for example, one works more or harder and income increases more than directly observed K when the children come along because of transaction costs in borrowing. Then the observed extra income and consumption may not measure increased utility. Of course, not all spending on children is "necessary." Some is clearly for (attempted) quality improvement, or discretionary. How should this be netted out?

Analogous problems arise with health care expenditures. If the demand for medical services is perfectly inelastic with a given amount necessary to maintain health, and amounts beyond that provide no utility, then income net of health expenditure is the appropriate measure. If demand for health care is not completely inelastic, actual health expenditures are only a proxy for true health needs, and subtracting all expenditures will understate "net" income. Again, observed income may rise to compensate for greater medical costs (if he or she is able), further complicating the story.

Health expenditures rise substantially as a share of income in old age. Further, the bulk of the costs are paid for by Medicare and Medicaid. If we do not include at least the insurance value of Medicare in

the retirement income, we ought to subtract net health insurance premiums from earnings during work years.

Because the out-of-pocket hospital and physician expenditures for
the elderly are small relative to the total, it may well be that adding
the average Medicare payment to the incomes of the elderly, as is often
done, would overstate the proper adjustment.

While each of these problems is nontrivial, it is clear that ignoring
the public transfers in the insurance value of Medicare as income sources
for the elderly without netting health care costs for work years will,
on average, lead to an understatement of replacement rates. Thus, the
empirical results presented below probably understate replacement rates.

Another important conceptual issue in comparing a certain income
stream from social security to an uncertain earnings stream is the discount for risk in the earnings, or equivalently, the "certainty bonus,"
for social security (aside from its annuity value). At one extreme,
capital markets may be so imperfect, and informal intrafamily arrangements nonexistent, that *annual* fluctuation in earnings may be quite a
problem. Even with perfect capital markets, however, the risk in career
earnings from occupational choice, and so on, may be substantial.
Define the equivalent certain income as that which satisfies

$$E\ U(\bar{y}) = U(y),$$

where $\bar{y}$ denotes a random income and y certain income. If y has mean
m and variance σ^2, taking a Taylor series expansion of U about m yields

$$y \approx m - \frac{\sigma^2}{2\ R(m)},$$

where $R(m) \equiv -[U'(y)/U''(y)]$, what is called the risk tolerance in the
finance literature, or the reciprocal of the Arrow-Pratt measure of absolute risk aversion. The difference between the mean and the equivalent certain income is a "risk charge." Alternatively, one can "gross
up" the certain income with a certainty bonus in comparison with risky
income flows. We make such an adjustment below. To our empirical
results we now turn.

5.4   Results

We have computed replacement rates for the Retirement History
Survey population in a number of different ways, for various years,
and for several subpopulations. Table 5.1 displays the results for a
conventional measure similar to that frequently reported by the Social
Security Administration. Two figures are given for those retired in the
1971 through 1979 Survey waves;[2] first, the ratio of social security

retirement benefits received to the average of the highest 3 years of price-indexed earnings in the 10 years prior to retirement and second, the ratio of total income (pensions, interest, dividends, rental income, earnings, transfers, social security, etc.) in retirement to the same average high-three earnings figure. The numbers are calculated separately for widows and for married couples. The widows in our tables are those whose spouses died since the survey began in 1969. This permits us to compare retirement benefits with the combined earnings records of both spouses. These combined earnings histories are the basis for the denominator for both widows and married couples.

The social security numbers in table 5.1 seem rather modest, ranging for married couples from 22% replacement in 1971 to 37.4% in 1979. They are lower for widows by a factor only slightly different than two-thirds, which is what we anticipated. Our priors were based on the fact that single-earner married couples who wait until 65 years of age to collect retirement receive 150% of their "Primary Insurance Amount," while the surviving spouse receives 100%.[3] The average social security replacement rate for married couples in this population increased by more than 50% from 1971 to 1979. This reflects a number of facts. First, at the later dates both spouses are more likely to be collecting social security rather than just one. Second, those who retire at later dates and ages receive actuarial adjustments in their annuities. Third, as this population ages, it works less and therefore fewer of the retired give back their social security benefits via the earnings test. Fourth, the real level of benefits was increased in 1972 and rose further for those who worked in the double indexing period of 1973–77. Despite the rise in the social security replacement rate for married couples, their total unadjusted replacement rate remained virtually constant at 70%. This may indicate that the population is decumulating private assets in a way which offsets their increased social security receipts. The significant difference between the average total replacement rates in table

Table 5.1   **Unadjusted Replacement Rates Relative to High-3 Average Annual Indexed Earnings, By Household Type**

	1971	1973	1975	1977	1979
Married couples:					
Social security	22.4	30.6	34.0	36.5	37.4
Pension and social security	34.1	42.2	45.6	47.7	47.6
Total	70.6	72.3	69.0	68.7	68.6
Widows:					
Social security	. . .	18.0	21.3	22.6	23.9
Pension and social security	. . .	25.1	29.5	28.0	28.4
Total	. . .	60.3	47.6	48.9	44.0

5.1 and the average social security replacement rates indicates that those who rely totally on social security have reasonably low resources available to them in retirement relative to their pre-retirement earnings.

Table 5.2 compares retirement income with 1951–74 career average real earnings where earnings have been indexed using the Personal Consumption Expenditure deflator of the National Income Accounts. The pattern of the figures in table 5.2 is very similar to those in table 5.1, but the level is increased by roughly 50%.[4] Interestingly, the average total replacement rate for married couples is 100% by 1979 when the denominator is career average indexed earnings. The social security replacement rate with this basis for comparison is over 50% by 1979. The 50% increase in replacement rates of table 5.2 versus table 5.1 reflects both the issues previously mentioned: income variability and the extraordinary real wage growth that members of this generation experienced near the ends of their careers.

Tables 5.3 and 5.4 show social security, social security plus private pensions, and total replacement rates where the denominator is average high-three out of the 10 years prior to retirement. The figures are calculated for different income groups, where the income-classifying variable is career average real earnings expressed in 1983 dollars. The figures in parentheses are sample sizes. The numbers indicate that the poor have by far the highest social security replacement rates, and even have the highest total replacement rates. By 1979, the total replacement rate was 100% even relative to the average of the high-three earnings years for those with average career earnings below $7,500. Social security replacement rates (in 1979) are 57.4% for married couples with low earnings histories, but only 19.4% for those whose high earnings years were between $30,000 and $50,000. We also see that private pensions are an important component of total retirement income, although less so for those in the lowest earnings history category.[5]

Tables 5.5 and 5.6 contain the same information except that the standard of comparison is the 1951–74 career average indexed earnings.

Table 5.2   **Unadjusted Replacement Rates Relative to Career Average Annual Indexed Earnings, By Household Type**

	1971	1973	1975	1977	1979
Married couples:					
Social security	31.8	44.0	49.2	53.3	54.5
Pension and social security	47.4	60.5	65.8	69.3	69.2
Total	102.8	105.5	101.2	101.0	101.5
Widows:					
Social security	. . .	26.4	32.6	33.1	34.7
Pension and social security	. . .	35.9	43.2	40.9	41.4
Total	. . .	82.5	71.8	75.1	65.1

Table 5.3   **Unadjusted Replacement Rates Relative to High-3 Average Annual Indexed Earnings By Income Class for Married Couples**

Average Annual Indexed Earnings	1971	1973	1975	1977	1979
Less than $7,500:					
Social security	32.6 (48)	46.8 (111)	52.6 (193)	55.6 (241)	57.4 (273)
Pension and social security	37.5 (47)	50.2 (111)	57.6 (191)	60.6 (240)	62.1 (270)
Total	88.4 (33)	97.5 (92)	100.2 (132)	96.3 (175)	100.0 (200)
$7,500–$12,500:					
Social security	25.1 (61)	36.5 (133)	40.0 (233)	43.9 (314)	44.4 (364)
Pension and social security	34.0 (58)	44.7 (133)	49.2 (233)	52.7 (312)	52.8 (356)
Total	76.7 (35)	77.4 (103)	78.8 (142)	77.5 (241)	76.3 (274)
$12,500–$20,000:					
Social security	21.4 (53)	26.9 (166)	32.4 (370)	36.4 (550)	37.1 (671)
Pension and social security	36.0 (50)	42.4 (162)	45.0 (362)	47.5 (531)	47.3 (658)
Total	58.9 (40)	64.3 (130)	61.1 (248)	64.4 (411)	64.3 (494)
$20,000–$30,000:					
Social security	15.5 (23)	22.2 (78)	23.8 (216)	26.2 (359)	27.8 (431)
Pension and social security	37.6 (22)	39.4 (76)	39.3 (214)	40.9 (354)	41.0 (422)
Total	62.4 (18)	55.1 (58)	53.5 (147)	54.8 (251)	56.2 (331)
$30,000–$50,000:					
Social security	9.4 (18)	14.2 (51)	17.0 (84)	18.8 (125)	19.4 (95)
Pension and social security	30.8 (17)	31.8 (50)	35.3 (81)	36.9 (116)	35.8 (138)
Total	55.1 (10)	54.3 (35)	55.6 (55)	54.0 (87)	54.4 (95)
More than $50,000:					
Social security	2.2 (10)	5.4 (19)	6.7 (27)	6.7 (34)	7.2 (39)
Pension and social security	6.2 (10)	12.0 (18)	16.3 (26)	20.5 (32)	16.6 (37)
Total	65.7 (7)	58.0 (13)	34.2 (15)	45.0 (18)	36.3 (23)

NOTE: The numbers in parentheses are sample sizes.

Now the total replacement rate is 88.2% for the middle-income ($12,500–$20,000) group of married couples in 1979; higher for the lower earnings groups and lower for the higher earnings groups. The total replacement rate is *over* 100% even for widows in the lowest earnings category. Perhaps a surprising finding of tables 5.3–5.5 is that those in the lowest earnings category have substantial non-social-security income sources, at least relative to their own pre-retirement earnings histories. We did an investigation of their retirement income sources and found that the largest non-social-security component was earnings. Income composition by earnings class for married couples in 1979 is shown in table 5.7. Those with low career average earnings are far more likely to work part-time in retirement. Those in the lowest category were still making more than one-third of their pre-retirement earnings in 1979, while the corresponding figure was less than 10% for all those with incomes greater than $20,000. Among those with low earnings histories, a non-trivial fraction have substantial amounts of interest, dividends, and rents, as indicated by the substantial average amounts in table 5.7.[6]

Table 5.4   Unadjusted Replacement Rates Relative to High-3 Average
                   Annual Indexed Earnings By Income Class for Widows

Average Annual Indexed Earnings	1973	1975	1977	1979
Less than $7,500:				
Social security	24.8 (26)	35.0 (50)	29.7 (68)	35.2 (97)
Pension and social security	35.6 (26)	53.0 (49)	37.3 (66)	41.9 (69)
Total	88.6 (22)	69.4 (36)	75.8 (51)	61.9 (82)
$7,500–$12,500:				
Social security	18.5 (23)	21.9 (54)	28.6 (86)	28.4 (128)
Pension and social security	20.7 (23)	27.1 (52)	34.0 (84)	32.7 (128)
Total	61.9 (20)	51.4 (39)	52.6 (70)	50.0 (98)
$12,500–$20,000:				
Social security	16.9 (36)	20.0 (81)	22.0 (139)	22.4 (179)
Pension and social security	19.6 (36)	24.6 (81)	25.6 (133)	25.6 (178)
Total	39.9 (31)	40.9 (54)	43.4 (99)	39.6 (146)
$20,000–$30,000:				
Social security	9.8 (13)	12.3 (37)	14.6 (71)	14.6 (98)
Pension and social security	29.1 (13)	21.6 (37)	20.9 (69)	18.2 (97)
Total	59.6 (9)	36.7 (28)	35.5 (55)	29.8 (83)
$30,000–$50,000:				
Social security	8.0 (4)	6.9 (13)	9.0 (19)	12.0 (27)
Pension and social security	15.7 (3)	11.1 (13)	16.7 (18)	20.3 (27)
Total	47.4 (1)	31.5 (7)	31.0 (11)	37.0 (21)
More than $50,000:				
Social security	0.0 (0)	2.8 (5)	3.5 (5)	4.4 (5)
Pension and social security	3.0 (0)	3.5 (4)	5.7 (4)	8.3 (7)
Total	10.0 (0)	10.6 (4)	11.2 (4)	32.9 (6)

NOTE: The numbers in parentheses are sample sizes.

Tables 5.8–5.12 show the effect of making three of the adjustments we discussed above for married couples with different levels of career average earnings. The replacement rates are relative to 1951–74 career indexed average earnings. The three adjustments reflect taxes, the costs of raising children, and the welfare effects of uncertainty of income and wealth. The tax adjustments take into account the payroll tax, the mildly progressive average income tax rates in the United States (Pechman 1983), and the facts that social security benefits were untaxed until 1984 and the elderly enjoy double personal exemptions. The children adjustment is only a rough approximation of the necessary costs of raising children. While children presumably generate utility for their parents, it is implausible that a couple with grown children requires the same resources in retirement as they did when raising the children to achieve the same standard of living. Whether all costs of raising children should be deducted from pre-retirement resources before making the comparison with post-retirement income is open to question,

Table 5.5   **Unadjusted Replacement Rates Relative to Career Average Annual
Indexed Earnings By Income Class for Married Couples**

Average Annual Indexed Earnings	1971	1973	1975	1977	1979
Less than $7,500:					
Social security	54.2 (48)	73.7 (111)	86.5 (193)	96.4 (241)	99.8 (273)
Pension and social security	61.8 (47)	79.8 (111)	95.9 (191)	104.0 (240)	107.5 (270)
Total	146.3 (33)	152.3 (92)	162.7 (132)	164.2 (175)	175.8 (200)
$7,500–$12,000:					
Social security	32.1 (61)	51.4 (133)	57.4 (233)	65.0 (314)	65.4 (364)
Pension and social security	43.5 (58)	62.8 (133)	71.2 (233)	78.6 (312)	78.5 (356)
Total	111.1 (35)	113.7 (103)	117.4 (142)	117.9 (241)	116.3 (274)
$12,500–$20,000:					
Social security	28.2 (53)	36.4 (166)	43.8 (370)	48.7 (550)	49.8 (671)
Pension and social security	48.3 (50)	58.5 (162)	61.5 (362)	64.1 (531)	64.0 (658)
Total	81.4 (40)	90.9 (130)	83.9 (248)	88.4 (411)	88.2 (494)
$20,000–$30,000:					
Social security	20.0 (23)	29.6 (78)	31.6 (216)	35.4 (359)	37.3 (431)
Pension and social security	47.7 (22)	53.2 (76)	52.4 (214)	55.4 (354)	55.2 (422)
Total	78.5 (18)	73.8 (58)	73.0 (147)	73.3 (251)	76.1 (331)
$30,000–$50,000:					
Social security	12.0 (18)	19.7 (51)	22.4 (84)	24.7 (125)	25.6 (142)
Pension and social security	39.8 (17)	44.0 (50)	47.4 (81)	48.8 (116)	48.2 (138)
Total	71.6 (10)	76.4 (35)	76.6 (55)	72.3 (87)	69.9 (95)
More than $50,000:					
Social security	3.3 (10)	7.8 (19)	10.1 (27)	10.3 (34)	11.9 (39)
Pension and social security	10.7 (10)	20.0 (18)	24.2 (26)	31.0 (32)	27.1 (37)
Total	86.3 (7)	74.1 (13)	58.0 (15)	70.7 (18)	63.0 (23)

NOTE: The numbers in parentheses are sample sizes.

but that is roughly what we have done. We have assumed that the married couples had two children, that child-raising costs account for 28% of all consumption in child-raising years (for two-child families, see Lazear and Michael [1983]), and that child-raising years are roughly half of the adult work life, but the first half (and, therefore, count for more than half in present value). We have made a rough adjustment by lowering the denominator (career average earnings) by 20% because of child-raising expenses. This reduction is substantially less than the BLS estimates of expense differences for elderly couples relative to middle-aged families with children. The third adjustment is also very difficult to measure precisely. Certainly younger workers have substantial uncertainty about both next year's earnings and, more relevant perhaps, the value of their human capital. Retired couples, on the other hand, probably have less uncertainty about the value of their social security claim. We feel we have made a relatively conservative correction for the comparative certainty of social security. We have esti-

Table 5.6   Unadjusted Replacement Rates Relative to Career Average
                     Annual Indexed Earnings By Income Class for Widows

Average Annual Indexed Earnings	1973	1975	1977	1979
Less than $7,500:				
Social security	39.8 (26)	62.6 (50)	55.7 (68)	61.2 (97)
Pension and social security	54.5 (26)	84.6 (49)	67.4 (66)	72.8 (96)
Total	134.1 (22)	125.1 (36)	160.3 (51)	113.2 (82)
$7,500–$12,500:				
Social security	27.4 (23)	33.1 (54)	40.2 (86)	39.8 (128)
Pension and social security	32.1 (23)	41.2 (52)	48.2 (84)	46.0 (128)
Total	78.9 (20)	77.4 (39)	72.2 (70)	70.1 (98)
$12,500–$20,000:				
Social security	22.4 (36)	26.2 (81)	28.3 (139)	28.8 (179)
Pension and social security	26.1 (36)	32.6 (81)	33.4 (133)	33.4 (178)
Total	53.0 (31)	53.8 (54)	55.3 (99)	51.1 (146)
$20,000–$30,000:				
Social security	13.8 (13)	16.7 (37)	19.8 (71)	19.8 (98)
Pension and social security	35.2 (13)	27.4 (37)	27.6 (69)	25.1 (97)
Total	67.4 (9)	45.1 (28)	45.8 (55)	40.5 (83)
$30,000–$50,000:				
Social security	11.7 (4)	10.6 (13)	13.0 (19)	16.6 (27)
Pension and social security	24.0 (3)	16.8 (13)	22.9 (18)	26.3 (27)
Total	64.0 (1)	42.6 (7)	44.4 (11)	52.5 (21)
More than $50,000:				
Social security	0.0 (0)	4.4 (5)	5.7 (5)	6.7 (8)
Pension and social security	0.0 (0)	5.5 (4)	9.5 (4)	12.7 (7)
Total	0.0 (0)	17.9 (4)	19.8 (4)	51.5 (6)

NOTE: The numbers in parentheses are sample sizes.

mated the trend growth and variation about trend of earnings and taken the one-period utility function to be the natural log of consumption. Many estimates suggest that households display more risk aversion than this implies. The net effect of adding the "certainty bonus" is to raise the social security benefits by roughly 10% relative to other income sources.[7]

Table 5.8 shows the effect of these adjustments for our category with the lowest earnings history. The tax adjustment is small for this group. The replacement rates, after these three adjustments, however, are 50% higher and are, in general, extremely high. By 1979, the social security replacement rate is in excess of 150% and the total rate is 250%. Table 5.10 shows the same adjustments for those with career average earnings between $12,500 and $20,000. The total adjusted replacement rate is over 100% for all years and the social security adjusted replacement rate alone is over 75%. In fact, our adjusted total replacement rates exceed 100% of career average earnings for all income

Table 5.7 Composition of Income Sources By Earnings Categories

Source of Income	< $7,500	$7,500–$12,500	$12,500–$20,000	$20,000–$30,000	$30,000–$50,000	> $50,000
Wages	$1,728 (273)	$ 1,834 (382)	$ 1,735 (712)	$ 2,004 (493)	$ 2,026 (155)	$ 5,615 (37)
Pensions	372 (304)	1,321 (412)	2,279 (740)	3,955 (492)	7,753 (162)	10,958 (40)
Non-social-security disability	146 (304)	68 (424)	32 (761)	82 (526)	0 (174)	63 (43)
Interest and dividends	660 (260)	1,563 (346)	1,781 (603)	2,710 (434)	6,864 (129)	14,412 (31)
Rent	382 (271)	618 (383)	399 (694)	493 (485)	422 (151)	1,919 (40)
Social security	4,516 (288)	6,511 (405)	7,895 (733)	8,688 (483)	9,012 (157)	8,326 (41)
SSI	254 (305)	74 (424)	20 (765)	0 (527)	0 (174)	0 (43)
Other government transfers	53 (298)	42 (422)	24 (763)	51 (525)	60 (173)	0 (42)
Relatives	1 (306)	19 (425)	9 (764)	4 (526)	8 (173)	0 (43)
Other	74 (306)	123 (423)	31 (764)	32 (526)	8 (173)	166 (43)
Item: Career average earnings	$4,949 (308)	$10,062 (425)	$16,121 (770)	$23,804 (527)	$35,619 (174)	$75,094 (43)

NOTE: Dollar figures are averages for 1979 over all married couples who reported a valid value (possibly zero) for the relevant income source. The numbers in parentheses are sample sizes.

Table 5.8   **Replacement Rates for Career Average Annual Indexed Earnings Less Than $7,500 for Married Couples**

	1971	1973	1975	1977	1979
Unadjusted:					
Social security	54.2 (48)	73.7 (111)	86.5 (193)	96.4 (241)	99.8 (273)
Pension and social security	61.8 (47)	79.8 (111)	95.9 (191)	104.0 (240)	107.5 (270)
Total	146.3 (33)	152.3 (92)	162.7 (132)	164.2 (175)	175.8 (200)
Tax adjustment:					
Social security	56.4 (48)	76.9 (111)	90.4 (193)	100.7 (241)	104.3 (273)
Pension and social security	64.3 (47)	83.2 (111)	100.0 (191)	108.6 (240)	112.3 (270)
Total	151.2 (33)	157.7 (92)	168.8 (132)	170.4 (175)	182.3 (200)
Tax and children adjustments:					
Social security	71.3 (48)	97.2 (111)	114.2 (193)	127.3 (241)	131.8 (273)
Pension and social security	81.2 (47)	105.2 (111)	126.5 (191)	137.3 (240)	142.0 (270)
Total	191.1 (33)	199.4 (92)	213.4 (131)	215.5 (175)	230.6 (200)
Tax, children, and certainty bonus adjustments:					
Social security	82.3 (48)	112.0 (111)	131.5 (193)	146.7 (241)	152.3 (273)
Pension and social security	92.2 (47)	119.9 (111)	143.8 (191)	156.7 (240)	162.5 (270)
Total	203.0 (33)	213.2 (92)	231.0 (132)	235.5 (175)	250.4 (200)

NOTE: The numbers in parentheses are sample sizes.

Table 5.9   **Replacement Rates for Career Average Annual Indexed Earnings $7,500–$12,500 for Married Couples**

	1971	1973	1975	1977	1979
Unadjusted:					
Social security	32.1 (61)	51.4 (133)	57.4 (233)	65.0 (314)	65.4 (364)
Pension and social security	43.5 (58)	62.8 (133)	71.2 (233)	78.6 (312)	78.5 (356)
Total	111.1 (35)	113.7 (103)	117.4 (142)	117.9 (241)	116.3 (274)
Tax adjustment:					
Social security	34.7 (61)	55.4 (133)	62.1 (233)	70.3 (314)	70.8 (364)
Pension and social security	46.7 (58)	67.5 (133)	76.6 (233)	84.6 (312)	84.6 (356)
Total	115.8 (35)	120.1 (103)	124.7 (142)	125.5 (241)	123.2 (274)
Tax and children adjustments:					
Social security	44.3 (61)	70.7 (133)	79.3 (233)	89.7 (314)	90.4 (364)
Pension and social security	59.6 (58)	86.1 (133)	97.8 (233)	108.0 (312)	107.9 (356)
Total	148.1 (35)	153.2 (103)	159.3 (142)	160.2 (241)	157.2 (274)
Tax, children, and certainty bonus adjustments:					
Social security	49.5 (61)	79.2 (133)	87.8 (233)	98.6 (314)	99.6 (364)
Pension and social security	65.0 (58)	94.6 (133)	106.3 (233)	116.9 (312)	117.1 (356)
Total	153.3 (35)	162.1 (103)	165.5 (142)	169.3 (241)	166.5 (274)

NOTE: The numbers in parentheses are sample sizes.

Table 5.10   **Replacement Rates for Career Average Annual Indexed Earnings $12,500–$20,000 for Married Couples**

	1971	1973	1975	1977	1979
Unadjusted:					
Social security	28.2 (53)	36.4 (166)	43.8 (370)	48.7 (550)	49.8 (671)
Pension and social security	48.3 (50)	58.5 (162)	61.5 (362)	64.1 (531)	64.0 (658)
Total	81.4 (40)	90.9 (130)	83.9 (248)	88.4 (411)	88.2 (494)
Tax adjustment:					
Social security	31.9 (53)	41.2 (166)	49.5 (370)	55.1 (550)	56.3 (671)
Pension and social security	54.0 (50)	65.1 (162)	68.9 (362)	72.0 (531)	72.0 (658)
Total	87.9 (40)	98.8 (130)	93.0 (248)	98.0 (411)	97.7 (494)
Tax and children adjustments:					
Social security	41.2 (53)	53.3 (166)	64.0 (370)	71.2 (550)	72.8 (671)
Pension and social security	69.8 (50)	84.2 (162)	89.0 (362)	93.2 (531)	93.2 (658)
Total	113.5 (40)	127.7 (130)	120.2 (248)	126.6 (411)	126.3 (494)
Tax, children, and certainty bonus adjustments:					
Social security	44.6 (53)	57.8 (166)	68.4 (370)	75.6 (550)	77.3 (671)
Pension and social security	73.3 (50)	88.8 (162)	93.4 (362)	97.5 (531)	97.7 (658)
Total	117.0 (40)	132.7 (130)	124.9 (248)	131.1 (411)	131.1 (494)

NOTE: The numbers in parentheses are sample sizes.

Table 5.11   **Replacement Rates for Career Average Annual Indexed Earnings $20,000–$30,000 for Married Couples**

	1971	1973	1975	1977	1979
Unadjusted:					
Social security	20.0 (23)	29.6 (78)	31.6 (216)	35.4 (359)	37.3 (431)
Pension and social security	47.7 (22)	53.2 (76)	52.4 (214)	55.4 (354)	55.2 (422)
Total	78.5 (18)	73.8 (58)	73.0 (147)	73.3 (251)	76.1 (331)
Tax adjustment:					
Social security	23.5 (23)	35.0 (78)	37.3 (216)	41.7 (359)	44.0 (431)
Pension and social security	54.1 (22)	61.3 (76)	60.6 (214)	64.3 (354)	64.2 (422)
Total	87.2 (18)	84.2 (58)	83.0 (147)	842.2 (251)	87.0 (331)
Tax and children adjustments:					
Social security	30.8 (23)	45.8 (78)	48.9 (216)	54.6 (359)	57.6 (431)
Pension and social security	70.7 (22)	80.2 (76)	79.3 (214)	84.2 (354)	84.0 (422)
Total	114.0 (18)	110.3 (58)	108.7 (147)	110.2 (251)	113.9 (331)
Tax, children, and certainty bonus adjustments:					
Social security	32.8 (23)	48.9 (78)	51.9 (216)	57.8 (359)	60.9 (431)
Pension and social security	72.8 (22)	83.4 (76)	82.3 (214)	87.4 (354)	87.3 (422)
Total	116.1 (18)	122.8 (58)	111.5 (147)	113.4 (251)	117.3 (331)

NOTE: The numbers in parentheses are sample sizes.

Table 5.12   **Replacement Rates for Career Average Annual Indexed Earnings $30,000–$50,000 for Married Couples**

	1971	1973	1975	1977	1979
Unadjusted:					
Social security	12.0 (18)	19.9 (51)	22.4 (84)	24.7 (125)	25.6 (142)
Pension and social security	39.8 (17)	44.0 (50)	47.4 (81)	48.8 (116)	48.2 (138)
Total	71.6 (10)	76.4 (35)	76.6 (55)	72.3 (87)	69.9 (95)
Tax adjustment:					
Social security	14.5 (18)	23.9 (51)	27.3 (84)	30.0 (125)	31.2 (142)
Pension and social security	45.0 (17)	50.2 (50)	54.2 (81)	56.4 (116)	56.0 (138)
Total	80.4 (10)	84.3 (35)	84.8 (55)	82.0 (87)	80.1 (95)
Tax and children adjustments:					
Social security	19.1 (18)	31.6 (51)	36.0 (84)	39.7 (125)	41.3 (142)
Pension and social security	59.4 (17)	66.3 (50)	71.7 (81)	74.6 (116)	74.1 (138)
Total	106.1 (10)	111.4 (35)	112.2 (55)	108.4 (87)	106.0 (95)
Tax, children, and certainty bonus adjustments:					
Social security	20.9 (18)	34.4 (51)	39.7 (84)	43.3 (125)	45.5 (142)
Pension and social security	61.0 (17)	69.0 (50)	75.4 (81)	78.3 (116)	78.4 (138)
Total	107.4 (10)	114.9 (35)	115.5 (55)	112.0 (87)	110.1 (95)

NOTE: The numbers in parentheses are sample sizes.

classes in all years. It should be noted that several of the omitted adjustments would tend to raise replacement rates further. For example, while our tax adjustment does take into account social security contributions during the working life, we do not subtract from earnings the contributions to pensions or other means of retirement asset accumulation. Second, we have not annuitized wealth at all in the retirement period. Our total replacement includes capital income, but the principal is left intact as if the household were planning to live forever. This effect may be offset since inflation may exaggerate capital income. We have not corrected interest income or dividends for inflation. Neither have we attributed retained earnings to equityholders. It is our view that the sum of all the inflation adjustments would leave our figures little changed. The total evidence of tables 5.8 through 5.12, then, seems quite conclusive that retirement resources are at least adequate to finance consumption at the average pre-retirement consumption level.

Tables 5.13 and 5.14 divide the Retirement History population of couples by year of retirement. Table 5.13 shows the fully adjusted social security replacement rates, while table 5.14 shows fully adjusted total replacement rates. The first year after retirement is unusual for a number of reasons. We do not know the exact timing of retirement, so we may pick up some pre-retirement earnings and may have less than a full year of social security benefits. Also, there may be some severance pay or lump sum settlements of retirement plans. Thus the main di-

Table 5.13   **Replacement Rates for Career Average Annual Indexed Earnings More Than $50,000 for Married Couples**

	1971	1973	1975	1977	1979
Unadjusted:					
Social security	3.3 (10)	7.8 (19)	10.1 (27)	10.3 (34)	11.9 (39)
Pension and social security	10.7 (10)	20.0 (18)	24.2 (26)	31.0 (32)	27.1 (37)
Total	86.3 (7)	74.1 (13)	58.0 (15)	70.7 (18)	63.0 (23)
Tax adjustment:					
Social security	4.4 (10)	10.5 (19)	13.5 (27)	13.8 (34)	15.9 (39)
Pension and social security	12.8 (10)	24.3 (18)	29.2 (26)	36.4 (32)	32.8 (37)
Total	91.8 (7)	81.7 (13)	66.8 (15)	79.0 (18)	72.6 (23)
Tax and children adjustments:					
Social security	6.1 (10)	14.3 (19)	18.5 (27)	18.8 (34)	21.8 (39)
Pension and social security	17.5 (10)	33.2 (18)	40.0 (26)	49.7 (32)	44.9 (37)
Total	125.5 (7)	111.6 (13)	91.3 (15)	107.9 (18)	99.2 (23)
Tax, children, and certainty bonus adjustments:					
Social security	7.0 (10)	16.6 (19)	22.2 (27)	22.5 (34)	25.8 (39)
Pension and social security	18.5 (10)	35.5 (18)	43.3 (26)	52.9 (32)	48.9 (37)
Total	126.8 (7)	113.9 (13)	93.9 (15)	110.5 (18)	103.0 (23)

NOTE: The numbers in parentheses are sample sizes.

Table 5.14   **Fully Adjusted Social Security Replacement Rates Relative to Career Average Annual Indexed Earnings By Year of Retirement for Married Couples**

Year of Retirement	1969	1971	1973	1975	1977	1979
1968 or earlier	33.1	49.4	67.7	81.5	89.2	94.0
1969 or 1970	. . .	29.2	69.6	80.0	89.7	91.0
1971 or 1972		. . .	41.2	73.1	78.8	82.1
1973 or 1974			. . .	51.1	80.5	78.8
1975 or 1976				. . .	74.0	87.1
1977 or 1978					. . .	75.4

agonal elements are the least dependable numbers. Table 5.13 shows that the social security benefits of each wave of retirees rose in the year following retirement. This is due to the spouse's collecting benefits at a later point in time, the increase in the generosity of the system in 1972, and the gradual reduction in the effect of the earnings test. By 1979, the fully adjusted social security replacement rates were over 80% for all vintages of retirees. Table 5.14 gives the same picture for total income. The figures are essentially constant with time since retirement, in contrast to the social security numbers, and are at least 150% for all retirement cohorts.

Table 5.15   Fully Adjusted Total Income Replacement Rates Relative to
                      Career Average Annual Indexed Earnings By Year of Retirement
                      for Married Couples

Year of Retirement	1969	1971	1973	1975	1977	1979
1968 or earlier	162.4	145.4	155.9	153.3	166.1	169.4
1969 or 1970	. . .	165.1	149.9	153.6	158.9	152.7
1971 or 1972		. . .	159.2	143.4	141.6	144.0
1973 or 1974			. . .	156.0	142.7	144.2
1975 or 1976				. . .	164.5	152.5
1977 or 1978					. . .	168.8

Such high replacement rates seem to us most consistent with the notion that these cohorts of elderly retirees did not fully anticipate their social security wealth windfalls and hence, in an ex post sense, oversaved. Had they known how large their benefits would become, they may well have preferred to consume more earlier in life, saving less for retirement and driving total replacement rates toward unity. Our numbers seem to contradict Hammermesh's (1982) contention that consumption cannot be maintained in retirement, but that is with the benefit of several more years worth of data. Since we find it implausible that the rate of time preference plus the mortality hazard rate falls short of the interest rate for these households, we prefer the interpretation that this apparent "oversaving" was unplanned, not the careful foresight suggested by Kotlikoff et al. (1982).

5.5 Conclusion

5.5.1 Summary

Our results suggest that by the late 1970s our sample had quite high average replacement rates, as adjusted.[8] The income available to them usually exceeds that available on average during their working lives. Indeed, had they anticipated their social security benefit growth, they probably would have consumed more earlier in their lifetime.

Traditional measures of replacement rates are quite misleading today. Just replacing "high-three" average earnings by career average earnings increases replacement rates by 50%. Calculated either way, social security replacement rates increased about 50% from 1971 to 1979.

Replacement rates are substantially in excess of one by 1979 for most income classes. Social security alone fully replaces average earnings for the elderly poor and replaces over half for middle-income elderly couples once adjustments are made for child-rearing costs, taxes, and risky earnings.

5.5.2 Further Research

We hope the previous discussion and analysis prove useful in reevaluating concepts and measures of earnings replacement. But, we view the above as the first part of a larger research agenda. Among the important issues (in addition to improving the current measures) we hope to address are the following:

1. The distribution of replacement rates with special emphasis on those with low rates in the low earnings categories;

2. The differences between and implications of anticipated and unanticipated social security benefit growth and replacement rates for cohorts of different ages;

3. The relationship of the ratio of the length of the retirement period to the working period and replacement rates. Just examining the ratio for a typical year is only part of the story. The ratio could be high, say two, but if R is only a few years and W many, the implications of such ratios are quite different.

4. Alternative saving scenarios and public/private retirement income substitution assumptions and their implications for replacement rates;

5. The annuity value of social security under alternative assumptions concerning private annuities markets;

6. Variations in replacement rates by occupation/industry and their implications;

7. The cracks in the safety net—who falls through due to lack of coverage, marital status, earnings histories, and so on. For example, widows of uncovered workers may not have adequate protection from private insurance/pensions/saving.

Appendix

This appendix briefly describes the Retirement History Survey data, the criteria used to select our subsample, our definition of replacement rate, the adjustments applied in deriving our improved measures of replacement rates, and our methods for aggregating replacement rates.

5.A.1. Data

The Retirement History study was a 10-year longitudinal survey of the retirement process conducted for the Social Security Administration. In 1969, 11,153 persons born between 1905 and 1911 were selected for the survey. There was substantial attrition (by placement in nursing homes or loss of contact as well as by death) for each successive biennial survey, so that 7,352 original respondents or their widows remained to answer the last survey in 1979.

Respondents were surveyed in odd-numbered years concerning current family composition, labor force participation, health, activities, and assets and wealth and concerning the previous (even-numbered) years' income and benefits. Replacement rates are calculated here for the years prior to the survey years.

The Social Security Administration prepared a matched data set of its records of the survey respondents' and spouses' covered earnings through 1974. It is this information which was used to determine the earnings histories which formed the denominator in the calculation of replacement rates.

Social Security Administration records consider only the earnings for each year in each job which totaled less than the year's maximum taxable earnings. In cases where reported covered earnings equaled or exceeded the taxable maximum, the following imputation procedures were used:

The few cases of covered earnings above the taxable maximum were taken as given. In these instances the person paid taxes in two or more jobs. We assumed that earnings in neither job exceeded the taxable maximum.

In cases where covered earnings equaled the taxable maximum, we assumed that the taxable maximum was attained in the middle of the last quarter in which taxes were paid. If, for example, the respondents finished paying social security taxes in the third quarter, we imputed his year's wage income to be 8/5 times the taxable maximum. This method should prove relatively unbiased, if inexact.

5.A.2 Selection of Subsample

Our estimates understate pre-retirement earnings for workers who spent a substantial portion of their career in jobs not covered by social security. To limit this bias, we sought to restrict our subsample to Retirement History Survey respondents who had spent most of their working lives in the social security system. This required four categories of excluded households:

1. We dropped from the sample 284 households that received federal or military pension income.
2. We excluded households which never retired. We define retirement as occurring in the year before the first Retirement History Survey in which the respondent reports being either completely or partly retired and the spouse (if any) reports an employment status of "keeping house," "retired," "unable to work," or "other" as opposed to "working," "with a job but not at work," or "looking for work." A total of 2,225 households failed to satisfy these

criteria before the Retirement History Survey study was completed or the respondent and spouse (if any) both died.

3. Because they paid no social security taxes between 1958 and 1974, 715 households were dropped from the survey.

4. We eliminated households with unusually high replacement rate values—any households with a social security income replacement rate above 250%, a pension income replacement rate above 200% or a total income replacement rate above 400%. These 1,154 excluded households typically had low career average earnings. About half had career average earnings—as estimated from social security tax payments—of less than $1,000 in 1983 dollars, indicating that most had spent a substantial fraction of their working lives in sectors of the economy not covered by social security.

Because the "retirement date" is somewhat ambiguous (we do not know exactly *when* during the period the person retired), the interpretation of actual annual earnings and social security benefits is difficult. To minimize this problem, we "skip" one survey wave to make certain we are not confounding retirement with part of a year's work. Thus, for each year reported in the tables, the percentage of the sample already retired might appear low; however, the data refer to those who had retired by the next 2 (2-year) earlier wave; for example, for 1971, the retirement occurred by 1968 and does not include those who retired in 1969 and 1970. For example, in table 5.5, about 10% of the total sample is counted retired in 1971. Actually, an additional 268 households in our sample retired between 1969 and 1971, and thus the total actually retired (as opposed to having "clean data" for the year) by 1971 was 29%.

Since replacement rates can be most sensibly compared within groups of relatively homogeneous composition, we limit our subsamples to (1) married couples who remain alive and together for all six surveys from 1969 to 1979 and (2) widows who lose their husbands between 1969 and 1979 and live until 1979. Replacement rates for widows are calculated starting with the year of retirement or the year of widowhood, whichever is later.

Finally, households with missing values for social security, pension, or total income were excluded from calculations of the replacement rates using that type of income in the numerator.

5.A.3   Replacement Rate Definitions

The replacement rate numerators used in this paper were derived from data on post-retirement income reported in the Retirement History Surveys. For each Retirement History Survey wave starting with retirement, we calculated: (1) social security income, (2) social security plus pension income, and (3) total income from all sources. Married couples' figures include the incomes of both husband and wife. Total income was constructed by summing the households' income from wages, interest and dividends, rent, annuities, pensions, relatives, disability benefits, state welfare benefits, workers' compensation, AFDC, unemployment insurance, SSI, and social security (old age, disability, survivor's, and black lung benefits).

In a typical Retirement History Survey wave, between 5% and 10% of our subsample households report missing values for social security income or social security plus pension income. Because total income is "missing" if any of its many components is badly reported, about one-third of the subsample households do not have usable values for total post-retirement income. However, social security and pension income replacement rates do not differ significantly between households with valid and invalid values for total income. Thus, within a given set of replacement rates for social security income, social security plus pension income, and total income, the three replacement rates may be compared even though they are averages based on somewhat different samples.

Like all other dollar figures used in this paper, the Retirement History Survey post-retirement income data in these numerators were converted to constant 1983 dollars using the Personal Consumption Expenditure deflator.

A description of how we netted income taxes out of the numerator in our replacement rate calculations is presented below.

The replacement rate denominator attempts to measure a household's pre-retirement standard of living. We focus on two basic denominators, calculated from wage earnings estimated from social security tax payments. For each year from 1951 to 1974, the respondent's wage earnings (plus those of spouse, if any) were inflated to 1983 dollars. Then two averages were computed. "Career Average Annual Indexed Earnings" is average earnings over all years from 1951 to retirement or 1974, whichever is earlier. "High-Three Average Annual Indexed Earnings," on the other hand, is the average of the 3 highest years' earnings in the 10 years before the most recent year of positive social security tax payments. This 10-year period is 1965–74 at the latest, as 1974 is the last year for which we have social security tax data.

In all but our unadjusted replacement rates, taxes are netted out of the numerator and the denominator. Census Bureau data were used to estimate average effective tax rates for our six income classes. We derived the following average rates for federal income, state income, and social security taxes for the pre-retirement period 1951–74:

Income	Rate (%)
< $7,500	3.89
$7,500–$12,500	6.22
$12,500–$20,000	10.49
$20,000–$30,000	14.74
$30,000–$50,000	17.44
> $50,000	25.37

Our estimated post-retirement average tax rates for federal and state income taxes for 1968, 1970, 1972, 1974, 1976, and 1978 are

Income	Rate (%)
< $7,500	0.47
$7,500–$12,500	2.81
$12,500–$20,000	7.09
$20,000–$30,000	11.47
$30,000–$50,000	15.48
> $50,000	24.43

Households were assigned to a pre-retirement tax bracket based on their career average annual indexed earnings augmented by 14% to allow for unearned income. A household's post-retirement tax bracket depended on its total Retirement History Survey income and could vary from survey to survey. Retirees were allowed an extra personal exemption, further reducing their effective tax rates.

Replacement rates which include the "children's adjustment" were based on denominators that were reduced by 20 percent of the pre-tax value of the denominator. The size of this adjustment is derived from Lazear and Michael (1983).

The fully adjusted replacement rate figures reported in this paper include social security income augmented by a certainty bonus, as described in the main body of the paper.

5.A.4   Aggregation of Replacement Rates

The replacement rates reported in each cell of our tables are means of the replacement rates of the households in the relevant cell. For example, in table 5.1 we see that, on average, for married couples who satisfy all our selection criteria, the (indexed) social security income reported in the 1979 Retirement History Survey wave replaced 37.4% of high-three average annual indexed earnings.

In all tables, except tables 5.14 and 5.15, cell averages exclude households that just became retired or widowed. A household whose status has just changed tends to have higher replacement rates than a similar household that became retired or widowed in an earlier survey. Often this difference is spurious, resulting, for example, from pre-retirement wage income being reported in the same Retirement History Survey in which retirement first occurs.

Notes

1. As documented in U.S. Bureau of the Census, Current Population Reports, ser. P-23, no. 128.

2. This time period was somewhat unusual for at least two reasons. First, the very substantial growth in real social security benefits from 1969–73 was almost certainly not anticipated. Thus, these "windfalls" might have a different impact on behavior, e.g., private asset accumulation for retirement, than benefit increases which were anticipated enough in advance to allow a very different lifetime consumption/saving plan to be followed. Future beneficiaries may save a smaller proportion of their income and have less capital income in retirement. Second, real wages grew at unusually rapid rates in the 1960s, and thus both the benefits and the "high-three" earnings years may be somewhat high relative to a normal wage growth history.

3. The widow's benefit was increased to 100% of PIA in 1972.

4. Data from the continuous work history survey indicate the peak earnings year was 3–5 years prior to retirement. Thus "high-three" in the last 10 boils down to the peak of the life-cycle earnings pattern.

5. We have data on pension income, not the terms of the pension payments. Some (unknown) fraction of these payments are not annuities and may cease prior to the recipient's date of death.

6. We hope to explore who are, and why, these respondents with low career average earnings but high property income in subsequent work.

7. Of course, other risk-sharing devices exist, such as unemployment insurance, AFDC, etc., so variable earnings in many cases have an income floor.

8. Recall the provisos mentioned in n. 4 about the special nature of our sample and time period.

References

Blinder, A.; Gordon, R.; and Wise, D. 1980. Reconsidering the work disincentive effect of social security. *National Tax Journal* 33:431–42.

Boskin, M., and Hurd, M. 1985. Indexing social security: A separate price index for the elderly? *Public Finance Quarterly* 13:436–49.

Bureau of Labor Statistics. 1968. Revised equivalence scale. Bulletin 1570-2. Washington, D.C.

Fox, A. 1982. Earnings replacement rates and total means: Findings from the retirement history study. *Social Security Bulletin* (October).

Fuchs, V. 1984. Though much is taken: Reflections on aging, health, and medical care. Milbank Memorial Fund Quarterly *Health and Society* 62:143–66.

Hammermesh, D. 1982. Consumption during retirement: The missing link in the life-cycle. NBER Working Paper no. 914.

Hay/Huggins Company, Inc. 1983. *Social Security Booklet* 23. Philadelphia (March).

Henle, P. 1972. Recent trends in retirement benefits related to earnings. *Monthly Labor Review.*

Hurd, M., and Boskin, M. 1984. The effect of social security on retirement in the early 1970s. *Quarterly Journal of Economics* 99:767–90.

Hurd, M., and Shoven, J. 1982. The economic status of the elderly. In *Financial aspects of the United States pension system,* ed. Z. Bodie and J. Shoven. Chicago, University of Chicago Press.

———. 1985. The distributional impact of social security. In *Pensions, labor, and individual choice,* ed. D. Wise. Chicago: University of Chicago Press.

Kotlikoff, L.; Spivak, A.; and Summers, L. 1982. The adequacy of savings. *American Economic Review* 72:1056–69.

Lazear, E., and Michael, R. 1983. Allocation of income within the household. University of Chicago. Mimeographed.

Moon, Marilyn. 1977. *The measurement of economic welfare.* New York: Academic Press.

Pechman, J. 1983. *Federal tax policy.* 4th ed. Washington: Brookings Institution.

Schultz, J., et al. 1974. Providing adequate retirement income. Waltham, Mass.: Brandeis University Press.

United States Bureau of the Census. 1983. *Current population reports.* Ser. P-23, no. 128. Washington, D.C.

United States Department of Health and Human Services, Social Security Administration. 1980. *Social security bulletin, annual statistical supplement.* Washington, D.C.

Weisbrod, B., and Hansen, W. L. 1968. An income–net worth approach to measuring economic welfare. *American Economic Review* 58:1315–29.

Comment   Alan L. Gustman

It is a pleasure to be asked to comment on a paper concerning social security by Professors Boskin and Shoven. For some time now, they have been examining a number of the problems associated with the social security system as it is currently constituted, helping us to understand the roots of these problems, and searching in the most creative and constructive way for appropriate reforms.

Alan L. Gustman is professor of economics, Dartmouth College, and research associate, National Bureau of Economic Research.

In this paper the authors have considered the scope of the redistribution over the life cycle which is fostered by the social security system in concert with other sources of income in retirement. The authors provide us with a road map of how to get from here to there. "Here" is the conventionally measured replacement rate, a ratio of social security benefits to peak earnings at the end of the life cycle. "There" is a fraction, with a numerator equal to total retirement income after taxes augmented by the utility value of the reduced risk from having the certain income from social security rather than an uncertain earnings stream, and with a denominator equal to average lifetime earnings, after taxes, with the earnings adjusted downward for the costs of child rearing. These adjustments take us from a social security replacement rate for peak earnings of married couples which ranges from a fifth to a little over a third, to an augmented full replacement rate ranging from 140% to 170% depending on year of retirement and wave of the survey. Along the way detailed statistics are presented for average replacement rates for individuals grouped not only by year of retirement and by year of the survey wave, but also by the level of the family's covered lifetime earnings and by source of retirement income. Information is also presented for a number of the many cells which are created when individuals are grouped by more than one of these criteria at once.

The novel aspect of this paper is the set of adjustments in replacement rates which are calculated by the authors. The value of the contribution made by the paper will be determined both by the usefulness of their general approach and by the appropriateness of the specific calculations the authors make. Although I have some questions about the general approach, I think it is important and useful. I do, however, have more serious doubts about the appropriateness of some of the particular calculations which the authors present.

Consider first an adjustment which is designed to make pre- and post-retirement incomes more comparable in terms of the utility value these incomes generate. Despite the caveat in their note 4, social security is held by Professors Boskin and Shoven to be a certain source of income, while earnings are a variable source of income. Hence social security is deemed to be more valuable. More specifically, the authors compute the trend in earnings and the variance around the trend, and then use these figures in an expected utility framework to calculate a certainty bonus of 10%, which they add to the value of social security, increasing the value of the replacement rate accordingly. I have no quarrel with the idea that the inflation protection provided by social security and the low risk of default enhance the value of social security benefits. However, there is also a great deal of uncertainty associated with social security which the authors ignore in this calculation. This is so for the group of recipients examined in this study whose pre-retirement period is the start-up period for social security, and it is true for later cohorts whose benefits may be adjusted to permit adequate financing of a mature system. A start-up period must involve great uncertainty, defined, as by the authors, either as realized deviations around a trend, or defined in an ex ante sense. Even those who fully understand the financing arrangements for the social security system have no way of telling when large increases in the benefit formula would stop, when it is that demographic and financial realities would finally take hold and a majority coalition would develop which favors limiting further growth in real benefits. Indeed, a major conclusion of the authors pertaining to the sample of retirees used in their study is that these cohorts of elderly retirees did not fully anticipate their social security wealth windfalls and hence, in an ex post sense, oversaved. Moreover, even for those who have already retired, their benefits have a substantial risk component. This risk is reflected in political reactions to the financial problems of the system, reactions which take the form not only of continuous study of the system, but also of legislated changes in benefit formulas. For example, potential reforms, including those proposed elsewhere by Boskin, may have large effects on the benefits of those at or near retirement age. (See Aaron 1983). Adjustments for uncertainty, although difficult to determine in practice, are appropriate. However, it is particularly inappropriate to adjust earnings but not social security, both for cohorts experiencing the start up of the social security system and for those whose retirement will coincide with the maturation of the system.

There are other adjustments employed by the authors which, although they have some merit, nevertheless raise troublesome questions. For example, I find the adjustment which reduces the value of pre-retirement earnings to reflect all costs of raising children to be more questionable than the authors do. As the authors note, the adjustment treats children as a durable good, with no special effect on one's utility from having the children home rather than having already grown up. Accordingly, the assumption they make is that, on average, costs are entirely concentrated during the period of child raising but benefits are spread over the lifetime. By focusing the cost on the period of child raising, but not allocating a disproportionate (although certainly not the entire) share of the utility gained from children to this period, the authors' adjustment for costs of child rearing leads to an overstatement of the replacement rate in retirement.

The largest single adjustment in replacement rates follows from the substitution in the denominator of the replacement rate fraction of a measure of career average earnings for high 3-year earnings—which according to the authors usually occur a few years before retirement. Yet nothing in the conceptual discussion presented by the authors provides any guidance as to which earnings measure—average earnings or full-time earnings just before retirement—is more appropriate. The theoretical model they present has a completely flat earnings profile; there is no bequest motive; there are no adjustment costs to altering the consumption stream; and capital markets are perfect.

To understand a set of questions I have about the effects of substituting a measure of career average real earnings for high 3-year averaged indexed earnings in the denominator of the replacement rate, it is useful to review some specifics about the authors' calculations. According to their note 6, the high 3-year earnings occur 3–5 years before retirement, and at the latest, are computed for the 10-year period from 1964 to 1974. Career average earnings are measured from 1951 to the earlier of the retirement year (i.e., the year that an individual without a working spouse first reports he is either partially or fully retired), or 1974. Thus, for example, it might be assumed that for a person who retired in 1975, high 3-year earnings would be centered around 1971, while career average earnings would be centered around 1963. In this example, the dates on which these alternative earnings measures are centered are 8 years apart. Alternatively, for a person who retired in 1979, the difference between the center of the peak earning period and the period over which average lifetime earnings are computed might be around 10 years apart, while for a person who retires in 1971, the difference might be around 6 years.

The authors find that the replacement rates decline by about 50% when career average earnings are substituted for high 3-year earnings. The reason for this decline is that the high 3-year earnings exceed career average earnings by that proportion. Although the yearly growth rate in real earnings that would generate a 50% difference of this sort depends on the exact shape of the age-earnings profile (e.g., very low earnings right before retirement would pull down the lifetime average), the underlying growth rates are very large. For example, if 8 years separate the centers of peak earnings and career average earnings, a very rough estimate of the growth rate in real earnings which would generate the observed difference between peak and average lifetime earnings is 5% per year. The period over which these relevant earnings computations are made for the cohorts in this study is, as the authors concede, a very unusual one. It is the period of the sixties, which was characterized by a continuing expansion from trough to peak of economic activity. Real median income for year-round full-time male workers grew 23% between 1962 and 1970 (*President's Economic Report* 1984, table B27).

The conclusion I draw is that, other things the same, using the authors' sample to calculate the effects on replacement rates of substituting a measure of career average earnings for peak earnings may lead to an overstatement of the increase in replacement rates which would be observed were data for a more normal period of economic activity used instead.

As the paper is presently written, the reader will have to exercise great care in interpreting the detailed tables. There are two problems here, which happen to have opposite implications for replacement rates computed with aggregated data. It can be seen by dividing replacement rates in table 5.5 by the replacement rates reported in corresponding cells in table 5.3 that for four of the six of the detailed earnings groups, ratios of peak to average earnings are higher for late retirees, sometimes substantially so, than are similar ratios for early retirees. For the other two categories of earners, the ratios for late retirees are lower, but only slightly so. One can also see from the counts presented in table 5.5 that the mix of retirees by lifetime earnings class changes over time. For example, using counts for the total retirement income category, it can be seen that those from the two lowest lifetime earning categories (individuals, who, in addition to high social security replacement rates probably have high ratios of wages offered for work while partially retired compared to wages paid on the main job while not retired) constitute 47% of the retirees in the sample in 1971, but only 33% of those in the 1979 group. When the characteristics of the retired group change over time, as appears to be the case for the sample in the paper, more attention needs to be paid to separating the effects of the changing composition of the sample from the effects of such changes in public policy as increases in social security replacement rates over time.

Let me conclude with a brief summary. I agree with the overall thrust of the adjustments of replacement rates advocated by Boskin and Shoven. High replacement rates in retirement are a problem we should be alert to, because the social security system is large and costly, because, as the authors point out, high replacement rates may be inefficient in that they force "too much consumption" into the retirement period, and because of other distortions they may cause. I also agree with their emphasis on the value of making the course of social security benefits over time more predictable as one way of avoiding an inefficient concentration of consumption after retirement. However, there are problems with too many of the adjustments made on the road to a 150% replacement rates for this paper to be used, as yet, by policymakers. Some problems result because the decade preceding retirement of their sample, as well as the one immediately following, both have unique features which have important implications for the replacement rate adjustments. Earnings growth was extremely rapid in the 1960s, while the early seventies are characterized by an unusual and extremely rapid increase in social security replacement rates (see Committee on Finance 1982, table 39). Other problems arise because some of the adjustments the authors have made, adjustments which have the effect of raising the replacement rate, appear to be questionable. On the other hand, there are factors which have not been mentioned, such as the gap between the year at which peak earnings occur and the center of the period over which they calculate average earnings, a gap that will increase in future years with an increase in the fraction of the lifetime covered by social security, that might lead the authors' calculations to understate the effects on the replacement rate of the adjustments they make. Given the potential importance of the outstanding questions, I believe that further work along the lines of this paper is required before we can determine with reasonable confidence the appropriate size of any adjustments in replacement rates so that the adjusted rates provide a useful comparison of earnings, consumption or utility differences between pre- and post-retirement periods.

References

Henry Aaron, 1983. "Comment." In *Behavioral Simulation Methods In Tax Policy,* edited by Martin Feldstein, pp. 237–46. Chicago: University of Chicago Press. U.S. Senate Committee On Finance. 1982. *Staff Data and Materials Related to Social Security Financing.*

6   Pension Plan Integration As Insurance Against Social Security Risk

Robert C. Merton, Zvi Bodie, and Alan J. Marcus

6.1 Introduction

According to recent surveys, more than half of private pension plans and a significant fraction of public plans in the United States today are explicitly integrated with social security.[1] The manifest purposes of this integration are (1) to ensure retirement income adequacy for all covered employees and (2) to ensure retirement income equity, defined as equal total replacement rates for all employees regardless of salary level. Integrated plans seek to achieve these goals by taking into account the amount that the retiree will be receiving from social security and then providing a benefit from the plan sufficient to produce a combined plan-plus–social security benefit that constitutes approximately the same percentage of the employee's preretirement compensation independent of his position on the pay scale.

Virtually all of the existing literature on integration and integrated plans has been concerned with the issues of adequacy and equity of integrated plans versus nonintegrated plans. The focus of this study is quite different. One of the primary side effects of plan integration is the alteration or the change in the risk-bearing relationships among

Robert C. Merton is J. C. Penney Professor of Management, Sloan School of Management, Massachusetts Institute of Technology, and research associate, National Bureau of Economic Research. Zvi Bodie is professor of finance, Boston University, and research associate, National Bureau of Economic Research. Alan J. Marcus is associate professor of finance, Boston University School of Management, and faculty research fellow, National Bureau of Economic Research.

This paper was funded by a grant from the U.S. Department of Health and Human Services. It was presented at the NBER Pension Conference at the Del Coronado Hotel in San Diego, California, April 13, 1984. The research reported here is part of the NBER's research project in pensions. Any opinions expressed are those of the authors and not of the National Bureau of Economic Research.

employees, employers, and the government vis-à-vis social security benefits. In effect, an integrated plan causes the employer to insure his covered employees against adverse changes in the social security benefit to which they will be entitled. Specifically, the employer provides a contingent liability against the firm in return for the claim which the employee currently has on the social security system, and thus substitutes in part the risks inherent in holding liabilities of the firm for the risks inherent in holding the claim on the social security system.

There exists in the United States today considerable uncertainty surrounding the future structure of the social security system and the level of benefits which that system will provide. The issue of social security risk and schemes for providing insurance against that risk is therefore of substantive importance from a policy perspective. Prior analyses of integration have addressed the issues of retirement-income adequacy and equity of integrated plans exclusively and thereby left the risk-sharing implications of integration as "unintended consequences" of those schemes. We therefore have chosen to focus on these risk-sharing aspects.

In two previous papers, one of us (Merton 1983a,b) addressed the issues of retirement income risk and adequacy and the role of social security. The specific normative questions analyzed in those papers were whether social security should be a mandatory or voluntary system, how it should be funded, and what form contributions and/or benefits should take. This paper, while related to the previous ones in its general perspective and methodology, focuses on the positive questions about integration surrounding the interaction between employer-provided pensions and social security.

The plan of the paper is as follows: in section 6.2, we briefly explain how integration works. In section 6.3 we present a stylized formal model of an integrated plan which seeks to explore and highlight the insurance and risk-sharing aspects of integration and to determine its costs and benefits. The model uses the tools and the analytical framework of contingent claims analysis in order to quantify the trade-offs involved. In section 6.4 we extend the formal model in several directions in order to add greater realism. Finally, the concluding section summarizes our main results and presents our agenda for future research on the integration issue.

6.2 How Integration Works

As noted, the general purpose of integration is to provide a retiree with a combined benefit that will constitute approximately the same percentage of the employee's preretirement compensation independent of his position on the pay scale. Since the social security benefit formula is highly progressive, or tilted toward the lower end of the pay scale, the effect of integration is to provide a benefit from the employer which is tilted in the opposite direction. There are two main approaches that can be and are used to produce this result. One is the "offset" approach and the other the "excess" approach.

In offset plans, a portion of an individual's social security benefit is subtracted from the benefit to which he is entitled according to some defined benefit formula to determine the amount the employer will have to provide. Thus a typical defined benefit plan might provide for a benefit which is equal to 2% of the worker's final average salary per year of service. For a worker with 25 years of service and a final average salary of $24,000, this plan leads to an annual benefit of $12,000 per year. If the social security benefit to which that worker is entitled comes to $7,000, and if there is a full 100% offset under the plan, the employer would have to pay the worker only ($12,000 − 7,000 or) $5,000 per year. The Internal Revenue Service, however, does not currently permit a full 100% offset. The maximum allowed offset presently is 83⅓% of an employee's primary insurance amount (PIA). Whatever the offset percentage is, once the benefit payable by the employer is determined, it is then frozen at that level throughout the retirement period and will not be lowered if there are subsequent increases in social security. The effect of an offset plan is illustrated in table 6.1, which is taken from Schulz and Leavitt (1983).

The table illustrates the effect on total replacement rates of an integrated plan with an 83⅓% offset. The last column of table 6.1A illustrates the "progressivity" of the tilt associated with social security replacement rates, falling from 70% for the lowest-paid worker to 9% for the highest paid. Column 5 in table 6.1B illustrates the impact of the social security offset. Through the offset, the lowest-paid workers in effect lose all of their private pension, while the highest-paid retain almost all. The ultimate impact of integration is to make the total replacement rates shown in column 7 more equal across salary levels than they otherwise would be.

The other form of integration is the so-called excess approach. Unlike offset plans, excess plans do not directly use social security benefits in calculating pension benefits. Instead they use social security contributions or, to be more precise, the taxable wage base for social security. Plan benefits are computed and paid only on earnings in excess of an "integration level," which is directly related to the social security taxable wage base (also called "covered compensation"). Under defined benefit plans, the pension benefit accrual rate is applied only to earnings in excess of the plan integration level. In defined contribution plans, the contribution rate is applied only to earnings in excess of the integration level. In the case of step-rate excess defined contribution

Table 6.1   **Effect of an Offset Plan on Replacement Rates**

A. Social Security Benefits and Replacement Rates for Workers
Retiring at Age 65 in 1982[a]

	Average Annual Earnings[b] ($)	Final Year's Earnings ($)	Social Security Benefit ($)	Social Security Replacement Rate[c] (%)	
Worker 1[d]	6,000	6,599	4,611	70	Worker 1
Worker 2[e]	12,000	13,198	7,149	54	Worker 2
Worker 3[f]	22,540	29,700	8,148	27	Worker 3
Worker 4[g]	67,620	89,100	8,148	9	Worker 4

[a]Assumed to retire at the beginning of 1982.

[b]Average of highest 5 years of earnings, which in these hypothetical examples are the last 5 years.

[c]Benefit divided by final year's earnings.

[d]Annual earnings are assumed to be $5,429 in the fourth year before retirement. Earnings are assumed to change at a rate of 5% per year.

[e]Annual earnings are assumed to be $10,858 in the fourth year before retirement. Earnings are assumed to change at a rate of 5% per year.

[f]Worker earns the taxable wage base in all years.

[g]Worker earns three times the taxable wage base in all years.

plans, contributions on earnings below the integration level, while not zero, are lower than they are on the earnings above the integration level. Excess plans have a similar effect to offset plans on the profile of combined replacement rates.

It should be clear that offset plans are by their nature defined benefit plans, while in the case of defined contribution plans the excess approach is the only one which can be used to perform integration. In the stylized model which we present in the next section of the paper, we assume for simplicity a defined benefit plan with a 100% social security offset. The same mode of analysis can be applied to examine the effects of an excess plan.

6.3   A Formal Model of Pension Integration

To analyze the effects of integration, we first describe the equivalent nonintegrated plan to be used as a basis for comparison. In a nonintegrated pension plan, the firm's payments to retirees are independent of the payments made by the social security system. We will denote social security payments at time t and S_t. B will denote the firm's promised payments in the nonintegrated plan, the level of which, we

B. Pension Benefits, Total Benefits, and Replacement Rates for
Workers in a Pension Plan with an 83⅓% Offset[h]

Gross Benefit Prior to Offset ($) (1)	Social Security Benefit ($) (2)	Offset = (2) × .833 ($) (3)	Final Pension Benefit = max [0, (1) − (3)] ($) (4)	Pension Replacement Rate[i] (%) (5)	Total Benefit (2) + (4) ($) (6)	Total Replacement Rate[i] (%) (7)
3,000	4,611	3,841	0	0	4,611	70
6,000	7,149	5,955	45	—[j]	7,194	55
11,268	8,148	6,787	4,481	15	12,629	43
33,804	8,148	6,787	27,017	30	35,165	40

Source: Schulz and Leavit (1983), p. 11.

[h]Calculations assume workers retire at age 65 in 1982. Calculations also assume that plan provides a benefit equal to 50% of final average earnings, minus 83⅓% of social security benefits. Final average earnings represent the average of the highest 5 years, which in these hypothetical cases are the last 5 years. See table 6.1A for the value of the high-5 average and final year's earnings in each case.

[i]Benefit divided by final year's earnings.

[j]Less than 1%.

will assume, is currently known. Once the individual retires, the stream of total income will be $B + S_{T+\tau}$ where T is the date of retirement and $\tau > 0$.

Our stylized integrated plan involves an offset provision: once social security payments exceed a stipulated minimum level, further increases in those benefits entitle the firm to reduce benefits paid via the pension fund. The offset provisions of integrated plans thus shift a portion of the risk and return of uncertain future social security payments from workers to employers. S_t evolves stochastically over time since social security benefits are linked to uncertain future wage or price levels and are subject to unforeseen legislative changes.

In practice, the offset is less than one-for-one, so that total benefits (i.e., pension plus social security) increase with the level of social security payments. For analytic simplicity, we first compare the polar cases of fully integrated plans that incorporate one-for-one offset provisions with fully nonintegrated plans. In section 6.4, we show how the analysis is modified to accommodate partially integrated plans.

Fully integrated plans guarantee workers a minimum *combined* retirement income from social security and pension payments of F dollars per period. At the date of retirement, T, if social security payments fall short of F, the employer is obliged to pay retirees $F - S_T$ dollars in each subsequent year of retirement. Therefore, when $S_T < F$, every dollar increase in the initial retirement year's social security payment, S_T, reduces the employer's required payment by an equal amount. In this regime, employers capture the entire benefit of increases in social security. Once $S_T = F$, however, the employer's obligation is reduced to zero, so that workers capture the benefits of further increases in social security. Total retirement income at T in the integrated plan equals the maximum of the guaranteed floor or current social security benefits, that is, max (F, S_T).

An important feature of integrated plans as currently implemented is that the employer's stream of pension obligations is fixed at time T. Future increases or decreases in social security benefits which occur after commencement of the retirement period do *not* induce offsetting changes in employer-provided pension payments. Thus, as with a non-integrated plan, the employee receives a fixed life annuity from his employer at retirement. Unlike the nonintegrated plan, the level of the fixed annuity payments in the integrated plan, max $(O, F - S_T)$, depends upon the level of the social security payment in the year of retirement, S_T. The total retirement income from social security and private pension received by the employee in year τ of his retirement is given by $S_{T+\tau}$ + max $(O, F - S_T)$.

This institutionally established feature of integrated plans leads to a simplification of the analysis by permitting the transformation of what would appear to be a dynamic multiperiod problem into a one-period problem. To see this and prepare for the analysis to follow, we develop the valuation equations for future social security payments and life annuities. If we denote by g the expected (real) rate of growth of social security payments, then it follows that

$$(1) \qquad E_t(S_T) = S_t e^{g(T-t)},$$

where E_t is the conditional expectation operator, conditional on information available at time t. If there were a traded financial claim which paid its owner $\$S_T$ at time T, then its market price at time t would be $E_t(S_T)\exp[-\alpha(T - t)]$, where α is the market equilibrium expected rate of return for a security in this risk class. It follows from (1) that the present value of the social security payment at time T can be written as

$$(2) \qquad V_0 = S_0 e^{-\delta T},$$

where $\delta \equiv \alpha - g$.

At retirement, the present value of the worker's lifetime social security benefits can be written as

$$(3) \qquad PV(S_T) = \int_0^\infty E_T(S_{T+t}) e^{-\alpha t} \Pr(t) dt,$$

where $Pr(t)$ is the probability that the retiree is alive t years after retiring. If the mortality table remains stable over time, then from (1) we can rewrite (3) as

$$(3') \qquad\qquad PV(S_T) = S_T h(\delta),$$

where $h(\delta)$ does not depend on S_T or time. Similarly, at retirement, the present value of a riskless life annuity of \$$A$ per year can be written as

$$(4) \qquad\qquad PV(A) = Ah(r),$$

where $h(\ )$ is the identical function as in $(3')$ and r is the riskless real rate of interest.

At the employee's retirement, S_T will be known, and hence, the value of employer-provided benefits at time T can be written as

$$(5) \qquad\qquad PV = \max(0, F - S_T) h(r).$$

Thus, because there are no further adjustments to these payments as the result of subsequent post-retirement changes in social security benefits, the analysis of this type of integrated plan need only focus on a single date, T. The multiple-period framework required to analyze alternative versions of integration is presented in section 6.4.

Armed with these basic valuation relations, we turn now to the changes in risk bearing caused by a change from a nonintegrated to an integrated plan. From the perspective of the employer, the firm changes from a commitment to pay \$$B$ a year during the retirement period to a commitment to pay \$$\max(0, F - S_T)$. When the worker retires, the firm knows precisely what the level of annuity payments will be in either plan. At that time, from (4), the value of the liability is $Bh(r)$ for the nonintegrated plan and $\max(0, F - S_T) h(r)$ for the integrated plan. However, when viewed from dates earlier than T, the level of annuity payments for the integrated plan is uncertain because S_T is unknown. A convenient interpretation of the provisions of the integrated plan can be used to determine the value of the firm's pension liability prior to the worker's retirement. The structure of the contingent liability payment, $\max(0, F - S_T)$, is formally equivalent to a European put option of maturity date T with an exercise price F on a stock with a price at time T given by S_T. This equivalence permits the use of established results from the put option pricing literature to value the obligations of the employer under the provisions of the integrated plan.[2]

The employer's major policy variable under an integrated plan is the level of guaranteed combined retirement income, F. To focus on the risk-sharing aspects of integration, we impose the constraint that the present value or cost of (contingent) employer payments over the life of any retiree be equal for integrated and comparable nonintegrated plans. That is, the present value or cost of the two plans is the same.

In the nonintegrated plan, the worker receives from the firm a stream of payments in retirement of B per year. From (4), the present value of this liability to the firm at time T is $Bh(r)$. If today's calendar date is normalized to zero and we neglect pre-retirement mortality, then the current value of this liability is $Bh(r)e^{-rT}$.

In an integrated plan, the worker receives from the firm a stream of payments of $\max(0, F - S_T)$ per year and the corresponding present value of this liability to the firm at time T is $\max(0, F - S_T)h(r)$. Neglecting pre-retirement mortality, the current value of this liability is $P(F, S_0, T)h(r)$ where P denotes the current (time 0) value of a European put option that gives its "owner" (the employee) the right to sell the social security payment at T for F, when the social security benefit level is currently at S_0.

Under the hypothesized condition that the current value of the pension cost to the employer is the same for the integrated and nonintegrated plans, it follows that F must be chosen so that

$$(6) \qquad P(F, S_0, T) = Be^{-rT}.$$

Given a valuation formula for the put, (6) can be used to solve for the level of the floor on combined retirement income, F, that equates the present value of the firm's obligations in the integrated and nonintegrated plans.

From the viewpoint of the employee, the effect on risk bearing of changing from a nonintegrated to an integrated pension plan is to provide the employee with an implicit insurance scheme. To see this, we compare the value of the worker's combined social security and private pension benefits at retirement for the nonintegrated plan to the corresponding value at retirement for the integrated plan. From (3') and (4), the value at time T under the nonintegrated plan can be written as

$$(7) \qquad S_T h(\delta) + Bh(r) = [h(\delta) - h(r)]S_T + h(r)\{S_T + B\}.$$

Similarly, the value at time T under the integrated plan can be written as

$$(8) \quad S_T h(\delta) + \max(0, F - S_T)h(r) = [h(\delta) - h(r)]S_T$$
$$+ h(r)\{S_T + \max(0, F - S_T)\}$$
$$= [h(\delta) - h(r)]S_T$$
$$+ h(r)\{\max(F, S_T)\}.$$

By inspection of (7) and (8), the difference in benefits to the employee between the two plans is the difference in the terms in curly brackets. For the integrated plan, the worker receives the social security payment of S_T, plus contingent lifetime annuity payments from the firm equal to the shortfall, if any, between S_T and the guaranteed combined income, F. The worker, therefore, receives insurance (the put option) from the employer against low levels of the social security benefit. If S_T is below the "insured value," F, the employer-provided insurance policy pays off and makes up the difference.[3]

As is evident from (7), the nonintegrated plan also provides a "floor" on combined retirement income, namely, B. However, if the floor F in the integrated plan is chosen so as to satisfy (6), then it is straightforward to show $F > B$ whenever $B > 0$ and $S_0 > 0$. Moreover, in practical cases, $F >> B$. That is, the combined minimum guaranteed level of benefits in the integrated plan will be much higher than in the nonintegrated plan. By more formal measures of risk such as the variance of the employee's retirement benefit, it is straightforward to show that $\text{var}(S_T + B) > \text{var}[\max(F, S_T)]$. Thus, it is appropriate to characterize the change from a nonintegrated to an integrated plan as providing the employee with insurance and reducing the uncertainty about his combined retirement income.

The insurance provided by integration does not come to the employee for "free." The price paid is that the employee gives up his nonintegrated plan claim of B in return for the integrated plan's insurance on the value of S_T. By inspection of (7) and (8), the employee will, ex post, be worse off in an integrated plan if $S_T > F - B$. Thus, it cannot be claimed, as a normative matter, that all risk-averse employees would prefer an integrated plan over a comparable-in-value nonintegrated plan. From (6) and the well-known put option price property that $0 \leq \partial P / \partial F \leq e^{-rT}$, it does follow, however, that $d(F - B) / dB > 0$. Hence, for a fixed probability distribution for S_T, the larger is B, the smaller is the probability that the worker will experience (ex post) regret for having chosen an integrated plan over a nonintegrated one.

To obtain solutions for F in (6) that are amenable to comparative-static analysis, we continue the examination of the properties of integrated plans under the simplifying assumption that S_t follows a geometric Brownian motion.[4] That is, the dynamics of S_t are assumed to be described by the stochastic differential equation

$$(9) \qquad dS = gSdt + \sigma S\, dz,$$

where, as previously defined, g is the expected rate of growth of social security payments; σ^2 is the instantaneous constant variance rate for the percentage change in S; and dz denotes a Wiener process.

From (2) and (9), arguments along the lines presented in Constantinides (1978) can be used to show that the put option price can be expressed as

(10) $P(F, S_0, T) = Fe^{-rT}[1 - N(d_2)] - S_0 e^{-\delta T}[1 - N(d_1)]$

where

$$d_1 = \frac{\ln(S_0/F) + (r - \delta + 1/2\ \sigma^2)T}{\sigma\ \sqrt{T}}$$

$d_2 = d_1 - \sigma\ \sqrt{T}$

$N(.)$ is the cumulative standard-normal distribution function.

Equation (10) is formally equivalent to the well-known Black-Scholes (1973) put option formula on a dividend-paying stock. The "dividend adjustment," δ, reflects the difference in the expected rate of "capital gains" on S, g, and the total required rate of return, α, given its risk characteristics. Some relevant comparative-static properties of $P(F, S_0, T)$ are presented in table 6.2. Equation (10) can be used to determine the floor levels, F, that equate $P(F, S_0, T)$ and Be^{-rT}.

There is considerable controversy over the issue of whether benefits accruing under a defined benefit plan ought to be viewed as fixed in real or nominal terms.[5] While this controversy has potentially significant implications for the *magnitude* of the effects we are examining, it is essentially unrelated to our main thrust. However, with this controversy in mind, we do present tables of analysis which reflect the two polar extremes: (1) the case in which employer-provided benefits are fixed in real terms (i.e., indexed to the price level), and (2) the case in which they are fixed in nominal terms, as argued by Bulow (1982). By analyzing the extremes we are in essence covering all the cases in between as well.

Table 6.3 presents floor levels corresponding to several possible combinations of social security and nonintegrated benefit levels. The table presents results for case 1, in which both employer-provided and social security benefits are interpreted as real obligations. Column 1 of table 6.3 contains hypothetical employer-provided benefits of various amounts. Column 2 of table 6.3 contains the expected real social security benefit, which we fix at \$10,000. Therefore, the different rows of table 6.3 may be interpreted as corresponding to different scenarios

Table 6.2   **Change in Floor Income of Integrated Plan in Response to Increase in Various Parameters**

Variable Increasing	Response of Floor Income
s_0	Increase
σ	Decrease
T	Indeterminate

Table 6.3   **Integrated Floor-Benefit Levels ($) (Real Contracting)**

Employer-provided Pension Nonintegrated Benefit (1)	Social Security Benefit (2)	Total Nonintegrated Benefit [(1) + (2)] (3)	Floor Benefit for Corresponding Integrated Plan (4)	(5)	(6)
			$\sigma = .01$	$\sigma = .025$	$\sigma = .05$
A. Time to retirement 15 years					
0	10,000	10,000	0	0	0
100	10,000	10,100	9,880	9,205	7,955
500	10,000	10,500	10,480	10,205	9,435
1,000	10,000	11,000	11,000*	10,900	10,400
5,000	10,000	15,000	15,000*	15,000*	14,990
10,000	10,000	20,000	20,000*	20,000*	20,000*
B. Time to retirement 25 years					
0	10,000	10,000	0	0	0
100	10,000	10,100	9,765	8,840	7,260
500	10,000	10,500	10,450	10,005	8,930
1,000	10,000	11,000	11,000*	10,785	10,015
5,000	10,000	15,000	15,000*	15,000*	14,935
10,000	10,000	20,000	20,000*	20,000*	20,000*
C. Time to retirement 35 years					
0	10,000	10,000	0	0	0
100	10,000	10,100	9,660	8,545	6,725
500	10,000	10,500	10,415	9,825	8,515
1,000	10,000	11,000	10,990	10,670	9,675
5,000	10,000	15,000	15,000*	15,000*	14,855
10,000	10,000	20,000	20,000*	20,000*	19,990

*In these cases the value to the employee of receiving social security payments in excess of the floor, while always positive, has a present value of less than $5.

in which private (nonintegrated) pension plan benefits as a fraction of social security benefits differ widely. These comparisons are of interest because (as demonstrated in table 6.1), employer-provided pension payments for low-income individuals are small relative to social security, while for high-income individuals, private pension benefits exceed social security, at least under the assumption that they are real.

The third column of table 6.3 is simply the sum of private plus expected social security benefits in the nonintegrated plan. This value is a useful benchmark against which to compare the guaranteed floor benefit of the integrated plan. Under certainty ($\sigma = 0$), and with no expected real growth in social security benefits, $\alpha = r = \delta$, and the guaranteed floor would be exactly $B + S_0$, which is in fact column 3. Of course, S_T is uncertain; hence, with $\delta = r$, column 3 is interpreted as the *expected* level of total combined benefits in the nonintegrated plan.[6] Column 3 and columns 4–6 compare the guaranteed *minimum* incomes in the integrated plan with this combined *expected* benefit from the nonintegrated plan.

Columns 4–6 are the minimum real income levels that the employer would provide in an integrated plan with the same present value as the nonintegrated plan, computed using standard deviations for the real percentage change in S_t of 1%, 2.5%, and 5% per year. Panel A of the table uses a time to retirement of 15 years, while panels B and C use 25 and 35 years, respectively.

To facilitate the comparison of integrated and nonintegrated benefits, note that the annuity levels in column 3 are equal to the guaranteed annuity the employer would provide if the employee would assign all his rights to future social security benefits to the employer. That is, an extreme form of risk shifting would be that the worker transfers all of his social security benefits to the employer in return for a guaranteed annuity. This sale causes the employer to bear all social security risk and to receive all of its benefits.

What level annuity would the employer offer in return for the social security benefit? From (2) and (3′), the current value of the employee's stream of social security benefits is given by $S_0 h(\delta)e^{-\delta T}$. From (4), the current value of a life annuity of \$A beginning at time T is $Ah(r)e^{-rT}$. Under the assumed condition of table 6.3 that $\delta = r$, it follows, therefore, that the level of annuity payments, A, which the firm would exchange in return for the employee's social security benefits is given by $A = S_0$. Thus, under the posited conditions, the number reported in column 3, $B + S_0$, is the guaranteed annuity level associated with the market value of the combined benefits in the nonintegrated plan.

In actual integrated plans, of course, the worker does not transfer all rights to social security benefits: if S_T exceeds F, the worker collects the additional amount $S_T - F$. In effect, the worker retains rights to the upper tail of the social security distribution. Whereas the worker would receive a guaranteed annuity level of payments $F' \equiv B + S_0$ in the hypothetical extreme case in which social security benefits are actually sold to the employer, in the integrated plan, the worker receives $F + \max(0, S_T - F)$ as his annuity at retirement. Thus, unlike the hypothetical sale in which the employer receives $S_T + B$ in exchange for the guaranteed floor, F, the employer actually receives $\min(F, S_T + B)$, which is always less than or equal to $S_T + B$. For the nonintegrated and corresponding integrated plans in table 6.3 to have equal present value of costs it must therefore be the case that the floor promised under the integrated plan not exceed the guaranteed annuity in the case of an outright sale, that is, $F \leq F' \equiv S_0 + B$. Thus column 3 provides an upper bound on the guaranteed benefit levels in columns 4–6. If there is no chance that S_T will exceed $S_0 + B$ then $F = S_0 + B$, otherwise F will be less than $S_0 + B$.

As table 6.3 demonstrates, individuals who would receive small private pension benefits relative to social security in nonintegrated plans will be offered a guaranteed combined benefit that is significantly less than the current combined benefit. This effect is more pronounced for large uncertainty rates (high σ) and for longer times to retirement. At the limit of zero private pension benefits, the floor integrated replacement benefit is zero. In this extreme case, the employer has no obligations in the nonintegrated scenario and thus the value of the insurance (the put) provided by the employer must also be zero. The floor benefit guarantee with equivalent present value in the integrated plan is zero, and the employer provides no insurance against declines in social security benefit levels. As employer-provided nonintegrated benefits increase, the corresponding floor benefit level rises. For private nonintegrated pension benefit levels of $100, the employer offers a floor level that is significantly below the current (and expected future) level for social security of $10,000. The $100 nonintegrated benefit given up by the employee to the employer can buy only "disaster" insurance which will pay off only if social security falls significantly below its current level.

For higher employer-provided pension levels, the minimum benefit guarantee rises and indeed can exceed the current level of social security of $10,000. For the highest employer-provided nonintegrated benefit considered in table 6.3 ($10,000), the employer offers a corresponding benefit floor in the integrated plan of $20,000.[7] Under the posited dynamic process for social security, there is virtually no chance that S_T will exceed the $20,000 floor. Thus, almost surely the employer will end up paying at T the floor benefit equal to $20,000 and will receive the social security benefit, S_T. In effect, the employer has purchased the employee's social security benefit.

The differences between the combined nonintegrated benefit levels and the floor income thus have a straightforward interpretation. For large floors, say greater than twice S_0, the social security benefit level must double in real terms before the employer fails to capture all the benefits from social security. Thus, the employer will almost certainly end up receiving the employee's social security benefit. In this regime, the employee has simply sold his rights to social security to the employer, who will pay $F - S_T$ in pension benefits at time T. In order to provide the employee with an integrated benefit level equal to the obligation B in the nonintegrated plan, the floor level must approximately satisfy $F - S_0 = B$, or $F = B + S_0$. Therefore, the benefit guarantees in columns 4–6 approach the values in column 3. As B

declines relative to S_0 there is a significant chance that S_T will be less than $S_0 + B$ and therefore as we have seen, the guaranteed minimum benefit, F, must be strictly less than $S_0 + B$.

All of these conclusions assumed that employer-provided benefits are fixed in real terms. Table 6.4 provides the same analysis as in table 6.3, but computed under the assumption suggested by Bulow (1982) that promised employer-provided benefits are fixed in nominal terms. Thus, for the same level of nominal benefits, B, the real level of benefits must be deflated by the rate of inflation. An inflation rate of 6% is assumed in table 6.4.

Columns 1 and 2 give the nominal and associated real employer-provided benefit levels corresponding to column 1 of table 6.3. For the same nominal benefits, the real benefit levels will, of course, fall as one considers longer times to retirement. Column 3 of table 6.4 presents the sum of the $10,000 real social security benefit plus the real employer-

Table 6.4   **Integrated Floor Levels ($) (Nominal Contracting)**

Employer-provided Nominal Benefit (1)	Employer-provided Real Benefit** (2)	Total Real Nonintegrated Benefit (3)	Real Floor Benefit for Corresponding Integrated Plan		
			(4) $\sigma = .01$	(5) $\sigma = .025$	(6) $\sigma = .05$
A. Time to retirement 15 years					
0	0	10,000	0	0	0
100	41	10,041	9,671	8,811	7,371
500	203	10,203	10,092	9,577	8,517
1,000	473	10,407	10,374	10,040	9,200
5,000	2,033	12,033	12,033*	12,026	11,806
10,000	4,066	14,066	14,066*	14,066*	14,032
B. Time to retirement 25 years					
0	0	10,000	0	0	0
100	22	10,022	9,374	8,124	6,239
500	112	10,112	9,799	8,904	7,349
1,000	223	10,223	10,049	9,344	7,989
5,000	1,116	11,116	11,113	10,938	10,218
10,000	2,231	12,231	12,231*	12,202	11,827
C. Time to retirement 35 years					
0	0	10,000	0	0	0
100	12	10,012	9,086	7,491	5,306
500	61	10,061	9,501	8,257	6,327
1,000	122	10,122	9,734	8,674	6,905
5,000	612	10,612	10,533	10,044	8,819
10,000	1,225	11,225	11,225*	10,978	10,089

*Present value of social security payments in excess of the floor is less than $5.
**Nonstochastic inflation rate of 6% used to deflate nominal quantities.

provided benefit, while columns 4–6 present real floor benefits for the nonintegrated plan. (Our analysis ignores price level risk; hence, the only source of uncertainty is social security risk.)

The floor benefit levels in table 6.4 are, as expected, lower than those in table 6.3. This pattern results from the decreased real value of employer-provided benefits when those benefits are nominally fixed. As is perhaps not surprising, the difference in floor levels is most pronounced for high values of σ and for panel C, in which time to retirement equals 35 years. In these cases, the floor benefits range from approximately 50% to 85% of their corresponding values in table 6.3, in which the employer-provided pension benefit is fixed in real terms.

To perhaps provide further intuition for the comparative statics results presented in tables 6.3 and 6.4, we note that the key expression in curly brackets in (8), max (F, S_T), can be rewritten as $F + \max(0, S_T - F)$. Max $(0, S_T - F)$ is the functional form of the payoff to a call option of maturity date T with an exercise price of F on a security whose price at time T is given by S_T. In this formulation, the employee's claim in the integrated plan is equivalent to a risk-free payment of F plus an implicit call option to buy back from the employer the social security benefit at time T for exercise price F. For large floor levels relative to the expected level of social security benefits, the employee's call will be significantly out of the money, and F must be near F'; since the call is unlikely to be exercised, the floor benefit must approach the combined nonintegrated benefit.

6.4   Extensions of the Model

In the previous section we used contingent claims analysis to value guaranteed replacement rates in a simple one-period model induced by the current institutional form of integrated plans. The contingent claims approach and the insights it yields are quite flexible, however, and are easily extended to handle both more realistic models of the current system and alternative types of integrated plans. In this section we illustrate that flexibility with a few important extensions to the basic model.

As was described in the introduction, the current practice for integrated plans is to provide only a partial offset for social security payments with a maximum of an 83⅓% offset. It is, however, straightforward to modify the 100% offset model of the previous section to accommodate this partial offset feature. If γ denotes the fraction of offset provided by a specific plan, then the level of life annuity payments provided by the employer is given by max $(0, F - \gamma S_T)$. Thus, as with the full offset plan, the structure of the firm's liability in a partial offset plan is equivalent to a put option. Therefore, the same formal analysis which led to the determination of the minimum guaranteed combined income, F, for the full offset plan can be applied to determine the floor for the partial offset one. If $F(\gamma)$ denotes the floor for a plan with a γ offset, then from (6), $F(\gamma)$, will satisfy

(11) $$P[F(\gamma),\gamma S_0,T] = Be^{-rT}.$$

Because the value of a put option is an increasing function of its exercise price and a decreasing function of the price of its underlying security, it follows from (11) that $dF(\gamma)/d\gamma > 0$. Therefore, a partial offset plan ($\gamma < 1$) will have a lower guaranteed retirement income level, $F(\gamma)$, than a full offset plan ($\gamma = 1$). A general property of put option prices is that they are first-degree homogeneous in these two variables. That is, $P[F(\gamma), \gamma S_0,T] = \gamma P[F(\gamma)/\gamma,S_0,T]$. It follows from (11) that the value of the put in all comparable integrated plans must equal Be^{-rT}; therefore $\gamma P[\dfrac{F(\gamma)}{\gamma},S_0,T] = Be^{-rT} = P[F(1), S_0, T]$. Because the value of a put is an increasing function of its exercise price, for $\gamma < 1$ this equality can be maintained only if $\dfrac{F(\gamma)}{\gamma} \geq F(1)$, or $F(\gamma) \geq \gamma F(1)$. Hence, although the partial offset plan has a lower income floor than a full offset plan, it is less than proportionately lower.

In summary, we can bound the guaranteed retirement income in a partial offset plan in terms of the floor level in a corresponding full offset plan by

(12) $$\gamma F(1) \leq F(\gamma) \leq F(1) , \gamma \leq 1.$$

In the previous section, we also assumed that the employer-provided benefit is riskless and that the only source of uncertainty is the level of social security payments received in retirement. A more realistic model would take into account that the employer-provided benefit (in either the nonintegrated or integrated plan) is also uncertain. However, because the payoff structure to the employee in an integrated plan is still given by $\max(F,S_T)$, the same basic methodology of section 6.3 can be used to extend the model to this more general case. Fischer (1978) has derived a valuation formula for the price of a contingent claim whose terminal value is $\max(F,S_T)$ when both F and S_T are stochastic. Hence, by replacing $P(F,S_0,T)$ in equation (6) by this more general valuation formula and reinterpreting Be^{-rT} in (6) as the present value of the uncertain benefit provided in the corresponding nonintegrated plan, one could proceed to analyze the impact on risk bearing of integration when both private and social security benefits are uncertain.

As a third illustration of the flexibility of the approach presented here, consider the case of an integrated plan in which the employer-provided benefit is not fixed after retirement but is adjusted each period to reflect post-retirement changes in social security benefits. Despite the fact that integrated plans in the United States do not currently work this way, this case is of interest for at least two reasons.

First, many employers do provide post-retirement benefit increases even though they are not contractually bound to do so.[8] These increases are typically made on an ad hoc basis, and employers explain their rationale as stemming from a concern for maintaining a floor beneath the retirement income of their former employees. Indeed, some researchers view these ad hoc increases as part of an implicit contract between employer and employees. Given their expressed purpose, there can be little doubt that the magnitude and frequency of these ad hoc increases depend on the magnitude and frequency of changes in social security benefits. The second reason for examining this case is that while formal integration may not work this way right now, it is possible that it might at some point in the future or in some other national setting. This is especially relevant since the normative implications of integrated plans have not yet received a full review.

In this version of an integrated plan, the firm's obligation at each date t during the retirement period equals $\max(0, F - S_t)$ so that the present value of contingent payments as of time 0 equals

$$(13) \qquad \int_T^\infty \Pr(t)\, P(F, S_0, t)\, dt.$$

Given mortality tables for $\Pr(t)$, and a formula for P, we can compute the level of F by equating the value in (13) to $Bh(r)e^{-rT}$ in a way that is similar to (6) in the previous section. By way of example, however, we compute the firm's reservation level for F, given B, for a particularly simple pattern for $\Pr(t)$. Suppose, for example, as described in Merton (1983b), that the probability of dying at t is determined by a Poisson-distributed random variable with characteristic parameter λ. Under this assumption, $\Pr(t) = \lambda e^{-\lambda t}$; the expected time until death is $1/\lambda$ and $h(r) = 1/(r + \lambda)$. Expression (13) can be written as

$$(14) \qquad \int_T^\infty \{Fe^{-(r+\lambda)t}[1 - N(d_2)] - S_0 e^{-(\delta+\lambda)t}[1 - N(d_1)]\} dt,$$

where d_1 and d_2 were defined in (10). The integral can be approximated numerically by setting the upper limit of integration equal to a large positive value. One then can search over F for the benefit floor guarantee that equates (14) to $e^{-rT}B/(r + \lambda)$.

Guaranteed combined benefit rates corresponding to combined income rates in the nonintegrated plan were computed using (14) under the assumption that $\delta = r$. For values of $\lambda = .0667$ and $\delta = .025$, and times to retirement of 15 and 35 years, we found that benefit floors were virtually identical to those in table 6.3.[9]

Another issue surrounding integrated plans that requires further study and clarification is the procedure for aggregating the worker's total private pension benefits when he has worked for more than one employer. For nonintegrated plans, the worker's total private pension annuity benefit, B', is the sum of the annuity benefits earned from all plans, $\Sigma_1^n B_i$, where B_i is the annuity benefit from employer i, $i = 1, \ldots, n$. As noted in the introduction, the typical nonintegrated plan determines the retirement benefit in terms of the number of years of service to the firm and some type of average salary during that service. Hence, as has been widely discussed in the pension literature, for the same wage profile, the total private retirement benefit received by a worker who participates in more than one nonintegrated plan will in general be different than if he had participated in only one plan for his entire work life.

With integrated plans, the issue of aggregating benefits is considerably more complex. In addition to the effect on the level of benefits found in nonintegrated plans, the same aggregation procedure when applied to integrated plans has a substantial impact on the risk characteristics of the worker's total retirement income.

To illustrate this point, consider two workers both of whom earn the same constant wage throughout their work life. Worker 1 has a single employer and worker 2 works an equal number of years for each of n firms. Under these specialized conditions, worker 1 and worker 2 would have the same total retirement income if the plans were nonintegrated. That is, worker 1 would receive B' and worker 2 would receive $B_i = B'/n$ from each firm i, $i = 1, \ldots, n$. If, however, each of the firms' plans is integrated with social security, then the private pension benefits to the two workers will be quite different.

Worker 1 with a single lifetime employer fits the assumed conditions of our model in section 6.3. His private pension annuity is given by max $(0, F - S_T)$ where F is determined from the solution of equation (6) with $B = B'$. This implicit put option insures him against low levels of social security payments by compensating him dollar for dollar for payments below F. Hence, he has a total retirement income floor of F. If the minimum guaranteed income floor for each plan i, F_i, is determined separately according to (6) with $B = B_i = B'/n$, $(i = 1 \ldots, n)$, then the aggregate private pension benefit for worker 2 is given by $\Sigma_1^n \max[0, F_i - S_T] = n \max(0, F' - S_T)$ where $F' = F_i$ $(i = 1, \ldots, n)$ is the common solution to (6) with $B_i = B'/n$.

In effect, worker 2 has been given a put option on his social security benefit by *each* of his employers and therefore has an aggregate of n put options on his single social security benefit. Thus, unlike worker 1's single put option, once worker 2's options are "in the money" (i.e., $S_T < F'$), he receives n dollars in private annuity benefits for each dollar decline in S_T below F'. He will, therefore, receive a larger total retirement income if $S_T < F'$ than if $S_T = F'$ (which corresponds to his minimum retirement income).

Worker 2, of course, pays for this "extra" benefit received for very low levels of social security. By analysis similar to that used to derive (12), $F/n \le F' \le F$ where, in general, $F' << F$ for $n \ge 2$. Hence, worker 2 has no protection against declines in the level of social security payments for $F' \le S_T \le F$ whereas worker 1 is "fully insured" in this regime. Thus, even for a worker with a large total nonintegrated private pension benefit B, the amount of "useful" insurance provided by integrated plans may be rather modest if the worker has had many employers and each $F_i << F$.

In summary, for a single-employer worker under an integrated plan, the schedule of total first-year retirement income as a function of the social security benefit, $\max(F,S_T)$, exhibits the standard insurance pattern of a "protective put" strategy. In contrast, the corresponding schedule of total income for an n-employer worker, $\max[nF' - (n - 1)S_T,S_T]$, is a piecewise linear function of S_T which is decreasing with slope $-(n - 1)$ for $S_T < F'$; reaches a minimum at $S_T = F'$; and is increasing with slope 1 for $S_T > F'$.

It is difficult to believe that this "vee-shaped" schedule of retirement income for multiple-employer workers is an intended consequence of integrated pension plans. Although the normative aspects of integrated plans is not the focus of this paper, our brief analysis here surely suggests that a widespread change from nonintegrated to integrated plans under current aggregation rules could have a significant and largely unintended effect on worker mobility.

6.5   Summary, Conclusions, and Agenda for Future Research

Our most robust finding in the previous section can be stated simply as follows. For extremely low values of B/S, that is, the ratio of employer benefits to social security in the nonintegrated scenario, the value of F in the integrated scenario is very low, indicating that integration would not in that situation provide much insurance. At the other extreme, for high ratios of employer-provided benefits to social security benefits in the nonintegrated scenario, integration results in virtually complete elimination of social security risk through employer insurance.

One's position on whether accruing benefits under a defined benefit plan are real or nominal thus has a significant impact on the degree of risk shedding achieved through integration. If the benefit is real, then all but those with virtually no private benefit in the nonintegrated scenario will by switching to an integrated plan in effect sell all their rights to social security. If the benefit is nominal then a greater proportion of individuals will retain a claim to at least some meaningful part of the distribution of social security benefits after integration.

Our analysis does not address the issue of whether or not integration under the offset plan examined here is desirable. Indeed, under the usual assumption of continuously differentiable preference functions, one would not expect that a "kinked" schedule of income—for example, max (F, S_T)—would be an unconstrained optimum. Such schedules can, however, be optimal if there are constraints such as that the worker cannot sell his human capital. For example, under just this constraint, Diamond and Mirrlees (1985) have examined the role of transferable private pensions in improving the risk-sharing opportunities for workers when they are mobile. As shown in Merton (1985), under certain conditions, the Diamond-Mirrlees optimal transferable pension schedule is formally identical in structure to the one derived here for an integrated pension plan. Hence, neglecting the problems associated with worker mobility, a normative study may well find that integrated pension plans like those analyzed in sections 6.3 and 6.4 do have optimal risk-bearing properties. If, however, worker mobility is taken into account, then based on the analysis in section 6.4, we conjecture that the optimal pension policy will be to integrate *all* pension plans, both private and public.

Thus, while the focus here has been to highlight what we believe to be some of the unintended consequences of integration in its current setting, the analysis also provides a footlight on the trade-offs that are likely to be encountered in a normative evaluation of integration.

One, presumably unintended consequence of integration is that it allows for a de facto sale of social security benefits by participants in even moderately generous private pension plans. Our tables suggest that for typical profiles this sale is effectively complete despite the de jure prohibition against such assignment embodied elsewhere in the law. A related consequence is that the risk shedding available to those with low employer-provided benefits is inferior to that of retirees who are more generously provided for. Since low-income individuals generally also have the lowest pension benefits relative to social security, this risk-sharing pattern would appear to be somewhat regressive. Finally, we note our finding that integrated plans have unintended consequences for worker mobility beyond those already identified for nonintegrated plans.

The analysis in this paper is our first step in exploring the issue of integration of employer-provided pensions as a means of insuring workers against retirement income risk. In addition to the normative analysis already noted, there are a number of extensions of the analysis which are on our agenda for future research.

First of these is to perform a study similar to the one presented here for excess plans, and in particular for defined contribution excess plans. Second, we plan to examine in greater depth the nature of social security risk and how it affects the value of the insurance provided through plan integration. For example, uncertainty regarding social security benefits, which are determined in large part through the political process, is not likely to be the same across all income levels.

As described briefly in section 6.4, a third obvious extension is to deal explicitly with other sources of retirement income risk in addition to social security and to see how they interact under plan integration. One major factor is inflation risk. Since the employer-provided benefit is usually fixed in nominal terms at least after retirement, its real value is risky because of price-level uncertainty. The latter risk can be reduced and indeed entirely eliminated through indexation, and a considerable literature on this issue already exists.[10] We therefore have chosen to ignore this issue in this paper, focusing exclusively on social security risk and integration. However, there clearly is an interaction between inflation risk and social security risk, and any full analysis of the issues of integration and indexation would have to consider the interaction between the two.

Fourth, we have considered only social security benefits and the risk associated with them and have ignored social security taxes or contributions. Clearly, changes in social security benefits in the future imply changes in social security contributions under the pay-as-you-go funding system currently in place. In that sense our model is partial equilibrium in its analysis of the changes in risk sharing between employer and worker. Future research will take account of the feedback between benefit changes and contribution changes in the future in assessing the risk profiles resulting from integration.

Finally, our model and the option pricing methodology which we have applied have clear implications for the actuarial methods used to cost integrated pension plans. To our knowledge the actuarial profession does not currently employ this methodology, and we plan to explore the implications of its use in a more detailed setting than the one used in this paper.

Notes

1. See Schulz and Leavitt (1983), p. 26. According to the 1980 Bankers Trust Survey as many as 87% of private defined benefit plans with pay-related formulas were integrated.

2. For an explanation of options and how they work, see the seminal paper by Black and Scholes (1973). For a survey of the options literature and its application to nontraded assets, see Mason and Merton (1984). Because social security benefits change over time, while employer-provided benefits in integrated plans are linked to the level of social security at the time of retirement and are not thereafter adjusted, employees might engage in strategic retirement behavior. For example, it might pay to retire immediately prior to a large increase in social security benefits, so as to obtain larger private pension benefits. This gaming issue is absent from our analysis, because we set the retirement date exogenously. However, strategic behavior could easily be incorporated into the analysis. If retirement dates are chosen by optimizing employees, then the implicit option conferred to employees is simply American rather than European. While closed-form solutions for the values of these options are generally unavailable, the exercise decision is well understood and several numerical valuation algorithms are available to value such options.

3. For a further discussion of the analogy between put options and insurance schemes, see Merton et al. (1982).

4. The quantitative properties of integrated plans can be sensitive to the particular stochastic process assumed for S. However, the important qualitative properties of integration are independent of the particular process postulated. Geometric Brownian motion is the prototype process examined in the finance literature and has the benefits of familiarity and simplicity.

5. For a full presentation of the view of defined benefit pension accruals as a nominal asset see Bulow (1982). For a good discussion of why they might best be viewed as real see Cohn and Modigliani (1983).

6. If the uncertainty surrounding the real value of future social security payments is diversifiable, then α also equals r, and the *actual* expected growth rate g is zero. If α exceeds r because of a risk premium associated with social security uncertainty, then $g = \alpha - r > 0$, and col. 3 is interpreted as the "risk-corrected" or "certainty-equivalent" expected level of total benefits.

7. The entries in col. 4 are accurate to $5. Floor levels equal to col. 3 thus result from rounding error. Actual floor levels must be somewhat less than the corresponding entry in col. 3.

8. See, for example, Clark et al. (1983).

9. We set the upper limit of the integral in (14) equal to 40 years. The value of the sum of the integrand using yearly increments for dt was no longer increasing noticeably at this point.

10. See, for example, Feldstein (1983), Summers (1983), and Bodie and Pesando (1983).

References

Black, Fischer, and Scholes, Myron. 1973. The pricing of options and corporate liabilities. *Journal of Political Economy* 81:637–54.

Bodie, Zvi, and Pesando, James. 1983. Retirement annuity design in an inflationary climate. In *Financial aspects of the United States pension system,* ed. Zvi Bodie and John Shoven. Chicago: University of Chicago Press.

Bulow, Jeremy. 1982. The effect of inflation on the private pension system. In *Inflation: Causes and effects,* ed. Robert E. Hall. Chicago: University of Chicago Press.

Clark, R. L.; Allen, S. G.; and Sumner, D. A. 1983. Inflation and pension benefits. North Carolina State University, Raleigh. Mimeographed.

Cohn, Richard A., and Modigliani, Franco. 1983. Inflation and corporate financial management. Paper presented at the Conference on Recent Advances in Corporate Finance: Implications for Corporate Financial Management Practice, NYU Graduate School of Business Administration.

Constantinides, George. 1978. Market risk adjustment in project valuation. *Journal of Finance* 33:603–16.

Diamond, P., and J. Mirrlees. 1985. Insurance aspects of pensions. In *Pensions, labor, and individual choice,* ed. David A. Wise. Chicago: University of Chicago Press.

Feldstein, Martin. 1983. Should private pensions be indexed? In *Financial aspects of the United States pension system,* ed. Zvi Bodie and John Shoven. Chicago: University of Chicago Press.

Fischer, Stanley. 1978. Call option pricing when the exercise price is uncertain and the valuation of index bonds. *Journal of Finance* 33:169–76.

Mason, S., and Merton, R. C. 1984. The role of contingent claims analysis in corporate finance. Harvard Business School Working Paper. February.

Merton, Robert C. 1985. Comment on "Insurance aspects of pensions by P. A. Diamond and J. A. Mirrlees." In *Pensions, labor, and individual choice,* ed. David A. Wise. Chicago: University of Chicago Press.

————. 1983a. On the role of social security as a means for efficient risk sharing in an economy where human capital is not tradable. In *Financial aspects of the United States pension system,* ed. Zvi Bodie and John Shoven. Chicago: University of Chicago Press.

————. 1983b. On consumption indexed public pension plans. In *Financial aspects of the United States pension system,* ed. Zvi Bodie and John Shoven. Chicago: University of Chicago Press.

Merton, Robert C., Scholes, M., and Gladstein, M. 1982. The returns and risks of alternative put option portfolio investment strategies. *Journal of Business* 55:1–55.

Schulz, James H., and Leavitt, Thomas D. 1983. *Pension integration: concepts, issues and proposals.* Washington: Employee Benefit Research Institute.

Summers, Lawrence. 1983. Observations on the indexation of old age pensions. In *Financial aspects of the United States pension system,* ed. Zvi Bodie and John Shoven. Chicago: University of Chicago Press.

Comment   Jeremy I. Bulow

This paper introduces two important issues to the NBER's discussion of private pensions. The first is the issue of social security integration,

Jeremy I. Bulow is associate professor of economics, Graduate School of Business, Stanford University, and faculty research fellow, National Bureau of Economic Research.

and the second is the role of risk sharing in determining pensions and other benefits.

A majority of private defined benefit pension plans are integrated, and this integration has many consequences. First, as Robert Merton pointed out in his discussion, the integration of social security with growing private pension benefits may alter the political interests of various groups in "protecting" the social security system. For example, workers aged 50–65 might care less if social security were cut, if their benefits were effectively insured by their employers.

There is a major qualification to this argument, however. The way integration works, once an employee is retired and drawing a private pension benefit, that benefit cannot be reduced by increases in social security benefits. Therefore already retired employees would still be just as badly hurt by any cut in the growth of nominal benefits as if there were no integration.

A second important characteristic of integration is that it is a major neglected issue in the general area of pension liability valuation. With nonintegrated plans we have some reasonably well-developed theories of how to value employee benefits, theories that do not depend heavily on projections of the future. However, if benefits are tied to social security, then projections must be made about what social security benefit levels will be in the future and how integration rules may change. That is, if a worker in an integrated plan were to quit the firm today we cannot estimate the present value of that worker's future private pension benefits without making projections about social security.

Third, social security integration introduces a related, equally important issue. Firms provide health benefits to retired workers that insure against costs not paid by medicare. Such firms bear the same kind of risk in their medical programs that integration brings with social security. The methods of analyzing the social security problem should thus be readily applicable to another, equally important problem. These two primary retirement benefits are special because changes in the rules which raise firms' costs cannot be balanced by offering employees lower salaries. About the only hedge that firms readily have against such changes is the ability to cut down on voluntary benefit increases for retirees if some increases are mandated by law.

Why do firms integrate their pension plans? Perhaps the two most commonly given reasons are what might be called "non-economist" reasons. First, some firms may simply wish to deceive unknowledgeable employees into believing they are accruing a valuable private pension benefit when in reality the workers will get very little because of the mathematics of integration. Second, there is some notion of "equity" in pension benefit replacement rates. If the objective of private pensions is to provide workers with an adequate pension, defined as some percentage of pre-retirement income, then integration may help attain that goal by smoothing total replacement rates.

The deception issue mentioned above is one which we economists are poorly equipped to discuss. The "pension adequacy" issue of the firm desiring to provide target replacement rates seems dubious for two reasons:

First, as economists, we tend to believe that private pay arrangements are determined largely by market considerations, not equity. We believe that workers negotiate compensation packages, and efficiency requires that the reason compensation comes in a particular form is that given the cost to the firm of a pay package the compensation must be distributed to maximize worker utility. As the authors point out, the discussion should center on why workers choose to take their compensation in a given form, rather than on what is an equitable pension benefit.

Second, given that highly paid workers will generally have more wealth and at least somewhat greater social security benefits upon retirement, it is not so obvious that "equity" would require the tremendous skewing of private pension benefits to highly paid workers that occurs with integration.

The authors suggest a third reason for integration, one that is consistent with economic thinking. They propose that integration may be employed for its favorable risk-sharing consequences. In their model, low-paid workers essentially have no private pension and bear the risk of changes in their social security benefits. Wealthier workers sell their social security benefit to the firm and are thus hedged (ignoring taxes) for changes in the value of their benefits. The authors argue that it is reasonable for more highly paid workers to have a greater interest in insuring against social security benefits because those workers probably have the greatest uncertainty about what their social security benefits will be.

There is a major difficulty with the notion of integration's primary purpose being to share risks efficiently. While there is some risk in social security wealth this risk would seem to be less than in most other forms of investment for retirement. Workers hold nominal annuities through defined contribution pension plans and thus bear inflation risk. We do not see workers demanding real instead of nominal private pensions. The employees who would be insuring against social security risk with integration—higher-paid retired salaried employees— also own a good deal of stock, which is vastly riskier than social security wealth. Thus it seems doubtful that risk sharing in social security would be of major importance to these employees.

Why then do firms have integrated plans? Probably the primary reason is for institutional tax considerations. There are many reasons why low-paid workers might not want much of their compensation in the form of a private pension while highly paid workers may favor deferred compensation. First, highly paid workers may have a bigger tax incentive to "smooth" taxable income than lower- paid workers. Second, the desirability of having the firm invest money in a pension account at a pre-tax rate of return is greater for workers in a high tax bracket. Third, because social security payments do replace a higher percentage of working income for lower-paid employees lifetime smoothing would dictate more non–social security retirement saving for highly paid workers.

ERISA has nondiscrimination provisions which limit the degree to which benefits can be skewed to highly paid employees. The way that firms can most effectively discriminate between high-paid and low-paid workers is by having an integrated plan. As the authors show, such plans will have a much higher ratio of private benefits for highly paid versus lower-paid workers than nonintegrated plans. I suspect that the true motivation for integration is to achieve a greater skewing of benefits than may be possible with nonintegrated plans.

In summary, the authors have introduced some important issues to our study of private pensions. They are correct in looking at social security integration in the context of maximizing economic behavior rather than in an "equity" context. However, I am not yet convinced that risk sharing is really an important consideration in establishing an integrated private pension plan.

III   Pensions and Savings Behavior

7 Uncertain Lifetimes, Pensions, and Individual Saving

R. Glenn Hubbard

7.1 Introduction

Attempts to measure the impacts of pensions on household saving have occupied much of the literature in empirical public finance over the past decade. From a theoretical perspective, identifying the channels through which pensions affect the intertemporal consumption decision can help to distinguish among motives for saving (e.g., for retirement consumption or for bequests) and to explain empirical findings of the relationship between wealth and lifetime earnings. Proper quantification of the effects of pensions on saving is important for analyses of intergenerational equity, bequests and income distribution, and tax policy and saving.

Most of the attention in the pension-saving controversy has focused on the social security system, beginning with the time series studies of Feldstein (1974).[1] The theoretical argument of Feldstein (and of Barro 1974, 1978) has centered around the funding status of social security, that is, the degree to which an unfunded social security system reduces private saving. Empirical tests of the effects of social security on saving in this vein have been conducted in the perfect certainty version of the life-cycle model (Modigliani and Ando 1957; Modigliani and Brumberg 1954).[2] In that approach, social security affects wealth accumulation

R. Glenn Hubbard is assistant professor of economics and urban affairs, Northwestern University, and faculty research fellow, National Bureau of Economic Research.

This paper was presented at the NBER Pensions Conference in San Diego, April 13–14, 1984. I benefited from comments on an earlier draft of this paper from Andrew Abel, Benjamin Friedman, Jerry Hausman, Mervyn King, Laurence Kotlikoff, Michael Marrese, Paul Menchik, Olivia Mitchell, George Sofianos, Lawrence Summers, Mark Warshawsky, and members of the Macro-Labor Workshop at Northwestern University. The usual disclaimer applies.

only through its impact on individual intertemporal budget constraints. Disposable income falls by the amount of the tax. To the extent that the present value of benefits exceeds the present value of taxes paid, an increase in lifetime resources is generated, raising consumption in all periods.

This paper focuses on the distinction of precautionary saving against uncertainty over length of life in the life-cycle framework and on the annuity insurance aspects of social security and private pensions. The development of public and private pensions is examined in response to missing markets for providing insurance for consumption in the facet of uncertain lifetimes. A simple life-cycle model is put forth in section 7.2 to show that even an actuarially fair, fully funded social security system can reduce individual saving by more than the tax paid. Hence, previous partial equilibrium estimates of the impact of social security on saving drawn solely from consideration of the intergenerational wealth transfer at the introduction of the system are, if anything, too small.[3]

A related finding stems from the fact that under current United States law, social security taxes and benefits are calculated only up to an earnings ceiling. High-income individuals have incomplete access to the social security annuity system. Hence, even in the absence of an explicit bequest motive, the ratio of wealth to lifetime earnings could rise with the level of lifetime earnings. Constrained access to publicly provided pension annuities may provide an impetus to the growth of private pension annuities. This potential ''annuity rationing'' provides a motivation for integrating social security and private pension benefit formulas.

Individual wealth-age profiles are constructed in section 7.3 given uncertain lifetimes and social security. The large partial equilibrium saving impacts found in section 7.2 are mitigated when initial endowments are considered. Specifically, accidental bequests, which arise in the model because of lifetime uncertainty, provide an intergenerational link for saving decisions. To the extent that the introduction of social security reduces the size of accidental bequests, the net effect of social security on the consumption of subsequent generations is diminished.

Section 7.4 extends the approach to private pensions. The fifth section addresses empirical issues arising from the models of sections 7.3 and 7.4, primarily with respect to how one should interpret econometric estimates of ''offsets'' to individual saving attributed to pensions. Using a model specification for individual wealth accumulation from the literature, potential offsets are interpreted according to the presence or absence of a bequest motive and according to the ability of individuals to adjust their participation in private pensions to counteract involuntary changes in social security. Some conclusions and directions for future research are given in section 7.6.

7.2   Social Security and Savings in a Life-Cycle Model

7.2.1   Consumer Saving Decisions

The solution to an economic agent's intertemporal consumption problem subject to a lifetime resource constraint requires the equalization of expected marginal utilities of consumption across time. Otherwise, an increase in consumption at one point in his life at the expense of consumption at another time would raise lifetime utility, indicating that the initial allocation was suboptimal. The introduction of uncertainty generates a demand for insurance to diversify risks. Where insurance markets are incomplete or missing, the first-best optimum may be unattainable.

The type of uncertainty considered here is that over longevity; agents do not know when they will die. Yaari's (1965) seminal paper showed that with an uncertain lifetime, intertemporal utility maximization can dictate saving for the possibility of living longer than the expected lifetime to avoid deprivation in old age (excessively high marginal utility of future consumption).[4] That excess saving can be large. Kotlikoff and Spivak (1981, p. 379) found that for plausible underlying parameter values, the present expected value of unintended bequests represented almost 25% of initial wealth for a single male aged 55.

To emphasize this point, consider the following simple model. Agents are assumed to be selfish, in the sense that no bequests are desired. The retirement age Q is taken as exogenous, and individuals live Q periods for certain. The probability of having died in the interval $[0,t]$ is p_t for each t; by assumption, p_t is equal to zero in the interval $[0,Q]$. Individuals have an expected lifetime of D years, with $D' > D$ being the maximum age to which one can survive. That is, D is just the weighted average of the years t in $(Q + 1, D']$, with weights $(1 - p_t)$ for each t. Individuals receive a gross wage w_t in each period t during their working period; wages are assumed to grow at rate g. Income taxes on wages are levied at rate θ.

Following Yaari (1965) and Barro and Friedman (1977), let utility be additively separable, and let $U(C_t)$ be evaluated contingent on being alive at time t. That is, the consumer's intertemporal choice model is given by

$$(1) \qquad \max \sum_{t=0}^{D'} (1 - p_t)\, U(C_t)\, (1 + \delta)^{-t}$$

subject to

$$\sum_{t=0}^{D'} C_t (1 + r)^{-t} = K_0 + (1 - \theta)\, w_0 \sum_{t=0}^{Q} \left(\frac{1 + g}{1 + r} \right)^t,$$

where C, δ, and r represent consumption and the (constant) subjective discount rate and real interest rate, respectively. K_0 represents initial resources from unplanned bequests from the previous generation.

Carrying out the optimization in (1) assuming $U(C) = (1/\gamma)C^\gamma$ yields an optimal consumption stream of

$$(2) \qquad C_t = C_0 \left(\frac{1 + r}{1 + \delta} \right)^{t/(1-\gamma)} (1 - p_t)^{1/(1-\gamma)},$$

where

$$(3) \qquad C_0 = \frac{K_0 + (1 - \theta)\, w_0 \sum\limits_{t=0}^{Q} \left(\dfrac{1 + g}{1 + r} \right)^t}{\sum\limits_{i=0}^{D'} (1 + r)^{i\gamma/(1-\gamma)} (1 + \delta)^{-i/(1-\gamma)} (1 - p_i)^{1/(1-\gamma)}}.$$

The extent to which uncertainty over length of life affects the stream of consumption depends on agents' degree of relative risk aversion, a transformation of γ, the elasticity of the marginal utility function. The higher is an individual's degree of relative risk aversion (or, equivalently, the lower is his intertemporal elasticity of substitution in consumption), the slower will his consumption grow over time.

7.2.2   The Introduction of Social Security

Access to a fair annuity market could remove the influence of lifetime uncertainty on consumption. Individuals could exchange a portion of their labor income when young to smooth consumption in old age. This role of annuities as a mechanism for sharing uncertainty about longevity is an integral part of Diamond's (1977) evaluation of the social security system, in which he focuses on the absence of complete markets for such contracts. Merton (1983) considers Pareto-improving social security programs in an intertemporal model in which human capital is not tradable. Eckstein et al. (1985) consider the Pareto-improving potential of mandatory social security in the context of market failure in competitive insurance markets in the presence of adverse selection in the paradigm of Rothschild and Stiglitz (1976) or Wilson (1977).

If all individuals were identical in terms of their probabilities of survival,[5] then (with risk-neutral insurers) a competitive equilibrium in the provision of fair annuities would be possible. The existence of a competitive equilibrium may be precluded by asymmetries of information between individuals and insurers. This is, of course, the familiar "adverse selection" phenomenon discussed by Rothschild and Stiglitz (1976).[6] There may be additional "moral hazard" or "free-rider" barriers to the existence of an annuities market. If individuals conjecture that the state will support them in deprivation, the need to purchase annuities is diminished. A rigorous development of optimal second-best provision of annuities is beyond the scope of this paper.

Public provision of the annuities through public pensions is one possibility.[7] Moral hazard problems still make voluntary participation difficult. Consider, though, a public pension system ("social security") of the following form. Individuals are compelled to pay a payroll tax at rate t_s on gross wages, from which the social security system is funded. During retirement they receive annuity benefits S in each period t until death. The budget constraint in (1) becomes

$$(4) \quad \sum_{t=0}^{D'} C_t(1 + r)^{-t} = K_0 + (1 - \theta - t_s) \sum_{t=0}^{Q} w_0 \left(\frac{1 + g}{1 + r}\right)^t$$
$$+ \sum_{t=Q+1}^{D'} S_t(1 + r)^{-t}.$$

If benefits are set according to a replacement rate of the terminal wage, (i.e., where $S = Rw_Q$, where R is the earnings replacement rate) then the economy-wide actuarially fair benefit S satisfies the condition that[8]

$$(5) \quad S \sum_{t=Q+1}^{D'} (1 - p_t) (1 + r)^{-t} = t_s \sum_{t=0}^{Q} w_0 \left(\frac{1 + g}{1 + r}\right)^t.$$

Substituting the actuarially fair social security benefit into the budget constraint in (4) yields

$$(6) \quad \sum_{t=0}^{D'} C_t(1 + r)^{-t} = K_0 + [1 - \theta + t_s (\omega - 1)] \sum_{t=0}^{Q} w_0 \left(\frac{1 + g}{1 + r}\right)^t,$$

where ω arises because of the difference in discount rates under certainty and uncertainty and is equal to

$$\left(\sum_{t=Q+1}^{D'} (1 + r)^{-t} \right) \Big/ \left[\sum_{t=Q+1}^{D'} (1 - p_t)(1 + r)^{-t} \right].$$

Since ω is greater than unity, the system generates an increase in lifetime resources. Note that this increase in resources occurs even in a system which is actuarially fair and fully funded (i.e., in which contributions are invested and earn the market rate of return r in each period).[9] In reality, the initial cohorts participating in social security received a rate of return greater than the actuarially fair return (see Hurd and Shoven 1983). This analysis focuses only on an actuarially fair system to point out that the negative impact of social security on individual saving does not hinge on such initial transfers.[10]

We can compare the gains to individuals from the "insurance" features of social security, which would exist even in a fully funded system, with the transfer gains to initial participants from an unfunded system emphasized by Feldstein (1974) and Kotlikoff (1979a). Hurd and Shoven (1983) note that the "median return ratio" (i.e., the ratio of social security benefits to contributions) for single individuals in the Retirement History Survey fell from 2.91 in 1969 to 2.73 in 1975 to 2.41 in 1979. Despite the large gains for older retirees, their simulations of gains for future retirees indicate that projected internal rates of return decline markedly after 1980. In the model outlined above, this ratio for the funded system would be ω. Assuming a real rate of interest of 4% yields a return ratio of 2.1, which is approximately the same size as the current transfer effect and potentially much larger than the future transfer effect.

As shown in table 7.1, depending on assumptions about the real interest rate and the social security payroll tax rate, the percentage increase in lifetime resources generated by an actuarially fair social security system can be large. Using actual data on survival probabilities for the U.S.,[11] when $r = .04$ and $t_s = 0.10$, a 21% increase in lifetime resources is afforded by an actuarially fair social security system. If initial resources were on average equal to 25% of initial lifetime earnings, this translates into a 16.9% increase in lifetime consumption. Individual saving is reduced by more than the amount of the tax paid.

Suppose that not everyone has equal access to the retirement annuities provided by social security, and that effective participation is higher for low-income individuals than for high-income individuals. Let $\bar{w}$ represent the ceiling on taxable income; the growth rate of the taxable wage base and the determination of the replacement rate are as before. The budget constraint in (6) then becomes

$$(7) \quad \sum_{t=0}^{D'} C_t (1 + r)^{-t} = K_0 + \sum_{t=0}^{Q} [1 - \theta + \tilde{t}_s(\omega - 1)]w_0\left(\frac{1 + g}{1 + r}\right)^t,$$

where $\tilde{t}_s$ is equal to $t_s(\bar{w}/w_0)$. The impact of social security on an individual's lifetime resources depends on his income. As an annuity, social security administered in this way generates a smaller reduction in saving for high-income people than for low-income people.

7.3   Social Security and Dynamic Wealth Accumulation

7.3.1   Individual Saving Behavior

We can use the derivation from the previous section of the impact of mandatory actuarially fair social security on saving to study individual wealth accumulation over time. For any time t, the present value (at time 0) of an individual's accumulated stock of wealth, K_{0t} (i.e., the present value of the "accidental bequest" of an individual who died in period t), can be expressed as

$$(8) \qquad K_{0t} = K_0 + \sum_{i=0}^{t} (1 + r)^{-i}[(1 - \theta - t_s)w_i + S_i - C_i].$$

Wages and social security benefits are the sources of income to the individual. w_t is zero in the interval $[Q + 1, D']$, and S_t is zero in the interval $[0,Q]$. Using the expressions derived before for w_t, S_t, and C_t, we can rewrite (8) as

$$(9a) \qquad K_{0t} = K_0 + (1 - \theta - t_s)w_0 \sum_{i=0}^{t} \left(\frac{1 + g}{1 + r}\right)^{i}$$

$$- [1 - \theta + t_s (\omega - 1)]\left(w_0 \sum_{i=0}^{Q} \left(\frac{1 + g}{1 + r}\right)^{i}\right) \times$$

$$\left(\frac{\sum_{i=0}^{t} (1 + r)^{\frac{i\gamma}{1-\gamma}} (1 + \delta)^{\frac{-i}{1-\gamma}}(1 - p_i)^{\frac{1}{1-\gamma}}}{\sum_{i=0}^{D'} (1 + r)^{\frac{i\gamma}{1-\gamma}} (1 + \delta)^{\frac{-i}{1-\gamma}} (1 - p_i)^{\frac{1}{1-\gamma}}}\right), \; t \; \varepsilon \; [0,Q],$$

and

$$(9b) \qquad K_{0t} = K_0 + (1 - \theta - t_s)w_0 \sum_{i=0}^{Q} \left(\frac{1 + g}{1 + r}\right)^{i}$$

$$+ t_s \left[w_0 \sum_{i=0}^{Q} \left(\frac{1 + g}{1 + r}\right)^{i}\right] \frac{\sum_{i=Q+1}^{t} (1 + r)^{-i}}{\sum_{i=Q+1}^{D'} (1 - p_i)(1 + r)^{-i}}$$

$$- [1 - \theta + t_s (\omega - 1)]\left(\sum_{i=0}^{Q} w_0\left(\frac{1 + g}{1 + r}\right)^{i}\right)$$

$$\left(\frac{\sum_{i=0}^{t} (1 + r)^{\frac{i\gamma}{1-\gamma}} (1 + \delta)^{\frac{-i}{1-\gamma}}(1 - p_i)^{\frac{1}{1-\gamma}}}{\sum_{i=0}^{D'} (1 + r)^{\frac{i\gamma}{1-\gamma}} (1 + \delta)^{\frac{-i}{1-\gamma}} (1 - p_i)^{\frac{1}{1-\gamma}}}\right), \; t \; \varepsilon \; [Q + 1, D'].$$

To provide an intuitive framework for considering an individual's wealth accumulation over the life cycle, note that if we denote the present values of lifetime labor income and social security taxes by V_L and V_S, respectively, we can rewrite (9a) and (9b) as

$$\text{(10a)} \quad \frac{K_{0t}}{V_L} = K_0 + \frac{(1 - \theta - t_s)w_0 \sum_{i=0}^{t}\left(\frac{1+g}{1+r}\right)^i}{V_L}$$

$$- \left[1 - \theta + \frac{V_S}{V_L}(\omega - 1)\right]\left(\frac{\sum_{i=0}^{t}(1+r)^{\frac{i\gamma}{1-\gamma}}(1+\delta)^{\frac{-i}{1-\gamma}}(1-p_i)^{\frac{1}{1-\gamma}}}{\sum_{i=0}^{D'}(1+r)^{\frac{i\gamma}{1-\gamma}}(1+\delta)^{\frac{-i}{1-\gamma}}(1-p_i)^{\frac{1}{1-\gamma}}}\right),$$

and

$$\text{(10b)} \quad \frac{K_{0t}}{V_L} = \frac{K_0}{V_L} + 1 - \theta - \frac{V_S}{V_L} + \frac{V_S}{V_L}\left(\frac{\sum_{i=Q+1}^{t}(1+r)^{-i}}{\sum_{i=Q+1}^{D'}(1-p_i)(1+r)^{-i}}\right)$$

$$- \left[1 - \theta + \frac{V_S}{V_L}(\omega - 1)\right]\left(\frac{\sum_{i=0}^{t}(1+r)^{\frac{i\gamma}{1-\gamma}}(1+\delta)^{\frac{-i}{1-\gamma}}(1-p_i)^{\frac{1}{1-\gamma}}}{\sum_{i=0}^{D'}(1+r)^{\frac{i\gamma}{1-\gamma}}(1+\delta)^{\frac{-i}{1-\gamma}}(1-p_i)^{\frac{1}{1-\gamma}}}\right).$$

The ratio K_{0t}/V_L tracks an individual's accumulated stock of assets relative to lifetime earnings. In a world of no uncertainty over longevity, K_{0t}/V_L is simply a function of age, and the results of the basic life-cycle model are reproduced, as long as the present values of social security contributions and benefits are equal. With lifetime uncertainty, wealth is still built up relative to earnings during the working period, but the rate at which consumption draws down accumulated wealth depends on survival probabilities and relative risk aversion. Because an actuarially fair social security system generates an increase in individual lifetime resources, lifetime consumption rises. Much of this increase in consumption comes during an individual's working life, as the need to save for retirement is reduced. Depending on risk aversion, while

Table 7.1   **Percentage Increase in Lifetime Consumption Generated by Actuarially Fair Social Security**

	$t_s = 0.10$	$t_s = 0.12$	$t_s = 0.14$
$r = 0.02$	29	35	41
$r = 0.04$	21	26	32
$r = 0.06$	16	19	23

NOTE: It is assumed that individuals receive no initial bequest.

retirement consumption is higher in the presence of social security, dissaving in retirement is likely to be less than in the certainty case.[12]

The problem becomes more complicated when the insurance coverage provided by social security is not the same across individuals. Suppose again that there is a ceiling on the level of earnings against which payroll tax rates and replacement rates are calculated. If that ceiling is $\bar{w}$ in period 0 and grows at the same rate as the wage base, then the effective tax rate is not t_s, but $\tilde{t}_s = t_s (\bar{w}/w_0)$. In that situation, equation (10) reveals that the ratio of wealth to lifetime earnings rises with the level of lifetime earnings, though at a decreasing rate.[13] This nonlinearity of saving rates with respect to lifetime earnings occurs in the absence of any explicit bequest motive. The implications of this effect for studies of the relationship between bequests and lifetime resources will be discussed later.

A related problem surfaces in the consideration of received bequests which augment lifetime resources. If we let K_0 represent the initial bequest, then we can rewrite equation (10) as

(11a)
$$\frac{K_{0t}}{V_L} = \frac{K_0}{V_L} + \frac{(1 - \theta - t_s)w_0 \sum_{i=0}^{t} \left(\frac{1+g}{1+r}\right)^i}{V_L}$$

$$- \left[1 - \theta + \frac{V_S}{V_L}(\omega - 1)\right] \left(\frac{\sum_{i=0}^{t} (1 + r)^{\frac{i\gamma}{1-\gamma}}(1 + \delta)^{\frac{-i}{1-\gamma}}(1 - p_i)^{\frac{1}{1-\gamma}}}{\sum_{i=0}^{D'} (1 + r)^{\frac{i\gamma}{1-\gamma}}(1 + \delta)^{\frac{-i}{1-\gamma}}(1 - p_i)^{\frac{1}{1-\gamma}}}\right),$$

and

(11b)
$$\frac{K_{0t}}{V_L} = \left(1 - \theta + \frac{K_0}{V_L} - \frac{V_S}{V_L}\right) + \frac{V_S}{V_L}\left(\frac{\sum_{i=Q+1}^{t} (1 + r)^{-i}}{\sum_{i=Q+1}^{D'} (1 - p_i)(1 + r)^{-i}}\right)$$

$$- \left[1 - \theta + \frac{V_S}{V_L}(\omega - 1)\right] \left(\frac{\sum_{i=0}^{t} (1 + r)^{\frac{i\gamma}{1-\gamma}}(1 + \delta)^{\frac{-i}{1-\gamma}}(1 - p_i)^{\frac{1}{1-\gamma}}}{\sum_{i=0}^{D'} (1 + r)^{\frac{i\gamma}{1-\gamma}}(1 + \delta)^{\frac{-i}{1-\gamma}}(1 - p_i)^{\frac{1}{1-\gamma}}}\right).$$

As in the case of labor income, the rate at which lifetime resources are consumed depends on survival probabilities and risk aversion. The initial capital endowment K_0, which comes here from an accidental bequest from the previous generation, raises the individual's lifetime resources, increasing the consumption out of the present value of labor income and reducing the ratio of accumulated wealth to lifetime earnings. In the case in which participation in social security annuities is higher for low-income individuals, initial wealth endowments may smooth the nonlinearity in earnings of savings rates brought about by such a social security system.

To quantify the impact of social security and bequests on individual consumption and wealth-age profiles, the model embodied in equation (11) can be simulated for plausible parameter values. Simulations were performed over a set of different values of r, g, δ, and γ. The following relationships among the parameters are assumed: $r > g$, $r > \delta$, and $\delta > 0$.[14] There is some evidence on the value of γ in the literature. In their study of household portfolio allocation, Friend and Blume (1975) estimated the coefficient of relative risk aversion to be in excess of 2.0, implying a value of γ of at most -1.0. Farber's (1978) estimation of preferences of United Mine Workers from collective bargaining agreements yielded estimates of the coefficient of relative risk aversion of 3.0 and 3.7. Here we use three alternative values of γ: 0.25, -1.0, and -3.0; g is assumed to equal 0.02, while $r = 0.04$, and $\delta = 0.03$.[15]

Table 7.2 reports K_{0t}/V_L for selected ages. The optimization begins at age 20; individuals are assumed to retire at age 65. Figures are expressed as differences from the no-social-security case. Column 1 reports values in the absence of social security, but with an initial bequest equal to 25% of lifetime earnings. Column 2 reports the reduction in K_{0t}/V_L when the individual participates in a social security system in which $\bar{t}_s = t_s = 0.14$. The third column shows the reduction in K_{0t}/V_L for an individual whose effective tax rate (participation) in the system is only half of the nominal rate. Finally, the fourth column shows the change in the wealth-age profile for an individual with an initial bequest equivalent to 25% of his lifetime earnings and for whom $\bar{t}_s = t_s = 0.14$.

Several interesting patterns emerge. As expected, higher values of relative risk aversion (lower values of γ) encompass higher wealth in all periods, particularly in old age. Given uncertainty over longevity with no social security, an initial bequest of 25% of lifetime earnings is almost completely consumed by age 75 when $\gamma = 0.25$. When $\gamma = -1.0$, however, about 13% remains; nearly 20% remains in the case in which $\gamma = -3.0$.

The second and third columns, which address the implied resource gains made possible by access to actuarially fair social security, display the reduction in K/V_L attributable to social security (when $t_s = 0.14$). When the effective tax rate is less than the nominal tax rate, the reduction in K/V_L is smaller. Hence, effective participation in social security which declines with increases in income, ceteris paribus, leads to saving rates which rise with earnings (and, a fortiori, stocks of wealth which rise with earnings). As γ is decreased (higher relative risk aver-

Table 7.2   **Social Security and K_0/V_L**

Age	$t_s = 0, \dfrac{K_0}{V_L} = .25$	$\bar{t}_s = t_s = .14$	$\bar{t}_s = .07, t_s = .14$	$\bar{t}_s = t_s = .14, \dfrac{K_0}{V_L} = .25$
		$\gamma = 0.25$		
40	.150	−.208	−.104	−.057
50	.104	−.296	−.148	−.192
65	.041	−.393	−.196	−.337
70	.025	−.336	−.168	−.311
75	.014	−.273	−.137	−.260
80	.006	−.222	−.111	−.215
		$\gamma = -1.00$		
40	.155	−.201	−.101	−.046
50	.114	−.282	−.141	−.168
65	.060	−.386	−.193	−.326
70	.044	−.330	−.175	−.306
75	.031	−.321	−.161	−.290
80	.020	−.298	−.150	−.279
		$\gamma = -3.00$		
40	.160	−.195	−.097	−.035
50	.122	−.272	−.136	−.150
65	.072	−.362	−.181	−.307
70	.057	−.333	−.177	−.276
75	.044	−.304	−.152	−.260
80	.033	−.282	−.141	−.250

NOTE: Entries represent differences in K_0/V_L from the no-social-security case.

sion), the social security system permits greater wealth decumulation in old age. In other words, the more risk averse the individual, the less of the "income effect" of social security participation consumed prior to retirement. Those findings are intuitive, since the value of annuity is highest for very risk-averse individuals.

The last column of table 7.2 shows the combined impact on the wealth-age profile of the combination of effective participation in social security at the nominal rate (14% here) and the receipt of an initial bequest. From the information in the first column of table 7.2 and from a comparison of the second and fourth columns, most of the impact of initial bequests on consumption occurs prior to retirement. That is, the differences in K/V_L in old age (with respect to the no-social-security case) are almost invariant to the initial bequest (at least in the range examined here).

We can now consider the issue of the consumption pattern of the elderly, addressed earlier by Mirer (1979) and by Davies (1981). Given uncertainty over length of life, the rapid reduction in consumption (relative to lifetime resources) in old age confirms the findings in Davies (1981) that positive net worth may continue indefinitely after retirement. The resulting slow decline (or possible increase) in net worth in retirement ignores, however, the decline in the value of the social security annuity. Since the model implies that individuals acknowledge the actuarial value of their social security holdings, that dissaving must take place.

For each year t in retirement, withdrawals to finance consumption relative to lifetime earnings can be expressed as

$$(12) \quad \frac{C_t}{V_L} = \frac{K_0 + [1 - \theta + t_s(\omega - 1)] \left(\frac{1 + r}{1 + \delta}\right)^{\frac{t}{1-\gamma}}(1 - p_t)^{\frac{1}{1-\gamma}}}{\sum_{i=0}^{D'} (1 + r)^{i\gamma/(1-\gamma)} (1 + \delta)^{-i/(1-\gamma)} (1 - p_i)^{1/(1-\gamma)}}.$$

Correspondingly, in each year t, the decline in the annuity value of social security relative to lifetime earnings is

$$(13) \quad \frac{\Delta V_{St}}{V_L} = \frac{S(1 - p_t)}{V_L} = \frac{t_s (1 - p_t)}{\sum_{i=Q+1}^{D'} (1 - p_i)(1 + r)^{-i}}.$$

The relationship between these two uses of total (pension plus non-pension wealth) depends on γ and the distribution of survival probabilities. To see the importance of considering the "dissaving" of annuity wealth, table 7.3 contrasts consumption and annuity revaluations in retirement of the case of $\gamma = -1$, $t_S = 0.14$, $r = 0.04$, and $\delta = 0.03$.[16] Note that annuity dissaving (the reduction in the actuarial value of the social security annuity) is substantially greater than the reduction in nonpension wealth.

To estimate correctly the net effect of social security on individual consumption and wealth accumulation after the commencement of the system, we must also consider its impact on intergenerational transfers (here, accidental bequests). By affecting the accidental bequests of

Table 7.3   **Annuity and Nonannuity Dissaving in Retirement**

Age	C_t/V_L	$\Delta V_{St}/V_L$	$\Delta V_{St}/C_t$
66	.033	.084	2.55
70	.032	.072	2.25
75	.029	.055	1.90
80	.026	.038	1.46
85	.020	.021	1.05

previous generations, social security further influences individual consumption patterns. It is to this issue which we now turn.

7.3.2   Long-Run Effects on Individual Saving

Given uncertainty over length of life, an actuarially fair social security system can reduce individual saving by more than the amount of the taxes paid. For plausible underlying assumptions about individual discount rates, survival probabilities, and the intertemporal elasticity of substitution in consumption, the magnitude of that reduction is substantial. The partial equilibrium conclusion is clear—estimates of the reduction in individual saving brought about by social security which focuses only on the extent to which the system delivers a present value of anticipated benefits greater the present value of taxes paid are, if anything, an underestimate. Before discussing general equilibrium interpretations of this finding (in the sense that the wage rate and real interest rate are endogenous and respond to changes in the saving rate), it is important to address the issue raised in the simulation exercises of the links among generations provided by accidental bequests.

An initial bequest from an "early death" of one's parent raises the beneficiary's consumption relative to lifetime earnings. In the model, the size of that bequest depends on the testator's coverage by social security and his age at death. By facilitating greater consumption out of lifetime earnings, social security reduces the accidental bequest. On that account, the initial resources available to the heir (and, from table 7.2, consumption when young) are lower. Even within the partial equilibrium analysis, the impact of social security on the consumption and saving patterns of individuals in a given generation depends on the balance between the effective increase in lifetime resources made possible by access to a fair annuity and the reduction in inheritances because of that impact on the saving of the previous generation.[17]

To see this more clearly, note that for an individual receiving an accidental bequest from a "parent" who died at age t in the interval $[Q + 1, D']$, the reduction in the bequest because of the parent's participation in social security is[18]

$$
(14) \quad \frac{dK_0}{dV_S} = (1 + r)^t \left[-1 + \left(\frac{\sum\limits_{i=Q+1}^{t} (1 + r)^{-i}}{\sum\limits_{i=Q+1}^{D'} (1 - p_i)(1 + r)^{-i}} \right) \right.
$$

$$
\left. - (\omega - 1) \left(\frac{\sum\limits_{i=0}^{t} (1 + r)^{\frac{i\gamma}{1-\gamma}}(1 + \delta)^{\frac{-i}{1-\gamma}}(1 - p_i)^{\frac{1}{1-\gamma}}}{\sum\limits_{i=0}^{D'} (1 + r)^{\frac{i\gamma}{1-\gamma}} (1 + \delta)^{\frac{-i}{1-\gamma}}(1 - p_i)^{\frac{1}{1-\gamma}}} \right) \right].
$$

We know from the individual's optimization problem that social security generates an increase in lifetime resources of $V_S(\omega - 1)$. If the "parent" and "child" have the same lifetime earning potential (i.e., the same w_0), then the net effect of social security is to increase lifetime resources by the amount E, where

$$(15) \qquad E = V_s(\omega - 1) \left[1 - (1 + r)^t \times \right.$$

$$\left(\frac{\sum_{i=0}^{t} (1 + r)^{\frac{i\gamma}{1-\gamma}} (1 + \delta)^{\frac{-i}{1-\gamma}}(1 - p_i)^{\frac{1}{1-\gamma}}}{\sum_{i=0}^{D'} (1 + r)^{\frac{i\gamma}{1-\gamma}} (1 + \delta)^{\frac{-i}{1-\gamma}} (1 - p_i)^{\frac{1}{1-\gamma}}} \right)$$

$$\left. + (1 + r)^t(\omega - 1)^{-1} \left(\frac{\sum_{i=Q+1}^{D'} (1 + r)^{-i}}{\sum_{i=Q+1}^{D'} (1 - p_i)(1 + r)^{-i}} - 1 \right) \right].$$

Note that if the parent lived to the maximum age, then E = 0. In general, the net increment to lifetime resources E made possible by social security depends on the age at which the parent died (magnitude of the accidental bequest).[19] To consider the net effect of social security on saving n generations after its introduction, an n-generational analogue to equation (15) could be constructed given the ages of death of previous testators. The role of family mortality history is important here, as individuals whose "ancestors" all died early will receive large bequests relative to those whose parent lived a long time.

Members of the first generation to participate in the social security system benefit in two respects, as their lifetime resources are augmented both by the bequests from the (uninsured) previous generation and the gains from participation in the social security annuity system. The reduced value of accidental bequests permits smaller consumption gains for subsequent generations. While it is true that social security reduces individual saving to a lesser degree in the generations after its introduction, there is still a reduction in the long-run capital stock. Ultimately, to consider the potential welfare gains from compulsory pensions, the trade-off between the benefits to early participants from access to the annuities and the costs to generations that follow of a lower capital stock must be examined.

7.3.3   General Equilibrium Effects of Social Security on the Capital Stock

The partial equilibrium effects of social security on individual saving will be dampened in a general equilibrium analysis of the impact of social security on aggregate capital formation.[20] The reduction in individual wealth accumulation brought about by social security will induce changes in factor returns, exhibiting both income and substitution effects on consumption. A higher real interest rate decreases lifetime resources; in addition, a higher rate of interest reduces the price of consumption in old age.

Kotlikoff (1979a), using a life-cycle model with no uncertainty over longevity and a Cobb-Douglas production technology, considered the impact of a pay-as-you-go social security system on the capital stock in a general equilibrium. For plausible parameter values, he found that the positive lifetime wealth increment traceable to social security (because of growth of the wage base) caused a 20% steady-state reduction in the capital stock in the general equilibrium.[21] While this is certainly substantial, it is roughly half of his partial equilibrium effect, which is directly related to the extent to which benefits are unfair (i.e., to the extent that the present value of benefits exceeds the present value of social security taxes paid).

While detailed general equilibrium simulations are not performed here, some simple calculations illustrate the basic points outlined above. Suppose output is produced according to a Cobb-Douglas production function in capital and effective labor, with a capital share of one third. Factor markets are assumed to be competitive, so that capital and labor are paid their marginal products. Again, labor is inelastically supplied, and labor-augmenting technical change is assumed to occur at a constant rate of 2%; let the population growth rate be 1%. Let the individual's optimization problem be parameterized by $r = 0.06$, $\delta = 0.03$, and $\gamma = -1.00$; the average propensity to consume out of total income[22] of about 0.82.

A fully funded, actuarially fair social security system with $t_s = 0.10$ reduces the capital stock by about 60%, implying an increase in the interest rate of 40% and a reduction in output of about 20%. Those changes are, of course, upper bounds to the true steady-state changes, as both the saving rate and the increase in lifetime consumption afforded by social security (indexed by ω) are sensitive to the interest rate. The calculations do, however, point up the need to consider in welfare comparisons both the increase in propensity to consume made possible by social security and the effects on consumption of the reduction in output accompanying a smaller capital stock. Access to the social security annuities facilitates an increase in the average propensity to consume (out of total income) of about 16%. Because of the fall in output, consumption per capital actually falls in the new steady state. If the output-reducing effect were large enough, lifetime welfare of a representative agent could actually decline in the new steady state following the introduction of social security.

7.4 Application to Private Pensions

To the extent that high-income individuals (those for whom $w_0 > \bar{w}$) are constrained to less than their desired participation in social security, there is excess demand for social security annuities. Adverse selection and the possibility of multiple insurance[23] still render unlikely the provision of such annuities by competitive insurance companies. Employer-sponsored private pension funds may act to fill this gap. Employers are likely to have better information on individual workers' life expectancies than would a disinterested insurance company. Second, by definition, such annuities can only be purchased at an individual's place of work; multiple insurance is not possible. Finally, the pension instrument may provide an added degree of freedom for the firm in influencing worker behavior.[24]

The tax treatment of pension plans is an important consideration. Social security taxes are levied on gross earnings, and prior to the 1983 amendments to the Social Security Act, benefits were not considered taxable income. For private pension plans, employer contributions are a deductible business expense and are not regarded as taxable income to employees until benefits are paid. Pension fund earnings accumulate tax-free until disbursement. Upon distribution, taxes paid on benefits are presumably less than corresponding wage tax payments, since earnings (and hence tax rates) are lower in retirement. Moreover, special retirement income credits further diminish effective tax rates on pension benefits.

At this point, we will assume that covered workers take their participation in plans as given; the implications of relaxing that assumption will be discussed later. For simplicity, let P be the actuarially fair pension benefit in retirement (determined by the product of a replacement rate and the terminal wage) corresponding to an implicit reduction in wages at rate t_p.[25]

In the context of this model, the worker bears only $(1 - \theta)t_p$ of the wage reduction, where θ is the marginal income tax rate. Benefits are taxed at rate $\hat{\theta}$, where $\theta > \hat{\theta}$. We introduce a parameter β to measure the extent to which benefits received are actuarially fair. That is, an actuarially fair pension benefit P can be constructed just as in the case of social security annuity benefits in equation (5). Benefits received are equal to βP, where P solves

(16) $\qquad P \sum_{t=Q+1}^{D'} (1 - p_t)(1 + r)^{-t} = t_p \sum_{t=0}^{Q} w_0 \left(\frac{1 + g}{1 + r}\right)^t.$

For received annuity payments to be actuarially fair, it must be the case that $\beta = 1$; less than fair benefits are associated with $\beta < 1$.

Given participation in social security, the budget constraint in (7) can be rewritten as

$$(17) \quad \sum_{t=0}^{D'} C_t(1 + r)^{-t} = K_0 + (1 - \theta - \tilde{t}_s)(1 - t_p) \sum_{t=0}^{Q} w_0 \left(\frac{1 + g}{1 + r}\right)^t$$

$$+ [S + (1 - \hat\theta)\beta P] \sum_{t=Q+1}^{D'} (1 + r)^{-t}$$

$$= K_0 + (1 - \theta - \tilde{t}_s)(1 - t_p) \sum_{t=0}^{Q} w_0 \left(\frac{1 + g}{1 + r}\right)^t$$

$$+ [\tilde{t}_s + (1 - \hat\theta)\beta t_p] \sum_{t=0}^{Q} w_0 \left(\frac{1 + g}{1 + r}\right)^t \left[\frac{\sum_{t=Q+1}^{D'} (1 + r)^{-t}}{\sum_{t=Q+1}^{D'} (1 - p_t)(1 + r)^{-t}}\right]$$

$$= K_0 + \{1 - \theta + \tilde{t}_s(\omega - 1) + t_p [(1 - \hat\theta)\beta\omega$$

$$- (1 - \theta - \tilde{t}_s)]\} \sum_{t=0}^{Q} w_0 \left(\frac{1 + g}{1 + r}\right)^t.$$

As shown before, $\omega > 1$. As long as β is close to unity, for any reasonable assessment of the relationship between θ and $\hat\theta$, $(1 - \hat\theta)\beta\omega > 1 - \theta - \tilde{t}_s$. This is certainly true for the estimated tax rates used by the Treasury in calculating the tax expenditure associated with pension tax subsidies, namely, $\theta = 0.23$ and $\hat\theta = 0.115$ (see Munnell 1982, p. 44, for details). Because of the tax deductibility of pension contributions, even in a world of certainty over longevity ($\omega = 1$), a funded private pension can still generate an increase in lifetime resources for the individual.

The tax treatment of pension contributions reinforces the role of private pension annuities in alleviating the rationing of public annuities. The effective contribution rates (participation rates) in the public and private pension systems both depend on the income of the individual. Recall that $\tilde{t}_s = t_s (\bar{w}/w_0)$, where $\bar{w}$ is the ceiling on taxable earnings. Under a progressive tax system, the marginal tax rate also depends on income, that is, $\theta'(w_0) > 0$. Hence for given (assigned) nominal participation rates in social security and private pensions, high-income individuals receive a greater effective increase in lifetime resources from private pensions of the sort described here. This effect may be desirable if one reason for the private pension system is to supplement the rationed access to social security annuities for high-income workers. Capital-market imperfections and borrowing restrictions would still limit the demand for pension annuities.

We can now reconstruct the wealth-age profiles given both social security and private pensions. Wages and public and private pension annuity payments are the sources of income to the individual. In the interval $[Q + 1, D']$, w_t is zero and S_t and P_t are zero in the interval $[0,Q]$. Using the expressions derived before for w_t, S_t, P_t, and C_t and denoting the present values of lifetime labor income, social security taxes, and implicit wage reductions to finance private pensions by V_L, V_S, and V_P, respectively, we can construct wealth-age profiles relative to lifetime earnings. That is,

$$
(18a) \quad \frac{K_{0t}}{V_L} = \frac{K_0 + (1 - \theta - t_s)(1 - t_p) w_0 \sum_{i=0}^{t} \left(\frac{1 + g}{1 + r}\right)^i}{V_L}
$$

$$
- \left\{1 - \theta + \frac{V_S}{V_L}(\omega - 1) + \frac{V_P}{V_L}[(1 - \hat{\theta})\beta\omega - (1 - \theta - \tilde{t}_s)]\right\} \times
$$

$$
\left[\frac{\sum_{i=0}^{t} (1 + r)^{\frac{i\gamma}{1-\gamma}} (1 + \delta)^{\frac{-i}{1-\gamma}} (1 - p_i)^{\frac{1}{1-\gamma}}}{\sum_{i=0}^{D'} (1 + r)^{\frac{i\gamma}{1-\gamma}} (1 + \delta)^{\frac{-i}{1-\gamma}} (1 - p_i)^{\frac{1}{1-\gamma}}}\right], \, t \, \varepsilon \, [0,Q],
$$

and

$$
(18b) \quad \frac{K_{0t}}{V_L} = \frac{K_0}{V_L} + \left(1 - \theta - \frac{V_S}{V_L}\right)\left(1 - \frac{V_P}{V_L}\right)
$$

$$
+ \left[\frac{V_S}{V_L} + (1 - \hat{\theta})\beta\frac{V_P}{V_L}\right]\left(\frac{\sum_{i=Q+1}^{t} (1 + r)^{-i}}{\sum_{i=Q+1}^{D'} (1 - p_i)(1 + r)^{-i}}\right)
$$

$$
- \left\{1 - \theta + \frac{V_S}{V_L}(\omega - 1) + \frac{V_P}{V_L}[(1 - \hat{\theta})\beta\omega - (1 - \theta - \tilde{t}_s)]\right\} \times
$$

$$
\left[\frac{\sum_{i=0}^{t} (1 + r)^{\frac{i\gamma}{1-\gamma}} (1 + \delta)^{\frac{-i}{1-\gamma}} (1 - p_i)^{\frac{1}{1-\gamma}}}{\sum_{i=0}^{D'} (1 + r)^{\frac{i\gamma}{1-\gamma}} (1 + \delta)^{\frac{-i}{1-\gamma}} (1 - p_i)^{\frac{1}{1-\gamma}}}\right], \, t \, \varepsilon \, [Q + 1, D'].
$$

The addition of private pension annuities complicates the evaluation of the effect of a change in compulsory social security holdings on nonpension wealth. Suppose that individual participation in private pension annuities is not invariant to changes in social security annuities. Let ψ_{ps} represent the magnitude of that discretionary adjustment, that is,

$$(19) \qquad \psi_{ps} = dV_p/dV_s.$$

Then from equation (18a), the impact of a change in social security wealth on the nonpension wealth of a nonretired individual is

$$(20) \quad \frac{dK_{0t}}{dV_S} = -\{\omega - 1 + \psi_{ps}[(1 - \hat{\theta})\beta\omega - (1 - \theta - \tilde{t}_s)]\} \times$$

$$\left[\frac{\displaystyle\sum_{i=0}^{t} (1 + r)^{\frac{i\gamma}{1-\gamma}} (1 + \delta)^{\frac{-i}{1-\gamma}} (1 - p_i)^{\frac{1}{1-\gamma}}}{\displaystyle\sum_{i=0}^{D'} (1 + r)^{\frac{i\gamma}{1-\gamma}} (1 + \delta)^{\frac{-i}{1-\gamma}} (1 - p_i)^{\frac{1}{1-\gamma}}} \right].$$

If $\psi_{ps} = 0$, then the impact of a change in holdings of social security annuities has the same influence on lifetime resources as before. When $\psi_{ps} < 0$ (i.e., increases in involuntary social security annuitization can be at least partially undone through changes in private pension participation), the impact of social security on individual wealth accumulation will also depend on the extent to which private pension annuities are actuarially fair (i.e., on the value of β) and on the tax advantages of pensions as compensation (values θ and $\hat{\theta}$).

When coverage by social security is higher for low-wage earners than for high-wage earners, we can use equation (13) to examine the impact on nonpension wealth of change in the social security payroll tax rate (index of participation). First, since the effective tax rate $\tilde{t}_s = t_s (\bar{w}/w_0)$, a given increase in the nominal tax rate translates into a smaller increase in V_S (and, ceteris paribus, a smaller displacement of nonpension wealth) for high-income workers (for whom $w_0 > \bar{w}$) than for low-income workers (for whom $\bar{w} > w_0$). When private pension participation is responsive to changes in social security annuity holdings (i.e., when $\psi_{ps} < 0$), then for a given offset factor ψ_{ps}, high-income individuals receive a smaller total offset than low-income individuals.[26]

In the next section, we take up issues associated with empirical treatment of forms of (18), emphasizing the role of assumptions about the structure of social security and private pensions, the presence or absence of a bequest motive, and the extent to which participation in private pension annuities is voluntary.

7.5 Empirical Issues

Gathering econometric evidence of the impact of social security and private pension annuities on household saving in the context of lifetime uncertainty entails estimation of the wealth profiles consistent with equation (18). Suppose one has a cross-section of household or individual data with information on earnings, assets and liabilities, pensions, and individual and labor-market characteristics. Most previous empirical examinations of the impact of social security on nonpension wealth have employed versions of the following specification:

$$(21) \qquad W_i = f(Y_i^*, A_i, Z_i) - \lambda PW_i,$$

where i refers to the individual and W, Y^*, A, Z, and PW are nonpension wealth, lifetime earnings, age, a vector of socioeconomic variables and individual characteristics, and the actuarial present value of anticipated pension benefits, respectively.

Consider for example a wealth accumulation equation of the following form:

$$(22) \quad \left(\frac{W}{Y^*}\right)_i = g(Y_i^*) + j(A_i) - a_s\left(\frac{SSW}{Y^*}\right)_i$$
$$- a_p\left(\frac{PPW}{Y^*}\right)_i + \gamma' Z_i + \varepsilon_i.$$

Anticipated pension benefits are divided into two components, social security (SSW) and private pensions (PPW), to allow for different effects on saving; a_s and a_p are coefficients to be estimated, j is a function of age. Finally, the function g can be specified to test the nonlinearity in income of the ratio of wealth to permanent income.[27]

Recalling the wealth-age profiles constructed from the theoretical model in the previous section, the specification of wealth accumulation in (22) illustrates the importance of the inclusion of the pension variables. With respect to social security, if individual earnings replacement rates are negatively correlated with earnings for high-income workers (as in the United States system), the measured effect of Y^* on W/Y^* would be biased upward if the social security variable were omitted. The correlation of PPW/Y^* with Y^* is less clear. Similarly, if one wanted to use (22) to interpret the impact of social security on saving, then omitting the private pension variable biases the estimate of a_s toward zero. The extent of the the bias depends on the degree of "integration" of the benefits of the two systems and on the extent to which private pension participation is discretionary.

Many recent empirical studies have tried to isolate the impact of pensions on the level of nonpension saving (using cross-section data) in models similar to (21) or (22). Estimating a version of (22) in level form, Feldstein and Pellechio (1979) found that an extra dollar of social security wealth reduced nonpension wealth by approximately a dollar, using data from the Federal Reserve Board's 1962 Survey of Consumer Finances; they had no data on private pensions. Some of their specifications also found a positive relationship between the ratio of net worth to permanent income and the level of permanent income. Using data from the Retirement History Survey, Diamond and Hausman (1984) found a social security offset of 30–50 cents (with a smaller nonpension wealth reduction for changes in private pension wealth). They also found evidence of a positive relationship between W/Y^* and Y^*.

Employing a logarithmic form of (22) for Canadian data, King and Dicks-Mireaux (1982) estimated the offset to nonpension wealth from a \$1 increase in social security wealth to be 24 cents (10 cents for private pensions), with offsets of approximately dollar for dollar for individuals in the top decile of the wealth distribution. Hubbard (1983) estimated a similar model for the United States (using data from the President's Commission on Pension Policy), finding a mean offset for social security wealth of 33 cents (16 cents for private pensions), with social security offsets in excess of dollar for dollar for those in the top decile of the wealth distribution.

Whether the versions of (21) and (22) used in the empirical studies described above can be justified according to a consistent set of economic assumptions depends on the structure of annuity markets and on whether or not a bequest motive exists. The basic model presented earlier assumes complete market failure in the private provision of annuities and the absence of a bequest motive. Theoretical possibilities encompass assumptions along the dimensions of "perfectness" of private annuity markets and the presence or absence of a bequest motive.

In addition, econometric estimates of the impact of private pension annuities on nonpension wealth accumulation as well as of the links between changes in social security annuities and private pension participation are necessary for an empirical consideration of the impact of the social security system on individual saving. The latter link is both important and not often noted. That annuity markets are extremely imperfect in the real world is not evidence per se of a severe market failure, as individuals have some control over their participation in private pensions either explicitly (for participants in defined contribution plans) or implicitly (through choice of employer). To the extent that individuals adjust their pensions for variation in social security annuities, the effective annuity market may be quite large. The magnitude of that adjustment must be resolved empirically.

As an empirical proposition, it is important to ascertain the degree of discretion in individual private pension plan participation. We can consider an auxiliary model of the form

(23)
$$\left(\frac{PPW}{Y^*}\right)_i = \gamma'Z_i - \psi_{ps}\left(\frac{SSW}{Y^*}\right)_i,$$

where ψ_{ps}, as before, represents the adjustment of private pension annuities to involuntary changes in social security annuities. Again, apart from issues of substitutability (i.e., if $\beta = 1$), a value of zero for ψ_{ps} indicates no discretion in pension participation; $\psi_{ps} = -1$ indicates complete discretion.

Given the assumption of market failure in the provision of nonpension annuities, four potential cases can be considered along the two dimensions of (1) bequest motives and (2) discretion in private pension participation. As a first case, suppose that there is no bequest motive and that private pension participation is exogenous to individual decisions. The offset to nonpension wealth of a change in compulsory social security annuities corresponds to the level described earlier; that is, the present value of anticipated (actuarially fair) social security benefits should displace nonpension wealth by more than dollar for dollar (in the absence of capital market restrictions). If effective replacement rates are nonlinear in earnings, high-income individuals are rationed in their access to social security annuities, and saving rates will rise with the level of permanent income.

Second, suppose that while there is no bequest motive, private pension participation is completely under individual control. In the limit, if private pension annuities are also actuarially fair ($\beta = 1$ in eq. [17]), there would be no restricted access to fair annuities, and W/Y^* would be independent of the level of Y^*. Involuntary increases in compulsory annuities (social security) would be completely reflected in reduced holdings of private pension annuities and not in the level of nonpension wealth. For intermediate versions of this second case, both a smaller offset to nonpension wealth from a change in social security benefits and a smaller effect of Y^* on W/Y^* would be expected relative to the first case.

The existence of a bequest motive changes the predicted effect of changes in compulsory social security annuities on the level of nonpension wealth and complicates the distinction of "annuity rationing" effects from the data. The third and fourth cases embody the sort of "bequest motive" described above, evidenced by levels of nonpension wealth realtive to permanent income that rise with permanent income.[28]

The third case is described by the existence of an operative bequest motive in conjunction with discretionary private pension participation.

In this case, involuntary changes in social security participation will have no impact on nonpension wealth; the changes are counteracted by offsetting movements in private pension holdings. With discretion in pension participation, there is no restriction of "fair" annuity purchases, so that a nonlinear relationship between W/Y^* and Y^* is traceable to the desire to leave bequests.

The fourth case combines a bequest motive with exogenous participation in private pensions. Again, the reduction in nonpension wealth attendant to an increase in holdings of social security annuities will be less than in the first case. An observation that saving rates out of permanent income increase with permanent income could reflect a combination of a bequest motive and rationed access to pension annuities.

The cases are summarized with respect to interpretations of the offset parameter a_s and nonlinearity of the ratio of nonpension wealth to permanent income with respect to permanent income in figures 7.1 and 7.2 below. Note that the predicted effects of changes in social security wealth and of changes in permanent income on individual wealth accumulation depend greatly on assumptions about bequest motives and on the size of the effective private annuity market afforded by access to private pensions. In reality, of course, the degree of discretion in private pension annuity holdings can vary anywhere between "none" and "complete." Estimation of the impact of changes in compulsory

	Complete Discretion in Pension	No Discretion in Pension
Bequest motive	$a_s = 0$	$a_s > 0$ but less than value below
No bequest motive	$a_s = 0$	$a_s > 1$

Fig. 7.1   Offset to Nonpension Wealth from Involuntary Increase in Social Security Annuities

	Complete Discretion in Pension	No Discretion in Pension
Bequest motive	Any nonlinearity due to bequest motive	Combination of annuity rationing and bequest motive
No bequest motive	W/Y^* independent of Y^*	Any nonlinearity due to annuity rationing

Fig. 7.2   Interpretation of Nonlinearity of W/Y^* with Respect to Y^*

social security annuities on holdings of private pension annuities (e.g., eq. [23] above) can help to allocate observed nonlinearities of saving rates with respect to the level of earnings between annuity rationing and bequest motives.[29]

The theoretical results in sections 7.2–7.4 and the summary of implications in figures 7.1 and 7.2 factilitate interpretation of the coefficients of (22). We can infer information about bequest motives and the impact of involuntary changes in social security annuities on nonpension wealth. First, consider the case in which the wealth-earnings relationship exhibits little nonlinearity in earnings. As ψ_{ps} approaches minus one, the model implies no bequest motive (of the sort outlined here) and no substantial impact of changes in social security on the level of nonpension wealth. As ψ_{ps} approaches zero, the implication of no bequest motive is joined by the prediction of a significant impact of a change in social security on nonpension wealth.

Second, suppose that the ratio of wealth to permanent income increases with permanent income. As ψ_{ps} approaches unity in absolute value, a bequest motive is ratified (since discretionary pensions provide an effective annuity market); the impact of involuntary changes in social security will fall almost entirely on holdings of private pension annuities. The closer is ψ_{ps} to zero, the greater will be the impact of changes in social security on nonpension wealth, so that the observed nonlinearity in the wealth-income relationship reflects both a bequest motive and incomplete access to retirement annuities outside social security.

7.6 Conclusions and Extensions

Assessing the impact of social security and private pensions on individual wealth accumulation is important for many analyses of welfare, capital formation, and equity in the distributions of income and wealth. Previous research efforts along the lines of Feldstein (1974) have addressed the funding status of social security and pensions. The focus here is on insurance features of pension annuities with respect to the problem of uncertainty over length of life.

The first part of the paper considers the introduction of social security into an economy with market failure in the provision of private annuities. The principal findings are three. First, in such a world, even an actuarially fair, fully funded social security system can substantially reduce individual saving, though individual welfare is initially improved. Hence, partial equilibrium estimates of the impact of social security on saving which rely solely on the extent to which individuals earn a more than fair return on social security are underestimates of the true effect.

Second, under current United States law, social security taxes and benefits are calculated only up to an earnings ceiling. High-income individuals have incomplete access to the social security annuity system. Hence, even in the absence of an explicit bequest motive, the ratio of wealth to lifetime earnings would rise with the level of lifetime earnings. Constrained access to publicly provided pension annuities may provide an impetus to the growth of private pension annuities.

Third, the partial equilibrium impact of social security and private pension annuities on nonpension saving is reduced when initial endowments are considered. For example, to the extent that the introduction of social security reduces the size of accidental bequests, the net effect of social security on the consumption of succeeding generations is mitigated. In addition, general equilibrium considerations, primarily the endogeneity of factor returns, can be expected to reverse part of the partial equilibrium impact. Because of these two considerations, the impact of social security on the steady-state capital stock is likely to be smaller than the partial equilibrium impact.

To provide an interpretation of econometric measures of the impact of pensions on nonpension saving, two additional considerations are important. Theoretical possibilities encompass assumptions along the dimensions of "perfectness" of private annuity markets (in this case, the ability to adjust private pension participation in response to involuntary changes in social security annuities) and the presence or absence of a bequest motive. Four cases are generated, as shown in figures 7.1 and 7.2 in the text. The predicted effects of changes in social security wealth and of changes in permanent income on individual wealth accumulation depend on assumptions about bequest motives and on the size of the effective private annuity market afforded by access to private pensions.

Three immediate extensions to the models presented here are left as tasks for future research. First, when capital-market imperfections are added to the model, so that nonpension wealth is required to be nonnegative in all periods, the impact of social security on lifetime consumption is reduced substantially. Significant welfare gains may be achievable by changing the structure of the payroll tax so as to shift intertemporally the burden of payroll taxation over the life cycle (see the discussion in Hubbard and Judd, 1985). Second, additional research is needed on private annuity markets to determine the actual extent of market failure. Finally, given the current political environment, introducing uncertainty over future social security benefits may be appropriate. That uncertainty would modify the wealth impacts derived here.

The debate over the influence of pensions on individual saving brings together questions of consumer choice under uncertainty and the effectiveness of fiscal policy. Researching the relationships among social security, private pensions, annuity markets, and bequests facilitates close empirical scrutiny of models of individual and aggregate saving, permitting consideration of the welfare effects of compulsory pensions.

In addition, while this paper has concentrated on annuity insurance, similar approaches could be used to study the impacts of other social insurance programs on national saving.

Notes

1. Earlier studies for private pensions include those of Cagan (1965), Katona (1964), and Munnell (1974). Feldstein's results have by no means gone unchallenged; see, e.g., Leimer and Lesnoy (1982) and the reply in Feldstein (1982). Microeconomic (cross-section) evidence has generally been supportive of the proposition that social security has reduced individual saving. See Feldstein and Pellechio (1979), Kotlikoff (1979b), Blinder, Gordon, and Wise (1981), Diamond and Hausman (1984), King and Dicks-Mireaux (1982), and Hubbard (1983).

2. Empirical tests of the life-cycle model under certainty have tested the hypothesis of a hump-shaped wealth-age profile, but results have by no means unambiguously validated the model. See, e.g., White (1978), Mirer (1979), and Kurz (1981). Even after controlling for the effects of permanent income, Blinder et al. (1981), Diamond and Hausman (1984), King and Dicks-Mireaux (1982), and Hubbard (1983) found results only mildly supportive of the basic theory. Other studies have addressed the possibility of other motives for saving. Kotlikoff and Summers (1981) reject the ability of the life-cycle model to explain wealth accumulation in the United States, putting forth a major role for bequests.

3. Abel (1985) takes up the intergenerational consequences of this point in a 2-period overlapping-generations model, with the implication that the insurance features of social security may reduce inequality in the distribution of wealth.

4. The precise direction of the influence of this uncertainty for saving is unclear. Heightened uncertainty over the length of life may lead to more saving (because of a longer than expected lifetime) or to less saving (to maintain present consumption). In the argument of Yaari (1965), two individuals with identical tastes, income, and investment opportunities are compared. The difference between them is that one lives T periods for certain while the other faces an uncertain lifetime of t periods, up to a maximum of T periods. Given a shorter expected life, uncertainty over length of life unambiguously leads to increased initial consumption. Champernowne (1969) and Levhari and Mirman (1977), on the other hand, consider two agents with identical expected lives but differing in the distribution of length of life. In either case, the impact of uncertainty over the length of life on wealth accumulation of a risk-averse individual is ambiguous and depends on the parameters of the model.

5. Note that this does not require that they *actually* die at the same time.

6. Rothschild and Stiglitz (1976) show that there will be no "pooling equilibrium," where all buy the same contract. They illustrate conditions under which a "separating equilibrium" occurs, in which different contracts are purchased by the risk groups. Following their argument and that of Riley (1979), if there is a fairly continuous distribution of survival probabilities, there is little hope for an equilibrium. Eckstein et al. (1985) consider the Pareto-improving potential of mandatory social security in the context of market failure in competitive insurance markets in the presence of adverse selection.

7. Previous work in this area in the context of pensions includes the contributions of Davies (1981) and Sheshinski and Weiss (1981). Davies used a life-cycle model under uncertain lifetime to address the phenomenon of slow dissaving in retirement. The presence of pensions in his simulation model (using Canadian data) reduced, but by no means eliminated, the effect of uncertainty on retirement consumption. In the model of Sheshinski and Weiss, the ultimate impact of social security on saving depends on the availability of a private annuity market. (The problem will arise here in sec. 7.4 in the context of discretion in private pension participation.) They found that, at the optimum, Yaari's (1965) result holds, namely, that private savings are reserved for bequests, while social security benefits are used to finance retirement consumption.

8. The actuarially fair benefit is constructed with respect to economy-wide survival probabilities. It is true that individuals who believe they will die "young" will want to purchase less than the "average optimal" amount of social security annuities, while those who expect to live a long time will want more. Both groups are better off, however, with the mandatory social security than without it, since in its absence, adverse selection is assumed to foreclose the possibility of a market of private annuities. A discussion of the potential separating equilibria in the private provision of annuities which may arise after the imposition of mandatory social security is given in Eckstein et al. (1985).

9. While the imposition of the social security system increases lifetime resources, nothing has been said about the optimal tax rate. Current law prohibits the explicit leverage of anticipated social security benefits. The ability to implicitly borrow against future benefits will depend on differences in w_0 (differences in ability to procure "unsecured" loans). Under the assumption of complete (explicit and implict) nonmarketability of benefits, we can demonstrate that there is an interior solution ($0 < t_s < 1$) for the individual's optimal tax rate (a sufficient statistic of participation as long as benefits are actuarially fair). The intuition is that while the purchase of "social security retirement annuities" increases resources available in old age, it decreases the resources available for current consumption.

10. Uncertainty over future social security benefits would mitigate the effect shown here. Watson (1982) discusses the influence of uncertainty over benefits in assessing the impact of social security on saving. Merton et al. (1984) show that many private pension integration arrangements remove much of this uncertainty.

11. A retirement age of 65 was assumed. Probabilities for survival were taken from Faber (1982).

12. This effect is most pronounced in the absence of explicit capital-market restrictions. With no initial endowment (and, hence, binding restrictions on the nonmarketability of social security when young), relative impacts on "working-period" and "retirement-period" consumption will depend on the relationship of the individual's actual and optimal tax rate (participation). The importance of (accidental) bequests as intergenerational links will be discussed later.

13. This nonlinearity has surfaced in some recent studies of the impact of social security on saving. See, e.g., Diamond and Hausman (1982) and Hubbard (1983).

14. For a more complete discussion of the implications of the choice of parameter values, see Levhari and Mirman (1977) or Davies (1981).

15. As in table 7.1, survival probabilities are taken from Faber (1982).

16. Note that if participation in social security is rationed by income, low-income individuals have more of their retirement dissaving in the form of reduction in the value of their social security annuity than do high-income

individuals. This analysis assumes that annuity and non-annuity holdings are perfect substitutes in dissaving. The studies cited in the beginning of the paper have found good but not perfect substitutability of social security for nonpension wealth in accumulation. Empirical evidence in Hubbard (1986) suggests that the substitutability is greatest for high-income individuals.

17. In a world with capital-market restrictions, then, a social security system of this type may *increase* saving, since received initial bequests are more liquid than anticipated social security benefits. The impact of social security on intergenerational transfers is an important component of the system's net effect on individual saving.

18. The implicit assumption, of course, is that the parent dies at the beginning of the child's (optimizing) life, age 20 here. This assumption is made to highlight the point that the existence of social security for the previous generation mitigates the impact of the present generation's participation in social security on its own wealth accumulation. More general assumptions about the timing of a testator's death would complicate expressions like (14) in the text, but the qualitative point would remain.

19. This damping through intergenerational transfers of the impact of social security on wealth accumulation is mitigated if "children" earn more on average than their "parents" (because of productivity growth).

20. The consumption of individuals of each age can be calculated from eq. (18a) and (18b), given the initial wage. The growth rate of the population will determine the relative number of persons at each age. Aggregate consumption can be calculated by summing consumption over ages, weighted by the relative population size.

21. Kotlikoff's (1979a) analysis also incorporates the influence of social security on retirement age, which is taken as exogenous here. To the extent that social security lowers the desired retirement age, the partial equilibrium wealth replacement effect of social security on saving is dampened.

22. The calculation was performed as follows. Let Y, YL, and n represent total income, labor income, and the population growth rate, respectively; then

$$\frac{C}{Y} = \left(\frac{YL}{Y}\right)\left(\frac{C}{YL}\right)$$

$$= \frac{2}{3}\left[\frac{\left(\sum_{i=0}^{Q}\left(\frac{1+g}{1+r}\right)^i\right)\left(\sum_{i=0}^{D'}((1+g)(1+n))^{-i}\left(\frac{1+r}{1+\delta}\right)^{\frac{i}{1-\gamma}}(1-p_i)^{\frac{1}{i\gamma}}\right)}{(1+r)^{\frac{i\gamma}{1-\gamma}}(1+\delta)^{\frac{-i}{1-\gamma}}(1-p_i)^{\frac{1}{1-\gamma}}}\right].$$

Given the assumed values for g, r, n, and δ in the text, $\frac{C}{\gamma} \cong 0.82$.

23. The idea here is that an individual who thinks he will live a long time would buy several small annuities rather than one large one in order to misrepresent his assessment of his longevity. Companies know his participation in social security, but not the extent to which he has obtained insurance from other private sources. Pauly (1974) and Wilson (1977) discuss certain situations in which market equilibria might occur after a compulsory insurance program is imposed.

24. Lazear (1983) has focused particularly on this point, emphasizing the role of pensions in influencing turnover, retirement, and investment in human capital. Many arguments for the existence of private pensions have emphasized their favorable federal tax treatment. Tax treatment cannot be the complete explanation, since defined contribution plans would dominate. Defined benefit

plans are instead prevalent. Munnell (1982) emphasizes both the tax benefits (to employers and to employees) and the inadequacy of social security in explaining the growth of private pension plans.

25. This ignores the possibility that firms may be willing to offer "more than fair" plans to achieve some other impact on worker behavior. See Lazear (1983).

26. This is just the characteristic of "integration" of the benefits of social security and private pension annuities. Since the passage of the Revenue Act of 1942, Congress has allowed public (social security) and private benefits to be considered together in determining whether a private plan discriminates in favor of low-income workers. For descriptions of typical integration provisions and discussions of their prevalence in the United States pension system, see Munnell (1982) and Kotlikoff and Smith (1983).

27. Note that empirical evidence of saving rates increasing with income does not validate the hypothesis the bequests are a luxury good (even if data on bequests are known), because of, among other things, rationing of the purchase of pension annuities by income.

28. Such a bequest motive is usually grounded in work in the human capital literature (see, e.g., Becker and Tomes 1976, 1979). That is, if human capital investment initially yields a higher rate of return than that on financial assets, parents who "care" about their children invest first in human capital up to the level at which the returns to additional investment just equal the market return. Further transfers are exclusively financial. Hence observed (financial) bequests will be higher for children whose parents had significant resources than for children with access to low parental resources. Despite serious data limitations, there have been some recent efforts to estimate the relationship between bequests and lifetime resources. The finding that the ratio of bequests to earnings rises with the level of earnings is corroborated in the careful empirical study of Menchik and David (1983).

29. The problem of isolating a relationship between wealth (or bequests) and lifetime resources is further complicated by the fact that price effects may be present as well (e.g., a correlation between earnings and after-tax financial returns). Government retirement saving policy can bring about those price effects—e.g., tax-favored treatment of IRAs and Keogh plans (see Hubbard 1984). To the extent that changes in government pension policy involve trade-offs among policy options (e.g., liberalized ceilings on tax-deductible IRA or Keogh contributions in exchange for a reduction in social security benefits), the stability of any observed relationship between wealth and earnings is all the more tenuous.

References

Abel, A. B. 1985. Precautionary saving and accidental bequests. American Economic Review 75:777–91.

Barro, R. J. 1974. Are government bonds net wealth? *Journal of Political Economy* 82:1095–1117.

———. 1978. *The impact of social security on private savings: Evidence from the U.S. time series*. Washington: American Enterprise Institute for Public Policy Research.

Barro, R. J., and Friedman, J. W. 1977. On uncertain lifetimes. *Journal of Political Economy* 85:843–49.

Becker, G. S., and Tomes, N. 1976. Child endowments and the quantity and quality of children. *Journal of Political Economy* 84 (p. 2): S143–S162.

———. 1979. An equilibrium theory of the distribution of income and inter-generational mobility. *Journal of Political Economy* 87:1153–89.

Blinder, A. S.; Gordon, R. H.; and Wise, D. E. 1981. Social security, bequests, and the life cycle theory of saving: cross-sectional tests. Working Paper no. 619. National Bureau of Economic Research.

Cagan, P. 1965. *The effect of pension plans on aggregate saving: Evidence from a sample survey.* Occasional Paper 95. New York: Columbia University Press (for NBER).

Champernowne, D. G. 1969. *Uncertainty and estimation in economics.* San Francisco: Holden Day.

Davies, J. B. 1981. Uncertain lifetime, consumption, and dissaving in retirement. *Journal of Political Economy* 89:561–78.

Diamond, P. A. 1977. A framework for social security analysis. *Journal of Public Economics* 8:275–98.

Diamond, P. A., and Hausman, J. A. 1984. Individual retirement and savings behavior. *Journal of Public Economics* 23:81–114.

Eckstein, Z.; Eichenbaum, M.; and Peled, D. 1985. Uncertain lifetimes and welfare enhancing properties of annuity markets and social security. *Journal of Public Economics* 26:303–26.

Faber, J. F. 1982. *Life tables for the United States: 1900–2050.* United States Department of Health and Human Services, Social Security Administration. Actuarial Study no. 87.

Farber, H. S. 1978. Individual preferences and union wage determination: The case of the United Mine Workers. *Journal of Political Economy* 86:923–42.

Feldstein, M. S. 1974. Social security, induced retirement and aggregate capital accumulation. *Journal of Political Economy* 82:905–26.

———. 1982. Social security and private saving: Reply. *Journal of Political Economy* 90:630–41.

Feldstein, M. S., and Pellechio, A. J. 1979. Social security and household wealth accumulation: New microeconomic evidence. *Review of Economics and Statistics* 61:361–68.

Friend, I., and Blume, M. E. 1975. The demand for risky assets. *American Economic Review* 65:900–22.

Hubbard, R. G. 1984. Do IRAs and Keoghs increase saving? *National Tax Journal* 37:43–54.

———. 1983. *The financial impacts of social security: A study of effects on household wealth accumulation and allocation.* Monograph 1983–3. Monograph Series in Finance and Economics, Salomon Brothers Center for the Study of Financial Institutions, New York University.

———. 1986. Pension wealth and individual saving: Some new evidence. *Journal of Money, Credit, and Banking* 18:167–68.

Hubbard, R. G., and Judd, K. L. 1985. Social security and individual welfare: Precautionary saving, borrowing constraints and the payroll tax. NBER Working Paper 1736.

Hurd, M. D., and Shoven, J. B. 1983. The distributional impact of social security. NBER Working Paper 1155. June.

Katona, G. 1964. *The Mass-Consumption Society.* New York: McGraw-Hill.

King, M. A., and Dicks-Mireaux, L. 1982. Asset holdings and the life cycle. *Economic Journal* 92:247–67.

Kotlikoff, L. J. 1979a. Social security and equilibrium capital intensity. *Quarterly Journal of Economics* 94:233–53.
———. 1979b. Testing the theory of social security and life cycle accumulation. *American Economic Review* 69:396–410.
Kotlikoff, L. J., and Smith, D. E. eds. 1983. *Pensions in the American economy*. Chicago: University of Chicago Press.
Kotlikoff, L. J. and Spivak, A. 1981. The family as an incomplete annuities market. *Journal of Political Economy* 89:371–91.
Kotlikoff, L. J., and Summers, L. H. 1981. The role of intergenerational transfers in aggregate capital accumulation. *Journal of Political Economy* 90:706–32.
Kurz, M. 1981. The life-cycle hypothesis and the effects of social security and private pensions on family savings. Technical Report no. 335 (rev.). Institute for Mathematical Studies in the Social Sciences, Stanford University. December.
Lazear, E. P. 1983. Incentive effects of pensions. NBER Working Paper 1126.
Leimer, D. R., and Lesnoy, S. D. 1982. Social security and private saving: New time-series evidence. *Journal of Political Economy* 90:606–29.
Levhari, D. and Mirman, L. 1977. Savings and consumption with an uncertain horizon. *Journal of Political Economy* 85:265–81.
Menchik, P. L., and David, M. 1983. Income distribution, lifetime savings, and bequests. *American Economic Review* 73:672–90.
Merton, R. C. 1983. On the role of social security as a means for efficient risk-bearing in an economy where human capital is not tradeable. In *Financial aspects of the United States pension system*. ed. Z. Bodie and J. B. Shoven. Chicago: University of Chicago Press.
Merton, R. C.; Bodie, Z.; and Marcus, A. J. 1984. Pension plan integration as insurance against social security risk. In this volume.
Mirer, T. W. 1979. The wealth-age relationship among the aged. *American Economic Review* 69:435–43.
Modigliani, F. and Ando, A. 1957. Tests of the life-cycle hypothesis of savings. *Bulletin of the Oxford Institute of Economics and Statistics* 19:99–124.
Modigliani, F. and Brumberg, R. 1954. Utility analysis and the consumption function: An interpretation of cross-section data. In *Post-Keynesian economics*, ed. K. Kurihara. New Brunswick; N.J.: Rutgers University Press.
Munnell, A. 1982. *The economics of private pensions*. Washington; Brookings Institution.
———. 1974. *The effects of social security on personal saving*. Cambridge, Mass.: Ballinger.
Pauly, M. V. 1974. Overinsurance and public provision of insurance: the role of moral hazard and adverse selection. *Quarterly journal of Economics* 88:44–54.
Riley, J. G. 1979. Informational equilibrium. *Econometrica* 47:331–59.
Rothschild, M., and Stiglitz, J. E. 1976. Equilibrium in competitive insurance markets: an essay on the economics of imperfect information. *Quarterly Journal of Economics* 90:629–50.
Sheshinski, E., and Weiss, Y. 1981. Uncertainty and optimal social security systems. *Quarterly Journal of Economics* 96:189–206.
Watson, H. 1982. Saving, social security, and uncertainty. *Southern Economic Journal* 49:330–41.
White, B. B. 1978. Empirical tests of the life-cycle hypothesis. *American Economic Review* 68:547–60.

Wilson, C. 1977. A model of insurance markets with incomplete information. *Journal of Economic Theory* 16:167–207.

Yaari, M. E. 1965. Uncertain lifetime, life insurance, and the theory of the consumer. *Review of Economic Studies* 32:137–58.

Comment   Olivia S. Mitchell

In recent years there has been a great deal of attention devoted to the effect of social security on savings, initiated primarily by Martin Feldstein's seminal paper 10 years ago on this topic. The paper I am to discuss today is very much in the mainstream tradition. Hubbard's goal is to discuss the implications of new theoretical structures for empirical modeling of the effect of social security on savings. The paper does not actually report estimates; instead Hubbard refers readers to others' work as well as to his own previous papers.

In commenting on this paper, I wish to focus on one empirical and two theoretical matters that I believe warrant further attention, given the proliferation of studies following Feldstein's. Regarding theory, two matters deserving more discussion are the nature of uncertainty modeled, and the degree to which theoretical models are informative about economic institutions they purport to explain. Regarding empirics, I will focus on the econometric links between theoretically preferred savings functions and equations usually used for empirical estimation. Each point is taken up in turn.

7.C.1   The Nature of Uncertainty in Social Security/Savings Models

In this paper Hubbard contrasts the life-cycle consumption path arising in a certainty world with that arising when the consumer is uncertain about when he will die. This type of uncertainty is tractable in the standard life-cycle framework, for it reduces to an additional discount factor in the lifetime utility function. As in his previous working paper, Hubbard posits a utility function separable across periods and with constant relative risk aversion. The only argument affecting utility is consumption; retirement is assumed to be exogenous.

Hubbard's findings in this setup seem sensible given earlier work he cites by Kotlikoff and Spivak (1981), Sheshinski and Weiss (1981), and Eckstein et al. (1985). If no annuities are available, people will oversave for retirement so that they do not outlive their assets. If fair public or private annuities are available, individuals smooth consumption by buying insurance (where the demand for insurance depends on interest and

Olivia S. Mitchell is associate professor of labor economics, Cornell University, and research associate, National Bureau of Economic Research.

time preference rates, risk aversion, and expected mortality patterns). An institution enabling risk-averse individuals to avoid "living too long" increases lifetime utility and consumption as compared to the no-insurance case; thus insurance will reduce lifetime savings. Thus on theoretical grounds, Hubbard predicts that an actuarially fair social insurance system reduces savings.

One question arises at this juncture: What has been sacrificed to generate unambiguous theoretical predictions regarding the effect of a social insurance scheme on savings? To begin with, I would find useful some sensitivity analysis using other functional forms for the utility function (e.g., what happens if utility includes leisure as well as consumption), the tax structure (e.g., what happens if taxes are progressive), and so forth.

Equally important, I question whether uncertainty about when one will die is one of the more important and/or interesting forms of uncertainty older individuals face. The answer appears to be both yes and no. Practically speaking, fear of living too long does seem to motivate a great deal of behavior including the peculiar savings patterns detected among older workers by Kotlikoff et al. (1982). On the other hand, this is only one of several types of uncertainty-generating savings behavior. Champernowne's model (1969), as in Levhari and Mirman (1977), considers differences across individuals in the distribution of the length of life. Watson (1982) and Merton (in this volume) build in uncertainty over wages, prices, and even future social security benefits. Many analysts in the implicit contracts literature emphasize uncertainty over work productivity, perhaps because of health surprises or macroeconomic surprises (e.g., Nalebuff and Zeckhauser 1985). Not least important is the fact that many private pensions are underfunded, which burdens workers with different types of uncertainty.

No doubt most listeners could extend this tabulation of sources of uncertainty not included in Hubbard's current model. Even if we stop here, however, including just these features would already complicate matters so greatly that the ability to make clear-cut predictions probably would be lost. For instance, it appears that allowing for variability in social insurance benefit levels means that such a system will have an ambiguous effect on savings; so too does allowing somewhat different formulations of mortality patterns. The point is that, in this case, simple theory generates unambiguous predictions—and yet the simple theory is far removed from processes generating empirical data.

A purist coming to this conclusion would of course give up further prospect of empirical work, and perhaps this is the shortest path to heaven. On the other hand, Hubbard (and I) would actually like to evaluate how social insurance schemes affect savings—theoretically and quantitatively. What can be done?

At this juncture, I believe that a most useful product would be a paper which systematically and carefully examines the implications of various kinds of annuity structures on savings, using several different formulations of uncertainty. I have earlier alluded to studies which could be used as pieces of the larger puzzle; there are no doubt others. The first goal of such a project would be to derive savings functions under alternative scenarios which could then be compared across model types, as Hubbard has begun to do with one particular uncertainty setup. A second goal would be to assess whether these savings functions (a) generate testable implications for empirical work, and (b) enable the econometrician to determine which model(s) is (are) more compatible with the data. I believe that the time is right for such a comprehensive exercise, ten years after Feldstein's seminal piece.

7.C.2   The Link Between Theory and Institutions

Pressing further in the quest for empirically testable models of social security and savings, I turn now to a discussion of several facts about the world generating the data before us. One problem is that the social security system as it exists in the United States is far from the actuarially neutral insurance plan Hubbard models. Since its inception, social security has operated as an underfunded "pay-as-you-go" method of transferring income across generations. Hurd and Shoven (1985) find that current retirees receive a positive real rate of return of well over 5%, implying that contributions to social security were a better investment than any other financial asset for that generation. In addition, half of all money contributed to social security avoided income taxes (until 1983), another factor making social security appealing as a savings vehicle. Under these circumstances, I would rephrase Hubbard's question: Why did people save anything at all, outside of the social security system? Most current retirees are not at the benefit maximum and could have saved more via social security. In general, models which assume an actuarially neutral social insurance scheme cannot begin to explain savings patterns over the last 40 years.

Another fact that should be recognized in empirically motivated theory is that retirement behavior is endogenous. Hubbard's model, like many in the public finance literature, assumes that one's retirement age is not subject to choice. This simplification is clearly useful since it generates unambiguous theoretical predictions. On the other hand, a more general framework could easily reverse his conclusions. For instance, workers might retire earlier and consume more leisure rather than reducing savings when social security comes into play. Research by Crawford and Lilien (1981) is informative along these lines. The point, of course, is that allowing retirement to be endogenous may weaken or even break the link between social security and savings, a conclusion that empiricists should recognize.

A third and related fact that an applied theorist should include in modeling is that an individual's wealth value of pensions and social security depends on when he retires. Many analysts have overlooked this institutional fact because existing data sets make it difficult to see. However, my own work with Gary Fields (1984) shows that social security wealth for the average 60-year-old in our LRHS sample was only 70% as large as it would have been if the worker waited to retire until age 65. Nonneutral patterns show up in private pensions as well; for instance, the pension wealth for a retiree at age 65 was 80% smaller than pension wealth at age 60 in our sample of covered workers. These total income values were computed for the *same* person at two different points in time, so they are not contaminated by selectivity bias present in self-reporting data. Using other data, Kotlikoff and Wise (in this volume) indicate similar patterns. Theoretical models should allow for these nonneutralities so that estimating equations using actual wealth values move beyond single "social security and pension wealth" variables.

7.C.3 Econometric Links

Hubbard's theoretical model generates two savings equations labeled (11a) and (11b) in his paper. Generally speaking, the dependent variable in each case is the ratio of accumulated wealth at time t, to lifetime earnings. Explanatory variables include lifetime pension and social security savings, which enter nonlinearly along with interest rate and other parameters. The form of the function should vary before and after retirement, which accounts for the two savings equations.

Empirical studies in this genre never really confront these equations (or even facsimiles thereof) with data. Instead, linearizations such as Hubbard's equation (15) are employed, where nonpension wealth values are regressed on arbitrary measures of pension wealth and other variables. Hubbard's model should be applauded for including the private pension term since many earlier formulations have ignored this important form of saving. However, the fact remains that the econometric links between theory and data are weak. For instance, theory nowhere motivates the addition of an error term. In addition he explicitly notes that theory does not imply that right-hand-side variables should enter additively. A great deal of work remains to be done in carefully linking theory and data.

7.C.4 Concluding Remarks

Feldstein's model of social security and savings has attained its tenth birthday in good health, judging from the important and interesting extensions that writers such as Hubbard are devising. Hubbard's paper is indeed a contribution to this growing field; worth special mention is his recognition of the jointness in social security, private pension, and other asset accumulation decisions. I especially liked his suggestion that private pensions may be integrated with social security benefit formulas to avoid "annuity rationing." More implications should be teased out of the framework in order to explain the data, and I am sure Hubbard will do so in future work.

I would also encourage analysts to cast wider nets if they wish to understand the quantitative effects of social security on savings. It is simpler not to focus on all of the different forms of uncertainty affecting older individuals' behavior, and the institutional features of social security and pensions as well. On the other hand, an empiricist must concern himself with the processes actually generating data.

I would like to add one more suggestion in closing. To date, apparently no empirical study has explored how savings patterns respond to realizations of uncertainty through time. It seems quite important to embed empirical savings models in a dynamic context. This type of analysis would be a valuable and welcome extension of Feldstein's seminal work.

References

Crawford, V., and Lilien, D. 1981. Social security and the retirement decision. *Quarterly Journal of Economics* 96:505–29.

Fields, G., and Mitchell, O. 1984. *Retirement, pensions and social security.* MIT Press.

Hurd, M., and Shoven, J. 1985. The distributional impact of social security. In *Pensions, labor, and individual choice,* ed. D. Wise. Chicago: University of Chicago Press.

Kotlikoff, L.; Spivak, A.; and Summers, L. 1982. The adequacy of savings. *American Economic Review* 72:1056–69.

Nalebuff, B., and Zeckhauser, R. 1985. Pensions and the retirement decision. In *Pensions, labor, and individual choice,* ed. D. Wise. Chicago: University of Chicago Press.

Watson, H. 1982. Saving, social security and uncertainty. *Southern Economic Journal* 49:330–41.

8   Annuity Markets, Savings, and the Capital Stock

Laurence J. Kotlikoff, John B. Shoven, and Avia Spivak

8.1 Introduction

This paper examines how the availability of annuities affects savings and inequality in economies in which neither private nor public pensions exist initially. The absence of widespread market or government annuity insurance clearly describes many less developed countries in the world today; it was also characteristic of virtually all countries prior to World War II. While there is now a considerable body of literature addressing the savings impact of funding or not funding government pensions (Barro 1974; Feldstein 1974; and numerous others), the effect of the insurance provision per se has received less attention.

Sheshinski and Weiss (1981) is the first analysis of the pure insurance effects of social security on national saving. They demonstrate that when private arrangements are unavailable, the government's provision of fully funded old age annuities alters household consumption possibilities. In their model in which agents have a bequest motive, the short-run saving impact of such provision is ambiguous. Hubbard (1983) points out that this provision unambiguously reduces national saving if agents have no bequest motive. Fuller descriptions of life cycle (zero

Laurence J. Kotlikoff is professor of economics, Boston University, and research associate, National Bureau of Economic Research. John B. Shoven is professor of economics, Stanford University, and research associate, National Bureau of Economic Research. Avia Spivak is senior lecturer, Department of Economics, Ben Gurion University, and visiting professor, Department of Economics, University of Pennsylvania.

This paper was originally prepared for presentation at the Econometric Society Winter Meetings, December 28–30, 1983, San Francisco. We thank Zvi Eckstein, Truman Bewley, Linus Yamane, and Ludo Van der Heyden for very helpful discussions and Linus Yamane for excellent research assistance. The research reported here is part of the NBER's research program in pensions. Any opinions expressed are those of the authors and not those of the National Bureau of Economic Research.

bequest motive) economies in the absence of annuity insurance are presented in Eckstein et al. (1985) and Abel (1985). Both papers independently derived the stochastic steady state properties of economies in which agents involuntarily leave bequests to their children. Abel also considers the effects of introducing a fully funded social security system into such an economy; his chief finding is that such a policy reduces savings.[1]

The assumption entertained by Eckstein et al. (1985) and Abel (1985) that completely selfish parents with no interest in their children leave involuntary bequests to their own children seems rather arbitrary. Clearly parents have the option to bequeath their wealth to surviving spouses, friends, other relatives, or charitable organizations. In addition, the notion that bequests are completely involuntary seems implausible. An alternative assumption is that selfish parents and selfish children collectively pool the risks of the parents' date of death in a manner that is mutually advantageous. There are three reasons why cooperative (voluntary) risk pooling seems a more realistic assumption. First, cooperative risk pooling Pareto dominates noncooperative behavior. Second, as described in Kotlikoff and Spivak (1981), the risks of uncertain longevity appear to be very large; the amount of resources that mildly risk-averse, selfish individuals would surrender to have access to fair annuity insurance is potentially quite sizable. This suggests a very substantial demand for market insurance if selfish parents cannot make comparable risk-pooling arrangements with their children, friends, or other relatives. Third, pooling longevity risk with even a single child can capture a large fraction of the gains from perfect insurance (Kotlikoff and Spivak 1981); hence, such risk pooling with children appears well "worth the trouble," with the gains far exceeding any reasonable transaction costs.

This paper models cooperative risk pooling of selfish parents and children taking into account the arrival of future selfish family members, namely, unborn grandchildren, great grandchildren, great great grandchildren, and so on. At each point in time the anticipated arrival of additional agents with whom young family members can share risks influences the set of current risk-sharing arrangements that are of mutual advantage to young and old family members. As a consequence the solution to the bargaining problem between currently living family members takes account of the infinite sequence of bargains struck by family descendants.

In addition to modeling the process of sequential generational risk sharing, we calculate, for the CES utility function, the stochastic steady state level and distribution of wealth. These calculations suggest that perfecting annuity insurance can have major impacts on national savings. For our preferred set of parameter values, the introduction of perfect annuity insurance reduces wealth by 35%–60% in the long run. The exact percentage reduction in savings within this range depends on assumptions about the cooperative bargaining solution. These figures are large, and larger still if one assumes a greater degree of risk aversion.

Given our parameterization of preferences, the 35%–60% range should, however, be viewed as an upper bound for the impact of introducing what amounts to a fully funded social security system in an economy with family risk sharing. There are two reasons why these figures are likely to considerably overestimate the actual outcome. First, they are partial equilibrium estimates, that is, they do not take account of potential changes in factor prices (wages and interest rates) that would arise, in a closed economy, from a major reduction in national wealth. Such price changes can significantly dampen savings reductions in models of this kind. Second, in order to highlight the impact of insurance provision, we assume that at most two family members are alive simultaneously. This generates the smallest possible risk sharing within families. Obviously, a sufficiently large number of family members is capable of pooling virtually all risks of uncertain longevity. With large enough families sharing mortality risks, the effect on aggregate wealth of perfecting insurance provision could be quite small.

While these numbers are partial equilibrium estimates and intentionally biased upward by our modeling of family size, they are surprisingly large relative to our prior beliefs. They suggest that the insurance aspects of social security are potentially as important in altering national savings as is the method of social security finance. It is also worth pointing out that the transition to the full annuity insurance equilibrium is completed once the initial generation of young family members reach old age. In real time, this is 40–50 years, but one would expect to see most of the ultimate change in savings occurring within the first 20 years. A final point that aids in evaluating these findings is that full insurance, while generating a Pareto-efficient steady state, may involve a steady state level of welfare that is lower than the minimum level of welfare in the family insurance stochastic steady state. This somewhat paradoxical result is explained as follows: the provision of full insurance transfers resources to the first cohort of elderly at the expense of initial young and future generations. While the new steady state is efficient, it has a smaller stock of resources, in this case capital, because of the initial transfer. This transfer to the initial elderly is not effected by explicit redistribution across age groups. It arises more subtly, namely, from the inability of young family members to continue selling insurance to their parents in exchange for their parents' potential bequests. Rather than bargain at less than fair insurance terms with children, provision of perfect annuities, which involves each cohort's pooling risk with its own members, permits the initial generation of elderly to consume at a higher rate. The initial set of children as well as all future generations are better off because of the perfection of the insurance market, but worse off because they no longer receive inheritances. Since all children in this paper are born with identical endowments, eliminating inheritances by providing perfect insurance also eliminates inequality.

The next section presents the infinite-horizon bargaining model; the zero bargaining, involuntary bequests model is also presented for purposes of comparison. This section also describes the algorithm used to solve the bargaining problem. Section 8.3 discusses the process of wealth transmission in the stochastic steady state. Section 8.4 compares long-run stocks of wealth under (1) perfect annuity markets, (2) three alternative parent-child bargaining solutions, and (3) no-insurance arrangements with involuntary transfers made to children. This section also considers how the presence of additional children would alter the findings. Section 8.5 summarizes the paper and discusses ideas for additional research.

8.2 The Model

As a prelude to presenting the selfish family, infinite-horizon bargaining problem, this section briefly reviews wealth accumulation under perfect annuity markets. In the subsequent modeling of family risk sharing, each selfish parent reaches a bargain with a single selfish child regarding the risk of long life. This is the simplest of family structures, but the associated intergenerational bargaining problem remains moderately complicated. The final part of this section describes how our stylized economy operates when family bequest-annuity agreements do not exist, but where involuntary bequests are made to children as in Eckstein et al. (1985) and Abel (1985). In this case it is everyone for himself; that is, there are no risk-pooling opportunities to ameliorate the risk of long life.

In comparing the economy under these three insurance arrangements—perfect insurance, self-insurance between parent and child, and no insurance—it is important to distinguish between transition effects and steady state comparisons. Clearly, if we move from no insurance to a family deal or from a family bargain to perfect insurance, the first generation gains. These gains are due to the fact that the generation alive during the switch received an inheritance from its parent but gives none or one of smaller expected value to its children. Kotlikoff and Spivak (1981) estimated that these gains to the first generation could be very substantial. For instance, consider a completely selfish 55-

year-old male who gains no pleasure from leaving bequests and whose time-separable consumption preferences are isoelastic, with a relative risk aversion coefficient of .75. This individual would consider the introduction of a perfect annuities market equivalent to an increase in his (her) wealth of 47%; with perfect annuities, there is no need to maintain precautionary balances to provide for an extraordinarily long life, and the individual can, therefore, enjoy a higher consumption stream for the remainder of his (her) life. The gains to those who first get access to a perfect annuities market increase with the age and degree of risk aversion of the individual. For uninsured individuals the gains to deals within the family are also large. With two participants the gain is roughly half that offered by perfect insurance, and with three it is roughly 70% as great. Hence, one would also expect significant start-up gains in moving from zero to family insurance.

This paper, in contrast to Kotlikoff and Spivak (1981), concentrates on steady state comparisons of the three insurance environments. In the case of family insurance we look at situations where a parent is insuring with a child, the child later makes a deal with his child, and so on. The analysis of aggregate wealth requires consideration of the entire family history of insurance arrangements and mortality experience. Obviously, the consumption and saving of current family members depends on their inherited wealth, which depends on the sequence of wealth and death dates of all previous ancestors.

There are 4 periods of life in this model. People live with certainty for the first 3 periods and survive to the fourth with probability P. So, the fraction $(1 - P)$ of the population live only 3 periods, while P live 4 periods. Children are 1 period when their parents are 3. Any negotiation or deal, explicit or implicit, between parent and child takes place before the parent and child engage in their respective third- and first-period consumption.

Individuals are exogenously endowed with earnings. The time pattern of the receipt of these earnings greatly influences saving and wealth in the economy. We assume that no earnings are received in the fourth period of life and examine a number of patterns of income receipt in the first 3 periods. Consumers are modeled as maximizing expected lifetime utility subject to one or more budget constraints. Utility is taken as separable in consumption (C_t) over time.

The perfect annuities case is by far the simplest to analyze since an individual's choice problem is separate from that of his parents and children. In this case each individual at age 1 maximizes

(1) $$EU = \sum_{t=1}^{4} P_t U(C_t) \alpha^{(t-1)}$$

subject to

$$\sum_{t=1}^{4} P_t C_t R^{(t-1)} = W_1,$$

where P_t is the probability of surviving to period t ($P_1 = P_2 = P_3 = 1$, and $0 < P_4 < 1$), C_t is consumption in period t, R is the discount factor (one divided by one plus the interest rate), α is the pure time discount factor, and W_1 is the present value of earnings. Throughout this paper we use the isoelastic form for $U(C_t)$,

$$(2) \qquad\qquad U(C_t) = \frac{C_t^{1-\gamma}}{1 - \gamma},$$

where $1 - \gamma$ is the elasticity of utility with respect to consumption. The parameter γ measures the (constant) degree of relative risk aversion.

The solution to the consumer's problem in the case of perfect annuities takes the form

$$(3) \qquad\qquad C_t = \frac{W_1 (R\alpha)^{(t-1)\gamma}}{\sum_{j=1}^{4} R^{(j-1)(1-\gamma)/\gamma} \alpha^{(j-1)/\gamma} P_j}.$$

Knowing C_t and the time pattern of earnings one can derive the accumulated wealth of each cohort. Total wealth in the economy equals the sum of each cohort's wealth holdings.

The family insurance solution where each member acts solely out of self-interest is much more complicated. When the bargaining takes place the parent is age 3 with one more period of certain life followed by one period of uncertain life. The agreement reached by parent and child can be thought of as the parent's buying an annuity from the child. In return for some money in period 3 (the price of the annuity) the child promises to offer a specified level of support for the parent in period 4 in the event that the parent lives that long. Equivalently, the deal can be arranged such that the child gives the parent some money before period 3 in return for being made beneficiary of the will of the parent. The equivalence can be seen in the following example which assumes a zero rate of interest for simplicity: say the parent pays $1 for an annuity that gives him $2 in period 4 of his life should he live. In the equivalent support-for-bequest arrangement the child gives the parent $1 in period 3 in return for the parent's agreeing to save $2 for this fourth period and makes the child his beneficiary should he die at the end of period 3. In both of these arrangements the child makes a net transfer of $1 to the parent if the parent lives to old age and receives $1 if the parent does not. Regardless of how the bargain is explicitly or implicitly specified, the parent and child share the risk of the parent's life span. Perhaps the simplest way to think about these deals is the first way, the purchase of annuity insurance by the parent from the child. The next issue to address is what is the price of this insurance.

Both the parent and the child can be made better off by striking a bargain. However, there is some indeterminacy as to how the surplus will be divided. One can imagine the price of the annuity being set sufficiently high that the parent's utility is just the same as if no deal had been struck, and, therefore, all of the gains from trade go to the child. At some low price, all of the gains from trade would go to the parent. An additional complication is that the child, in striking an arrangement with the parent, considers the third-period bargain he will make with his own child. The expected utility from that future bargain is denoted $\hat{V}$ and depends on the child's level of third-period wealth, W_{s3}, that is, $\hat{V} = \hat{V}(W_{s3})$. Throughout the paper we assume that successive children all earn identical amounts with certainty in the first three periods of their lives. Hence, the resources of the grandchild, with whom the child will bargain, is suppressed as an argument of $\hat{V}$.

The frontier of the utility possibilities space with intergenerational bargaining is located by solving the following problem:

Maximize

$$
(4) \quad \frac{C_{f3}^{1-\gamma}}{1-\gamma} + \frac{\alpha P C_{f4}^{1-\gamma}}{1-\gamma} + \frac{\theta C_{s1}^{1-\gamma}}{1-\gamma} + \theta P \left[\frac{\alpha C_{s2,a}^{1-\gamma}}{1-\gamma} + \alpha^2 \hat{V}(W_{s3,a}) \right]
$$

$$
+ \theta(1-P) \left[\frac{\alpha C_{s2,d}^{1-\gamma}}{1-\gamma} + \alpha^2 \hat{V}(W_{s3,d}) \right]
$$

subject to

$$
C_{f3} + C_{s1} + R(C_{f4} + C_{s2,a}) + R^2 W_{s3,a} = W_{s1} + W_{f3}/R
$$

and

$$
C_{f3} + C_{s1} + R C_{s2,d} + R^2 W_{s3,d} = W_{s1} + W_{f3}/R,
$$

where C_{f3} and C_{f4} are the parent's certain and contingent consumption in periods 3 and 4, respectively; C_{s1} is the child's first-period consumption, and $C_{s2,a}$ and $C_{s2,d}$ are the child's second-period consumption contingent upon the parent being alive or dead in period 4, respectively. The child's certain present value of resources is W_{s1}, and his (her) parent's third-period wealth is W_{f3}. Finally, $W_{s3,a}$ and $W_{s3,d}$ are the third-period levels of wealth of the child, that he or she uses in bargaining with the grandchild, contingent upon the parent being alive or dead in period 4.

Problem (4) involves maximizing a weighted sum of the two participants' expected utility where the weight θ, applied to the child's utility, potentially ranges from zero to infinity. The child considers his consumption in periods 3 and 4 under two eventualities: either his parent dies early, and he, therefore, does not have to pay off on the annuity insurance agreement (this is reflected in the final term of eq. [4] which is weighted by the $[1 - P]$ possibility of its occurrence), or the parent dies late and, hence, the child does have to pay off on the annuity insurance (the fourth term in eq. [4]). As stated, the $\hat{V}(W)$ function gives the expected utility the child experiences from his third- and fourth-period consumption discounted to period 3 of his life as a function of his wealth in period 3.

Equation (4) has two budget constraints because total consumption plus savings for the child's third period equals total initial wealth of the parent and child under both lifetime possibilities for the parent. The weight θ reflects the terms of trade in this bargaining problem. In general one would expect θ to be a function of the resources of both the parent and the child, W_{f3} and W_{s1}, respectively. However, since W_{s1} is constant in our analysis, we express $\theta = \theta(W_{f3})$.

Solving problem (4) for different values of θ traces out the utility possibility frontier for family deals shown in figure 8.1. Obviously, not all values of θ will generate outcomes that are in the core. We have labeled as θ_s the critical value for θ for which the parent receives none of the gains from trade (i.e., the child receives all gains from trade).

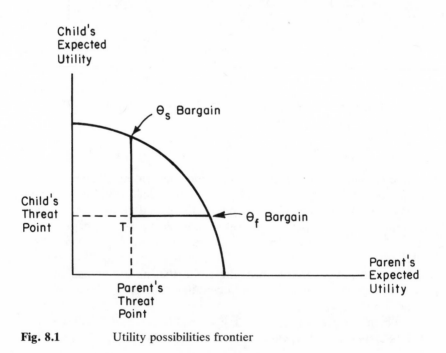

Fig. 8.1   Utility possibilities frontier

We define θ_f symmetrically with the parent getting all of the surplus. The point T is the threat point, indicating the parent's and child's expected utility levels if they fail to bargain with each other. As is clear from problem (4), figure 8.1 depends on the respective resources of the father and the son, W_{s1} and W_{f3}, and on the function $\hat{V}_s(\cdot)$.

Since we consider a stationary environment in which tastes and endowments of children remain unchanged, we will limit ourselves to stationary bargaining solutions. That is, we assume that the $\hat{V}$ function will be the same for the bargaining of each successive pair of generations. An implication of stationarity is that the parent's expected utility in (4) expressed as a function of his wealth, W_{f3}, equals the child's expected utility function, $\hat{V}$, when the child becomes a father. An immediate property of stationarity is that the child reaches the same deal with his child as his parent did with him if respective resources are the same. More formally, a stationary solution is defined as a bargaining function $\theta(W_{f3})$ and an expected utility function $V(W)$ such that if C_{f3}^*, C_{f4}^* are optimal values of consumption derived from solving problem (4), where $V(W_{s3})$ is substituted for $\hat{V}(W_{s3})$, then

$$V(W_{f3}) = \frac{1}{1-\gamma}C_{f3}^{*1-\gamma} + \alpha P \frac{1}{1-\gamma}C_{f4}^{*1-\gamma}.$$

Solving problem (4) involves searching for a fixed-point function V and an associated $\theta(W_{f3})$ function that produces outcomes that are in the core. We consider and compute three solutions to problem (4). In the first solution, denoted θ_s, the child receives all the gains from trade; furthermore, all successive bargains involve children receiving all gains from trade. In the second, θ_f solution, the initial and all successive fathers receive all gains from trade. In the third solution the gains from trade are always divided between child and son according to John Nash's (1953) two-person bargaining solution.

In the θ_s solution parents receive their threat-point level of expected utility. This is the expected utility received by the parent if he acts on his own and is given by the solution to (5). Maximize

(5)
$$\frac{C_{f3}^{1-\gamma}}{1-\gamma} + \frac{\alpha P C_{f4}^{1-\gamma}}{1-\gamma}$$

subject to

$$C_{f3} + R\,C_{f4} = W_{f3}/R.$$

The structure of the problem is very much like that with perfect annuities, except that providing for C_{f4} costs R instead of only PR. The advantage of annuity markets is precisely this reduced cost of consumption in periods where survival is uncertain. Denote $V_s(W_{f3})$ as the maximum utility that the parent with wealth W_{f3} can achieve on his own by solving (5). Thus, $V_s(W_{f3})$ is the indirect utility function when no deal is struck and is given by

$$V_s(W_{f3}) = k\frac{W_{f3}^{1-\gamma}}{1 - \gamma},$$

where

$$k = R^{\gamma-1}[(1 + (\alpha P)^{1/\gamma}R^{\frac{(\gamma-1)}{\gamma}}]^{\gamma}.$$

Naturally, $V_s(W_{f3})$ is the minimum the parent is willing to accept in an annuity bargain with his child. In addition, V_s is the expected utility function of the child in the θ_s bargain with his own child. Replacing V_s for $\hat{V}$ in (4) and choosing θ_s for each value of W_{f3} such that

$$V_s(W_{f3}) = \frac{C_{f3}^{*1-\gamma}}{1 - \gamma} + \alpha\frac{PC_{f4}^{*1-\gamma}}{1 - \gamma}$$

provides a proof by construction that V_s is a fixed-point function for the θ_s problem. In addition the computed values of θ_s for different values of W_{f3} determine the function $\theta_s(W_{f3})$. While parents, in this θ_s bargain, receive their threat-point levels of expected utility, their actual pattern of consumption differs from what they would choose on their own. As described below, C_{f3}^* is smaller and C_{f4}^* greater than the respective solution values to problem (5).

Although the V_s function was obtained analytically, this is not generally possible. For the θ_f and Nash (denoted θ_n) solutions an iterative technique described below is used to find fixed-point functions and their associated θ functions. Both the θ_f and θ_n solutions require specifying the child's threat point. Given our assumption of a cooperative, efficient solution to father-son bargaining, the child, if he fails to bargain with his father, can credibly assert to his father that he will be able to reach a deal with his child. The child's threat point, EU_s^T, is the solution to problem (6); it involves the child's consuming C_{s1} and C_{s2} in his first two periods, respectively, and bargaining with his child in period 3 based on third-period wealth, w_{s3}.

Maximize

(6) $$EU_s^T = \frac{C_{s1}^{1-\gamma}}{1 - \gamma} + \frac{\alpha C_{s2}^{1-\gamma}}{1 - \gamma} + \alpha^2\hat{V}(W_{s3})$$

subject to

$$C_{s1} + RC_{s2} + R^2W_{s3} = W_{s1}.$$

In the case of $\hat{\theta}_f$ bargaining, $\hat{V}$ is replaced by V_f in (6) as well as (4). The θ_f solution proceeds by first guessing a function V_f. Next we solve (6) to determine the son's threat-point utility EU_s^T. Given the guess of V_f and the derived value of EU_s^T, θ is chosen in (4) such that the son's expected utility in the solution to (4) equals EU_s^T. This last calculation is repeated for different values of W_{f3}, thereby generating a function $\theta_f(W_{f3})$. In addition to computing a θ_f function based on the initial guess of V_f, the solution to (4) based on $\theta_f(W_{f3})$ determines the father's expected utility in the bargain. The maximizing values of

$$\frac{C_{f3}^{*1-\gamma}}{1-\gamma} + P\alpha\frac{C_{f4}^{*1-\gamma}}{1-\gamma}$$

for different values of W_{f3} provide an expected utility function for the parent in his θ_f bargain with his child. This function is used as the next guess of the V_f function, and the calculations are repeated. The iteration proceeds until the guess of the V_f function equals the father's expected utility as a function of W_{f3}, that is, until we have found a function V_f, which is a fixed point of the mapping described.

In the Nash bargaining case a very similar solution technique is applied. The Nash solution involves choosing θ in (4) to maximize the quantity $(EU_f - EU_f^T)(EU_s - EU_s^T)$, where EU_f and EU_s are the expected utilities obtained by the parent and child, respectively, and EU_f^T equals V_s, the parent's threat point. To find V_n, the Nash fixed-point function, we again choose an initial guess of V_n and solve (6) to find EU_s^T. We also solve (5) to find EU_f^T. Next the guessed value of V_n is substituted for $\hat{V}$ in (4), and θ_n is chosen to maximize $(EU_f - EU_f^T)(EU_s - EU_s^T)$. Repeating this last step for alternative values of W_{f3} generates a function $\theta_n(W_{f3})$ as well as an expected utility function of the father arising from Nash bargaining. This latter function is used as the second guess of the V_n function. The iteration continues until we find a fixed-point function V_n. In this bargaining solution as in the previous θ_s solution, the $\theta_f(W_{f3})$ and $\theta_n(W_{f3})$ functions calculated in the last round of the iteration correspond to the correct bargaining functions for the functions V_f and V_n, respectively.

The V_s function is used as the initial guess of the V function for the θ_f and Nash bargaining solutions. In each iteration we computed the solution to (4) for 80 different values of W_{f3}. We then fit a fifth-order polynomial in W_{f3} to these points and used the resulting regression as the guess of V in the next iteration. The iterative procedure for determining V converged roughly by the eighth iteration; 12 iterations each were used for the θ_f and Nash cases. By "rough convergence" we mean that economic choice variables were identical to at least the second digit between iterations. For a range of intermediate values of

W_{f3} the calculated consumption terms are identical to five digits between iterations. While we believe more accurate values of the V_s and V_n functions could be obtained, the computation costs of achieving the additional accuracy is considerable; solving (4) for any one of the 80 values of W_{f3} in any one of the 12 iterations requires rather extensive computation.

8.2.1   The Involuntary Bequest Model

The next case we examine is the situation in which there are no insurance arrangements but unintentional bequests are made to children. This case has been examined in 2-period models by Eckstein et al. (1985) and Abel (1985). The solution differs from that of the threat points because the child inherits money unspent by the parent. The child in period 1 of his life can observe the wealth of his parent and can calculate the potential inheritance, I, he will receive should his parent die young. The child is assumed to solve the following problem.

Maximize

$$(7) \quad \frac{C_{s1}^{1-\gamma}}{1 - \gamma} + P\left[\frac{\alpha C_{s2,a}^{1-\gamma}}{1 - \gamma} + \alpha^2 V_s(W_{s3,a})\right]$$

$$+ (1 - P)\left[\frac{\alpha C_{s2,d}^{1-\gamma}}{1 - \gamma} + \alpha^2 V_s(W_{s3,d})\right]$$

subject to

$$C_{s1} + RC_{s2,a} + R^2 W_{s3,a} = W_{s1}$$

and

$$C_{s1} + R\,C_{s2,d} + R^2 W_{s3,d} = W_{s1} + I,$$

where

$$I = W_{f3}/R - C_{f3}.$$

The child maximizes his welfare subject to the certain earnings endowment, W_{s1}, and the inheritance I left by the parent if he dies young. The V_s function gives the level of expected utility the child can receive in periods 3 and 4 with no deal with his child, that is, the solution to problem (5) above.

8.3   The Transmission of Wealth in the Stochastic Steady State

Figure 8.2 graphs the wealth of children in their third period (when they are parents) against their parents' wealth, W_{f3}, for the case of family insurance bargains. The amount of wealth the child brings into

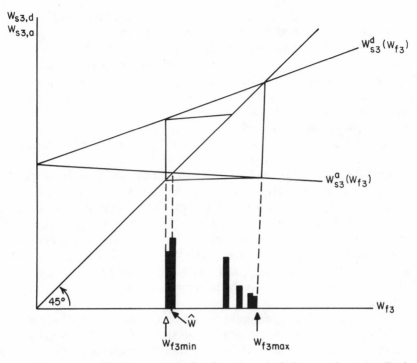

Fig. 8.2   Wealth transmission functions and the steady state distribution of parents' wealth

his third period depends, of course, on the age at which his parent dies. The curves $W_{s3}^d(W_{f3})$ and $W_{s3}^a(W_{f3})$ indicate the third-period wealth of the child if his own parent lives for 3 periods and 4 periods, respectively. Note that the two curves intersect on the vertical axis, since a child whose parent has no wealth engages in the same consumption regardless of the date of his parent's death.

The exact position and shapes of these curves depend on the specification of the utility function as well as the parent-child bargaining solution. For the examples we describe here, the curves were constructed by fitting fifth-order polynomials to the values of $W_{s3}^d(W_{f3})$ and $W_{s3}^a(W_{f3})$ calculated for 80 different values of W_{f3}. The intercepts in each regression were constrained to equal the amount of resources a child would save for period 3 assuming he engages in no bargain with his parent. In each calculation, the estimated curves were essentially straight lines, with $W_{s3}^d(W_{f3})$ and $W_{a3}^a(W_{f3})$ monotonically increasing and decreasing W_{f3}, respectively.

Intuitively, $W_{s3}^d(W_{f3})$ rises with W_{f3} because a fraction of the parent's increased resources will be allocated to the parent's contingent fourth-period consumption, C_{f4}. If the parent dies after period 3, the additional

C_{f4} is passed on to the child. For the child the inheritance is allocated to larger second-period consumption as well as larger third-period savings, $W_{s3}^d(W_{f3})$, that is, used in the bargain with his own child. The decline in $W_{s3}^a(W_{f3})$ as W_{f3} increases is explained as follows: regardless of the bargaining solution between the parent and child, the parent's contingent bequest rises with W_{f3}. Part of the price the child pays for the larger contingent bequest is somewhat lower values of second-period consumption and third-period wealth in the case the parent does not die young. This permits the parent to consume more in period 3 and, potentially, in period 4.

Assuming, as is verified in our actual calculation, that the slope of W_{s3}^d (W_{f3}) is everywhere positive and less than unity, W_{f3max} is the unique limiting value of a parent's third-period wealth when *all* his forefathers have died early. For values of W_{f3} above W_{f3max}, successive early deaths of parents lead to smaller values of W_{f3} for each successive parent until the sequence converges to W_{f3max}. Similarly, starting with a value for W_{f3} below W_{f3max} and assuming that all successive parents die early leads to successively larger values of W_{f3} until W_{f3max} is reached.

We next turn to the minimum bound on the stochastic steady-state distribution of a parent's wealth. If the slope of $W_{s3}^a(W_{f3})$ is between 0 and -1, which is the case in the examples presented below, then $\hat{W}_{f3}$ is the unique limit of the value of a parent's wealth as successive parents in a family continue to live through period 4. In this case the sequence of W_{f3}s, starting at any particular value, converges as a "Cobb-web" to $\hat{W}_{f3}$; that is, each successive parent with more wealth than $\hat{W}_{f3}$, who lives to period 4, has a child who has less than $\hat{W}_{f3}$ when the child becomes a parent.

In the stochastic steady state W_{f3min} is the lower bound on a parent's third-period wealth. Values below W_{f3min} cannot arise in the stochastic steady state; any parent with W_{f3} below W_{f3min} will have a child whose wealth as a parent is between W_{f3min} and W_{f3max}. Once the W_{f3} for a particular family falls within W_{f3min} and W_{f3max}, no parent in the family will ever appear with wealth outside this range. Values of W_{f3} below W_{f3min} and above W_{f3max} are nonrecurrent states in the Markov process that maps W_{f3} into $W_{s3}^d(W_{f3})$ with probability $1 - p$ and into $W_{s3}^a(W_{f3})$ with probability p. As can readily be seen by tracing out alternative p and $(1 - p)$ sequences, starting with values of W_f between W_{f3min} and W_{f3max}, the larger the value of W_f in the preceding generation, the smaller will be the W_{f3} in the next generation if the parent dies late. W_{f3min}, therefore, corresponds to the value of $W_{s3}^a(W_{f3})$ for W_{f3max}, that is, $W_{f3min} = W_{s3}^a(W_{f3max})$. Hence, if the richest parent survives to period 4, his child is the poorest parent when he reaches period 3. This extreme "riches to rags" result is quite intuitive. A parent with the largest possible wealth, W_{f3max}, provides the largest estate if he dies early but no estate if he dies late. In order to "purchase" the right to this largest potential estate the child pays the largest price in terms of reduced consumption and third-period wealth if his parent lives.

Since the Markov process described in figure 8.2 is nonrecurrent, there are large regions between W_{f3min} and W_{f3max} that have zero mass with respect to the steady state distribution of wealth. The shaded areas in figure 8.2 chart this distribution for the case θ's in which parents receive none of the gains from bargaining with their children. This distribution was constructed by giving 100,000 families the same initial value of W_{f3} and then simulating 25 successive generations using a 0.6 probability of a 4-period lifetime. The distribution of W_{f3} stabilized after roughly eight generations. Since we assume that a new generation is born every period, rather than every other period, there are also orphaned 2-period-old children as well as 2-period-old children with surviving parents who hold wealth at any point in time. Calculating the stochastic steady state's stock of wealth requires simply summing the wealth holdings of all age 3 parents, the wealth of orphaned children, and the wealth of 2-period-old children and their surviving 4-period-old parents. The wealth holdings of these latter two groups are derived from the distribution of wealth holdings of 3-period-old parents; the consumption of each of the 100,000 parents and their children, when these parents are age 3, is subtracted from the income of these families to compute their combined saving. This saving plus each parent's initial wealth represents the next-period wealth holdings of families consisting either of orphaned children or of children with surviving parents. Since this wealth distribution is stationary in the stochastic steady state, next period's wealth holdings of these groups is identical to this period's wealth holdings of such groups. Similar calculations are made for the case in which there are no insurance bargains between parents and children, but children nonetheless inherit their parents' estates.

Parameter values were chosen as follows: the time preference factor, α, and the discount factor, R, both equal .86. The coefficient of risk aversion, γ, equals 4, and the fourth-period survival probability, ρ, equals 0.6. If one thinks of each period as consisting of 15 years, then a discount factor of .86 corresponds to a 1% annual real rate of return. In addition, if we view parents as being age 50 and children age 20 when the bargains are struck, the 0.6 fourth-period survival probability is roughly equivalent to assuming an expected age of death of 74.

Table 8.1 presents the calculated values for a parent's third- and fourth-period consumption at alternative levels of W_{f3} under perfect insurance, the three alternative parent-child bargains (the θ_f, Nash, and θ_s solutions to [6]), and the case of no-insurance arrangements. In each of these cases, the parent's consumption increases with his third-period

Table 8.1   Parent's Consumption Under Alternative Insurance Arrangements

Parent's Third-Period Wealth (WF3)	Perfect Insurance		θf Bargain (Parents Receive All Gains from Trade)		Nash Bargaining Solution		θs Bargain (Children Receive All Gains from Trade)		No Insurance Arrangements	
	CF3	CF4	CF3	CF4	CF3	CF4	CF3	CF4	CF3	CF4
9.0	6.9	6.9	6.4	5.8	6.2	5.6	5.9	5.3	5.0	5.3
8.0	6.7	6.7	5.7	5.2	5.5	4.9	5.2	4.7	5.3	4.6
7.0	5.4	5.4	5.0	4.5	4.89	4.3	4.5	4.1	4.6	4.0
6.0	4.6	4.6	4.4	4.0	4.2	3.8	3.9	3.6	4.0	3.5
5.0	3.8	3.8	3.6	3.3	3.5	3.2	3.2	3.0	3.3	2.9
4.4	3.4	3.4	3.2	3.0	3.0	2.8	2.8	2.6	2.9	2.5

NOTE: Table assumes $\gamma = 4$, $P = .6$, $\alpha = R = .86$.

wealth. Access to perfect insurance results, for this parameterization of utility, in higher levels of consumption for the parent in both periods 3 and 4 relative to the other cases of partial or zero insurance. For example, if the parent's wealth is 4.4 at the beginning of period 3, he consumes 2.9 and 2.5 in periods 3 and 4, respectively, with no insurance, and 3.4 in both periods with perfect insurance. The present value difference in these consumption paths is 25%.

A parent-and-child bargain in which successive parents receive all gains from trade with successive children, the θ_f bargain, provides parents with consumption values that are roughly midway between those of perfect and zero insurance. Consumption values for the parent under the Nash bargaining solution lie between the θ_f and θ_s deals. This is the expected result since the Nash solution divides the gains from trade between parents and children. The θ_s bargain, in which the parent receives no benefits from dealing with his child, involves slightly less third-period consumption and slightly more fourth-period consumption when old than in the case of zero insurance.

Table 8.2 shows consumption and third-period wealth values of children in different insurance regimes. Under perfect insurance the child's consumption is 3.4 in each period; with no insurance arrangements and no involuntary bequests the child consumes 3.2 during the first 3 periods and 2.8 in the last period. Depending on the parent's wealth and longevity and the bargain struck between the two, the child can potentially consume well in excess of the perfect insurance values. As an example, take the case of a parent with wealth of 6.0 who agrees to a θ_s bargain with his child. The child's first-period consumption is 3.4, the same as under perfect insurance. If the parent dies after his third period, the child consumes 4.5 in period 2 rather than 3.4, the perfect insurance amount. Furthermore, the child's third-period wealth in this case is 7.9, substantially in excess of 4.4, the third-period wealth of a son under perfect insurance. With third-period wealth of 7.9, the child's third- and contingent fourth-period consumption values are, from table 8.1, roughly 5.5 and 4.9. For this child the total potential realized present value of consumption is 14.4, although the present value of his earnings is only 10.

8.4   The Savings Impact of Alternative Insurance Arrangements

Table 8.3 compares steady state per capita wealth stocks in the different insurance regimes under alternative assumptions about age-earnings profiles. Each of the age-earnings profiles has a present value of 10, which is received with certainty over the course of the first 3 periods. Since the child's resources are identical in each of these cases, the consumption decisions of the child and parent are the same for

Table 8.2 Child's Consumption Under Alternative Insurance Arrangements
Consumption and Wealth Values: Father-Son Bargains

Father's Wealth	θ_s Bargain (Children Get All Gains from Trade)					Nash Bargaining Solution					θ_f Bargain (Children Get No Gains from Trade)				
	CS1	CS2A	CS2D	WS3,A	WS3,D	CS1	CS2A	CS2D	WS3,A	WS3,D	CS1	CS2A	CS2D	WS3,A	WS3,D
9.0	3.4	3.1	5.2	5.4	9.1	3.4	3.1	5.5	4.6	8.3	3.3	2.9	5.1	4.4	8.5
8.0	3.4	3.1	4.9	5.4	8.7	3.5	3.1	5.2	4.6	7.9	3.3	3.0	4.9	4.4	8.1
7.0	3.4	3.1	4.7	5.4	8.3	3.5	3.1	5.0	4.6	7.5	3.3	3.0	4.7	4.5	7.7
6.0	3.4	3.1	4.5	5.4	7.9	3.5	3.1	5.0	4.6	7.1	3.3	3.0	4.5	4.5	7.3
5.0	3.3	3.1	4.3	5.4	7.5	3.4	3.1	4.5	4.7	6.8	3.2	3.0	4.3	4.5	6.9
4.4	3.3	3.1	4.1	5.4	7.3	3.4	3.2	4.4	4.7	6.6	3.3	3.0	4.2	4.6	6.7

Consumption Values

	Perfect Insurance				No Insurance Arrangements and No Involuntary Bequests			
	CS1	CS2	CF3	CF4	CS1	CS2	CF3	CF4
	3.4	3.4	3.4	3.4	3.2	3.2	3.2	2.8

NOTE: Table assumes $\gamma = 4$, $P = .6$, $\alpha = R = .86$.

Table 8.3   **Wealth Per Capita and Percentage Long-Run Decline in Wealth from Switch to Perfect Insurance**

Age-Earnings Profile	Perfect Insurance	θ_f Bargain (Parents Receive All Gains from Trade)		Nash Bargaining Solution		θ_s Bargain (Children Receive All Gains from Trade)		No Bargain Involuntary Bequests	
	Wealth	Wealth	Percentage Wealth Decline	Wealth	Percentage Wealth Decline	Wealth	Percentage Wealth Decline	Wealth	Percentage Wealth Decline
(10,0,0,0)	12.7	13.9	8.6	14.2	10.6	15.9	20.1	15.5	18.1
(5.0,5.8,0,0)	7.7	8.9	13.5	9.2	16.3	10.9	29.4	10.5	26.7
(3.3,3.9,4.5,0)	2.2	3.4	35.3	3.7	40.5	5.4	59.3	5.0	56.0
(3.0,5.8,2.7,0)	3.4	4.6	26.1	4.9	30.6	6.6	48.5	6.2	45.2
(2.0,5.8,3.5,0)	0.7	2.9	171.4	3.2	78.1	3.9	82.0	3.5	80.0

NOTE: Table assumes $\gamma = 4$, $P = .6$, $\alpha = R = .86$.

each of these earnings paths. Hence, the difference in stocks of wealth by row in table 8.3 are simply a function of the timing of the receipt of labor income.

The absolute size of these economies' wealth stocks may appear small in comparison to the level of earnings or income in a particular period. However, such stock-flow ratios must be adjusted for the fact that flows in this model are received over a period that corresponds to roughly 15 years. In the case of the third and probably the most realistic earnings profile in table 8.3, the ratio of wealth to one-fifteenth of a period's labor earnings is 6.9 in the case of the θ_s bargain. A wealth/earnings ratio of 6.9 is somewhat greater than that observed in the United States.

The percentage reductions in wealth from moving to perfect insurance reported in table 8.3 are very large. For the earnings profile in the third row the long-run wealth reduction is 59% starting from the θ_s (children take all) stochastic steady state. It is 41% in the case of an initial Nash bargaining equilibrium and 35% when the initial equilibrium involves θ_f (parents take all) bargain.

The values in table 8.3 are highly sensitive to the shape of the age-earnings profile. The smallest percentage wealth reduction arises when all earnings are received in the first period; in this case wealth falls by 20.1% starting from the θ_s bargain and by 13.9% starting from the θ_f bargain.

The percentage change in wealth appears relatively insensitive to variations in the degree of relative risk aversion, γ. For example, reducing γ from 4 to 1.5 lowers the percentage decline in wealth under row 3's earnings profile and initial θ_s bargaining from 59.3% to 50.7%. Raising γ to 8 increases the value to 63.2%. Under table 8.3's first age-earnings profile the percentage wealth reductions starting from θ_s economies are 15.1, 20.1, and 22.9 for values of γ equal to 1.5, 4, and 8, respectively.

There is considerably more sensitivity to changes in the fourth-period survival probability P; however, the sensitivity depends on the choice of earnings profile. For example, lower P from 0.6 to 0.3, which reduces the expected age of death from roughly 74 to roughly 69, converts the 59.3% θ_s reduction (row 3, table 8.3) to 83.6%. The same reduction in P raises table 8.3's row 1, θ_s value from 20.1% to only 23.4%.

The large differences in wealth stocks between the perfect insurance and family insurance regimes suggests that steady state welfare could actually be lower in the case of perfect insurance. This is indeed possible. Under θ_f (children take all) bargaining and assuming γ equals 1.5, the expected utility of even the child of the poorest parent exceeds the uniform, steady state expected utility under perfect insurance. Starting from a situation of zero insurance, achieving the perfect insurance expected utility level requires a 7% increase in resources; achieving the expected utility of the child with the poorest parent in the θ_s stochasic steady state requires an 8% increase in lifetime resources, starting from this benchmark regime. Attaining the level of welfare of the child whose parent in the θ_f steady state has the maximum potential wealth, W_{f3max}, requires a corresponding 12% increase in resources.

The steady state stocks of wealth in the case of no family arrangements, but involuntary bequests to children, are slightly smaller than those under θ_s bargaining. This is not surprising since in both cases parents receive their threat-point levels of utility and consume roughly similar amounts. In the θ_s deal, however, the child's insurance provision leads to a somewhat lower level of the parent's consumption in period 3 and a somewhat higher level in period 4 (see table 8.1). In addition, given W_{f3}, the child consumes slightly less in period 1 in the θ_s deal than in the involuntary bequest setting. This consumption pattern explains the larger wealth stock in the θ_s insurance regime.

Another question raised by table 8.3 is the extent to which imperfections in annuity markets can fully explain observed intergenerational transfers. Kotlikoff and Summers (1981) invoked the assumption of perfect insurance arrangements in estimating that roughly 80% of private U.S. wealth corresponds to accumulated inheritances of those currently alive. This assumption that annuity insurance is fairly well developed in the United States can be defended by pointing to social security and other government annuities, private pensions, old age labor earnings that are partly contingent on survival, and the potential for family risk sharing involving multiple members. Still, it is interesting to ask how their calculation turns out when it is applied to the two-member family insurance economy described above. Their technique involves subtracting accumulated consumption from accumulated earnings for each cohort and then summing across cohorts to get a total wealth stock. This "life-cycle" wealth is then compared with actual wealth holdings. If agents in the economy are selfish and annuity arrangements are perfect or very close to perfect, computed and actual aggregate wealth will be identical or extremely close to one another.

The two-person family regime is, however, quite far from that of perfect insurance. As described here, this imperfection produces a stochastic steady state in which observed consumption profiles often exceed what could be financed from one's own labor earnings even under perfect insurance. Hence, in this economy, subtracting, for all cohorts, accumulated consumption, part of which is financed by past intergenerational transfers, from accumulated earnings produces an underestimate of the economy's actual wealth. For the θ_s bargain, with γ equals 4 and with table 8.3's row 3 earnings profile, 1.5, the underestimate is close to 90% of actual wealth. Since Kotlikoff and Summers's (1981) calculation understates United States wealth by 80%, imperfections in annuity markets appear potentially capable of fully explaining actual intergenerational transfers in the United States.

8.5 Conclusion

The preceding calculations as well as the figures presented in table 8.3 must be viewed cautiously. They embed rather extreme assumptions concerning the size of the risk-sharing pool and, in the θ_s case, the nature of risk sharing. A more realistic model would contain two parents pooling risk with two or more children. Since the parents, by themselves, can provide each other with considerable insurance protection, their threat-point values of expected utility are greater in collective bargaining with their children. As a consequence one would expect parents, in such a model, to have an expected utility level considerably greater than that described by the θ_s solution. In addition, if they can extract most of the gains from trade from dealing with their children, they will end up with close to perfect insurance. In that case the impact of improving annuity arrangements on savings would be minor.

Extending the analysis to different configurations of families is an area for future research. To date we have considered the simplest case of multiple children dealing with a single parent under the θ_s bargain. For table 8.3's third earnings profile the percentage reduction in wealth is quite similar to the 50% figure in table 8.3 over a range of children numbering as great as 5 per parent. Since their earnings profile implies very little saving in period 1, the change in the earnings' age structure from a 1/5 ratio of children to parents has little impact on accumulated earnings of particular cohorts at a point in time. In addition, the consumption patterns of children and the parent are not greatly altered in moving from one to five children under the θ_s bargain. This would not, of course, be the case in the θ_f bargain. A θ_f bargain with five children would provide parents with close to the consumption levels available with perfect insurance.

While the findings should be viewed cautiously, they do suggest that the manner in which annuity markets function can significantly affect saving, wealth, and welfare in an economy. That each generation has large incentives to improve annuity arrangements was demonstrated in Kotlikoff and Spivak (1981). Here we find that the steady state welfare gains are significantly smaller and, in fact, may be negative. The first generations' gain results in a smaller inheritance and capital stock for future generations. This lower wealth may more than offset the welfare gains that each generation receives from the availability of long-life insurance.

We should reemphasize that we are addressing a different question from that of Feldstein (1974) and others who are largely concerned with the funding status of social security. While that line of research attempts to estimate the substitutability of social security wealth for private capital, we are here concerned with the insurance aspects of pensions and social security. It is our feeling, buttressed by the results of this paper, that a considerable amount of saving is potentially done for what could be loosely termed precautionary motives. In addition, the exact manner in which families self-insure can have major consequences for wealth accumulation. When more perfect insurance policies are made available, whether funded or not, less aggregate saving occurs. While we have focused on annuity insurance, the paper's findings suggest that the availability of unemployment insurance, disability insurance, and health insurance could also significantly affect national saving. In addition, the government's pooling of human capital risks through progressive income taxation may also be having a major impact. In general, the study of savings and government insurance provision is an important area for additional research.

Note

1. This paper reaches a similar conclusion about the savings impact of perfecting insurance arrangements, although we model the initial, no-market/government annuity economy quite differently. Abel's research and ours were conducted independently.

References

Abel, Andrew B. 1985. Precautionary saving and accidental bequests. *American Economic Review* 75:777–91.
Barro, Robert J. 1974. Are government bonds net wealth? *Journal of Political Economy* 82:1095–118.
Davies, J. B. 1981. Uncertain lifetime consumption and dissaving in retirement. *Journal of Political Economy* 89:561–78.
Eckstein, Zvi; Eichenbaum, Martin S.; and Peled, Dan. 1985. Uncertain lifetimes and welfare enhancing properties of annuity markets and social security. *Journal of Public Economics* 26:303–26.
Feldstein, Martin S. 1974. Social security, induced retirement, and aggregate capital accumulation. *Journal of Political Economy* 82:905–26.
Hubbard, Glenn R. 1983. Uncertain lifetimes, pensions, and individual saving. In this volume.

Kotlikoff, Laurence J., and Spivak, Avia. 1981. The family as an incomplete annuities market. *Journal of Political Economy* 89:372–91.

Kotlikoff, Laurence J., and Summers, Lawrence H. 1981. The role of intergenerational transfers in aggregate capital accumulation. *Journal of Political Economy* 90:706–32.

Nash, John F. 1953. Two-person cooperative games. *Econometrica* 21:128–40.

Sheshinski, E., and Weiss, Y. 1981. Uncertainty and optimal social security systems. *Quarterly Journal of Economics* 96:189–206.

Yaari, M. E. 1965. Uncertain lifetime, life insurance, and the theory of the consumer. *Review of Economic Studies* 32:137–50.

Comment   Michael Rothschild

Models like the one developed in this paper shed light on two issues. They can be used to assess how well different institutions work to share the risks of uncertain length of life. Because in the absence of perfect insurance people accumulate private wealth to insure themselves against poverty in their old age, these models are also used to analyze the effects of these different institutions on capital formation. My comments concern the first issue; I will discuss how I think the welfare consequences of different methods of intergenerational risk sharing ought to be measured. I will also indicate briefly how in one variant of the model analyzed in this paper, taxation can increase welfare.

One of the several virtues of this paper is that it explicitly calculates the distribution of wealth which results from the inheritance process. If there were perfect annuity markets, no one in this economy would leave an estate. Since everyone has the same ability to earn income, all people face the same lifetime budget constraint; all have, at birth, the same expected utility. When there are imperfect annuity markets, people leave estates. How much they leave depends on how long they live and how much they inherited from their parents. The bequest process thus induces a distribution of wealth. The characteristics of this distribution depend on the institutional structure; that is, it depends on the particular contract which fathers and sons make with one another. Because there is a distribution of wealth in societies with imperfect annuity markets, different individuals have different expected utility at birth. Expected utility is determined by one's father's wealth, and this varies from person to person.

This suggests using the following standard to compare welfare under different annuity arrangements: Suppose you were going to be born

Michael Rothschild is professor of economics, University of California, San Diego, and research associate, National Bureau of Economic Research.

into a society with a particular annuity structure. What is your expected utility if you assume a position in the wealth distribution according to the steady state distribution of wealth? This is, of course, the same thing as total utility in steady state using a utilitarian measure of welfare. This seems an appropriate criterion for this model as everyone is the same except for accidents of birth and length of life. Since they calculated the steady state distribution of wealth, Kotlikoff et al. could easily calculate this measure of welfare. It would be interesting to use this standard to compare the different imperfect annuity agreements discussed in the paper.

From this perspective there are three kinds of uncertainty in the model. The first is uncertainty about how long one will live. Call this length-of-life uncertainty; it is the primary source of uncertainty. Other kinds of uncertainty arise because people cannot completely insure themselves against a long life. The second kind of uncertainty is uncertainty about how wealthy one's father will be. ("Will be" because we are considering the thought experiment of being born into a random family.) Call this wealth uncertainty. Finally there is uncertainty as to how long one's father will live and thus what bequest one will actually get. Call this bequest uncertainty. Bequest uncertainty causes real misallocation of resources. Because I do not know what my wealth will be until bequest uncertainty is resolved, I cannot hope to allocate consumption over my lifetime as well as I could if I knew what my lifetime budget constraint would be before I started consuming.

With perfect annuity markets none of these kinds of uncertainty exist—or at least they can be perfectly insured against. If there are no annuity markets, then all three kinds of uncertainty exist. Intergenerational risk sharing mitigates length-of-life uncertainty; it does this at the expense of increasing bequest uncertainty. The size of bequest risk is determined by the difference between the amount the son gets if his father lives 3 periods and the amount (possibly negative) the son gets if his father lives 4 periods. This difference is larger if the son partially insures his father than if he doesn't. The larger, in the sense of second-degree stochastic dominance, are bequests, the greater is bequest uncertainty. I suspect that welfare is larger the smaller is bequest uncertainty. Bequests are smallest when fathers appropriate most of the gains from the annuity bargain. Thus, I think it likely that welfare or expected utility in steady state is highest when $\theta = \theta_f$. What makes this a hunch rather than a conjecture is my inability to speculate about the effect of different values of θ on wealth uncertainty.

One institution which would increase welfare from the no-insurance situation is a 100% inheritance tax, with proceeds distributed in a lump sum fashion. Such a tax would have almost the opposite effect of the imperfect annuities studied in this paper. It would do nothing to mitigate life uncertainty, but it would do away completely with both wealth uncertainty and bequest uncertainty. Such an inheritance tax would substitute for a market on which one could insure perfectly against bequest and wealth uncertainty. It would be interesting to compare expected welfare in a society which had no annuities but which did have inheritance taxes with expected welfare in a society with the imperfect annuities created by intergenerational risk sharing. An inheritance tax would make the imperfect annuity arrangements studied in this paper impossible. It would also entail more capital in steady state than would any intergenerational risk-sharing agreement.

9   Dissaving after Retirement: Testing the Pure Life Cycle Hypothesis

B. Douglas Bernheim

9.1   Introduction

Does wealth typically decline after retirement? Despite much recent research, this deceptively simple question has remained controversial. Previous investigators seem evenly divided on the issue of whether elderly individuals save or dissave, and no consensus about magnitudes has emerged even among those who agree on the direction of change.

There is as well widespread disagreement about the reasons for asking this question. Some (notably Mirer 1979) have argued that the life cycle hypothesis is inconsistent with rising or slowly declining wealth after retirement. Others (such as Davies 1981) have recognized that, in view of uncertainty concerning life spans, one cannot base a formal test of the life cycle hypothesis on this information alone. Such authors have, however, suggested that one could conduct an informal "test" by comparing empirical data with the results of simulations based upon plausible parameters values. Finally, one might altogether abandon the hope of inferring motives from information about the age-wealth profile, and instead simply treat such information as valuable per se. If, for example, wealth fails to decline rapidly after retirement, intergenerational transfers are likely to be significant. Regardless of motives, this

B. Douglas Bernheim is assistant professor of economics, Stanford University, and faculty research fellow, National Bureau of Economic Research.

This paper was presented at the NBER Pensions Conference in San Diego, April 13–14, 1984. Financial support from the Center for Economic Policy Research at Stanford University and the NBER pensions project is gratefully acknowledged. I am indebted to Lawrence Levin for able research assistance. I would also like to thank Martin Feldstein, Franklin Fisher, Victor Fuchs, Michael Hurd, Mervyn King, Daniel McFadden, and Lawrence Summers for helpful comments and discussions. The views expressed here are my own, and should not be attributed to any other individual or organization.

will have strong implications concerning the long run distribution of wealth (see, e.g., Stiglitz 1978; Loury 1981).

The appropriate definition of "wealth" will depend critically upon which of these purposes one has in mind. Information on bequeathable wealth-age profiles is by itself sufficient for drawing inferences about the magnitude of bequests. However, tests of the life cycle hypothesis must necessarily consider all forms of resources, including annuities (social security and pensions). It is therefore somewhat surprising that, with few exceptions (King and Dicks-Mireaux 1982, Dicks-Mireaux and King 1984; Hurd and Shoven 1985), studies of the age-wealth profile ignore annuities. Nor have any of these authors provided a theoretical discussion of how calculated rates of dissaving should be adjusted in the presence of annuities.

Accordingly, this paper has three objectives. First, we present new evidence on the relationship between age and bequeathable wealth holdings after retirement. While previous studies employ either cross-sectional survey or estate data, our approach is to follow a sample of retired individuals over time. We argue that this methodology is likely to produce superior estimates of dissaving after retirement. We find that bequeathable wealth declines relatively rapidly for single individuals (roughly 3%–4% per year), while for couples, the evidence is mixed (slight declines, on the order of 1%–2% per year, are observed for early retirees; otherwise, bequeathable wealth remains relatively constant after retirement). Changes in the composition of bequeathable wealth (specifically, the fraction held as residential housing) are also analyzed.

Our second objective is to develop and implement a technique for calculating meaningful rates of resource depletion when some positive fraction of wealth is held as annuities. Since survival probabilities decline with age, the use of actuarial values (as in King and Dicks-Mireaux 1982 or Dicks-Mireaux and King 1984) builds in a tendency for total wealth to decline quite rapidly after retirement. However, we argue that actuarial discounting is inappropriate for calculating meaningful rates of depletion. Instead, we show that simple discounting of benefit streams is (approximately) appropriate whenever behavior is governed by traditional life cycle concerns. Thus we find, contrary to King and Dicks-Mireaux, that, after adjusting for annuities, neither single individuals nor couples dissave significant fractions of their total resources after retirement.

Of course, this is not a formal test of the life cycle maximization principle. Our third objective is to construct such a test using information on the age-wealth profile. We show that the life cycle model has strong implications about how rates of accumulation and depletion will respond to the imposition of nondiscretionary annuities.[1] Implementation of these tests produces results which are unfavorable to the pure life cycle hypothesis.

The paper is organized as follows. In the next section, we describe the data source which is employed throughout. A discussion of the existing literature on bequeathable wealth-age profiles appears in section 9.3, along with our new estimates. Theoretical foundations for the valuation of annuity wealth are discussed in section 9.4, and adjusted estimates of accumulation and depletion are presented. Section 9.5 describes and implements a test of the life cycle hypothesis based on the behavioral response of changes in wealth to involuntary annuitization. The paper closes with a brief conclusion.

9.2 The Data

This study employs data from the Longitudinal Retirement History Survey (LRHS), which followed a sample of over 11,000 retirement-aged individuals (58–63 in 1968) for a period of 10 years, starting in 1969. Some information was also obtained from matching administrative records.

The LRHS collected extensive information on the net worth of respondents. Our measure of bequeathable wealth includes the value of owner-occupied housing (net of mortgage liabilities), equity in a business or farm, the net value of other property holdings, cash, and financial assets (including stocks, bonds, bank accounts, checking accounts, and money loaned to other), minus total household debt (excluding mortgage items already counted).[2]

While extensive in coverage, there is reason to believe that wealth data contained in the LRHS are not of high quality. In general, it is difficult to elicit accurate information about net worth in interview surveys.[3] A casual inspection of LRHS records indicates substantial misreporting of assets.[4] Deleting observations for which any component of wealth was incorrectly reported would drastically reduce the sample size, as well as induce a bias of unknown direction. Due to the relative magnitude of housing in the portfolios of most elderly individuals, we did insist that the completion code associated with this item indicated an unambiguous value. This probably biases our sample somewhat toward renters,[5] although the statistics presented in section 9.3 suggest that this bias is not large. Throughout the paper, it is important to bear in mind that wealth is poorly reported; we will return to this issue at various points.

Our study also requires extensive information on pensions and annuities. Private and government pension benefits are inferred from income data reported during the sample period. Fortunately, it is possible to distinguish one-shot, lump sum payments from annuities on the basis of recorded responses. For individuals retiring late, benefits from such pensions may commence after 1979 (the youngest respondent is 68 in that year), in which case no income is reported. For such individuals, we supplement income data with survey responses to questions concerning expected levels of future benefits. However, one should bear in mind that private pensions in particular are probably underreported for late retirees.

Social security benefits for each year were calculated on the basis of prevailing legislation in that year, using data on covered earnings obtained through matching administrative records. Benefits were calculated on the basis of *actual* retirement dates for respondent and spouse. For the purpose of this calculation, we assumed that all individuals still working in 1979 retired at the end of that year.

The matching administrative records were also used to calculate a measure of lifetime resources for each respondent. Unfortunately, this information is incomplete, since yearly earnings are only reported up to the taxable maximum. Since the records also indicate the quarter in which the taxable maximum was reached, we were able to extrapolate yearly earnings using the method described by Fox (1976). The resulting income stream was then accumulated at a 3% rate to a standard age, producing a measure of lifetime earnings.

Much of our analysis also requires us to know whether a particular individual is retired. Defining retirement is problematic. To reduce contamination arising from the presence of earned income, we created a relatively pristine sample of retirees. Thus, "retirees" report themselves as fully retired in both the retirement year and all successive years, and they report negligible earned income during this period.[6] A retired couple consists of two retired members, while a working couple need only have one worker.

In the following sections, our analysis focuses on the behavior of four samples. To minimize the effects of short-run fluctuations, it seemed desirable to look at changes in wealth over relatively long periods. Since the 1973 wave of the LRHS collected very incomplete data on asset holdings, we chose to compare the behavior of retirees and workers over the periods 1969–75 and 1975–79. For the first period, we constructed a sample of households who were retired as of 1969, and deleted all observations which had disappeared by 1975 (due to death or attrition) or for which household composition had changed (due to divorce, separation, or death). Similarly, we constructed a sample of households which still included working members as of 1975 and used these as a basis of comparison.[7] Note that our households are preselected on the basis of survival, and presumably overrepresent healthy individuals. This probably biases our estimate of asset decumulation downward a bit relative to the correct number for the entire population, but it should not affect the comparison of workers and retirees. The second period (1975–79) received identical treatment. Our basic samples consisted of 574 households retired by 1969 (270 single individuals,

504 couples), 1,360 households still working in 1975 (240 single individuals, 1,120 couples), 1,037 households retired by 1975 (173 single individuals, 864 couples), and 507 households still working in 1979 (96 singles, 411 couples).

Finally, all variables have been deflated to 1975 dollars. This, of course, affects the interpretation of magnitudes reported in the following sections.

9.3 Bequeathable Wealth

Although information about the bequeathable wealth-age profile does not by itself allow us to discuss the plausibility of life cycle motives, it is nevertheless of significant independent interest. In this section, we review the existing literature on dissaving among the elderly, arguing that previous studies suffer from significant biases. New estimates of dissaving from bequeathable wealth are then presented.

9.3.1 Previous Studies

Three different types of data sources have been used to estimate the extent of dissaving during retirement. These are: (1) interview surveys of saving among the aged, (2) cross-section interview surveys of net worth, and (3) estate data. We consider these in turn.

Typically, data from interview surveys of saving among the aged (Lydall 1955; Projector 1968; Mulanaphy 1974) have found positive or only slightly negative rates of accumulation. These findings can be criticized on several grounds. First, savings are defined by observable transactions. Thus, all capital gains and losses (including those induced by inflation) are omitted. Second, the data are highly aggregated. Both Projector and Lydall group all aged individuals (those over 65) together in a single category. Undoubtedly, many of these are still working, perhaps saving at a rapid rate in anticipation of retirement. This problem is compounded by the fact that mean values are reported—a small (perhaps wealthy) fraction of the sample saving large amounts may, in such a calculation, dominate the dissaving of a much larger fraction. Thus, the percentage of retirees dissaving at reasonably rapid rates may be much larger than these numbers would suggest.

A number of investigators, including Lydall (1955), Projector and Weiss (1966), Smith (1975), Mirer (1979), and King and Dicks-Mireaux (1982) have attempted to infer the bequeathable wealth-age profile from cross-section interview surveys of net worth. With the exception of King and Dicks-Mireaux, these studies confirm the findings reported above. However, this approach encounters a variety of difficulties.

First, none of these studies distinguish between workers and retirees. Physical assets understate the total wealth (human and nonhuman) available to nonretired individuals. Since the proportion of fully retired individuals in a cohort rises with the age of that cohort, this builds in a spurious positive correlation between observed wealth and age.[8]

To illustrate the potential significance of this effect, we regressed total bequeathable wealth on age and lifetime resources for four sub-samples (all single individuals, retired single individuals, all couples, and retired couples), using cross-section data from the 1975 wave of the LRHS. We chose the 1975 wave for two reasons: (1) in 1975, age of respondent ranges from 64 to 69, which facilitates comparison with other studies,[9] and (2) in 1969, there was very little spread in age of retirement due to the comparative youth of the sample.[10] Our results are presented in table 9.1.[11] Point estimates for the entire sample are roughly consistent with previous studies. However, when current workers are excluded, significant dissaving is observed for both single individuals and couples (note, however, that the coefficient is not statistically significant for couples).

Unfortunately, restricting attention to retired individuals within a cross-section induces a sample selection bias. Suppose we know that an individual of age A is retired, but we have not observed his date of retirement. It is straightforward to show that his expected age of retirement is increasing in A.[12] Thus, all else equal, we would expect older members of a cross-section to have retired later. Differences in age therefore overstate differences in years of retirement (time spent dissaving). This suggests that our estimates understate the true magnitude of dissaving.

A second difficulty encountered by studies employing cross-section interview surveys of net worth is that such surveys implicitly incorporate an important sample selection criterion: only surviving members of a particular cohort are represented. Ex ante, survivors are, on a average, healthier. Thus, as a cohort ages, the survivors will represent an increasingly healthy (in a lifetime sense) fraction of the original

Table 9.1   **Wealth Level Regressions for 1975 Cross-Section**

Variable	Singles		Couples	
	All	Retired	All	Retired
Constant	−10934	168757	34527	170171
	(36359)	(83408)	(37321)	(118587)
Age	379	−2442	65.6	−1925
	(593)	(1354)	(608.9)	(1930)
Y	0.0234	0.00892	0.0133	0.0196
	(0.0054)	(0.0134)	(0.0035)	(0.0102)
Sample size	1605	213	5960	964

sample.[13] This induces a correlation between age and lifetime health in cross-sections.[14] Healthier individuals in turn tend to accumulate more wealth to provide for longer retirement periods. As a result, a spurious positive correlation between wealth and age may be observed.

Third, with the exception of King and Dicks-Mireaux, studies employing cross-section surveys of net worth fail to control for lifetime resources. Since wealthier people tend to live longer, older members of any cross-section will, on average, have higher lifetime resources. This problem is compounded by the secular decline in retirement age (older individuals spent more years in the labor force). Rising productivity generates an offsetting "cohort effect"—on average, older members of any cross-section will have worked during periods of lower wages. The net effect is ambiguous; age may be positively or negatively correlated with age in cross-sections.[15]

King and Dicks-Mireaux recognize the importance of controlling for lifetime earnings, and employ the ratio of net worth to "permanent income" as their dependent variable. While this is an improvement over previous techniques, it fails to correct properly for the first two sources of bias mentioned in the preceding paragraph. Most obviously, since permanent income is a yearly figure, no adjustment is made for length of working life. In addition, this variable is constructed in a manner which fails to adjust for the correlation between wealth and survival probabilities. Specifically, permanent income is inferred from a cross-section regression explaining current earnings. Since retired individuals have no current earnings, the estimates are driven by the earnings of younger (and therefore, since the cohort effect is corrected for, lifetime poorer) individuals. This builds in a tendency to underpredict the permanent income of elderly individuals, or equivalently to understate the extent of dissaving.

Finally, we consider studies based on estate data. Since Atkinson (1971), Atkinson and Harrison (1978), and Brittain (1978) use this data to generate cross-section estimates of the age-wealth relation, their analyses suffer from the problems described above. In fact, different sample selection criteria imply that, in some cases, the bias will be much worse. For example, information on young individuals is observed only if those individuals die young. Since early death is highly correlated with poor health, there will be a strong correlation between age and lifetime health in such samples. In addition, estate data are heavily truncated, providing no information on a very large number of individuals who die with relatively little net worth. In effect, any individual who dissaves too rapidly is automatically excluded from these samples.

Shorrocks (1975) used a somewhat different approach, estimating the age-wealth relationship from estate data by following a particular cohort over time. While he corrects for potential biases based upon the correlation between wealth and survival probabilities, he does not adjust for the effects of attrition (individuals who dissave sufficiently never show up in estate data), and therefore understates the rate of resource depletion.

While most of these studies have focused on the relationship between total bequeathable wealth and age, some have also investigated changes in portfolio composition among the elderly. One question of particular interest is how the percentage of net worth held as owner-occupied housing changes with age. Attempts to infer an answer to this question based upon cross-section data are subject to the difficulties mentioned above. Portfolio composition may, for example, be related to total lifetime resources, which is correlated with age in cross-sections (see above). It is therefore not surprising that various studies, such as Mirer and King and Dicks-Mireaux, have reached very different conclusions.[16]

9.3.2   New Estimates

Since most objections to analyses of cross-section data are based on the premise that individuals at one age are systematically different from individuals at another age, one possible solution is to follow the same individuals over time, observing changes in their net worth. Thus, Mirer concludes that longitudinal data from retirement to death would be "ideal" for determining wealth holding profiles.[17] Diamond and Hausman (1984) have previously employed the National Longitudinal Survey (NLS, or Parnes data) to study individual savings behavior, in part generating an estimate of asset decumulation after retirement. Like the LRHS, the NLS followed a sample of households over a period of 10 years; however, NLS respondents are, on average, much younger.[18] Thus, Diamond and Hausman's estimates of decumulation are based on a relatively small,[19] and perhaps atypical,[20] sample of retirees. With the completion and availability of the LRHS, it is now possible to supplement the existing literature with new estimates based on more complete longitudinal data for the early retirement period. Our first objective is to provide this evidence.

While the use of panel data does allow us to overcome a variety of difficulties encountered by other approaches, it also raises a new set of problems. First, estimates are very sensitive to macroeconomic events. For example, in a period of supra (sub) normal stock market returns, respondents may experience significant *unanticipated* accumulation (depletion) of net worth (more on this below). The data, however, provide no way of distinguishing motives. It is worth noting that analyses of cross-section data encounter a similar difficulty, since different cohorts have encountered systematically different patterns of unanticipated gains and losses over the life cycle. Within the current context, we can partially correct for this effect by examining evidence based upon macroeconomically distinct time periods (specifically, we use 1969 through 1975 and 1975 through 1979). In addition, we can, for each period, isolate the net effect of retirement on accumulation by contrasting the behavior of retirees and workers.

A second problem concerns sample selection. For each period, our analysis is confined to households who "survived" the entire period. Presumably this implies that our data overrepresent healthy, wealthy, and domestically stable households. In addition, our requirement that households be retired at the beginning of the period, combined with the relative youth of respondents, implies that the sample is skewed toward early retirees.[21] It is critical to realize, however, that although our sample may be somewhat atypical relative to the entire population,[22] there is no reason to believe that our selection criteria bias estimates of dissaving for this group. The great advantage of panel data is that, by following the same households over time, we can hold exogenous factors (however selected) constant. In contrast, for cross-sections, dissaving is inferred from differences in the net worth of households of different ages, who are implicitly selected according to different criteria. We conclude that panel data, while not perfect, provides a superior source of evidence on asset accumulation.

We begin by inspecting the time pattern of mean bequeathable wealth for each of our subgroups. Results are presented in table 9.2.[23] Between 1969 and 1975, net worth declines by 21.1% ($3,176) for retired individuals, and 22.8% ($7,923) for retired couples. In the later period (1975–79), it declines by 6.8% ($1,393) for retired individuals and rises by 4.1% ($2,466) for retired couples. These figures are consistent with a 3%–4% yearly decline during the first period and either a 2% yearly decline or 1% yearly rise in the second period. It is difficult to determine whether differences between periods are attributable to sample differences (early vs. late retirees) or to changing macroeconomic circumstances.

It is noteworthy that, for each subgroup of working households, net worth always moves in the same direction as it does for the corresponding retired subgroup. In fact, it falls for all groups, except for couples between 1975 and 1979. This in itself is not surprising; hump-shaped income profiles may cause wealth to begin its decline prior to retirement. King and Dicks-Mireaux also find some evidence of dissaving within the pre-retirement group. However, since income falls discontinuously at retirement, the life cycle hypothesis at minimum predicts that the rate of accumulation (depletion) should fall (rise) at that time.[24] Is this prediction consistent with the data?

For single individuals, there is very little difference in either period between the absolute dollar value dissaved by retirees and workers.

Table 9.2   Bequeathable Wealth by Year and Retirement Status

Variable	Single Individuals				Couples			
	Retired by 1969	Not Retired by 1975	Retired by 1975	Not Retired by 1979	Retired by 1969	Not Retired by 1975	Retired by 1975	Not Retired by 1979
Bequeathable wealth in								
1969	15008	30003	21743	48768	34818	66719	61304	87374
1975	11832	27183	20601	37943	26895	64420	60144	75709
1979	—	—	19209	37071	—	—	62610	84480
Fraction of sample with positive bequeathable wealth in								
1969	0.685	0.858	0.821	0.896	0.915	0.938	0.957	0.949
1975	0.626	0.846	0.902	0.885	0.768	0.932	0.962	0.961
1979	—	—	0.879	0.885	—	—	0.954	0.951
1969 and 1975	0.415	0.675	0.671	0.719	0.621	0.818	0.855	0.827
1975 and 1979	—	—	0.688	0.750	—	—	0.861	0.844
Sample size	270	240	173	96	504	1120	864	411

However, since early retirees tend to be relatively poor, differences between rates of dissaving are substantial (mean net worth of workers fell 9.4% between 1969 and 1975 and 2.3% between 1975 and 1979). For couples, differences between both rates of change and absolute dollar values dissaved were substantial.[25] In interpreting these numbers, it is important to recall that the subgroups are based on different sample selection criteria, and differences may therefore reflect heterogeneous behavioral propensities.

One puzzling aspect of table 9.2 is the precipitous decline between 1969 and 1975 in the net worth of both single individuals and couples still working in 1979. During this period, mean dissaving of households retiring in the more distant future exceeded that of any other groups. This observation seems inconsistent with life cycle behavior; we will return to it at various point.

For a number of reasons, we are dissatisfied with estimates of accumulation and depletion based on mean values of net worth. Most importantly, these estimates will be heavily influenced by the potentially atypical behavior of households with high initial wealth. Suppose, for example, that the behavior of households i is given by[26]

$$W_{t,i} = \beta_i W_{t-1, i},$$

where $W_{t,i}$ is bequeathable wealth in period t. Our estimate $\hat{\beta}_1$, of the mean population dissaving rate, is

$$\text{(1)} \qquad \hat{\beta}_1 = \frac{\overline{W}_t}{\overline{W}_{t-1}}$$

$$= \sum_i^N \frac{W_{t-1,i}}{N\overline{W}_{t-1}} \beta_i .$$

That is, $\hat{\beta}_1$ is a weighted average of the β_i's, where the largest weights are accorded to individuals with high initial wealth. Such individuals may, for example, be atypically acquisitive, leading to a high estimated value of β.

A related problem concerns measurement error. Suppose that β_i has a common value, β, for all households, so that true wealth $W_{t,i}^*$ evolves according to

$$\text{(2)} \qquad W_{t,i}^* = \beta W_{t-1,i}^* .$$

Assume as well that wealth is observed with error:

$$\text{(3)} \qquad W_{t,i} = W_{t,i}^* \epsilon_{t,i},$$

where $E(\epsilon_{t,i}) = 1$, and $\epsilon_{t,i}$ is independent of $W_{\tau,i}^*$ and $\epsilon_{\tau,j}$ for all $(\tau, j) \neq (t, i)$. Then our estimate $\hat{\beta}_1$ can be written as

$$\hat{\beta}_1 = \sum_i^N \frac{W_{t-1,i}}{N\bar{W}_{t-1,i}} \tilde{\beta}_i \, ,$$

where

$$\tilde{\beta}_i = \beta \, \epsilon_{t,i}/\epsilon_{t-1,i} \, .$$

$\hat{\beta}_1$ is a consistent estimator of β. However, since it is a ratio of stochastic terms, its small sample properties are suspect. In particular, observations with a high value of $\epsilon_{t-1,i}$ (and therefore a lower value of $\tilde{\beta}_i$) will receive greater weight ($W_{t-1,i}/N\bar{W}_{t-1,i}$ will be higher). We would therefore expect our estimate of β to be biased downwards, toward high dissaving.

These considerations suggest that we should accord equal weight to the dissaving *rate* of each household. One alternative is to calculate the mean rate, $\hat{\beta}_2$:

$$\hat{\beta}_2 = \frac{1}{N} \sum_i \frac{W_{t-1,i}}{W_{t,i}}$$

(where N is the number of observations). When wealth is observed with error, this technique will produce inconsistent estimates of β. In particular, it is straightforward to verify that, under the appropriate regularity conditions,[27]

$$\text{plim } \hat{\beta}_2 = \beta \, E\!\left(\frac{1}{\epsilon_{t,i}}\right) ,$$

which generally exceeds β. The difficulty again arises from the appearance of a stochastic term in the denominator.

We suggest the following procedure. Equation (2) can be written as

$$\log W_{t,i}^*/W_{t-1,i}^* = \log \beta.$$

Substituting (3), we see that

$$\log W_{t,i}/W_{t-1,i} = \log \beta + \log \epsilon_{t-1,i} - \log \epsilon_{t,i} \, .$$

If the measurement error terms are, for example, independent[28] and lognormal, then the mean observed log rate of accumulation is an unbiased estimator of the log of β. With population heterogeneity, this procedure produces an unbiased estimate of the mean of $\log \beta_i$, but it is not possible to recover the population mean of β_i itself. However, if the β_i's are reasonably close together (we might expect them to be near unity), the mean of the logs will not be far from the log of the mean.

The problem with the procedure is that it requires us to drop all households for which measured wealth was nonpositive in either period

t or period $t - 1$. It is important to examine the resulting sample selection bias. If the sample is heterogeneous, the procedure excludes all observations for whom $\beta_i = 0$ or ∞. In addition, if the probability of falsely reporting 0 falls with wealth, then our estimate of the mean of log β_i will be biased upward.[29]

To determine the potential significance of this effect, we examined the frequency of movements to and from nonpositive levels of bequeathable wealth. Our findings are summarized in the second part of table 9.2. For most groups (especially couples), the percentage reporting zero wealth was relatively low. Moreover, net movements between positive and nonpositive wealth levels are typically quite small (on the order of 1% or 2%), with three exceptions. First, 6% (net) of retired single individuals moved from positive to nonpositive wealth between 1969 and 1975, as did 15% of retired couples. During the same period, 8% of single individuals who would retire by 1975 moved in the opposite direction. Thus, we observe some tendency for early retirees to completely exhaust their accumulated resources quickly after retirement. We also observe a significant fraction of single individuals accumulating appreciable resources only immediately prior to retirement.

There is, however, much noise in these data. While net movements between positive and nonpositive wealth levels are typically small, the total fraction of households moving in one direction or the other is quite large. To see this, note (in table 9.2) that the percentage of households reporting positive resources in two consecutive sample years is substantially smaller than the fraction reporting positive resources in either of those two years alone.

Table 9.3 presents sample statistics on log W_{75}/W_{69} and log W_{79}/W_{75} for each of our subgroups. Recognizing the conceptual difficulties generated by the sample selection bias described above, we have listed medians, as well as the fraction of each subsample for which bequeathable wealth declines during the period of observation. If inclusion of observations with zero wealth is desired, it is possible to adjust fractile statistics using the percentage movements to and from zero wealth reported in table 9.2.

The results are quite striking, and differ enormously from those based on wealth levels. The mean log rates of accumulation indicate statistically significant dissaving for every retired group, except couples from 1975 to 1979. Positive saving among this group may be an artifact of the precipitous, and probably unanticipated, rise in housing prices during the late seventies, combined with relatively widespread home ownership (see statistics below). In contrast, no dissaving is indicated in any currently working group, and in many such cases the estimated saving rates are statistically significant. Note that the "puzzle" of sig-

Table 9.3   Changes in Bequeathable Wealth by Year and Retirement Status

	Single Individuals				Couples			
Variable	Retired by 1969	Not Retired by 1975	Retired by 1975	Not Retired by 1979	Retired by 1969	Not Retired by 1975	Retired by 1975	Not Retired by 1979
Log W_{75}/W_{69}								
Mean*	−0.198	0.113	0.256	0.025	−0.125	0.171	0.123	0.077
	(0.108)	(0.131)	(0.143)	(0.180)	(0.066)	(0.038)	(0.043)	(0.063)
Median	−0.186	0.152	0.131	0.009	−0.086	0.181	0.149	0.170
Fraction < 0	0.580	0.444	0.457	0.507	0.527	0.381	0.407	0.418
Log W_{79}/W_{75}								
Mean*	—	—	−0.285	0.021	—	—	0.028	0.095
			(0.120)	(0.164)			(0.044)	(0.055)
Median	—	—	−0.104	0.176	—	—	0.074	0.133
Fraction < 0	—	—	0.546	0.375	—	—	0.415	0.403

*Estimated standard errors in parentheses.

nificant dissaving before retirement among late retirees no longer appears. Medians reveal a similar pattern, the only discrepancy in sign arising with respect to single individuals still working in 1979, during the first sample period. Adjustment of medians for movement to and from nonpositive wealth would not alter this pattern.

Rates of dissaving for retired single individuals are evidently quite high. Calculated means indicated a yearly decline of between 3% and 6%; medians confirm the lower end of this range. In contrast, couples dissave very little—perhaps 1% or 2% per year in the first period (early retirees), and not at all in the second period (although medians indicate that wealth may have risen by as much as 2% per year, the reader should bear in mind the above qualification concerning housing price inflation). The discrepancy between the behavior of single individuals and that of couples should not be surprising, since couples must provide for the possibility that either member survives for a long time. In addition, it may account for the diversity of previous estimates: Mirer studies couples, while King and Dicks-Mireaux include single individuals.

It is worth noting that saving is observed for a significant fraction (over 40%) of all retired samples, and that dissaving is observed for a significant fraction (over one-third) of all nonretired samples. While this phenomenon may reflect heterogeneity of behavior, we are inclined to attribute it primarily to the apparent extent of measurement error.

Only our highest estimates of depletion rates are roughly consistent with the 5.1% to 7.4% figures obtained by Diamond and Hausman (1984). These estimates are not, however, strictly comparable with ours, since they refer to hypothetical decumulation in the absence of annuity holdings (more on this in sections 9.4 and 9.5). In addition, Diamond and Hausman's sample may be unrepresentative. As mentioned earlier, NLS households are, on average, substantially younger than LRHS households. Individuals retiring during the NLS sample period will, by and large, be early retirees; our results indicate that early retirees tend to overrepresent single individuals,[30] and we have seen that single individuals deplete resources more rapidly than couples. In light of our findings, it would seem unwise to conclude on the basis of their study that typical married retirees dissave significant portions of their wealth.

We now examine the evolution of portfolio composition after retirement. Table 9.4 decomposes bequeathable wealth into four categories: owner-occupied housing, business and property, financial assets, and debt (other than mortgages). The last of these categories is insignificant. The extent of home ownership (fraction owner-occupants) is also indicated.

For both single individuals and couples retired by 1969, there is a decline in every significant asset category *except* housing. The data

Table 9.4   Breakdown of Bequeathable Wealth for Retirees

Type of Wealth and Year	Single Individuals		Couples	
	Retired by 1969	Retired by 1975	Retired by 1969	Retired by 1975
House*				
1969	6122	4175	13700	15013
	(0.307)	(0.260)	(0.688)	(0.627)
1975	6424	9893	13944	25481
	(0.322)	(0.468)	(0.581)	(0.791)
1979	—	8268	—	28934
		(0.416)		(0.775)
Business and property				
1969	1312	12042	6172	29625
1975	914	4575	3401	14013
1979	—	4143	—	14966
Financial wealth				
1969	7718	5790	15654	17635
1975	4646	6509	10119	21509
1979	—	6949	—	19076
Nonmortgage debt				
1969	143	263	709	969
1975	153	374	567	861
1979	—	192	—	366

*Percentage owning a home is given in parentheses.

indicate a slight increase in home ownership for retired individuals during this period and a slight decline for retired couples.

The behavior of households which were retired by 1975 is more interesting. More or less simultaneously with retirement (1969–75), both single individuals and couples liquidated large amounts of business and property wealth. At the same time, holdings of financial assets rose slightly, while large gains in housing wealth (especially in frequency of home ownership) were registered. This raises the possibility that households liquidated business and property holdings to finance purchases of homes.[31] During the post-retirement period, there is a slight dip in home ownership for both groups. Evidently, while many households purchase homes at retirement, a smaller but significant number of households sell homes within a few years subsequent to retirement.

The evidence also appears to indicate that a reasonably stable (perhaps slightly increasing) fraction of bequeathable wealth is held as owner-occupied housing during retirement. This confirms the finding of King and Dicks-Mireaux, contradicting that of Mirer. However, we should emphasize that these data only concern the early retirement period.

9.4 Annuities

A very large fraction of the total resources available to many retired individuals is locked into annuities (government and private pensions, social security). Studies which ignore this important component of wealth fail to provide sufficient information for judging the plausibility of life cycle motives.

It has frequently been argued that the inclusion of annuities would vindicate the hump-shaped wealth-age profile, since the actuarial value of survival contingent claims falls with age (single-year survival probabilities decline). Thus, Mirer (1979) concedes that, "to some extent, perhaps a great one for many people, pension and Social Security programs tend to institutionalize the tenets of the life cycle theory." Likewise, Dicks-Mireaux and King (1984) find evidence of "a clear life-cycle pattern" when the actuarial value of annuity claims are included in measures of net worth.

In this section, I argue that actuarial valuation is inappropriate if one wishes to infer an age-wealth profile in order to judge the plausibility of life cycle motives. Elsewhere (Bernheim 1984b), I have shown that the simple discounted value of future benefits (ignoring the possibility of death) is ordinarily a good approximation to the value (in terms of compensating variation) of an annuity. Here I establish that simple discounting is also appropriate within the current context. Since this measure changes very little with age, my analysis reverses the conclusions of King and Dicks-Mireaux: the inclusion of annuities reinforces earlier findings that resources decline only slightly, if at all, after retirement.

9.4.1 Theoretical Considerations

Actuarial valuation of annuities is appropriate under either of two conditions: (1) households are risk neutral, or (2) households have access to competitive annuity markets. The first of these conditions is unreasonably restrictive, and generates absurd behavioral predictions.[32] Under the second condition, there is a very simple test of pure life cycle motives: Do households hold positive levels of bequeathable wealth at all? In fact, if annuities yield any return in excess of the interest rate, pure life cycle consumers will annuitize 100% of their resources,[33] and the notion of dissaving will be vacuous. Thus, if we wish to use evidence on rates of dissaving to test the pure life cycle hypothesis, we must assume a complete absence of annuity markets.[34]

Under the assumptions of missing annuity markets and risk aversion, the value of an annuity will exceed its actuarial value by a risk premium. Our current task is to determine what this observation implies about the appropriate computation of age-wealth profiles.

We will assume the constant elasticity, intertemporally separable form of lifetime utility,

$$
(3) \qquad \frac{1}{\alpha} \int_0^\infty e^{-\lambda t} C_t^\alpha dt \ ,
$$

where λ captures the effects of discounting both through the pure rate of time preference and survival probabilities.[35] At time 0, the individual is endowed with some level of bequeathable wealth W_0, and receives some annuity payment A_0. Annuity payments grow geometrically at the rate g; the interest rate is r. Thus, the individuals choice is constrained as follows:

$$
(4) \qquad \int_0^\infty (C_t - A_t)e^{-rt} \, dt \le W_0
$$

and

$$
(5) \qquad W_t = e^{rt}W_0 - \int_0^t (C_\tau - A_\tau)e^{r(t-\tau)} \, d\tau \ge 0.
$$

Ignoring constraint (5) and maximizing (3) subject to (4), we obtain the following first-order conditions:

$$
(6) \qquad C_t = e^{\gamma t} C_0 \ ,
$$

where $\gamma \equiv (r - \lambda)/(1 - \alpha) < r$.[36] Suppose $\gamma \ge g$. Then continuing to ignore (5), it is easy to see that the optimal program is given by (6), along with

$$
(7) \qquad C_t = (r - g) \left(W_t + \frac{A_t}{r - g} \right)
$$

and

$$
(8) \qquad \left(W_t + \frac{A_t}{r - g} \right) = \left(W_0 + \frac{A_0}{r - g} \right) e^{\gamma t}.
$$

Since this program never violates (5), it is optimal.

The interpretation of (7) and (8) is straightforward: consumption in each period is a constant fraction of total wealth, and total wealth grows at the geometric rate γ. Note, however, that the annuity wealth term, $A_t/(r - g)$, is equal to the simple discounted value of future benefits (ignoring death). Thus, to make inferences about γ (the life cycle parameter of interest) from data on the age-wealth profiles, we should define total wealth to include the *simple* discounted value of annuities, *not* the actuarial value. Intuitively, unless an individual plans to consume his principal at some point in the future, he will be indifferent an annuity paying $1 per year, and an asset worth $1/r (both generate the same survival contingent income stream).

If $\gamma < g$, the problem is more complex. Ignoring (5), one again obtains (7) and (8), but in this case (5) will be violated for t sufficiently large (the individual will wish to borrow on future annuity benefits). Along the true optimal program, consumption will obey the first-order condition (6) as long as wealth is positive; however, once (5) binds, we will simply have $C_t = A_t$. Let T denote the age at which (5) first binds. Then the first-order conditions imply that

(9)
$$\begin{cases} C_t = e^{\gamma t} C_0 & t < T \\ C_t = A_t & t \geq T. \end{cases}$$

From the resource constraint, we have

(10)
$$W_0 = \int_0^T (C_t - A_t) e^{-rt} \, dt.$$

Finally, it is easy to see that, despite the binding constraint, consumption must be continuous in time, so that

(11)
$$e^{\gamma T} C_0 = e^{gT} A_0.$$

Equations (9), (10), and (11) together determine C_0 and T, from which the optimal program can be constructed.

In Bernheim (1984b), we calculated the compensating variation associated with the marginal annuity for the case of $\gamma < g$ (using eqq. [9]–[11]),

$$\left. \frac{dW_0}{dA_0} \right|_{U=U^*} = -\frac{1}{r-g}(1-\phi),$$

where

$$\phi = \left(1 - \frac{r-g}{\lambda - \alpha g}\right) e^{(g-r)T},$$

and established that $0 \leq \phi < 1$. Intuitively, since (5) may bind at some point, the annuity is worth less than an asset which yields the same yearly survival contingent income. As T goes to infinity (or γ to g), this event becomes more remote, so naturally the value of annuitization approaches $A_0/(r-g)$.

Hypothetical values of the proportional adjustment factor (ϕ) are given in Bernheim (1984b). For completeness, we reproduce two sample calculations here. We assume that $r = 0.03$, $g = 0$, $\alpha = 0$ (the logarithmic case), and $A_0/(r - g)W_0 = 2$ (i.e., two-thirds of total resources are held as annuities).[37] Since λ depends on the rate at which individuals discount future utility, it is the most difficult parameter to gauge. We employ values of 0.05 and 0.07.[38] The formula for γ is given above. Substituting (9) into (10), one finds that T is given by the implicit solution to

$$e^{(g-\gamma)T}[1 - e^{(\gamma-r)T}]\frac{r - g}{r - \gamma} - [1 - e^{(g-r)T}] = \frac{W_0(r - g)}{A_0} .$$

Calculated values of γ, T, and ϕ are presented in table 9.5. Ignoring nonnegativity constraints, wealth would decline by 2% and 4% per year, for λ equal to 0.05 and 0.07, respectively. The associated unconstrained intervals are 42 and 27 years. The marginal annuity is worth 89%, and 75% of its simple discounted value, respectively. Employing a "triangle approximation" for the value of inframarginal units, we find that the associated compensating variations for all annuity holdings are 94%, and 87% of their simple discounted values. In contrast, for these parameter values the actuarial discounted value of a benefit stream is only 37.5% of its simple discounted value.[39]

There is, of course, no reason to believe that it is appropriate to use the compensating variation as a measure of annuity valuation when calculating wealth trajectories (except in the limiting case where the nonnegativity constraints never bind). For this reason, we pose the question somewhat differently. Suppose we employ simple valuation, that is, define total resources,

$$R_t \equiv W_t + A_t / (r - g) ,$$

Table 9.5   **Wealth Trajectories for Hypothetical Parameter Values***

Calculated Parameter	Assumed Value of λ	
	0.05	0.07
γ	-0.020	-0.040
T	42	27
ϕ	0.114	0.254
ψ	0.027	0.090
γ^r	-0.016	-0.026
γ^w	-0.052	-0.093

*For these calculations, we assumed $r = 0.03$, $g = 0$, $\alpha = 0$ (i.e., the logarithmic case), $A_0/(r - g)W_0 = 2$, and $t = 6$.

and calculate rates of dissaving from R_t/R_0 (i.e., pretend the non-negativity contraints never bind). How well will our estimated dissaving parameter,

$$\gamma^r \equiv t^{-1} \ln(R_t/R_0) \, ,$$

approximate the parameter of interest (γ)?

Using our characterization of the optimal (constrained) program, it is possible to calculate that

$$W_t = e^{rt} (W_0 - A_0\{e^{(g-\gamma)T}[1 - e^{(\gamma-r)t}]/(r - \gamma) \\ - [1 - e^{(g-r)t}]/(r - g)\}) \, .$$

Substituting this into the expression for R_t, one can show (after some tedious manipulations) that

(12)
$$\frac{R_t}{R_0} = e^{\gamma t}[1 + \psi]$$

where

(13)
$$\psi = e^{(r-\gamma)t}\left[\frac{1 - e^{(\gamma-r)t}}{1 - e^{(\gamma-r)T}}\right]\left[\frac{A_0^{/(r-g)}}{R_0}e^{(g-r)T} - e^{(\gamma-r)T}\right].$$

Table 9.5 presents values of ψ and γ^r calculated for our sets of hypothetical parameter values (where $t = 6$). When $\lambda = 0.05$, ψ is 0.027, which indicates that γ^r understates the "true" rate of dissaving by approximately $\frac{1}{2}\%$ per year. Thus, rather than observing a decline of 2% per year, we should observe "total wealth" falling by $1\frac{1}{2}\%$ per year. When $\lambda = 0.07$, $\psi = 0.090$, which indicates that γ^r understates the true rate of dissaving by $1\frac{1}{2}\%$ per year. Thus, "total wealth" would fall by $2\frac{1}{2}\%$, rather than by 4%, per year.

These calculations suggest that γ^r will, for $\gamma < g$, understate the rate of dissaving, γ. We now prove that this inequality always holds.

PROPOSITION 1: For $\gamma \geq g$, $\gamma^r = \gamma$. For $\gamma < g$, $\gamma^r > \gamma$.

Proof: The first statement follows trivially from equation (8). We prove the second claim by showing that $\psi > 0$. Straightforward calculations reveal that, for $\gamma < g$, $dC_0/dA_0|_{R_0} < 0^{40}$ (intuitively, annuities have a negative income effect since the nonnegativity constraint binds; consumption is therefore depressed). Thus, $R_t > R_0 e^{\gamma t}$ (since the right-hand side indicates remaining resources in period t if nonnegativity constraints are ignored). Taking $t = T$ and rearranging, we see that $A_0 e^{gT}/(r - g) > R_0 e^{\gamma T}$. From equation (13), this is easily seen to imply that ψ is positive. Q.E.D.

Given this result, one possible approach is to adjust γ^r given an assumed value of ψ, corresponding to some set of reasonable parameter values. Unfortunately, ψ depends on γ, so we cannot estimate γ from

γ^r without knowing γ itself. Another alternative is to obtain a lower bound on γ, in addition to this upper bound.

How might we obtain a lower bound? One suggestion is to calculate rates of dissaving from W_t/W_0 (as in the preceding section):

$$\gamma^w \equiv t^{-1}\ell n(W_t/W_0) .$$

To motivate this suggestion, ignore (for the moment) nonnegativity constraints (eq. [5]). Equation (8) will then describe the evolution of total wealth. Simple manipulations reveal that

(14)
$$\frac{\dot{W}_t}{W_t} = \gamma + (\gamma - g)\frac{A_t/(r - g)}{W_t} .$$

Equation (14) has an important interpretation. If the individual holds no annuities, his bequeathable wealth grows at exactly the rate γ. Supposing as before that $\gamma < g$, as annuities increase, the rate at which bequeathable wealth declines will *accelerate*.[41] The reason is straight-forward: annuity wealth, $A_t/(r - g)$, declines at the rate g; to preserve a *total* rate of decline of γ, bequeathable wealth must fall at an accelerated rate. Thus, as long as $\gamma < g$, γ^w will overstate the extent of dissaving. Note that this is completely contrary to the assertions of earlier authors, who had argued that W_t/W_0 would understate dissaving due to the actuarial decline in annuity wealth.

Of course, the preceding analysis ignores the nonnegativity constraints. It is important to verify that our lower bound on γ is valid even when these constraints are considered explicitly. In particular, we prove:

PROPOSITION 2: When $\gamma < g$, $d(W_t/W_t)/dA_0 < 0$.

Proof: Using the accounting identity

$$\frac{\dot{W}_t}{W_t} = r + \frac{A_t - C_t}{W_t} ,$$

we see that

$$W_t^2 \frac{d(\dot{W}_t/W_t)}{dA_0} = W_t\left(\frac{dA_t}{dA_0} - \frac{dC_t}{dA_0}\right) - (A_t - C_t)\frac{dW_t}{dA_0} .$$

Appropriate substitution from equations (7) through (10) reveals that this is[42]

$$= A_t\, e^{(g-r)(T-t)} \cdot \left[\frac{e^{(r-\gamma)(T-t)} - 1}{r - \gamma}\right]\left[e^{rt} + \left(1 - \frac{r - \gamma}{r - g}\delta\right)\right]$$

$$+ \left[\frac{e^{(r-g)(T-t)} - 1}{r - \gamma}\right]\left[e^{\gamma t}\left(\frac{r - \gamma}{r - g} - 1\right)\delta - e^{rt}(1 - \delta)\right]$$

where

$$\delta = \frac{1 - e^{(g-r)T}}{1 - e^{(\gamma-r)T}} .$$

Using the fact that

$$\frac{e^{(r-\gamma)(T-t)} - 1}{r - \gamma} > \frac{e^{(r-g)(T-t)} - 1}{r - g} > 0 ,$$

it is then possible to show that[43]

$$\frac{d(\dot{W}_t/W_t)}{dA_0} < 0 ,$$

which is the desired result. Q.E.D.

Of course, if $A_0 = 0$, $\dot{W}_t/W_t = \gamma$, so for $\gamma > g$, $A_0 > 0$ implies $\gamma^w < \gamma$. It is convenient to summarize this conclusion, as well as much of the preceding analysis, in the following proposition.

PROPOSITION 3:
(i)   If $\gamma = g$ or $A_0 = 0$, $\gamma^r = \gamma^w = \gamma$.
(ii) If $\gamma > g$ and $A_0 > 0$, $\gamma^r = \gamma < \gamma^w$.
(iii) If $\gamma < g$ and $A_0 > 0$, $\gamma^w < \gamma < \gamma^r$.

Case iii is the most interesting, since (for $g = 0$) it concerns a dissaver who holds positive annuities. For such an individual, depletion of bequeathable wealth will overstate dissaving, while depletion of total wealth (including the simple discounted value of annuity benefits) will understate it.

Which of our two measure, γ^r or γ^w, will be closer to γ? In general, the answer depends upon particular parameter values. We can obtain some feel for magnitudes by using (12), along with the definition of R_t to obtain

(15)
$$\frac{W_t}{W_0} = \frac{e^{\gamma t}(1 + \psi) - \xi e^{gt}}{1 - \xi}$$

where

$$\xi = \frac{A_0/(r - g)}{R_0} .$$

Suppose $g = 0$. What happens as ξ rises? Ignoring the effect on ψ, we see that W_t/W_0 falls; in fact, it is equal to zero when $\xi = e^{\gamma t}(1 + \psi) < 1$. Thus, we would expect γ^w to significantly understate γ when the degree of annuitization is high.

The data presented below indicate that ξ is quite high—roughly on the order of 2/3 (while others have found much lower levels of annuitization relative to bequeathable wealth, this is due to the use of actuarial valuation). It is therefore not very surprising that γ^r significantly outperforms γ^w for our hypothetical parameter values. In table 9.5, we calculate values of γ^w, using equation (15). Increasing annuitization from zero to two-thirds of total resources accelerates the rate of bequeathable wealth depletion from 2% to 5.2% per year for $\lambda = 0.05$, and from 4% to 9.3% for $\lambda = 0.07$. In both cases, the true value of γ is much closer to our upper bound, γ^r. By incorporating data on annuities, we might therefore hope to learn much more about the implied behavioral rate of dissaving.

9.4.2   Analysis of the Data

In implementing the ideas described above, we encounter two conceptual difficulties. The first concerns expectations about future annuity benefits. In particular, substantial changes in social security legislation took place during the sample period. Should we assume that these were properly anticipated? If we assume myopic expectations at each point in time (constant real benefits from that point forward), social security wealth will be quite volatile. However, since by assumption this volatility is unanticipated, resulting changes in wealth should not be counted as saving or dissaving. In such a world, *planned* dissaving from social security is necessarily zero by definition.

In practice, we assume that all changes in social security legislation during the sample period were correctly anticipated, and that constant real benefits were expected after 1979. This tends to minimize changes in social security wealth induced by legislative action. We also assume that government and private pensions were expected to provide constant real and nominal benefits, respectively.[44]

A second difficulty concerns the proper treatment of couples. The model described above is out of its depth when household members can die at distinct points in time. If, however, annuities have full assumption of benefits by a surviving spouse, then our conclusion is essentially unchanged: if the household has no bequest motive, and if its members would never want to consume the principal of an asset, then it must be indifferent between that asset and an annuity which pays the same income stream. Thus, simple discounting is still appropriate. If the desire to consume the principal will arise only far in the future, then simple discounting must be a good approximation.

For government and private pensions, we assume full transfer of benefits, so the difficulty disappears. However, we know that this is counterfactual in the case of social security. We resolve this dilemma by decomposing social security into two streams: a certain stream (equal to the minimum benefit under any survival contingency), and a contingent stream (equal to the residual). By the preceding argument, simple discounting is approximately appropriate for the certain stream. In the following analysis, we simply ignore the contingent stream. We suspect that the insurance value associated with this contingent stream does not change enough over time to alter any of our qualitative conclusions.

In table 9.6, we present calculations of annuity wealth for the samples described in section 9.2. The presentation of these numbers is designed to facilitate comparison with the results on bequeathable wealth.

Note that between 1969 and 1975, annuity wealth rises steeply for most pre-retirement groups. Since pensions pay little or no income to such individuals during this period, pension assets effectively earn interest as the date of benefit eligibility approaches (the rise in pension wealth is due solely to this effect; in these calculations, continuing to work does not per se contribute to the value of benefits). Note that this effect is not very significant for working households between 1975 and 1979; evidently, most of these households began to receive benefits prior to full retirement.

For retired groups, annuity wealth changes very little, as expected. During the sample period there are two countervailing effects: legislation increases the real value of social security, while inflation erodes the value of private pensions. The first effect is not as large as one might expect, since we assume that future legislative changes are correctly anticipated. Thus, the social security wealth stream is relatively flat. Since private pensions are discounted at a much higher rate, social security dominates these calculations. Nevertheless, the erosion of private pension values contributes to a slight decline in total annuity wealth.

In table 9.7, we combine data on bequeathable wealth and annuities. Due to the size of annuities relative to bequeathable asset, the total wealth-age profile is relatively flat. For retired single individuals, total wealth appears to decline by at most 1% per year. In fact, between 1969 and 1975, total wealth increased for more than half of these households. Retired couples exhibit a slight decline (1%–1½% annual) in total wealth during the early sample period, but show virtually no change during the later period. In contrast, working households show slight increases (0%–2%) in total wealth for almost every period and subsample. Note that the "puzzle" concerning the precipitous decline between 1969 and 1975 in the bequeathable wealth of late retirees now acquires a new interpretation: this dissaving simply offset the implicit saving accompanying the approach of pension eligibility.

Contrary to King and Dicks-Mireaux, we have found that evidence of rapid dissaving among the elderly disappears when annuities are considered. Our calculations based on hypothetical parameter values in a simple life cycle model (table 9.5) suggest that the data on be-

Table 9.6   Changes in Annuity Wealth by Retirement Status

Variable	Retired by 1969	Not Retired by 1975	Retired by 1975	Not Retired by 1979	Retired by 1969	Not Retired by 1975	Retired by 1975	Not Retired by 1979
Annuity wealth								
1969	75002	80049	69885	64722	105699	95429	89340	94452
1975	73644	90580	77507	73048	100012	103500	95061	99762
1979	—	—	77131	72974	—	—	93910	100112
$\log A_{75}/A_{69}$								
Mean*	−0.0095	0.115	0.093	0.102	−0.040	0.076	0.065	0.051
	(0.0042)	(0.0036)	(0.005)	(0.007)	(0.005)	(0.003)	(0.003)	(0.006)
Median	0.006	0.147	0.114	0.147	0.002	0.080	0.067	0.068
Fraction < 0	0.311	0.032	0.019	0.023	0.442	0.090	0.141	0.164
$\log A_{79}/A_{75}$								
Mean*	—	—	−0.004	−0.005	—	—	−0.011	−0.007
	—	—	(0.001)	(0.005)	—	—	(0.002)	(0.003)
Median	—	—	−0.001	−0.001	—	—	−0.001	−0.001
Fraction < 0	—	—	0.963	0.943	—	—	0.904	0.802

*Estimated standard errors are in parentheses.

Table 9.7   Changes in Total Wealth by Retirement Status

Variable	Single Individuals				Couples			
	Retired by 1969	Not Retired by 1975	Retired by 1975	Not Retired by 1979	Retired by 1969	Not Retired by 1975	Retired by 1975	Not Retired by 1979
Total wealth								
1969	90009	110051	91600	113491	140516	162148	150643	181826
1975	85475	117763	98108	110989	126906	167920	155205	175471
1979	—	—	96340	110045	—	—	156520	183141
Log TW_{75}/TW_{69}								
Mean*	−0.067	0.0611	0.071	−0.021	−0.094	0.062	0.055	0.029
	(0.027)	(0.028)	(0.052)	(0.065)	(0.014)	(0.012)	(0.012)	(0.019)
Median	0.005	0.134	0.087	0.076	−0.044	0.097	0.071	0.065
Fraction < 0	0.450	0.228	0.237	0.337	0.624	0.302	0.328	0.370
Log TW_{79}/TW_{75}								
Mean*	—	—	−0.046	0.011	—	—	0.013	0.023
			(0.025)	(0.049)			(0.011)	(0.020)
Median	—	—	−0.003	0.004	—	—	0.005	0.027
Fraction < 0	—	—	0.586	0.467	—	—	0.479	0.424

*Estimated standard errors are in parentheses.

queathable and total wealth profiles (tables 9.3 and 9.7) together are consistent with a behavioral dissaving rate of less than 2% per year.[45] However, as noted before, this does not constitute a formal test of the life cycle hypothesis. In the next section, we investigate the possibility of basing a formal test on information about the age-wealth profile.

9.5 Testing the Pure Life Cycle Hypothesis

While rates of dissaving may not, by themselves, confirm or refute the life cycle hypothesis, the observed response of these rates to involuntary annuitization may provide a basis for doing so. This suggestion motivates the following analysis.

Returning to our formal model, let us assume that, as an approximation, we can ignore the effect of nonnegativity constraints (eq. [5]). Equation (14) will then describe the evolution of bequeathable wealth. It is useful to rewrite this as

$$(16) \qquad \frac{\dot{W}_t}{W_t} = \gamma \ + \ \xi(g)\frac{A_t}{W_t}$$

where

$$\xi(g) \ = \ \frac{\gamma \ - \ g}{r \ - \ g} \ .$$

Notice first that the sign of $\xi(g)$ is the same as that of $\gamma - g$. This simply reflects the phenomenon noted earlier: annuitization will accelerate (decelerate) the growth of bequeathable wealth if and only if $\gamma > g$ ($\gamma < g$). We illustrate this pattern in figure 9.1. Suppose that two individuals have different behavioral dissaving parameters (γ_1 and γ_2), but that their annuity benefit profiles have a common growth rate, g. If $\gamma_1 > g > \gamma_2$, annuitization will accelerate bequeathable wealth accumulation for individual 1, and slow it for individual 2. Proposition 2 confirms that explicit consideration of the nonnegativity constraints does not change this conclusion.

A test based on the behavioral response of accumulation rates to involuntary annuitization should have substantial power against major alternatives. The existence of an operative bequest motive would, for example, imply that annuitization *always* causes bequeathable wealth to accumulate more rapidly (decline more slowly).[46] A similar implication is generated by more simple-minded models, in which households save some constant fraction of current income.

Next, observe that, to a first-order approximation (expanding ξ around $g = 0$),

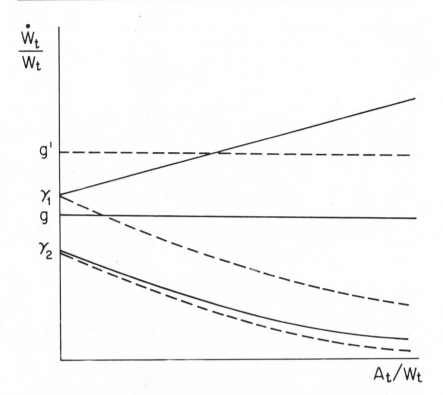

Fig. 9.1   The effect of annuitization on wealth accumulation

$$(17) \qquad \xi(g) \approx \frac{\gamma}{r} + \frac{\gamma - r}{r^2}g.$$

The transversality condition guarantees that the coefficient of g is unambiguously negative—in fact, for all $g < r$, $\xi'(g) < 0$; ξ falls as the growth rate of annuity benefits rises. Intuitively, increasing the value of g may shift an individual from the regime in which annuitization accelerates the growth of bequeathable wealth ($\gamma > g$) to the regime in which the effect of annuitization is reversed ($\gamma < g$). This is illustrated in figure 9.1: for $g' > \gamma_1 > g$, individual 1 belongs to the class of consumers who respond to annuitization by accumulating wealth at a slower rate (dashed lines indicate behavioral responses associated with an annuity benefit growth rate of g'). This implication is, as well, presumably testable.

Our data on bequeathable wealth profiles, of course, only allow us to measure discrete changes, rather than continuous rates of change.

In moving to our empirical implementation, we must therefore begin by converting (16) into its discrete analog:

$$\frac{W_{t+1}}{W_t} \approx (1 + \gamma) + \xi(g)\frac{A_t}{W_t}.$$

For reasons discussed in section 9.3, we prefer to use the log rate of accumulation as our dependent variable. Since the rate is presumed close to unity for most observations, we can employ the following approximation:

$$\ell n \ W_{t+1}/W_t \approx \gamma + \xi(g)\frac{A_t}{W_t}.$$

Finally, using our first-order approximation of $\xi(g)$ (eq. [17]) and adding a stochastic error term (representing among other things, the effects of the preceding approximations), we produce our basic specification:

$$(18) \qquad \ell n W_{t+1}/W_t = \gamma + \frac{\gamma}{r}\frac{A_t}{W_t} + \left(\frac{\gamma - r}{r^2}\right)g\frac{A_t}{W_t} + \epsilon_t.$$

Given cross-sectional data on bequeathable wealth and annuities (including the growth rate of benefits), one could estimate equation (18), alternatively ignoring and imposing (through a NLLS procedure) the implicit constraints on the coefficients. The model could then be tested by evaluating (statistically) the plausibility of these constraints, and by examining the sign of $\gamma - r$ in the constrained version. We eschew this approach for two reasons.

First, measurement error in W_t introduces significant spurious correlation between the dependent and independent variables. A more sophisticated estimation technique is therefore required. One could employ a two-stage procedure, instrumenting for A_t/W_t with A_t/Y_t (where Y_t is lifetime resources). In the results reported here, we simply substitute A_t/Y_t for A_t/W_t in the basic specification. Estimates based on instrumenting for A_t/W_t (not reported) differed very little from these results.

Second, data on g is extremely poor. Inference of g from successive observation of benefits received by the same individual is subject to enormous measurement error (due to variance in reporting). Alternatively, one might attempt to form an estimate of g based on the proportion of benefits which are unindexed. Presumably, this is closely related to the proportion of benefits received from private sources (PROP), since government pensions (including social security) are indexed, while most private pensions are not. However, the accuracy of this estimate would be questionable, particularly since many apparently unindexed private pensions are de facto indexed by "good will" increases in benefits. Although one would nevertheless expect PROP and g to be negatively correlated (due to the lack of ubiquitous indexing), the magnitude of this correlation is unknown. The use of PROP to proxy for g would only allow us to judge the directions of various effects, rather than their magnitudes.

These considerations lead us to estimate the following modified version of equation (18):[47]

$$(19) \qquad \ell n \ W_{t+1,i}/W_{t,i} = \beta_0 + \beta_1 \frac{A_{t,i}}{Y_i} + \beta_2 \ PROP_{t,i} \cdot \frac{A_{t,i}}{Y_i} + \epsilon_{t,i}$$

where i indexes household. Rather than attempt to recover γ and r and to test parameter restrictions, we simply inspect the pattern of coefficients. For a sample dominated by dissavers (savers), β_1 should be negative (positive). Since PROP is negatively correlated with g, β_2 should be positive. We will, in addition, estimate a version of (19) where $\ell n \ A_{t,i}/Y_i$ is substituted for $A_{t,i}/Y_i$. Since several levels of approximation have been used in deriving equation (19), we have no great attachment to any particular functional relationship; it is therefore important to determine whether or not the signs of estimated coefficients are sensitive to such alternative specifications.

Unfortunately, estimation of equation (19) may be contaminated by spurious correlation between PROP and ϵ. Individuals with large private pensions may, for example, be atypical (wealthier, less impatient). Alternatively, large values of PROP may reflect greater exposure to inflation risk, which would in turn have behavioral implications. We remedy these problems by including PROP as a separate right-hand side variable in the estimating equation:

$$\ell n \ W_{t+1,i}/W_{t,i} = \beta_0 + \beta_1 \frac{A_{t,i}}{Y_i} + \beta_2 \ PROP_{t,i} \frac{A_{t,i}}{Y_i} + \beta_3 PROP_{t,i} + \epsilon_{t,i}.$$

Our expectation is that the spurious effects described above will be captured in the estimated value of β_3: although there are many reasons to believe that PROP is systematically related to ϵ, it is much more difficult to explain why the partial correlation (controlling for PROP) between the interaction and error terms would be nonzero.

We estimated these specifications separately for single individuals and couples, using $t = 1975$ and $t + 1 = 1979$. The second period was chosen so that the samples would be more representative of typical retirees. Results are presented in tables 9.8 and 9.9.

Consider first the regressions for single individuals (table 9.8). Specification 1 corresponds to equation (19). Referring to equation (18), we see that the estimated intercept measures the 4-year (nonannuitized) dissaving rate. The particular value presented in table 9.1 implies a

Table 9.8   Single Individuals, Retired by 1975 (Dependent Variable: log W_{79}/W_{75})

Variable	Specification			
	1	2	3	4
constant	−0.235 (0.133)	−0.274 (0.131)	−0.609 (0.746)	−0.192 (0.706)
A/Y	0.031 (2.01)	0.227 (1.96)	—	—
Log A/Y	—	—	−0.076 (0.172)	0.017 (0.163)
PROP	—	8.47 (3.22)	—	−52.2 (13.3)
PROP · A/Y	−315 (95.2)	−735 (184)	—	—
PROP · log A/Y	—	—	0.425 (0.397)	−11.4 (3.04)

Table 9.9   Couples, Retired by 1975 (Dependent Variable: log W_{79}/W_{75})

Variable	Specification			
	1	2	3	4
Constant	0.0144 (0.0529)	0.0360 (0.0559)	0.531 (0.262)	0.763 (0.273)
A/Y	1.46 (1.20)	1.27 (1.21)	—	—
Log A/Y	—	—	0.113 (0.061)	0.165 (0.064)
PROP	—	−0.403 (0.339)	—	−3.55 (1.26)
PROP · A/Y	−25.7 (10.4)	−13.7 (14.3)	—	—
PROP · log A/Y	—	—	0.105 (0.054)	−0.665 (0.279)

yearly dissaving rate of about 6%, which is on the high end of the estimates presented in section 9.3. Since those estimates were not corrected for annuities, this leads one to suspect that annuitization increased the rate of accumulation for this group, contrary to our theoretical predictions. The point estimate of the coefficient on A/Y confirms this suspicion; however, it is estimated very imprecisely, and a range of magnitudes entirely consistent with the theory are well within a single standard deviation. Finally, we see that the coefficient of PROP.A/Y is negative, and statistically significant at a high level of confidence. This is, of course, inconsistent with the theoretical implications outlined above.

Adding PROP to this regression (specification 2) changes none of the qualitative conclusions, and in fact *increases* both the magnitude and statistical significance of the estimated coefficient on PROP.A/Y. Evidently, spurious correlation between PROP and ϵ have the effect of biasing this coefficient upward. Notice also that the coefficient of PROP is statistically significant—its inclusion in the regression is warranted.

The pattern of estimates using log A/Y is only slightly different. Although this alternative specification obscures the interpretation of the intercept, the signs of the remaining coefficients may again be revealing. As before, the separate effect of annuitization is estimated very imprecisely. Furthermore, when PROP is omitted (specification 3), the estimated coefficient of PROP.A/Y is positive, though statistically insignificant. However, the inclusion of PROP drives this coefficient significantly negative as before; furthermore, the inclusion of PROP seems warranted on statistical grounds (its t-statistic is approximately 4).

We turn now to the regressions for couples (table 9.9). The intercepts in specification 1 and 2 suggest a small positive saving rate, roughly consistent with that estimated in section 9.3. While one cannot reject the hypothesis that this term is negative, values lying within two standard deviations are consistent with, at most, a dissaving rate of 2% per year. We remarked earlier that couples may nevertheless have intended to dissave—the observed accumulation may have been due entirely to unanticipated housing price inflation during this period. If this is so, annuitization should depress the rate of accumulation for this group. The coefficients of A/Y reveal that exactly the opposite is the case. While these coefficients are not statistically significant at conventional levels, notice that these levels are surpassed by the estimated coefficients of log A/Y in specifications 3 and 4. Together, these estimates strongly suggest that annuitization increased accumulation rates for this group.[48] If so, there are two possibilities: either couples are intentional net savers after retirement (which requires us to accept somewhat implausible behavioral parameters to rescue the life cycle model), or the response among couples of saving to annuitization is inconsistent with life cycle motives.

Further evidence against the life cycle hypothesis is again generated by the estimated coefficients of PROP.A/Y and PROP.log A/Y. The pattern here closely resembles that for single individuals. In three of four specifications, the estimated parameter is negative; in two of these it is statistically significant at conventional levels. Once again, only specification 3 yields a point estimate consistent with theory. However, specification 4 reveals that the omission of PROP is unwarranted on statistical grounds.

Although we have reported relatively few regressions in this section, our estimates were quite robust with respect to the inclusion of other potentially important variables. Adding age of respondent, health, and number of living children did not, for example, substantively alter any of the results discussed above.

9.6 Conclusions

If, as suggested here, the pure life cycle hypothesis fails to account for savings behavior after retirement, then it is important to determine whether this behavior is consistent with other theories. One possibility is to maintain life cycle motives, while posing the problem of wealth accumulation within a different institutional setting. In particular, the models of Kotlikoff and Spivak (1981) and Bernheim et al. (1984) portray intergenerational transfers as a mechanism for facilitating intra-family exchange. Alternatively, one can supplement the life cycle model with a traditional bequest motive. Fortunately, these alternatives generate testable empirical implications. Bernheim et al. present econometric and other evidence to support a strategic bequest motive. My own work in progress (preliminary results are presented in Bernheim [1984a]) considers whether or not the data are also consistent with a model of household preferences augmented with intergenerational altruism.

Notes

1. These tests should not be confused with those of Feldstein (1974, 1977), Feldstein and Pellechio (1979), Kotlikoff (1979), and others who examine the effect of involuntary annuitization on levels of bequeathable wealth holdings.
2. Notice that this definition does *not* include the value of durable goods. It is quite likely that, as a result, the data understate the true rate of dissaving (elderly individuals probably engage in few purchases of new durable goods, while old goods depreciate). The resulting bias is, however, likely to be small.
3. Ferber et al. (1969) documents a tendency for misreporting of assets to be related to the respondent's level of wealth.
4. This can often be inferred from the corresponding completion codes, or from the implausibility of recorded values.
5. Presumably, if an individual does not own a home, it is straightforward to report 0.
6. Earned income does not exceed $1,000 per year in any year after retirement.
7. Note that this group is not contaminated by any households which retired in the interim.
8. Aware of this difficulty, Mirer reestimates his regressions for the subsample of individuals who are over 75 years old. Although this does not completely

eliminate the bias (in particular, many members of this subgroup may perform significant part-time work), and although this subsample may be dominated by outliers in the age spectrum, the robustness of Mirer's original estimates is suggestive.

9. Lydall and Projector and Weiss simply group together all individuals over 65. Mirer reports that 37% of his sample is between 65 and 67 years old.

10. Estimation using the 1969 wave yielded very imprecise estimates. However, it should be noted that the coefficient on age was slightly positive in all cases.

11. Note that the samples sizes here are larger than those reported in sec. 9.2. Since we employ cross-sectional data here, we do *not* insist that the households survive to a later sample year.

12. Suppose $A_1 > A_2$. Then, if R is age of retirement,

$$
\begin{aligned}
E(R|R \leq A_1) &= \text{prob}(R \leq A_2|R \leq A_1)\, E(R|R \leq A_2) \\
&\quad + \text{prob}(A_2 < R \leq A_1|R \leq A_1)\, E(R|A_2 < R \leq A_1) \\
&> [\text{prob}(R \leq A_2|R \leq A_1) + \text{prob}(A_2 < R \leq A_1|R \leq A_1)] \\
&\qquad \cdot E(R|R \leq A_2) \\
&= E(R|R \leq A_2).
\end{aligned}
$$

13. To put it another way, the probability of living to 70 conditional upon surviving to 69 is higher for the average 60-year-old who actually survives to 69 than it is for the average 60-year-old in general since the latter sample includes relatively unhealthy people with low conditional survival probabilities who are likely to die before they reach 69.

14. The secular rise in life expectancies may partially or completely offset this effect.

15. Mirer attempts to correct only for the "cohort effect" and finds, not surprisingly, more striking evidence of positive saving during retirement.

16. Mirer's procedure, in particular, seems seriously flawed: he regresses the ratio of net value in owner-occupied housing to total net worth on age and total net worth. Elsewhere, he concedes that there is likely to be substantial measurement error in net worth. This builds in a strong, spurious negative correlation between the dependent variable and observed total net worth (as reflected by its negative coefficient and enormous t-statistic). Presumably, all coefficients in this regression are then estimated inconsistently.

17. Mirer (1979), p. 439.

18. In the first sample year, NLS respondents are 45–59, as opposed to 58–63 for the LRHS.

19. Unfortunately, Diamond and Hausman do not report the total number of individuals retiring during their sample period. Their regressions were, however, based on approximately 1,200 observations. Assuming a uniform distribution of age, only 400 would have reached 65 by the end of the sample period. This may in part account for the large standard error of their estimate. In contrast, the youngest LRHS respondent was 68 in 1979.

20. Diamond and Hausman's sample will overrepresent early retirees. This may explain many of their findings; see the comments at the end of this section.

21. Since early retirees typically are poorer and less healthy, this somewhat offsets the other effects.

22. It would in any case be quite difficult to produce a "typical" sample, since the LRHS oversamples certain groups to begin with.

23. Note that for the "retired in 1969" and "not retired in 1975" samples, no value is reported for bequeathable wealth in 1979, since we do not require household survival past 1975.

24. This follows from smoothing of consumption.

25. The net worth of workers fell by 3.4% ($2,299) between 1969 and 1975, and rose by 11.6% ($8,771) between 1975 and 1979.

26. In a world without annuities, wealth would evolve in this way as long as preferences were homothetic.

27. The law of large numbers requires the existence of certain moments.

28. The assumption of independence deserves some attention. One might object that an individual who underreports assets in one year is likely to do so in the next as well. This creates no problems, as long as the fraction underreported by individual i does not change systematically with his wealth.

29. Observations with larger β_i's will (given the same level of initial wealth) be more likely to remain in the sample.

30. For example, over one-third of LRHS households retired in 1969 were single individuals; in 1975, this figure fell to one-sixth.

31. Thomas Gustafson has pointed out that the data presented here are too aggregated to test this hypothesis—we cannot tell if the *same* households which sell businesses and property also become new homeowners during this period. In fact, this pattern might seem somewhat unlikely, since households that do not own homes often have virtually no other assets. Alternatively, the rise in average housing wealth may be primarily attributable to the purchase of more expensive houses by those liquidating business and other property holdings (new homeowners may have virtually no equity). Another possibility is that individuals who move at retirement typically discover that their current house is worth more than expected; the decline in other assets should then be counted as dissaving. By disaggregating the data, it should be possible to distinguish between these possibilities. This is left for future work.

32. If the rate of time preference exceeds the discount rate, households will consume all resources immediately. If the inequality goes the other way, the transversality condition is violated, and no optimum exists. For equality, the household is completely indifferent between all consumption programs that exhaust his resources.

33. See Yaari (1965).

34. Households may still hold some bequeathable wealth if annuitization occurs through the family, as suggested by Kotlikoff and Spivak (1981). It is, however, unclear whether one can infer anything from rates of dissaving in the context of their model.

35. Implicitly, we assume that single year conditional survival probabilities are constant over time. In such a world, the actuarial value of an annuity does not change with age. In what follows, it should be clear that our central results do not depend upon this assumption. In particular, the argument which establishes that simple discounting is approximately appropriate depends only upon there being a relatively long interval before the nonnegativity constraint on bequeathable wealth binds. To take an extreme alternative, suppose death will occur at date T, with certainty. If an annuity contract promises to pay benefits past this date, those benefits are irrelevant. The appropriate value of an annuity (assuming either that the individual can borrow on benefits paid prior to T or that terminal benefits are not too large) is then just the simple discounted value of benefits, up to age T. In this very special case, actuarial valuation is exactly appropriate, and our technique (which includes benefits promised after T) is clearly in error. However, we have added the qualification that there must be a relatively long interval before the constraint on bequeathable wealth binds. Here, it binds as T, so if T is large, our method is, again, approximately

appropriate. In general, however, if there is some maximum age, one could always improve our measure by excluding benefits promised after the maximum age.

36. The transversality condition guarantees this inequality.

37. This is consistent with the calculations in the next section. Previous studies have obtained lower estimates of annuitization $[A_0/(r - g)W_0]$ specifically because they have employed actuarial valuation.

38. For elderly individuals, single year survival probabilities are approximately 95%, so one can think of $\lambda = 0.05$ as representing the case where all discounting is due to uncertain length of life.

39. While these calculations appear to confirm the superiority of simple discounting as a measure of value, the reader should bear in mind that any sample of elderly individuals may exhibit great behavioral heterogeneity. Thus, even if simple discounting is appropriate for the median household, it may be highly inaccurate when applied to rapid dissavers, who will reach a binding constraint quickly.

40. Details are available from the author.

41. If $\gamma > g$, the *growth* of bequeathable assets accelerates with annuitization. For this case, the nonnegativity constraints never bind, and (17) is exactly appropriate.

42. This requires an exceptionally large amount of tedious algebraic manipulation. Details are available from the author.

43. Again, details are available from the author.

44. I assumed inflation rates of 6% prior to 1969, rising to 9% by 1975, and 12% by 1979, remaining constant thereafter.

45. While this conclusion appears warranted for the *median* household, I have ignored sample heterogeneity. This is particularly important, since rapid dissavers will reach a binding constraint on bequeathable wealth quickly, thereby rendering the use of simple discounting perhaps very inaccurate. Unfortunately, it is not possible to distinguish behavioral heterogeneity from measurement error.

46. See Bernheim (1984a) for a discussion.

47. Note that since $\text{PROP}_{t,i} = P_{t,i}/A_{t,i}$ (where $P_{t,i}$ is private pension benefits), $\text{PROP}_{t,i} \cdot A_{t,i}/Y_i = P_{t,i}/Y_i$ (i.e., the $A_{t,i}$ terms cancel).

48. This finding is confirmed by Diamond and Hausman (1984).

References

Atkinson, A. B. 1971. The distribution of wealth and the individual life cycle. *Oxford Economic Papers* 23:239–54.

Atkinson, A. B., and Harrison, A. J. 1978. *The distribution of wealth in Britain*. Cambridge: Cambridge University Press.

Bernheim, B. D. 1984a. Annuities, bequests, and private wealth. Stanford University. Mimeographed.

———. 1984b. Life cycle annuity valuation. Stanford University. Mimeographed.

Bernheim, B. D.; Shleifer, A.; and Summers, L. 1984. Bequests as a means of payment. NBER Working Paper no. 1303.

Brittain, J. 1978. *Inheritance and the inequality of material wealth*. Washington: Brookings Institution.

Davies, J. B. 1981. Uncertain lifetime, consumption, and dissaving in retirement. *Journal of Political Economy* 89:561–78.

Diamond, P. A., and Hausman, J. A. 1984. Individual retirement and savings behavior. *Journal of Public Economics* 23:81–114.

Dicks-Mireaux, L., and King, M. A. 1984. Pension wealth and household savings: Tests of robustness. *Journal of Public Economics* 23:115–40.

Feldstein, M. S. 1974. Social security, induced retirement, and aggregate capital accumulation. *Journal of Political Economy* 82:905–26.

————. 1977. Social security and private savings: International evidence in an extended life-cycle model. In *The economics of public services,* ed. M. Feldstein and R. Inman. Proceedings of the International Economics Association Conference in Turin, Italy. London: Macmillan.

Feldstein, M. S., and Pellechio, A. 1979. Social security and household wealth accumulation: New microeconomic evidence. *Review of Economics and Statistics* 61:361–368.

Ferber, R. et al. 1969. Validation of a national survey of consumer financial characteristics: Savings accounts. *Review of Economics and Statistics* 51:436–44.

Fox, A. 1976. Alternative measures of earnings replacement for social security. In *Reaching retirement age*. Office of Research and Statistics, Social Security Administration. Research Report no. 47. Washington: Government Printing Office.

Hurd, M., and Shoven, J. 1985. The distributional impact of social security. In *Pensions, labor, and individual choice,* ed. D. Wise. Chicago: University of Chicago Press.

King, M. A., and Dicks-Mireaux, L. 1982. Asset holding and the life cycle. *Economic Journal* 92:247–67.

Kotlikoff, L. 1979. Testing the theory of social security and life cycle accumulation. *American Economic Review* 69:396–410.

Kotlikoff, L., and Spivak, A. 1981. The family as an incomplete annuities market. *Journal of Political Economy* 89:372–91.

Loury, G. 1981. Intergenerational transfers and the distribution of earnings. *Econometrica* 49:843–67.

Lydall, H. 1955. The life cycle in income, saving, and asset ownership. *Econometrica* 46:985–1012.

Mirer, T. W. 1979. The wealth-age relationship among the aged. *American Economic Review* 69:435–43.

Mulanaphy, J. 1974. *Statistical report: 1972–73 survey of retired TIAA-CREF Annuitants*. New York.

Projector, D. 1968. *Survey of changes in family finances*. Federal Reserve Board of Governors. Washington, D.C.

Projector, D., and Weiss, G. 1966. *Survey of financial characteristics of consumers*. Federal Reserve Board of Governors. Washington, D.C.

Shorrocks, A. F. 1975. The age-wealth relationship: A cross-section and cohort analysis. *Review of Economics and Statistics* 57:155–63.

Smith, J. D. 1975. White wealth and black people: The distribution of wealth in Washington, D.C. in 1967. In *The personal distribution of income and wealth,* ed. J. D. Smith. NBER Studies in Income & Wealth, No. 39. New York: Columbia University Press.

Stiglitz, J. E. 1978. Equality, taxation, and inheritance. In *Personal income distribution,* ed. W. Krelle and A. F. Shorrocks. Amsterdam: North-Holland.

Yaari, M. E. 1965. Uncertain lifetime, life insurance, and the theory of the consumer. *Review of Economic Studies* 32:137–50.

Comment   Michael Hurd

The main goals of Bernheim's paper are to give evidence about the saving behavior of the retired, to argue that the proper measure of annuity wealth in an equation that describes the trajectory of wealth is the simple discounted value of the annuity stream, and to test the pure life cycle of consumption. I believe that the first goal has been achieved successfully: the data on saving are interesting and mostly convincing. The second goal has less well been achieved, but certainly Bernheim has made an important point with the argument. I have considerable doubts about Bernheim's interpretation of the results pertaining to the final goal; in fact, I find nothing in the overall results of the paper to cast doubt on the pure life cycle hypothesis.

The saving of the elderly has been measured before; but, as Bernheim says in his literature review, the previous studies have flaws that make their interpretation difficult. In particular it is hard to believe that the wealth trajectories reported in those studies, most of which are based on cross-section data, are what the trajectories of individuals would be. The data in table 9.2 on bequeathable wealth are the first convincing evidence I have seen about the wealth changes of elderly individuals. Of those data, the entries for the already retired are the only ones with an easy interpretation because the theory relates to the trajectory of lifetime wealth, which is not known for workers. Over already retired individuals, four wealth changes can be calculated from table 9.2: by marital status, wealth changes between 1969 and 1975 for those retired by 1969, and wealth changes between 1975 and 1979 for those retired by 1975. Three changes are negative, and in some cases the decline is substantial. The fourth change is positive; but reference to table 9.4 shows that the increase is due almost solely to an increase in housing wealth of about $2,000 per couple despite a reduction of about 2% in the fraction owning a home. This fact points out a difficulty in aggregating different components of wealth: a category of wealth that has a consumption flow and that is lumpy will certainly not change over time in the same way as a more liquid kind of wealth. It seems reasonable to suppose here that the increase in wealth was due to the large increase in housing values that occurred in the latter part of the decade of the 1970s: couples were much more likely to hold a house than singles so they gained more than the corresponding singles category. I agree completely with Bernheim's statement that measures should be developed to reduce the importance of the very wealthy. I have reservations about the logarithm measure, however, because it requires observations with zero wealth in either the beginning or end of the period to be dropped.

Michael Hurd is associate professor of economics, State University of New York, and research associate, National Bureau of Economic Research.

This procedure will induce biases of an unknown magnitude and direction in the ratio of wealth.

Overall I interpret the data of table 9.2 to show that the wealth of the retired does decline as they age, and that the problems mentioned by Bernheim about previous studies have empirical importance.

The changes in total wealth reported in table 9.7 are mostly a reflection of the changes in bequeathable wealth because by construction annuity wealth cannot change by much for the already retired. The social security component of annuity wealth cannot change at all because it is just the simple discounted stream of a perpetuity which always pays the same amount. (There is no mortality adjustment.) Although the paper does not give a breakdown of annuity wealth between social security and private annuities, social security is probably almost all of annuity wealth. This is because social security is discounted at 3% whereas private annuities are discounted at 9%–15% from 1969 to 1979 and at 15% after 1979. Of course, this difference in the discount factor makes an enormous difference in the present value of the constant stream. Private annuity wealth can only change between 1969 and 1979 because the discount rate is smaller at the beginning of the period than at the end. This explains why the drop in annuity wealth is greater between 1969 and 1975 than between 1975 and 1979. In summary, little new information about the change in wealth can be found by looking at total wealth because by construction there can be very little change in annuity wealth.

The second major point of the paper is the argument that simple, not actuarial, discounting is appropriate for calculating annuity wealth. This is potentially an important point because it will apply to studies of retirement behavior as well as saving behavior. In particular, according to Bernheim's argument, any inducement to retire built into pension plans cannot arise from mortality rates. From this point of view the incentive effects of pensions reported by Wise and Kotlikoff in this volume are overstated. Whether simple discounting is accurate or not, however, depends critically on the boundary condition on bequeathable wealth, equation (5) in the paper. This equation says that an optimal consumption plan is not allowed to drive bequeathable wealth negative. Whether this condition will be satisfied by a plan that ignores the differences between annuity wealth and bequeathable wealth depends on the initial mix of wealth, and the parameters of the problem, the subjective discount rate, the risk aversion parameter, the interest rate, and the mortality rate. Bernheim argues that, with typical values, the year in which bequeathable wealth will go to zero is sufficiently far beyond the retirement date that the boundary condition can be ignored, and, therefore, simple discounting is appropriate. A substantial part of this argument rests on his illustrative calculations. His two examples in table 9.5 show that the marginal trade-offs, holding utility constant, between bequeathable wealth and annuity wealth, calculated by simple discounting of the flow of annuity payments, are .89 and .75; that is, for a typical mix of bequeathable and annuity wealth, and typical parameters, an additional dollar of annuity wealth is valued somewhat, although not greatly, less than an additional dollar of bequeathable wealth. This conclusion depends on the parameter values used to calculate the time until the boundary condition holds, and to calculate the trade-off. Bernheim used some typical parameter values to conclude that simple discounting is appropriate. Other, seemingly reasonable parameter values, however, do not lead to the same conclusion. For example, I used a risk aversion parameter of -2, an interest rate of .03, a subjective rate of time discount of .05, and a constant mortality rate of .04 to calculate roughly that an average single person who retired in 1969 would have exhausted bequeathable wealth in about 15 years under the consumption plan that ignores the boundary condition, and that the trade-off between the two kinds of wealth is about .4. Whether these calculations are strictly accurate or not, or whether the parameters are typical or not, the calculations show that there are surely a number of observations in the data for which the time period until bequeathable wealth is exhausted is short and the marginal valuation is not near unity. As Bernheim points out, however, this calculation of the marginal valuation of annuity wealth is irrelevant to the central question of the paper: What do the rates of asset decumulation tell us about utility function parameters? Because a central point of the paper is that simple discounting of annuities is the appropriate way to value them, he puts the question somewhat differently: What can the rate of decumulation of total wealth (calculated from simple discounting) tell us about a key utility function parameter? He shows that the observed rates of decumulation will equal the parameter of interest, which is negative in most cases, plus a positive number. In table 9.5, he gives two examples. In the first, the time until bequeathable wealth is exhausted, T, is 42 years. The true parameter is $-.02$ and the error is .005; that is, we would observe decumulation of .015 per year and interpret that to be the utility parameter (actually a combination of several parameters). We, therefore, make a 25% error in the parameter calculation. In the second example, T is 27 years, the true parameter is $-.04$, and the error is .015. We make a 30% error in the parameter estimate. What the error would be for my illustrative example, which has a T of 15, is unknown, but it undoubtedly would be greater than when $T = 27$. Again there are surely a number of observations in the data for which T is small and the error substantial. Even if T is large for average values of the parameters and wealth mix, which is by no means obvious because we do not know what average values of the parameters are, there is a serious aggregation problem. For many kinds of problems it is not enough to say that the typical or average observation in the data implies that simple discounting is justified: the aggregation problem requires that each case be examined. Unfortunately this creates substantial computation problems because usually one desires to estimate the utility function parameters, yet they must be known to decide whether simple discounting is appropriate or not. In summary, Bernheim has made a useful point; whether the conclusion should be applied in a particular study depends on the details of the study. It is certain, however, that estimation which makes use of annuity data will be much more complicated.

The third goal of the paper is to test the pure life cycle hypothesis of consumption. The idea behind the test is that people with a high ratio of pension wealth to bequeathable wealth will consume at a different rate than people with a low ratio. This kind of relationship is not easy to estimate, however. First, bequeathable wealth is not really exogenous: for example, if people have different rates of time preference both the trajectory of wealth and wealth will be a reflection of the rate of time preference. Second, the wealth trajectories are valid for steady states; but there were surely a number of unexpected shocks during the 1970s that affected wealth trajectories. Inflation and social security changes are examples. Third, the equation to test the hypothesis, equation (14), has an unobserved variable, the growth rate of pensions, that appears on the right-hand side. Bernheim solves this last problem by substituting for the growth rate, the ratio of annuity benefits from private sources to total annuity benefits. It is expected that if the model is correct and the life cycle hypothesis is valid the coefficient on this variable will be positive. According to the results in tables 9.8 and 9.9, however, that coefficient is generally negative. Bernheim interprets this to be good evidence against the life cycle hypothesis. I believe this strong conclusion is not warranted. As was mentioned earlier, the basic equation (14) refers to a steady state; yet the rate of inflation increased substantially over the time period of the data. The jump in inflation caused not just a decline in the growth rates of pensions but also a loss of wealth. The wealth loss was greatest for people who had a large value of private pension wealth. What effect this had on the estimated coefficients is not clear because several of the right-hand variables were affected; but in that there was a differential impact according to the value of a key right-hand variable, one would want to be cautious in the interpretation of the results. In a similar way there were windfall gains in social security that affected the sample differentially according to the ratio of private annuity benefits to social security benefits.

In summary, this paper presents some interesting data on the wealth trajectories of the elderly. In my view they provide good evidence that the elderly do not continue to save after retirement, and, therefore the claims made in some of the older literature are incorrect. The paper makes an important point about the computation of annuity wealth: depending on the application it may often be the case that annuity wealth should be the simple discounted flow of annuity payments. This point will have relevance in many other kinds of problems. Despite the test of the pure life cycle hypothesis, my general impression is that there is little evidence against the life cycle hypothesis here; rather, I view the wealth trajectories as providing support for the hypothesis.

IV Pensions and the Labor Market

10 The Incentive Effects of Private Pension Plans

Laurence J. Kotlikoff and David A. Wise

The proportion of workers covered by pensions has increased very substantially over the past two or three decades, and in particular the number of older workers with pensions continues to increase. During the same period, and especially in the past decade, the labor force participation of older workers has declined dramatically. The juxtaposition of these two trends suggests the possibility that they may be related. In this paper, we examine the stipulations of private pension plans with a view to analyzing the incentive effects created by their provisions. We find pension plans provide very substantial incentives to terminate work at the current job after the age of early retirement and even greater incentives to leave after the age of normal retirement. While analysis of the plan provisions suggests a potentially large effect of pension plans on labor force participation, the evidence does not directly demonstrate that pension-related work incentives did indeed cause workers to leave the labor force earlier. Such conclusions must rely on the association of individual retirement decisions with the provisions of individual pension plans—an analysis that must await data as yet withheld from public use. Nonetheless, examination of the structure of pension plans suggests the likelihood of a very sizable effect of plan provisions on labor force participation. The analysis of plan provisions also allows inferences about the cost in pension benefits of job

Laurence J. Kotlikoff is professor of economics at Boston University and research associate, National Bureau of Economic Research. David A. Wise is John F. Stambaugh Professor of Political Economy, John F. Kennedy School of Government, Harvard University, and research associate, National Bureau of Economic Research.

Gary Heaton accomplished the very substantial programming task that the paper required and served as a continuous source of information, explanation, and expertise. We thank Tom Gustafson for his very helpful comments.

283

change. In addition, the examination of plan provisions allows consideration of the differential cost of pension plans for men versus women. The wide diversity of plans and the corresponding wide diversity of the pension-related work incentives is a major theme of the paper.

In an earlier paper Kotlikoff and Wise (1984) emphasized the apparent inconsistency of pension accrual profiles with a spot market view of the labor market. The evidence in this paper, particularly the analysis of post–normal retirement benefit accrual and supplemental benefit formulas, provides even stronger demonstration of the inconsistency. In contrast to the earlier paper, which considered only a limited number of plans with earnings-related benefit formulas, this paper includes the entire universe of defined benefit pension plans.

10.1 Background

10.1.1 Vested Pension Benefit Accrual Profiles

Information on the value of annual vested accrual pension benefits for workers of different ages and with different amounts of service is useful for displaying a variety of pension incentive effects. Vested pension benefit accrual at age a, $I(a)$, equals the difference between pension wealth at age $a + 1$, $Pw(a + 1)$, and pension wealth at age a, $Pw(a)$, accumulated to age $a + 1$ at the nominal interest rate r, that is,

$$(1) \qquad I(a) = Pw\,(a + 1) - Pw(a)(1 + r).$$

Pension wealth at age a is defined as the expected value of vested pension benefits discounted to age a. Intuitively $PW(a)$ can be thought of as the worker's pension bank account. If $I(a)$ equals zero, the worker continuing employment with the plan sponsor at age a has exactly the same pension wealth at age $a + 1$ as an identically situated worker who terminates employment at age a. Pension accrual is thus the increment to pension wealth in excess of the return on the previously accumulated pension bank account. Throughout the paper we express pension accrual increments as a fraction of the worker's wage, $W(a)$. Specifically $R(a,t)$ denotes the ratio of $I(a)$ to $W(a)$ for a worker age a with t years of service.

The appendix presents formulas for pension benefit accrual for a very simple defined benefit pension plan, emphasizing the change in the formula at ages of full or partial vesting, at early retirement age, and after noral retirement. This analysis explains why many pension age–accrual profiles show sizable discontinuities at vesting and at early and normal retirement. It is useful here to provide a brief summary of the implications of these formulas. The discontinuities in age accrual profiles associated with vesting are fairly obvious; in the case of cliff vesting (100% vesting occurring at a particular age) $Pw(a)$ in (1) equals zero prior to the age of vesting and suddenly becomes positive at the full vesting age. Hence $I(a)$ is zero prior to cliff vesting and rises to a positive value at the cliff vesting age, a^*; on the other hand, $I(a^* + 1)$ is smaller than $I(a^*)$ because it represents the difference in two pension wealth numbers, rather than simply the value of one, $Pw(a^*)$.

Another discontinuity in $I(a)$ occurs, for most plans, at early retirement. This discontinuity occurs for plans that reduce early retirement benefits using a formula that is less than actuarially fair, and the lower the reduction the greater the decline in $I(a)$. To see this note that prior to the early retirement age $Pw(a)$ is not influenced by the early retirement reduction rate since workers are assumed to start collecting their vested benefits at the most lucrative date, which is almost invariably the age of early retirement; taking benefits at early retirement generally provides a larger present value of vested pension benefits accrued up to this age than opting to begin collecting these accrued benefits later. This reflects the use by pension plans of reduction rates in computing early retirement benefits that typically are lower than the actuarial rate. While $Pw(a)$ and $I(a)$ are independent of the reduction rate prior to early retirement, they are both functions of the reduction factor after early retirement. The smaller the reduction factor, the closer $Pw(a)$ will be to $Pw(a + 1)$, holding other factors constant, and the smaller will be $I(a)$. This is important since the reduction factors of most plans are fairly small, providing substantially less than an actuarial reduction.

A second, more fundamental reason for smaller increments after the early retirement age involves discounting. Prior to early retirement an extra dollar of benefits has a higher present value in the $Pw(a + 1)$ formula than in the $Pw(a)$ formula because at age $a + 1$ the worker is 1 year closer to receipt of these additional benefits than at age a. After the early retirement age benefits are available immediately and, ignoring the worker's shortening life span, an extra dollar of benefits at age $a + 1$ has the same present value as an extra dollar at age a. Stated differently, after early retirement there is no special advantage from raising benefits next year over this year because, like additional benefits earned next year, additional benefits earned this year become available immediately. This lack of discounting after benefits are available raises $Pw(a)$ relative to $Pw(a + 1)$ which implies a smaller annual pension accrual, $I(a)$, and smaller values of $R(a,t)$.

A third factor leading to a drop in $I(a)$ at early retirement is the shorter life span during which benefits will be collected if retirement from the plan is postponed. This factor does not enter into the calculus for $I(a)$ prior to early retirement because, conditional on reaching early retirement, both $Pw(a + 1)$ and $Pw(a)$ are based on the same potential life span of the worker.

Each of these three factors also plays a role in the significant decline in $I(a)$ at normal retirement. Most pension plans do not increase annual benefits for workers electing to postpone receipt of pensions in years after normal retirement. This implicit zero reduction rate means a smaller value of incremental accrued benefits. The second factor involved in the drop in $I(a)$ after early retirement is the change in discounting of $Pw(a)$ relative to $Pw(a + 1)$. This feature continues after normal retirement as well because benefits remain immediately available. Finally, beyond the normal retirement age there is a more rapid reduction in expected life span and, therefore, in the expected duration of benefit receipt if the worker postpones retiring. This feature also lowers $I(a)$ (see appendix).

While these three features help explain low and even negative values of $I(a)$ after normal retirement, other provisions produce sharp declines in $I(a)$ at normal retirement. According to data in the 1979 BLS Level of Benefits Survey, 23% of covered workers are enrolled in plans that do not credit service at all after normal retirement. Another 30% of covered workers are in plans that provide limited credit after normal retirement, and the remaining pension participants are in plans that credit all service during all years after normal retirement. Plans that provide limited credit typically credit service until the worker reaches a specified age, about age 70 on average.

Once plans stop crediting service they either (1) commence benefit payments immediately regardless of the recipient's work status, (2) defer pension benefits until the worker actually retires, or (3) defer payment until retirement, but actuarially increase the benefit. Of the participants in the plans that provide no or limited credit, 15% receive immediate payments, 76% receive deferred payments with no actuarial increase, and the rest receive deferred payments with an actuarial increase.

10.1.2 Implication of Pension Accrual Discontinuities for Viewing Labor Market Equilibrium

If the labor market exhibits spot market equilibrium, $I(a)$ plus the worker's nonpension compensation at age a, $W(a)$, equals the worker's marginal product at age a, $M(a)$:

$$(2) \qquad\qquad M(a) = W(a) + I(a).$$

Under the spot market assumption workers always receive $M(a)$ regardless of the firm or its pension plan. If $I(a)$ is smaller in one firm than another, $W(a)$ must be larger in the firm with the smaller value of $I(a)$ to insure equality of total annual compensation across firms. Since in a spot market equilibrium workers can freely move from one firm to another and firms can freely fire any worker demanding more than $M(a)$, only accrued vested benefits will have any economic value; if the value of this year's pension benefits reflected anything other than those to which the worker had legal title, either the worker or the employer would have an incentive to terminate the employment relationship. Note that the terms in (1) incorporate the spot market free mobility assumption in that workers are assumed to choose the most advantageous date to start collecting previously accumulated benefits since "retiring" for purposes of collecting a pension from one firm does not preclude subsequent work in another firm paying $M(a)$.

Obviously, if $W(a)$ is a smooth function of age, and $I(a)$ exhibits sharp discontinuities, $M(a)$ must exhibit sharp discontinuities at these same ages to satisfy (2). Casual empiricism suggests that $W(a)$ changes smoothly with age, or at least does not abruptly change precisely at ages when $I(a)$ exhibits sharp changes. There is also no reason to believe that $M(a)$ abruptly changes with age to satisfy (2); hence the sizable discontinuities reported here in the $I(a)$ profile appear strikingly at odds with the spot market condition (2).

10.1.3   Calculating Vested Benefit Accrual Profiles

This study calculates accrual profiles for 2,342 of the 2,492 plans identified by the BLS as usable.[1] Throughout the paper we focus on the age profiles of the ratios of $I(a)$ to $W(a)$; that is, we express the pension increments at age a as a fraction of the wage at age a. We utilize the survey's weights in presenting various average accrual profiles. The weights reflect the plan's fraction of total pension participants. To construct accrual profiles for plans which base their benefits on earnings we used a set of industry- and occupation-specific cross-section age earnings profiles estimated from CPS data. Longitudinal age earnings profiles were obtained by assuming 6% overall growth in wages and adding to this the wage growth by age estimated by the CPS cross section data. Kotlikoff and Wise (1984) describe these estimates in detail. In the analysis here we assume that wage earnings after age 65 remain constant in nominal dollars. Our actuarial calculations employ a 9% nominal interest rate and use a unisex mortality table, which represents an average of male and female mortality probabilities. Unlike the simple formulas in the appendix, our calculations take account of the worker's survival probabilities before retirement as well as after.

The BLS Level of Benefits Survey contains highly detailed information concerning the sampled pension plans' vesting provisions, requirements for early and normal retirement, the specifics of their normal and supplemental benefit formulas, and the crediting of service and payment of benefits for those working beyond the normal retirement age.

There is a very considerable amount of diversity in the particular provisions of private plans which generate sizable differences in vested pension benefit accrual. Many seemingly minor features of a plan can have very important effects on benefit accrual. For example, consider a stipulation that service is credited for only 25 years in a plan that permits early retirement at 62. For a worker hired at age 30 the accrual at age 55 will decline sharply to zero and remain at zero until the early retirement age. Without this ceiling on credited service, accrual between ages 55 and 62 could be very sizable; the weighted average ratio of pension accrual to the wage is roughly 15% in our sample of plans with age 62 early retirement. Other examples of very important "details" of pension provisions are age and service requirements for supplemental benefits, ceilings on the amount by which social security benefits can be used to offset pension benefits, maximum values of pension benefits, discontinuous changes by age in the rate of benefit reduction for early retirement, and maximum ages for plan participation. Each of these features, as well as numerous others not mentioned, can produce sharp discontinuities in $I(a)$ at ages other than the ages of vesting, early retirement, and normal retirement. Our calculations take into account each of the seemingly "minor" as well as major pension provisions included in the data.

The considerable variation in plan features within industry and occupation and, consequently, accrual profiles raises several important issues about the functioning of the U.S. labor market. First, equally productive workers are likely to face very different incentives to change jobs or retire because of pension plans. Second, the heterogeneity in accrual profiles across plans suggests that equally productive workers in the same industry and occupation, but in different plans, may be receiving quite different amounts of total compensation both on an annual and on a lifetime basis. Third, equally productive workers of different sexes or ages who join the same pension plan in a firm at the same time are likely to receive very different labor remuneration, even if the quality and quantity of their labor supply is equivalent. Fourth, the complexity of the calculations required to compute the accrual of vested benefits, and therefore the compensation one is currently receiving, calls into question the understanding of pension compensation both on the part of employers and workers.

10.2 Pension Accrual Profiles for Percent-of-Earnings Plans

Percent-of-earnings plans are discussed in this section and flat (non-earnings-related) plans in the next. Variation in pension accrual profiles by early and normal retirement ages is discussed first, followed by a discussion of the wide variation among plans holding early and normal retirement ages fixed. Next we consider the effect of social security offset provisions and also examine accrual profiles by industry and by occupation. Then the effects of alternative post–normal retirement provision are discussed. Finally there is an analysis of the effects on accrual profiles of early and normal retirement supplements. The cost in pension wealth of job change is discussed in section 10.4. Section 10.5 describes the differences in the pension cost of hiring women versus men.

10.2.1 The Decline in Pension Wealth Accrual at Early and Normal Retirement Ages

Average accrual profiles for the percent-of-earnings plans with 10-year cliff vesting are shown in table 10.1 by early and normal retirement ages. Three of these average profiles corresponding to plans with the respective early and normal retirement ages—55-55, 55-65, 65-65—are graphed in figure 10.1 In this and subsequent figures and tables, annual accrued pension benefits are expressed as a ratio of the wage. The graph depicts the very substantial declines in the rate of pension wealth accrual at several critical ages. The first is the age of normal retirement, which equals the age of early retirement for plans with no early retirement option. Second, there is also a sharp decline in the rate of accrual at the age of early retirement, but this decline is substantially lower than the decline at the normal retirement age.[2] Third, there is a very substantial decline between ages 65 and 66 in the average accrual rate no matter what the ages of early and normal retirement.

The actual declines in average accrual rates at these critical ages indicated in table 10.1 are highlighted in table 10.2. The ages of early and normal retirement are identical in columns, 1, 4, 6, and 8 of the table with respective retirement ages of 55, 60, 62, and 65. At these ages the accrual rates as a percentage of wages decline from .26 to 0, .27 to − .06, .25 to − .13, and .21 to − .19, respectively. Thus, at these ages the total annual compensation (wage plus pension accrual) from working declines by 21%, 26%, 30%, and 33% respectively. Surely then the incentive to continue work with the current employer past these ages is very substantially reduced.

In instances where early and normal retirement ages do not coincide, there is also a very substantial decline in the ratio of pension accrual to the wage at the age of normal retirement. For example, among plans with early retirement at 55 and normal retirement at 60 the decline is from .14 to − .09. There is also a decline at the age of early retirement for these plans, although it is considerably less substantial than the decline at the age of normal retirement. For example, of plans with early retirement at 55 and normal retirement at 65 the decline at 55 is from .10 to .07, while at 65 the decline is from .04 to − .15.

Table 10.1 Weighted Average Accrual Rates for Percent-of-Earnings Plans with 10-Year Cliff Vesting, by Early and Normal Retirement Age

	Retirement Age (Early/Normal)							
Age	55/55 (N = 152)	55/60 (N = 115)	55/65 (N = 513)	60/60 (N = 78)	60/65 (N = 53)	62/62 (N = 19)	62/65 (N = 8)	65/65 (N = 50)
40	**.244**	**.111**	**.071**	**.034**	**.047**	**.038**	**.054**	**.036**
41	.045	.022	.013	.007	.010	.016	.009	.010
42	.051	.026	.016	.008	.011	.017	.010	.011
43	.058	.029	.018	.010	.013	.120	.011	.012
44	.066	.033	.020	.011	.015	.029	.013	.014
45	.075	.036	.023	.013	.017	.036	.013	.016
46	.085	.043	.026	.016	.019	.042	.015	.018
47	.097	.050	.031	.028	.022	.047	.017	.021
48	.110	.057	.035	.039	.025	.054	.019	.024
49	.124	.064	.040	.056	.029	.060	.021	.027
50	.141	.077	.046	.065	.034	.068	.023	.031
51	.159	.072	.052	.084	.040	.077	.026	.033
52	.180	.087	.062	.091	.050	.090	.028	.043

53	.204	.099	.072	.105	.060	.101	.032	.050
54	.231	.113	.083	.117	.068	.114	.035	.055
55	.261	**.130**	**.097**	.149	.082	.128	.039	.065
56	-.003	.100	.068	.170	.094	.144	.036	.068
57	-.012	.111	.072	.192	.107	.162	.039	.076
58	-.020	.118	.076	.224	.127	.184	.044	.089
59	-.028	.129	.077	.241	.146	.208	.048	.105
60	-.038	**.143**	.079	**.269**	**.167**	.241	.054	.118
61	-.048	-.090	.068	-.061	.133	.220	.059	.128
62	-.058	-.091	.064	-.091	.115	**.248**	**.066**	.145
63	-.067	-.091	.056	-.114	.114	-.130	.017	.163
64	-.076	-.092	.053	-.121	.114	-.136	.012	.186
65	**-.085**	**-.094**	**.044**	**-.121**	**.112**	**-.144**	**.006**	**.211**
66	-.292	-.169	-.152	-.138	-.088	-.266	-.081	-.194
67	-.294	-.174	-.162	-.155	-.115	-.263	-.080	-.204
68	-.295	-.179	-.171	-.171	-.142	-.260	-.079	-.213
69	-.296	-.182	-.179	-.184	-.162	-.258	-.078	-.221
70	-.297	-.184	-.186	-.196	-.182	-.255	-.077	-.234

NOTE: Plans with early or normal retirement supplements are excluded.

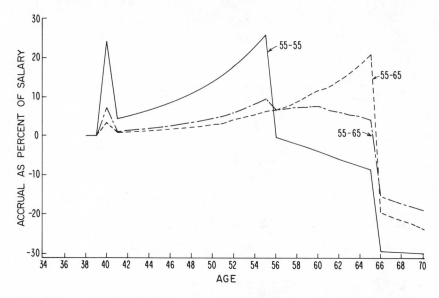

Fig. 10.1   Weighted average accrual rates for percent-of-earnings plans with 10-year cliff vesting, for selected early and normal retirement ages. Plans with early or normal retirement supplements are excluded.

Table 10.2

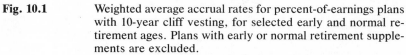

	Retirement Age (Early/Normal)							
	(1)	(2)	(3)	(4)	(5)	(6)	(7)	(8)
Age	55/55	55/60	55/65	60/60	60/65	62/62	62/65	65/65
40	.244	.111	.071	.034	.047	.038	.054	.036
55	**.261**	.130	.097					
56	−.003	.100	.068					
60		**.143**		**.269**	.167			
61		−.090		−.061	.113			
62						**.248**	.066	
63						−.130	.017	
65	−.085	−.094	**.044**	−.121	**.112**	−.144	**.006**	.211
66	−.292	−.169	−.152	−.138	−.088	−.266	−.081	−.194
70	−.297	−.184	−.186	−.196	−.182	−.255	−.077	−.234
65–66	20	8	19	2	20	12	8	40

Finally, in all cases there is a substantial decline in the rate of pension accrual between ages 65 and 66. The effective reduction in compensation ranges from 8% to 40% of the wage rate except for plans with early and normal retirement at 60, in which case the decline is from $-.12$ to $-.14$. Thus while the stipulations of plans vary tremendously, these plans, on average, seem to provide a substantial inducement to retirement after age 65, no matter what the inducement before this age.

The figure and the table also show a large variation in average pension accrual at 40, the age of cliff vesting. It is highest, on average, for plans with early and normal retirement at 55 and lowest, on average, for plans with early and normal retirement at 65. As mentioned, because the early retirement reduction typically is less than actuarially fair, pension wealth is generally greatest if benefits are taken at the age of early retirement. Thus the accrued wealth at the age of vesting is usually calculated by discounting benefits from the age of early retirement, assuming that the worker could begin to collect benefits at that age. Figure 10.1, for example, shows a vesting spike of almost 25% of earnings for 55-55 plans, 7% of earnings for 55-65 plans, and about 4% of earnings for 65-65 plans.

In summary, it seems apparent that continued participation in the labor force after the age of normal retirement and sometimes even after the age of normal retirement typically involves a substantial reduction in compensation because of the very large declines in the rate of pension wealth accrual. After the age of 65, there is typically a substantial loss in pension accrual, no matter what the ages of early and normal retirement. And, the sharp changes in average pension accrual at particular ages provides rather strong prima facie evidence against annual spot market clearing; neither wages nor marginal products appear to adjust at these critical ages to meet the spot market equilibrium condition written in (1).

10.2.2 Variation Among Plans

Even among plans with the same early and normal retirement ages there is wide variation in accrual rates at each age, particularly after the age of early retirement. To demonstrate this fact, average accrual rates for the 513 plans of table 10.1 with early retirement at 55 and normal retirement at 65, together with median, maximum, minimum, and upper and lower 5 percentile levels, are shown in table 10.3. The lower 5 percentile points for any age group for example is that accrual rate such that 5% of plans have accruals below that level. The upper 5 percentile point is defined analogously. Consider the accrual ratio at vesting. While the average vesting ratio for this sample is .071, the median is .021, the maximum is .383, and the minimum is zero. The ratio at the lowest fifth percentile is 0, while it is .201 for the largest

Table 10.3   **Dispersion of Accrual Ratios for Table 10.1 Plans with Age 55 Early Retirement and Age 65 Normal Retirement (N = 513)**

Age	Weighted Average Accrual Ratios	Median Accrual Ratios	Minimum Accrual Ratios	Maximum Accrual Ratios	Lowest Fifth Percentile	Largest Fifth Percentile
40	**.071**	**.021**	**0**	**.383**	**0**	**.201**
41	.013	.012	− .025	.071	0	.036
42	.016	.013	− .025	.080	0	.041
43	.018	.014	− .027	.091	0	.046
44	.020	.016	− .026	.103	0	.052
45	.023	.019	− .029	.116	0	.058
46	.026	.023	− .028	.131	0	.066
47	.031	.028	− .024	.162	0	.076
48	.034	.032	− .020	.167	0	.083
49	.040	.039	− .020	.188	0	.093
50	.046	.046	− .011	.212	0	.106
51	.052	.052	− .020	.240	0	.119
52	.062	.061	− .019	.270	0	.140
53	.072	.072	− .015	.305	0	.157
54	.083	.083	− .015	.344	0	.180
55	**.097**	**.100**	**− .005**	**.405**	**0**	**.208**
56	.068	.075	− .065	.424	0	.165
57	.072	.079	− .063	.363	0	.171
58	.076	.083	− .051	.248	0	.183
59	.077	.083	− .046	.286	− .0006	.190
60	.079	.086	− .064	.345	− .014	.204
61	.068	.074	− .156	.339	− .038	.181
62	.064	.068	− .154	.325	− .050	.190
63	.056	.062	− .192	.310	− .115	.191
64	.053	.060	− .221	.460	− .119	.210
65	**.044**	**.052**	**− .323**	**.326**	**− .148**	**.205**
66	− .152	− .136	− .558	.121	− .203	0
67	− .162	− .159	− .550	.060	− .406	0
68	− .171	− .179	− .541	.043	− .412	0
69	− .179	− .190	− .534	.029	− .414	0
70	− .186	− .197	− .618	.014	− .424	0

fifth percentile. A similarly large dispersion in annual accrual ratios is indicated for each of the ages 40 through 70. Weighted average accrual rates together with upper and lower 5 percentile levels are graphed in figure 10.2. While the average accrual rates between ages 55 and 65 are positive, for many plans the rates by 65 are very negative. Thus it is important to base judgment about the labor force participation incentive effects of pension plans on more than average accrual rates.

Additional evidence of the variability of pension accrued profiles is obtained by comparing profiles of particular plans. Figure 10.3 plots the accrual profiles of four of the sample's 30 largest plans. Plan 1

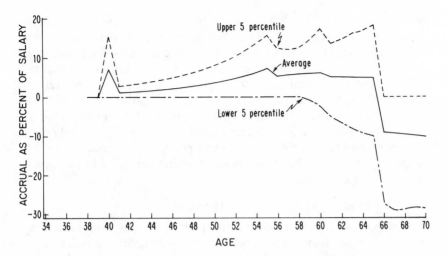

Fig. 10.2   Weighted average accrual rates and upper and lower 5 percentile levels for percent-of-earnings plans with 10-year cliff
vesting, early retirement at 55 and normal retirement at 65.
(Note: Plans with early or normal retirement supplements
are excluded.)

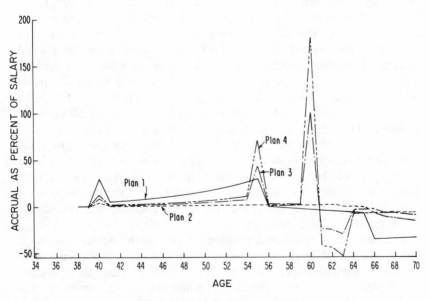

Fig. 10.3   Accrual profiles for four large plans.

exhibits a 29% vesting spike, a reduction of 30 percentage points in the accrual ratio at age 55 and a further major reduction at age 65 from $-.063$ to $-.351$. In contrast the vesting spike is only 4% for plan 2 in the figure. This plan also exhibits no major reduction in the accrual ratio at early retirement and only a minor reduction at normal retirement. Plan 3's vesting spike is much less than that of plan 1, but the drop off of the accrual ratio at age 55 is very much larger than that in plan 1. This plan also exhibits extremely sharp changes in accrual ratios at ages 60 and 63. Plan 4 exhibits even greater discontinuities in the accrual profile. Thus the plans' incentive effects on labor force participation also vary widely.

10.2.3   The Effect of Social Security Offsets

As described above, a substantial number of plans have social security offset provisions, under which pension benefits are reduced by an amount depending upon the recipients' social security benefits. The offset provisions vary widely among plans. In some instances the offset is enough to completely eliminate payment of pension benefits from the private pension plan. Private pension benefit payments are typically substantially lower with than without the offset provision. Accrual rates for percent-of-earning plans with 10-year cliff vesting and early retirement at 55 are shown in table 10.4 for selected normal retirement ages, with and without social security offset provisions. The average profiles for offset and non-offset plans with early retirement at 55 and normal retirement at 62 are graphed in figure 10.4. A noticeable difference between the two groups of plans is the relatively large spike at vesting for plans without the offset compared with the low rate of accrual at vesting or plans with the social security offset. In addition, the accrual ratio at 55 is larger for plans without the offset than for plans with it, and the drop in the rate of accrual is substantially larger for plans without than for plans with the offset. The accrual ratio for plans without an offset is .21 at 55 and drops by almost 60% to .09 at 56. In contrast, the accrual rate for plans with an offset is about 16% at 55 and drops by only about 26% to .12 at age 56. Both groups of plans show negative accrual rates after the age of normal retirement, 62, and both groups of plans show much larger negative accrual rates after 65. Table 5.4 indicates that the relative accrual rates of the two groups for plans with different normal retirement ages are similar to those shown in the figure.

The table also shows that pension accrual at the age of vesting is rather substantial for plans without a social security offset even among plans with normal retirement at 65. The average accrual rate at vesting for all plans with early retirement at 55 and normal retirement at 65 is .071, as shown in table 10.1 above. It can be seen in table 10.4 that

Table 10.4   Weighted Average Accrual Rates for Percent-of-Earnings Plans with 10-Year Cliff Vesting and Early Retirement at Age 55, by Normal Retirement Age and Social Security Offset

| | Normal Retirement Age | | | | | |
| | 55 | | 62 | | 65 | |
Age	Without Offset ($N = 135$)	With Offset ($N = 17$)	Without Offset ($N = 103$)	With Offset ($N = 84$)	Without Offset ($N = 254$)	With Offset ($N = 259$)
40	**.260**	**.073**	**.175**	**.030**	**.121**	**.016**
41	.049	.005	.034	.010	.022	.004
42	.055	.008	.039	.014	.026	.005
43	.062	.010	.044	.017	.029	.006
44	.071	.013	.049	.020	.033	.007
45	.080	.017	.064	.024	.037	.009
46	.090	.030	.064	.027	.041	.011
47	.102	.039	.074	.034	.078	.013
48	.115	.047	.086	.040	.052	.016
49	.130	.061	.100	.049	.058	.019
50	.147	.074	.112	.066	.065	.025
51	.166	.089	.127	.079	.072	.029
52	.187	.108	.143	.096	.081	.041
53	.211	.127	.165	.112	.091	.051
54	.238	.146	.185	.132	.102	.062
55	**.269**	**.175**	**.213**	**.155**	**.116**	**.076**
56	.008	.042	.090	.115	.078	.058

Table 10.4 (continued)

Age	Normal Retirement Age					
	55		62		65	
	Without Offset (N = 135)	With Offset (N = 17)	Without Offset (N = 103)	With Offset (N = 84)	Without Offset (N = 254)	With Offset (N = 259)
57	−.016	.036	.092	.120	.077	.065
58	−.025	.040	.103	.135	.076	.076
59	−.034	.034	.096	.140	.073	.082
60	−.043	.025	.087	.143	.069	.091
61	−.052	−.004	.090	.109	.071	.066
62	−.062	−.012	**.087**	**.110**	.061	.068
63	−.071	−.024	−.075	−.066	.047	.066
64	−.081	−.026	−.086	−.069	.040	.067
65	**−.090**	**−.032**	**−.098**	**−.074**	**.025**	**.066**
66	−.309	−.109	−.224	−.154	−.203	−.097
67	−.309	−.132	−.248	−.170	−.212	−.108
68	−.308	−.153	−.270	−.184	−.219	−.119
69	−.307	−.172	−.280	−.196	−.227	−.128
70	−.307	−.191	−.290	−.204	−.233	−.136

NOTE: Plans with early or normal retirement supplements are excluded.

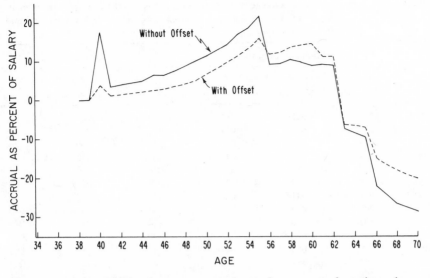

Fig. 10.4 Weighted average accrual rates for percent-of-earnings plans with 10-year cliff vesting, early retirement at 55 and normal retirement at 62, for plans with and without social security offsets. (Note: Plans with early or normal retirement supplements are excluded.)

the accrual is over 12% for plans without a social security offset while it is less than 2% for plans with an offset.

10.2.4 Accrual Ratios by Industry and Occupation

Industry

Accrual profiles for selected industries are shown in table 10.5. For purposes of comparison and for ease of exposition, profiles are presented only for plans with early retirement at 55, although profiles for three normal retirement ages, 55, 62, and 65, are shown. The most apparent difference among industries is in the proportion of plans with particular early and normal retirement ages. For example, in retail trade and services almost all plans have normal retirement at 65; only a few plans have early retirement at 55 or 62. On the other hand, almost 62% of plans in transportation have early and normal retirement at 55; approximately 20% of plans show normal retirement at 62 and 20% at 65. In manufacturing, 66% of plans have normal retirement at 65, 28% at 62, and about 6% at 55.

But among plans with the same early and normal retirement age, table 5.5 indicates little difference in average accrual profiles across industries. Table 10.6 isolates accrual ratios at critical ages, in particular

Table 10.5   Weighted Average Accrual Rates for Percent-of-Earnings Plans with 10-Year Cliff Vesting and Early Retirement at 55, by Industry and Normal Retirement Age

	Manufacturing			Transportation		
Age	55/55 (N = 22)	55/62 (N = 107)	55/65 (N = 256)	55/55 (N = 120)	55/62 (N = 37)	55/65 (N = 37)
40	.227	.091	.056	.257	.168	.122
41	.039	.019	.011	.048	.035	.021
42	.045	.024	.013	.055	.040	.024
43	.051	.028	.015	.062	.045	.027
44	.058	.032	.017	.070	.050	.030
45	.066	.037	.020	.079	.075	.034
46	.078	.041	.023	.090	.067	.035
47	.089	.050	.026	.101	.075	.040
48	.101	.060	.030	.114	.085	.045
49	.115	.073	.035	.129	.096	.052
50	.129	.080	.041	.146	.110	.060
51	.146	.092	.046	.165	.127	.067
52	.165	.103	.052	.187	.147	.081
53	.187	.119	.063	.211	.178	.098
54	.211	.134	.074	.238	.201	.111
55	.240	.158	.087	.269	.228	.127
56	−.008	.100	.067	−.003	.078	.091
57	−.178	.099	.072	−.011	.093	.094
58	−.025	.103	.079	−.019	.126	.100
59	−.035	.102	.081	−.028	.126	.103
60	−.046	.098	.084	−.036	.125	.109
61	−.057	.096	.074	−.045	.098	.093
62	−.068	.101	.074	−.054	.087	.086
63	−.079	−.080	.071	−.062	−.077	.063
64	−.088	−.087	.070	−.071	−.085	.062
65	−.099	−.095	.068	−.080	−.094	.058
66	−.288	−.158	−.141	−.300	−.242	−.206
67	−.288	−.174	−.152	−.301	−.276	−.217
68	−.288	−.189	−.161	−.302	−.309	−.227
69	−.288	−.204	−.170	−.302	−.320	−.237
70	−.288	−.216	−.177	−.302	−.329	−.246

NOTE: Plans with early or normal retirement supplements are excluded.

before and after the age of early retirement and before and after the age of normal retirement. Averages are only presented for cells with more than 10 plans. Two dashes indicate that there were fewer than 10. The cell was left blank if the corresponding age did not represent a critical age for the plan in question. Only in manufacturing and transportation were there a substantial number of plans with early and normal retirement at 55. In these two industries, the accrual profiles look very similar. Three industries had a significant number of plans with

Retail Trade			Finance			Services		
55/55 (N = 2)	55/62 (N = 6)	55/65 (N = 90)	55/55 (N = 2)	55/62 (N = 18)	55/65 (N = 70)	55/55 (N = 3)	55/62 (N = 3)	55/65 (N = 33)
.021	**.001**	**.080**	**.068**	**.086**	**.077**	**.251**	**.179**	**.068**
.020	.001	.014	.027	.020	.017	.047	.033	.013
.019	.001	.0126	.033	.023	.020	.053	.037	.015
.018	.001	.017	.039	.026	.023	.060	.042	.017
.017	.002	.019	.048	.031	.026	.068	.048	.019
.015	.002	.021	.057	.035	.030	.076	.054	.023
.016	.002	.023	.068	.041	.033	.086	.061	.027
.016	.003	.026	.080	.047	.038	.098	.069	.030
.016	.003	.028	.095	.054	.044	.110	.078	.034
.087	.007	.031	.109	.067	.050	.124	.087	.041
.110	.015	.035	.130	.117	.058	.140	.099	.048
.125	.020	.038	.152	.135	.066	.157	.111	.056
.140	.022	.043	.203	.172	.092	.178	.126	.064
.163	.025	.046	.230	.193	.104	.200	.142	.075
.172	.080	.050	.267	.220	.122	.226	.160	.086
.196	**.098**	**.056**	**.306**	**.250**	**.146**	**.254**	**.182**	**.098**
−.182	.087	.034	.092	.141	.092	−.010	.162	.082
−.176	.084	.032	.083	.140	.096	−.018	.161	.087
−.171	.114	.027	.083	.143	.104	−.027	.158	.096
−.167	.107	.018	.074	.140	.108	−.035	.153	.106
−.164	.097	.018	.064	.134	.110	−.045	.1248	.112
−.161	.070	.013	−.052	.054	.099	−.053	.277	.080
−.159	**.045**	.002	−.065	**.044**	.098	−.062	**.367**	.075
−.158	−.040	−.017	−.078	−.093	.097	−.072	−.075	.069
−.159	−.054	−.027	−.088	−.100	.098	−.081	−.086	.063
−.106	**−.068**	**−.059**	**−.099**	**−.108**	**.096**	**−.090**	**−.096**	**.054**
−.040	−.160	−.156	−.150	−.187	−.167	−.316	−.406	−.144
−.044	−.158	−.158	−.206	−.214	−.175	−.311	−.400	−.152
−.048	−.157	−.160	−.256	−.238	−.192	−.807	−.395	−.158
−.045	−.158	−.161	−.300	−.245	−.207	−.302	−.390	−.164
−.050	−.159	−.162	−.339	−.251	−.222	−.297	−.384	−.169

early retirement at 55 and normal retirement at 62, and again there seems to be little noticeable difference among the plans by industry. All industries have plans with normal retirement at 65. but even in this case, the profiles seem quite similar. The only possible exception seems to be retail trade, where pension accrual relative to the wage rate is less generous than in the other industry groups.

Nonetheless, a typical worker apparently faces a much greater incentive to leave the labor force early in some industries than in others.

Table 10.6   **Weighted Average Accrual Rates at Selected Ages for Percent-of-Earnings Plans with 10-Year Cliff Vesting Early Retirement at 55, Early and Normal Retirement Ages and Industry**

Early/ Normal Retirement Ages, Age	Industry				
	Manufacturing	Transportation	Retail Trade	Finance	Services
55/55					
40	.227	.257	—	—	—
55	.240	.269	—	—	—
56	− .008	− .003	—	—	—
62					
63					
65	− .099	− .080	—	—	—
66	− .288	− .300	—	—	—
70	− .288	− .302	—	—	—
55/62					
40	.091	.168	—	.086	—
55	.158	.228	—	.250	—
56	.100	.078	—	.141	—
62	.101	.087	—	.044	—
63	− .080	− .077	—	− .093	—
65	− .095	− .097	—	− .108	—
66	− .158	− .242	—	− .187	—
70	− .216	− .329	—	− .251	—
55/65					
40	.056	.122	.080	.077	.068
55	.087	.127	.056	.146	.098
56	.067	.091	.034	.092	.082
62					
63					
65	.068	.058	− .059	.096	.054
66	− .141	− .206	− .156	− .167	− .144
70	− .177	− .246	− .162	−222	− .169

For example, a large portion of workers covered by pensions in transportation would experience a 27% reduction in effective compensation by continuing to work between 55 and 56. Whereas at age 55 pension accrual would be equivalent to about 27% of wage rates for many workers in this industry, if the worker continued in the labor force until age 66, his annual loss in pension wealth would be equivalent to 30% of wage earnings at 66. A large proportion of workers in manufacturing have plans with early retirement at 55 and normal retirement at 65. In this case, the accrual at 55 averages about 9% of the wage at 55 and declines only to about 7% of the wage by 65. But then the accrual rate becomes negative, and if the worker were to continue in the labor force between 65 and 66, the decline in pension accrual would amount to an effective reduction in compensation of about 21%.

Occupation

Among plans with the same early and normal retirement ages, the pension accrual ratios do not differ noticeably by occupation. Accrual ratios for professions, clerical workers, and production workers are shown in table 10.7 for plans with early retirement at age 55 and three normal retirement ages—55, 62, and 65. Plans in the 55-65 group are graphed by occupation in figure 10.5. It seems clear from the table and the figure that given the age of normal retirement, there appear to be no substantial differences in accrual ratios by occupational group. Consider, for example, plans with normal retirement at age 55: at age 55, the accrual ratio is .29 for professionals, .25 for clerical workers, and .25 for production workers. At age 66, the accrual ratio has dropped to −.30 for professionals, −.30 for clerical workers, and −.29 for production workers. Similarly, close ratios are observed for the other two normal retirement ages. For example, at age 62 the accrual ratios for plans with normal retirement at 62 are .10 for professionals, .10 for clerical workers, and .10 for production workers. This is not to say that there are no differences in pension coverage by occupational groups. It simply says that conditional on having a plan with given early and normal retirement ages, the accrual ratios for the occupational groups are very similar. The data in table 10.7 may, however, be concealing intra-industry variation in accrual profiles by occupation for given retirement ages.

To address this potential ambiguity, accrual ratios for the same plans treated in table 10.7 are presented in table 10.8 but only for manufacturing. But here again there is very little difference in the accrual profiles by occupation. Consider, for example, the drop in accrual ratios between ages 55 and 66. For plans with normal retirement at age 55, the decline is .58 (.287 minus −.295) for professionals, .51 for clerical workers, and .50 for production workers. Analogous declines are .29 for professionals, .30 for clerical workers, and .35 for production workers, respectively, in plans with normal retirement at 62. Only among plans with normal retirement at age 65 is there a noticeable difference in the accrual ratios by occupation. In this case, the drop between age 55 and age 66 is .29 for professionals, .25 for clerical workers, but somewhat less than .18 for production workers. Thus we conclude that differences in pension accrual ratios by occupation are primarily due to different plan types or to differences in early and normal retirement, given the general type of plan. Production workers, for example, are more likely to have flat benefit plans than professionals.

Table 10.7   Weighted Average Accrual Rates for Percent-of-Earnings Plans with 10-Year Cliff Vesting and Early Retirement at Age 55, by Normal Retirement Age and Occupation

Age	Normal Retirement Age = 55			Normal Retirement Age = 62			Normal Retirement Age = 65		
	Prof. (N = 53)	Cler. (N = 51)	Prod. (N = 48)	Prof. (N = 75)	Cler. (N = 74)	Prod. (N = 38)	Prof. (N = 204)	Cler. (N = 199)	Prod. (N = 110)
40	**.251**	**.240**	**.242**	**.091**	**.111**	**.115**	**.072**	**.077**	**.062**
41	.047	.046	.044	.020	.023	.024	.015	.014	.011
42	.054	.052	.050	.026	.027	.028	.017	.017	.013
43	.061	.059	.056	.030	.031	.032	.019	.019	.016
44	.069	.066	.064	.035	.036	.036	.022	.022	.018
45	.078	.075	.073	.044	.044	.047	.025	.025	.020
46	.092	.084	.082	.045	.048	.047	.029	.028	.022
47	.105	.095	.093	.054	.057	.053	.036	.033	.025
48	.119	.107	.106	.062	.067	.063	.039	.036	.028
49	.135	.122	.120	.071	.078	.078	.045	.042	.033
50	.154	.137	.135	.086	.095	.089	.053	.048	.037
51	.175	.154	.153	.100	.108	.103	.060	.055	.041

Age									
52	.199	.175	.173	.116	.128	.117	.072	.068	.046
53	.226	.196	.196	.132	.147	.141	.083	.077	.055
54	.256	.220	.222	.155	.166	.160	.098	.089	.063
55	**.291**	**.248**	**.252**	**.177**	**.191**	**.187**	**.112**	**.104**	**.075**
56	.020	−.025	−.005	.102	.113	.093	.079	.070	.058
57	.012	−.036	−.012	.106	.115	.096	.082	.074	.060
58	.006	−.046	−.020	.116	.127	.112	.086	.080	.064
59	−.001	−.058	−.027	.119	.126	.109	.087	.081	.065
60	−.010	−.070	−.035	.118	.121	.104	.084	.082	.072
61	−.019	−.087	−.044	.103	.098	.097	.069	.072	.064
62	−.027	−.101	−.052	**.100**	**.098**	**.096**	.062	.067	.063
63	−.036	−.114	−.060	−.069	−.077	−.068	.053	.060	.055
64	−.042	−.128	−.068	−.074	−.087	−.074	.051	.052	.054
65	**−.049**	**−.140**	**−.075**	**−.080**	**−.098**	**−.083**	**.038**	**.042**	**.052**
66	−.295	−.295	−.290	−.171	−.203	−.199	−.167	−.157	−.133
67	−.298	−.298	−.289	−.185	−.223	−.224	−.175	−.169	−.143
68	−.303	−.300	−.288	−.199	−.242	−.247	−.184	−.180	−.149
69	−.306	−.302	−.287	−.206	−.252	−.260	−.193	−.190	−.156
70	−.310	−.304	−.286	−.214	−.261	−.272	−.201	−.199	−.160

NOTE: Plans with early or normal retirement supplements are excluded.

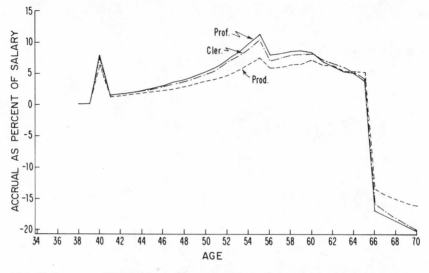

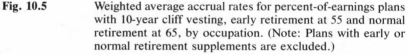

Fig. 10.5   Weighted average accrual rates for percent-of-earnings plans with 10-year cliff vesting, early retirement at 55 and normal retirement at 65, by occupation. (Note: Plans with early or normal retirement supplements are excluded.)

10.2.5   The Effect of Alternative Post–Normal Retirement Provisions on Pension Accrual

Accrual ratios for percent-of-earnings plans with early retirement at 55 are shown in table 10.9 for selected normal retirement ages and for alternative post–normal retirement provisions. The post–normal retirement provisions have been grouped into five categories:

1. *Full credit, deferred:* Plans providing full credit according to the standard formula for years worked past the age of normal retirement, but with benefits beginning only after retirement.
2. *No credit, deferred:* Plans with no credit given for work after the the age of normal retirement and with benefits beginning only after retirement.
3. *No credit, immediate payout or actuarial increase:* Plans with no credit given for additional work after the age of normal retirement, but with benefits beginning immediately or increased actuarially until benefits are taken.
4. *Limited credit, deferred:* Plans with limited credit given for work after the age of normal retirement or with full credit for service post normal retirement up to a specified age or number of years; benefits are deferred in these plans until retirement.
5. *Limited credit, immediate payout or actuarial increase:* Plans with provisions analogous to the third category above but with limited credit rather than no credit.

Table 10.8   Weighted Average Accrual Rates for Percent-of-Earnings Plans with 10-Year Cliff Vesting and Early Retirement at Age 55, by Normal Retirement Age and Occupation, for Manufacturing

Age	Normal Retirement Age = 55			Normal Retirement Age = 62			Normal Retirement Age = 65		
	Prof. (N = 9)	Cler. (N = 7)	Prod. (N = 6)	Prof. (N = 44)	Cler. (N = 45)	Prod. (N = 18)	Prof. (N = 101)	Cler. (N = 99)	Prod. (N = 56)
40	**.247**	**.213**	**.219**	**.082**	**.081**	**.108**	**.064**	**.059**	**.050**
41	.045	.037	.036	.018	.080	.022	.013	.009	.010
42	.051	.043	.042	.026	.021	.025	.016	.011	.012
43	.057	.049	.048	.030	.024	.028	.018	.012	.014
44	.064	.056	.054	.035	.028	.032	.021	.015	.015
45	.072	.065	.063	.040	.032	.036	.024	.017	.018
46	.091	.075	.071	.041	.039	.041	.029	.020	.020
47	.106	.085	.081	.053	.049	.046	.035	.023	.023
48	.120	.096	.091	.060	.061	.059	.040	.028	.026
49	.137	.109	.103	.068	.071	.078	.046	.034	.030
50	.155	.123	.116	.078	.077	.086	.055	.040	.034
51	.175	.139	.132	.089	.088	.099	.063	.047	.037
52	.198	.158	.148	.100	.100	.110	.072	.053	.040
53	.224	.180	.167	.114	.116	.126	.084	.064	.050
54	.253	.202	.188	.130	.131	.142	.102	.073	.058
55	**.287**	**.231**	**.216**	**.148**	**.155**	**.172**	**.117**	**.087**	**.070**
56	.003	.002	.018	.089	.113	.099	.085	.071	.055

Table 10.8 (continued)

Age	Normal Retirement Age = 55			Normal Retirement Age = 62			Normal Retirement Age = 65		
	Prof. (N = 9)	Cler. (N = 7)	Prod. (N = 6)	Prof. (N = 44)	Cler. (N = 45)	Prod. (N = 18)	Prof. (N = 101)	Cler. (N = 99)	Prod. (N = 56)
57	−.008	−.006	−.027	.088	.120	.093	.087	.084	.057
58	−.015	−.012	−.034	.093	.128	.093	.093	.095	.062
59	−.027	−.020	−.044	.095	.127	.087	.093	.102	.064
60	−.039	−.028	−.055	.094	.126	.077	.091	.107	.068
61	−.051	−.036	−.066	.092	.126	.076	.080	.101	.059
62	−.062	−.045	−.077	**.097**	**.139**	**.072**	.077	.099	.061
63	−.076	−.053	−.089	−.084	−.047	−.104	.070	.101	.057
64	−.081	−.062	−.100	−.088	−.053	−.113	.064	.098	.059
65	**−.092**	**−.070**	**−.111**	**−.094**	**−.061**	**−.124**	**.057**	**.095**	**.060**
66	−.295	−.280	−.286	−.142	−.148	−.176	−.176	−.151	−.114
67	−.304	−.276	−.282	−.151	−.176	−.198	−.182	−.166	−.127
68	−.314	−.272	−.278	−.161	−.193	−.217	−.194	−.179	−.133
69	−.323	−.270	−.273	−.171	−.211	−.235	−.203	−.189	−.141
70	−.329	−.268	−.270	−.179	−.224	−.250	−.212	−.198	−.146

NOTE: Plans with early or normal retirement supplements are excluded.

Table 10.9 Weighted Average Accrual Rates for Percent-of-Earnings Plans with 10-Year Cliff Vesting and Early Retirement at 55, by Normal Retirement Age and Post-Normal Retirement Provision

	Normal Retirement Age = 55			Normal Retirement Age = 62					Normal Retirement Age = 65				
Age	Full Credit, Defer. (N = 18)	No Credit, Defer. (N = 5)	Limited Credit, Defer. (N = 129)	Full Credit, Defer. (N = 76)	No Credit, Defer. (N = 7)	No Credit, Immed. Payout or Actuarial Increase (N = 2)	Limited Credit, Defer. (N = 66)	Limited Credit, Immed. Payout or Actuarial Increase (N = 35)	Full Credit, Defer. (N = 212)	No Credit, Defer. (N = 207)	No Credit, Immed. Payout or Actuarial Increase (N = 63)	Limited Credit, Defer. (N = 22)	Limited Credit, Immed. Payout or Actuarial Increase (N = 9)
40	**.186**	**.009**	**.252**	**.104**	**.120**	**.243**	**.105**	**.087**	**.077**	**.057**	**.082**	**.063**	**.023**
41	.035	.009	.046	.022	.034	.047	.021	.018	.016	.011	.012	.013	.007
42	.040	.009	.053	.028	.039	.053	.024	.021	.018	.012	.013	.015	.014
43	.045	.008	.060	.032	.044	.060	.028	.024	.021	.014	.015	.017	.016
44	.051	.008	.068	.036	.050	.068	.032	.028	.024	.016	.017	.020	.019
45	.058	.007	.077	.041	.057	.076	.050	.033	.028	.018	.019	.025	.022
46	.072	.007	.087	.045	.064	.086	.045	.038	.031	.019	.022	.029	.028
47	.085	.007	.098	.053	.073	.097	.054	.045	.036	.025	.025	.034	.037
48	.096	.007	.111	.063	.082	.110	.062	.051	.040	.026	.028	.039	.045
49	.110	.026	.125	.076	.093	.124	.072	.060	.046	.029	.031	.045	.052
50	.125	.048	.142	.091	.104	.139	.081	.081	.053	.035	.035	.052	.058
51	.143	.054	.160	.106	.119	.156	.094	.093	.060	.040	.039	.054	.067
52	.166	.060	.181	.123	.133	.176	.109	.109	.072	.048	.044	.066	.076
53	.188	.070	.204	.145	.150	.198	.125	.124	.081	.057	.054	.082	.087
54	.214	.074	.231	.164	.168	.223	.147	.140	.092	.068	.063	.094	.098
55	**.244**	**.084**	**.261**	**.191**	**.190**	**.250**	**.170**	**.161**	**.105**	**.081**	**.077**	**.112**	**.116**
56	.015	−.080	−.007	.119	.137	.091	.058	.094	.071	.051	.062	.097	.112

Table 10.9 (continued)

Age	Normal Retirement Age = 55			Normal Retirement Age = 62					Normal Retirement Age = 65				
	Full Credit, Defer. (N = 18)	No Credit, Defer. (N = 5)	Limited Credit, Defer. (N = 129)	Full Credit, Defer. (N = 76)	No Credit, Defer. (N = 7)	No Credit, Immed. Payout or Actuarial Increase (N = 2)	Limited Credit, Defer. (N = 66)	Limited Credit, Immed. Payout or Actuarial Increase (N = 35)	Full Credit, Defer. (N = 212)	No Credit, Defer. (N = 207)	No Credit, Immed. Payout or Actuarial Increase (N = 63)	Limited Credit, Defer. (N = 22)	Limited Credit, Immed. Payout or Actuarial Increase (N = 9)
57	.006	−.077	−.016	.116	.145	.073	.070	.094	.074	.054	.067	.098	.116
58	.008	−.075	−.024	.120	.152	.064	.098	.099	.076	.059	.068	.104	.128
59	−.007	−.073	−.033	.116	.161	.053	.097	.105	.075	.062	.071	.108	.127
60	−.017	−.071	−.042	.110	.169	.042	.093	.106	.074	.063	.082	.109	.122
61	−.039	−.070	−.051	.092	.158	−.079	.090	.073	.061	.057	.090	.071	.071
62	−.048	−.069	−.060	**.082**	**.216**	**−.091**	**.094**	**.066**	.053	.056	.088	.067	.063
63	−.058	−.068	−.069	−.064	−.378	0	−.033	−.051	.041	.052	.085	.052	.056
64	−.063	−.079	−.078	−.074	−.357	0	−.037	−.063	.038	.048	.083	.048	.049
65	−.071	−.016	−.087	−.085	−.337	0	−.045	−.074	**.027**	**.041**	**.080**	**.041**	**.037**
66	−.113	−.018	−.317	−.166	−.318	0	−.026	0	−.154	−.179	0	−.165	−.112
67	−.115	−.020	−.312	−.208	−.314	0	−.260	0	−.175	−.177	0	−.175	−.148
68	−.196	−.021	−.308	−.247	−.309	0	−.257	0	−.194	−.174	0	−.185	−.179
69	−.236	−.020	−.303	−.268	−.304	0	−.256	0	−.211	−.171	0	−.201	−.207
70	−.272	−.023	−.298	−.290	−.299	0	−.251	0	−.226	−.168	0	−.210	−.230

NOTE: Men only. There were no plans with the provisions corresponding to the two deleted categories under the 55 normal retirement heading.

With the exception of plans of type 3, these provisions typically lead to very negative accrual ratios after the age of normal retirement. Table 10.9 compares accrual ratios across these five types of plans with varying post–normal retirement benefit provisions. The table examines alternative normal retirement ages, with early retirement occurring at 55. The figures in table 10.9 are somewhat surprising, indicating quite negative accrual ratios for plans that fully credit post–normal retirement service; indeed, in certain cases, these negative accrual ratios are larger in absolute value than negative accrual ratios of plans that provide no credit.

To isolate the impact of the choice of post-retirement provisions, accrual ratios for percent-of-earnings plans with early retirement at 55 and selected normal retirement ages were calculated first assuming that all of the plans had a full credit provision and second assuming that all of the plans had a no-credit provision. These results are shown in table 10.10. The table indicates that the effect of crediting service after normal retirement depends importantly on the age of normal retirement. For plans with a normal retirement age of 55, negative accrual ratios are larger in absolute value under no crediting prior to age 66 and smaller in absolute value thereafter.

10.2.6   Early and Normal Retirement Supplements

Approximately 11.4% of plans have early and 7.5% have normal retirement supplements. The typical normal retirement supplement provides an addition to otherwise calculated benefits if the individual postpones retirement until the normal retirement age. The typical early retirement supplement provides an addition to benefits if retirement occurs after the age of early retirement. The average accrual rates for percent-of-earnings and flat plans with supplements and with 10-year cliff vesting and early and normal retirement at 55 and 65, respectively, are shown in table 10.11 by type of supplement. There are only two plans in the category with only normal retirement supplements, but nonetheless the effect of the supplements can be seen in the first column of the table. The accrual rate jumps from about 8% of the wage at age 64 to 60% of the wage at age 65. Thus the supplement apparently provides a relatively strong incentive to remain with the firm until age 65, but thereafter there is a sharp drop in the accrual rate to −18%. Accrual rates for plans with early retirement supplements are shown in the second column of the table. In this case there is a sharp increase in the accrual rate from .12 at age 54 to .44 at age 44, with a sharp drop thereafter. Again, the provision seems to provide a substantial incentive to remain with the firm to the age of early retirement, with a very substantial decline thereafter. Accrual rates for plans with both types of supplement are shown in the last column of the table. In this

Table 10.10   Weighted Average Accrual Rates for Percent-of-Earnings Plans with
                          10-Year Cliff Vesting and Early Retirement at 55, by Normal Retirement
                          Age, *Assuming* Full-Credit and No-Credit Post-Retirement Provisions

Normal Ret. Assumed Post-Normal Ret. Provision Age	Normal Retirement Age = 55		Normal Retirement Age = 62		Normal Retirement Age = 65	
	Full Credit ($N = 152$)	No Credit ($N = 152$)	Full Credit ($N = 187$)	No Credit ($N = 187$)	Full Credit ($N = 513$)	No Credit ($N = 513$)
40	.244	.244	.106	.106	.071	.071
41	.045	.045	.023	.023	.013	.013
42	.051	.051	.027	.027	.016	.016
43	.058	.058	.032	.031	.018	.018
44	.066	.066	.035	.035	.020	.020
45	.075	.075	.045	.045	.023	.023
46	.085	.085	.046	.046	.026	.026
47	.097	.097	.055	.055	.031	.031
48	.110	.110	.064	.064	.035	.035
49	.124	.124	.076	.076	.040	.040
50	.141	.141	.090	.090	.046	.046
51	.159	.159	.104	.104	.052	.052
52	.180	.180	.120	.120	.062	.062
53	.204	.204	.140	.140	.072	.072
54	.231	.231	.160	.160	.083	.083
55	**.261**	**.261**	**.185**	**.185**	**.097**	**.097**
56	− .002	− .244	.102	.102	.068	.068
57	− .011	− .229	.105	.105	.072	.072
58	− .019	− .215	.118	.118	.076	.076
59	− .027	− .202	.117	.117	.077	.077
60	− .037	− .139	.114	.114	.079	.079
61	− .049	− .178	.099	.099	.068	.068
62	− .059	− .167	**.098**	**.098**	.064	.064
63	− .068	− .157	− .060	− .284	.056	.056
64	− .077	− .148	− .069	− .267	.053	.063
65	− .086	− .139	− .079	− .252	**.044**	**.044**
66	− .133	− .130	− .150	− .237	− .132	− .225
67	− .177	− .128	− .192	− .233	− .153	− .222
68	− .219	− .127	− .231	− .232	− .172	− .219
69	− .261	− .124	− .260	− .227	− .190	− .216
70	− .301	− .123	− .285	− .223	− .205	− .212

case there is a rather large spike at the age of early retirement, equal
to 62% of the wage in that year, with a smaller but still noticeable spike
at about the age of normal retirement.

Accrual rates for percent-of-earnings and flat plans with either
type of supplement are shown in table 10.12 for selected early
and normal retirement ages. The spikes in the accrual rates are

Table 10.11   **Weighted Average Accrual Rates for Percent-of-Earnings and Flat Plans with 10-Year Cliff Vesting, Early and Normal Retirement at 55–65, and Early or Normal Retirement Supplement, by Type of Supplement**

	Type of Supplement		
Age	Normal ($N = 2$)	Early ($N = 10$)	Both ($N = 10$)
40	**.065**	**.111**	**.035**
41	.012	.197	.009
42	.013	.023	.011
43	.015	.026	.013
44	.017	.031	.018
45	.019	.035	.023
46	.022	.040	.030
47	.025	.047	.037
48	.028	.053	.044
49	.032	.060	.052
50	.036	.069	.060
51	.040	.079	.070
52	.045	.094	.081
53	.051	.106	.095
54	.057	**.121**	**.108**
55	.065	**.442**	**.621**
56	.047	$-.0007$	$-.051$
57	.051	$-.008$	$-.049$
58	.054	$-.014$	$-.043$
59	.058	$-.022$	$-.046$
60	.061	$-.011$	$-.051$
61	.066	$-.049$	$-.068$
62	.070	$-.058$	$-.072$
63	.074	$-.073$	$\mathbf{-.080}$
64	**.078**	$-.022$	.009
65	**.601**	$-.031$	**.008**
66	$-.181$	$-.247$	$-.092$
67	$-.180$	$-.213$	$-.167$
68	$-.179$	$-.207$	$-.164$
69	$-.179$	$-.204$	$-.163$
70	$-.178$	$-.201$	$-.160$

highlighted with dashed lines. Consider, for example, plans with early retirement at age 55. The spike created by the early retirement supplement is from .22 to .39 for plans with normal retirement at 55, from .12 to .50 for plans with normal retirement at 60, and from .11 to .48 for plans with normal retirement at 65. Of the 56 plans with normal retirement at age 60, the pension accrual rate at that age is on average equivalent to 100% of the wage rate. Similar discontinuities in the accrual ratios are evident

Table 10.12   **Weighted Average Accrual Rates for Percent-of-Earnings and Flat Plans with 10-Year Cliff Vesting and Early or Normal Retirement Supplements, by Early and Normal Retirement Ages**

Age	55/55 (N = 19)	55/60 (N = 56)	55/65 (N = 22)	60/60 (N = 37)	60/65 (N = 2)	62/62 (N = 19)
40	**.199**	**.136**	**.082**	**.078**	**.068**	**.056**
41	.039	.024	.015	.014	.012	.010
42	.045	.027	.018	.016	.013	.011
43	.052	.030	.021	.018	.015	.013
44	.059	.034	.025	.020	.017	.151
45	.068	.038	.030	.022	.019	.180
46	.077	.043	.036	.023	.022	.020
47	.088	.049	.041	.027	.025	.023
48	.100	.055	.048	.030	.028	.026
49	.114	.062	.056	.035	.032	.030
50	.129	.070	.064	.039	.036	.035
51	.148	.080	.074	.044	.040	.029
52	.167	.090	.087	.050	.046	.033
53	.191	.103	.099	.057	.053	.039
54	**.220**	**.117**	**.113**	.066	.061	.044
55	**.389**	**.498**	**.484**	.075	.069	.060
56	− .019	.071	.016	.086	.080	.064
57	− .078	.071	.019	.099	.092	.161
58	− .048	.071	− .021	.114	.107	.097
59	− .057	**.069**	− .026	**.132**	**.123**	.110
60	− .067	**1.079**	− .008	**.643**	**.233**	.127
61	− .085	− .292	− .049	− .208	.048	**.146**
62	− .093	− .301	− .056	− .212	.045	**.183**
63	− .108	− .353	− .067	− .227	.039	− .078
64	− .079	− .079	**− .006**	− .102	.072	− .086
65	− .086	− .043	**.018**	− .099	.194	− .094
66	− .124	− .088	− .182	− .100	− .048	− .169
67	− .141	− .116	− .195	− .088	− .064	− .111
68	− .150	− .124	− .191	− .092	− .072	− .112
69	− .151	− .132	− .188	− .097	− .112	− .113
70	− .151	− .141	− .186	− .102	− .120	− .114

NOTE: There are no plans in the 62–65 or in the 65–65 early-normal retirement groups.

for plans with other early and normal retirement ages. For example, of plans with early and normal retirement at age 60, the accrual rate at that age is equivalent to 64% of the annual wage for persons aged 60. Thus these special supplements create very significant one-time additions to pension wealth and therefore provide potentially very important incentives to remain with the firm until the age at which the special supplement is awarded. The special supplements also further dramatize the wide variation in the incentive effects implicit in the provisions of private pension plans.

10.3   Flat Benefit Plans

Accrual ratios for flat benefit plans with selected early and normal retirement are shown in table 10.13. This table can be compared to table 10.1 above, which presents comparable numbers for percent-of-earnings plans. The accrual profiles for flat plans with early-normal retirement at age 55-55, 55-60, 55-65 are shown graphically in figure 10.6. In general, the accrual profiles for the flat benefit plans look quite similar to those for percent-of-earnings plans. Recall that we have assumed that the flat benefit increases with the rate of inflation, assumed to be 6% annually in our calculations. While it is not possible to make comparisons for plans with each of the early and normal retirement combinations because of the relatively small sample sizes in some of them for flat benefit plans, for several early-normal retirement age combinations there are rather large numbers of plans of both types, for example, the combinations 55-60, 55-65, and 60-65. The average decline in the accrual ratio between the age of early retirement to age 66 is .30 for percent-of-earnings plans versus .39 for flat benefits plans in the case of the 55-60 retirement age combination. It is .25 versus .16 for the 55-65 combination, and .26 versus .17 for the 60-65 combination.

Accrual ratios at several critical ages for plans with early retirement at 55 and normal retirement at 65 are shown below for percent-of-earnings and flat benefit plans.

Age	Percent-of-Earnings Plans	Flat Plans
40	.071	.070
55	.097	.073
56	.068	.052
65	.044	.049
66	− .152	− .091
70	− .186	− .102

The accrual rates for these plans are graphed in figure 10.7. The evidence seems to indicate that the two types of plan provide rather similar incentive effects.

The provisions of flat rate plans, like those of percent-of-earnings plans, also yield widely different ratios, even among plans with the same early and normal retirement ages. Indications of the dispersion of the accrual ratios among flat plans with early and normal retirement at 55 and 65, respectively, are shown in table 10.14 and in figure 10.8. While the average accrual rate at age 55, for example, is 7% the minimum value is zero and the maximum is 24%. Similarly at age 56, while the average is about 5% the maximum is 20% and the minimum about

Table 10.13   Weighted Average Accrual Rates for Flat-Rate Plans with 10-Year Cliff Vesting, by Early and Normal Retirement Age

Age	55/55 (N = 3)	55/60 (N = 90)	55/65 (N = 106)	60/60 (N = 10)	60/65 (N = 48)	62/62 (N = 3)	62/65 (N = 17)	65/65 (N = 14)
40	**.304**	**.104**	**.070**	**.022**	**.046**	**.033**	**.025**	**.019**
41	.052	.027	.012	.004	.008	.006	.004	.006
42	.059	.031	.013	.004	.009	.007	.005	.006
43	.066	.035	.015	.005	.010	.007	.006	.006
44	.075	.039	.017	.006	.012	.008	.007	.007
45	.084	.044	.019	.006	.013	.009	.007	.007
46	.096	.049	.022	.007	.015	.010	.008	.007
47	.108	.052	.025	.029	.017	.011	.009	.008
48	.123	.058	.029	.053	.019	.013	.011	.009
49	.139	.064	.032	.063	.022	.015	.012	.009
50	.158	.073	.037	.067	.025	.016	.013	.010
51	.180	.093	.042	.079	.028	.018	.015	.011
52	.205	.105	.048	.084	.032	.021	.017	.012
53	.235	.121	.054	.098	.037	.024	.020	.014
54	.269	.138	.062	.110	.042	.027	.022	.015
55	**.308**	**.163**	**.073**	.150	.048	.030	.025	.017
56	−.121	.079	.052	.171	.055	.035	.028	.018
57	−.119	.077	.055	.189	.063	.040	.032	.020
58	−.118	.095	.058	.228	.073	.045	.037	.030
59	−.117	**.105**	.060	.258	.084	.052	.043	.036
60	−.117	.105	.061	**.285**	**.101**	.059	.050	.042
61	−.263	−.029	.050	.005	.061	.068	.058	.042
62	−.253	−.036	.050	−.012	.062	**.078**	**.068**	.049
63	−.244	−.052	.049	−.042	.063	−.014	.067	.058
64	−.235	−.091	.049	−.058	.034	−.015	.066	.069
65	**−.227**	**−.104**	**.049**	**−.079**	**.069**	**−.017**	**.063**	**.083**
66	−.280	−.131	−.091	−.174	−.074	−.085	−.037	−.074
67	−.275	−.164	−.093	−.267	−.076	−.083	−.040	−.074
68	−.271	−.175	−.096	−.255	−.078	−.082	−.042	−.074
69	−.267	−.181	−.099	−.246	−.080	−.081	−.046	−.074
70	−.263	−.203	−.102	−.244	−.083	−.080	−.049	−.074

NOTE: Plans with early or normal retirement supplements are excluded.

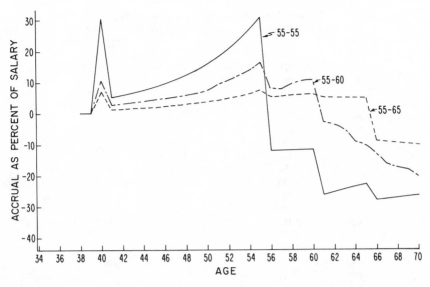

Fig. 10.6   Weighted average accrual rates for flat rate plans with 10-year cliff vesting, for selected early and normal retirement ages. (Note: Plans with early or normal retirement supplements are excluded.)

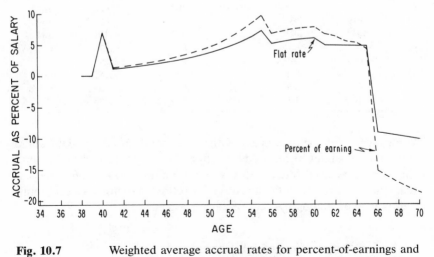

Fig. 10.7   Weighted average accrual rates for percent-of-earnings and flat rate plans with 10-year cliff vesting, early retirement at 55, and normal retirement at 65. (Note: Plans with early or normal retirement supplements are excluded.)

Table 10.14   Dispersion of Accrual Rates for Table 10.11 Plans with Age 55
                     Early Retirement and Age 65 Normal Retirement ($N = 106$)

Age	Weighted Average Accrual Ratios	Median Accrual Ratios	Minimum Accrual Ratios	Maximum Accrual Ratios	Lowest Fifth Percentile	Largest Fifth Percentile
40	**.070**	**.073**	**0**	**.260**	**0**	**.157**
41	.012	.013	0	.045	0	.027
42	.013	.015	0	.050	0	.030
43	.015	.016	0	.057	0	.034
44	.017	.018	0	.064	0	.038
45	.019	.021	0	.072	0	.043
46	.022	.024	0	.081	0	.049
47	.025	.027	0	.091	0	.055
48	.029	.031	0	.102	0	.062
49	.032	.035	0	.115	0	.071
50	.037	.039	0	.130	0	.080
51	.042	.045	0	.147	0	.092
52	.048	.041	0	.166	0	.104
53	.054	.058	0	.187	0	.119
54	.062	.067	0	.212	0	.137
55	**.073**	**.077**	**0**	**.240**	**.006**	**.157**
56	.052	.053	− .006	.195	0	.123
57	.056	.055	− .007	.192	0	.121
58	.058	.055	− .010	.189	0	.125
59	.060	.055	− .013	.183	− .008	.146
60	.061	.056	− .031	.184	− .024	.173
61	.050	.042	− .217	.204	− .051	.137
62	.050	.040	− .213	.226	− .066	.148
63	.049	.035	− .209	.400	− .082	.162
64	.049	.034	− .204	.561	− .093	.169
65	**.049**	**.029**	**− .198**	**.328**	**− .101**	**.184**
66	− .091	− .067	− .560	0	− .275	0
67	− .093	− .073	− .552	.008	− .291	0
68	− .096	− .079	− .545	.055	− .287	0
69	− .099	− .096	− .536	.045	− .283	0
70	− .102	− .101	− .528	.035	− .286	0

zero. At 65, the average is 5% with a maximum of almost 33% and a minimum of about − 20%. At 66, after the age of normal retirement, the average accrual rate is − 9% while the minimum is − 56% and the maximum is zero. Thus the incentive for retirement varies widely among flat as well as among percent-of-earnings plans.

10.4   The Pension Cost of Job Change

There are many ways to think about the effect of job change on pension accrual and the potential incentive effects of pension provisions

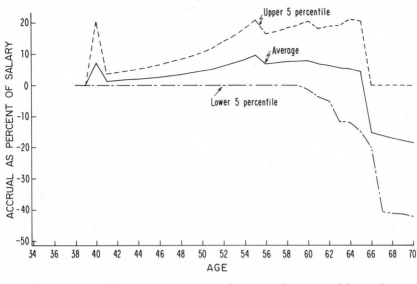

Fig. 10.8   Weighted average accrual rates and upper and lower 5 percentile levels for flat rate plans with 10-year cliff vesting, early retirement at 55, and normal retirement at 65. (Note: Plans with early or normal retirement supplements are excluded.)

on the job change decision. One approach is to consider the effect of job change on accrued pension wealth at the age of retirement, say the age of plan-normal retirement. Another way is to consider the expected loss in future pension wealth from changing job as a proportion of expected future wages. We shall consider variations of both measures.

10.4.1   If Change to a No-Pension Job

Consider a person who starts a job at some age, say 31. Suppose that at a given subsequent age the person could change to another job and obtain the same future wages as on the current job. Assume that his decision is either to stay on the current job until normal retirement or to switch to the second job and stay on that one until the age of normal retirement. But suppose that the new job has no pension. Then the loss in pension wealth is equal to the pension wealth that the worker would accrue if he were to stay with the current employer until the age of normal retirement. This loss relative to the present value of expected future wages is shown in tables 10.15, 10.16, and 10.17. Table 10.15 assumes that an individual begins employment with the first firm at age 31. Table 10.16 assumes a starting age of 41, and table 10.17 a starting age of 51. The tables present these loss ratios by plan-normal retirement age, and loss ratios are calculated through the age of normal retirement. To obtain a more concise picture of the losses, they are

Table 10.15   **Loss in Expected Pension Wealth If Change to No-Pension Job, as Percent of Expected Wages, by Age of Job Change and by Normal Retirement Age, Starting Initial Job at Age 31**

	Age at Normal Retirement			
Age	55 (N = 184)	60 (N = 446)	62 (N = 442)	65 (N = 858)
31	.072	.055	.048	.026
32	.076	.058	.050	.027
33	.080	.061	.053	.028
34	.084	.064	.055	.029
35	.089	.067	.058	.030
36	.095	.071	.060	.032
37	.101	.075	.064	.033
38	.108	.079	.067	.035
39	.116	.084	.071	.037
40	.106	.083	.069	.035
41	.111	.087	.072	.037
42	.116	.092	.075	.038
43	.122	.097	.078	.040
44	.128	.103	.081	.041
45	.134	.108	.083	.043
46	.140	.115	.086	.044
47	.145	.121	.089	.046
48	.151	.128	.092	.047
49	.156	.135	.094	.048
50	.161	.143	.095	.049
51	.163	.152	.097	.050
52	.163	.161	.097	.050
53	.154	.171	.096	.050
54	.124	.182	.093	.048
55		.182	.082	.044
56		.174	.080	.043
57		.199	.077	.042
58		.237	.071	.040
59		.310	.062	.037
60			.031	.032
61			.022	.030
62				.026
63				.023
64				.016
65				

shown for selected ages of job change in table 10.18. For plans with normal retirement at age 65, the loss in pension wealth relative to expected wages is relatively small, between 4% and 6% for all ages of job change, with the exception of job change at age 59 when joining the firm at age 51. In the latter case, the remaining working life of the individual is short and he is not yet vested. Thus the loss in potential pension accrual is relatively large compared to future earnings. Among

Table 10.16   **Loss in Expected Pension Wealth If Change to No-Pension Job, as Percent of Expected Wages, by Age of Job Change and by Normal Retirement Age, Starting Initial Job at Age 41**

	Age at Normal Retirement			
Age	55 (N = 57)	60 (N = 349)	62 (N = 546)	65 (N = 1009)
41	.079	.064	.062	.034
42	.086	.068	.066	.036
43	.093	.073	.071	.038
44	.103	.079	.076	.040
45	.114	.085	.082	.043
46	.127	.092	.088	.046
47	.143	.101	.096	.050
48	.164	.111	.104	.054
49	.191	.122	.114	.058
50	.117	.096	.097	.048
51	.121	.100	.102	.049
52	.122	.103	.106	.051
53	.119	.106	.110	.052
54	.103	.108	.115	.053
55		.104	.111	.052
56		.105	.106	.053
57		.105	.111	.053
58		.100	.119	.052
59		.085	.130	.051
60			.132	.047
61			.168	.046
62				.044
63				.040
64				.031
65				

plans with earlier normal retirement—55, 60, or 62—the potential loss in future pension accrual is considerably larger, typically on the order of 8%–20% of future earnings. The loss if one changes jobs just before normal retirement, however, is in some instances much larger than this, as high as 30%–50%. For example, if at age 31 one enters a plan with normal retirement at age 60, the loss ratio if one changes job at 59 is 31%. If the individual enters at 51 and leaves at 59, the loss is almost 50%.

The greater relative loss with earlier normal retirement is shown in figure 10.9, which presents loss ratios versus age for normal retirement at 55 and at 65, starting at age 31. The effect of starting age is shown graphically in figure 10.10 for plans with normal retirement at 60.

A limiting case of numbers like those presented in table 10.18 is the present discounted value of expected pension benefits at the age of hire as a proportion of expected wages at that time. These numbers of course

Table 10.17   **Loss in Expected Pension Wealth If Change to No-Pension Job, as Percent of Expected Wages, by Age of Job Change and by Normal Retirement Age, Starting Initial Job at Age 51**

	Age at Normal Retirement			
Age	55 (N = 32)	60 (N = 178)	62 (N = 451)	65 (N = 1287)
51	.000	.080	.094	.046
52	.000	.091	.105	.051
53	.000	.104	.118	.056
54	.000	.122	.134	.062
55		.146	.150	.069
56		.178	.169	.079
57		.229	.203	.090
58		.313	.251	.104
59		.482	.325	.122
60			.183	.059
61			.246	.060
62				.059
63				.055
64				.044
65				

Table 10.18   **Loss in Expected Pension Wealth If Change to No-Pension Job, as Percent of Expected Wages by Age of Job Change, Age of Starting Job, and Age of Normal Retirement**

Starting Age and Age	Age at Normal Retirement			
	55	60	62	65
31:				
44	.13	.10	.08	.04
49	.16	.14	.09	.05
54	.12	.18	.09	.05
59	—	.31	.06	.04
41:				
44	.10	.08	.08	.04
49	.19	.12	.11	.06
54	.10	.11	.15	.05
59	—	.09	.13	.05
51:				
44	—	—	—	—
49	—	—	—	—
54	—	.12	.13	.06
59	—	.48	.33	.12

NOTE: With expectations evaluated to plan normal retirement age.

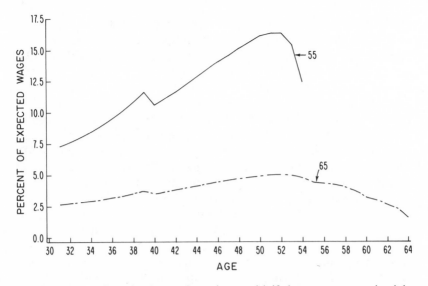

Fig. 10.9   Loss in expected pension wealth if change to no-pension job, as a percentage of expected wages, for normal retirement at 55 v. 65.

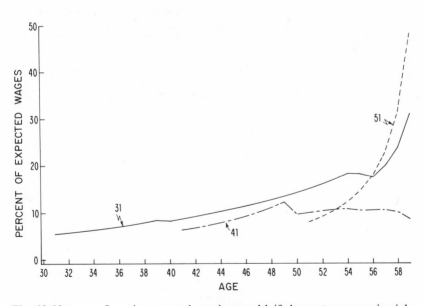

Fig. 10.10   Loss in expected pension wealth if change to no-pension job, as a percentage of expected wages, for normal retirement at 60, by age started job.

indicate the cost to the employer of pension benefits versus wages if a person stays with the employer from the time of hire to the age of early or normal retirement. Such ratios are presented in table 10.19 by age of initial employment and plan-normal retirement age. The ratios are presented first assuming that the individual remains with the firm until the age of early retirement and then assuming that the person remains until the age of normal retirement. It can be seen from the table that the present discounted value of pension versus wage compensation is small on average, ranging from about 2% to about 10%. The average proportion of compensation in pension benefits is typically larger the later the age of initial employment. For example, the ratio of pension benefits to wages for plans with normal retirement at 62 is .049 if one enters the firm at 31 and stays to the age of normal retirement. The ratio is .062 if one enters at 41, and .094 if one enters at 51. It is important to understand that while these ratios may appear relatively small, the pattern of pension accrual may still have a very substantial effect on worker labor force participation, as demonstrated above.

Possibly the most striking feature of these loss ratios is the wide variation among plans. To demonstrate the dispersion, the mean loss ratio and the minimum and maximum at each age are shown in table

Table 10.19   **Present Discounted Value of Expected Pension Benefits as a Proportion of Expected Wages, at Age of Hire, by Age of Hire and Plan Normal Retirement Age**

Age of Hire and Plan Normal Retirement Age	If Retire at Early Retirement Age	If Retire at Normal Retirement Age
31:		
All	.038	.044
55	.072	.072
60	.044	.055
62	.043	.049
65	.022	.026
41:		
All	.042	.049
55	.078	.079
60	.060	.064
62	.051	.062
65	.027	.034
51:		
All	.045	.060
55	—	—
60	.069	.080
62	.054	.094
65	.039	.046

10.20 for plans with normal retirement at 65 and for persons who enter the firm at age 31. Up to age 55—which is the age of early retirement for a substantial proportion of plans—the loss is close to zero for some plans and indeed is even negative for some. For other plans, however, the loss is very high, ranging up to 26% of future earnings at age 54. After 55, the maximum loss is typically over 30%, while the minimum is close to -20% at each age. Pension accrual after the age of early retirement is negative in many instances. For a member of such a plan,

Table 10.20   **Dispersion of Loss in Expected Pension Wealth If Change to No-Pension Job, for Plans in Table 10.15 with Normal Retirement at Age 65**

Age	Mean	Minimum	Maximum
31	.026	0	.098
32	.027	0	.101
33	.028	0	.105
34	.029	0	.110
35	.030	0	.115
36	.032	0	.120
37	.033	0	.125
38	.035	0	.131
39	.037	0	.137
40	.035	$-.010$	.139
41	.037	$-.009$	.145
42	.038	$-.008$	.152
43	.040	$-.007$	.158
44	.041	$-.005$	.166
45	.043	$-.003$	.173
46	.044	$-.004$	.182
47	.046	$-.005$	.190
48	.047	$-.005$	.199
49	.048	$-.007$	.209
50	.049	$-.012$	.219
51	.050	$-.022$	.229
52	.050	$-.034$	.240
53	.050	$-.049$	.252
54	**.048**	**$-.068$**	**.264**
55	.044	$-.182$	.276
56	.043	$-.181$	.289
57	.042	$-.178$	.301
58	.040	$-.175$	.313
59	.037	$-.187$	.325
60	.032	$-.229$	.335
61	.030	$-.221$	.341
62	.026	$-.233$	.339
63	.023	$-.248$	.321
64	.016	$-.220$	.367
65			

it would pay to leave this firm, taking early retirement benefits, and join another firm, assuming that one could join the second firm and obtain the same expected future wages.

10.4.2   Job Change and Pension Wealth at Age of Normal Retirement

Pension wealth at the age of normal retirement may be reduced very substantially by job change, as shown in table 10.21. A person who began work at 31 and changed to another job at 41 would have accrued, on average, only 72% of the pension wealth of a person who began at 31 and remained in the same firm. If he changed jobs at 41 and again at 51, he would accrue only 43% of the pension wealth of a person with no job change. This percentage ranges from a low of 30% on average in transportation to 60% in construction. Thus the loss in pension wealth with job change seems to provide a potentially large incentive against job mobility.

Because some plans place a limit on years of service that are credited in calculating benefits, it may in some instances pay to change jobs and begin to accrue benefits in a new plan. This leads to ratios that are greater than one in a few instances. The minimum and maximum values over all industries arise in anomalous plans, and these should not be given much weight; but they do suggest that there is substantial variation among plans in this respect, as well as in other respects discussed above.

Table 10.21   **Weighted Average Pension Wealth (or Ratio) at Normal Retirement, by Age of Initial Employment, and by Job Change, and by Industry, All Plans**

Industry (No. of Plans)	Age of Initial Employment			Pension Wealth at Normal Retirement Relative to Wealth Without Job Change If:		
	31	41	51	Change at 41	Change at 51	Change at 41 and 51
All industries (N = 2342)	32491	21410	10924	.72	.85	.43
Minimum	0	0	0	0	0	0
Maximum	197070	175899	117291	4.97	8.18	5.09
Mining (N = 39)	44856	27237	13147	.62	.81	.38
Construction (N = 9)	35778	28680	16837	.87	1.02	.60
Manufacturing (N = 1297)	31448	20393	10633	.73	.85	.44
Transportation (N = 328)	38680	22350	8598	.57	.81	.30
Wholesale trade (N = 100)	30836	21989	13135	.74	.87	.50
Retail trade (N = 260)	19453	13002	6024	.67	.80	.41
Finance (N = 7)	38864	30766	17309	.91	1.01	.58
Services (N = 8)	29993	22551	12520	.77	.87	.47

10.4.3   Pension Accrual Ratios and Age of Initial Employment

Pension accrual rates for percent-of-earnings plans with 10-year cliff vesting are shown in tables 10.22 and 10.23 for persons beginning employment at ages 41 and 51 respectively. The tables are analogous to table 10.1 above, presenting information by plan early and normal retirement ages. To provide an easier comparison of the accrual rates by starting age, accrual rates for selected ages are shown in table 10.24. The numbers are taken from table 10.1, table 10.22, and table 10.23. Accrual ratios for plans with early and normal retirement at 55 and 65 respectively are graphed in figure 10.11. The accrual rate at vesting is the most important difference across initial employment ages. For example, as shown in table 10.24, the accrual rate at vesting is .24 for persons beginning employment at 31, it is .62 for those beginning at age 41, and .92 for those beginning at age 51. The difference is simply due to the fact that the later the age of initial employment, the nearer is the time of benefit receipt at the age of vesting. The accrual rate at vesting increases with age of initial employment for each early-normal retirement age category. Otherwise, the pattern of accrual rates does not vary by starting age, except that the absolute value of the rates, both positive and negative, is smaller as the age of initial employment increases. Again, this is simply because potential benefits are lower with later starting ages and, thus, potential losses after the age of early or normal retirement are smaller. Notice that the accrual rate after the age of 65 is negative in each case. Plan provisions typically make the age of early and normal retirement dependent upon age and years of service. Thus in practice, the ages of early and normal retirement are typically somewhat higher for persons beginning employment at age 51. But in no case is the age of normal retirement greater than 65.

10.5   Pension Accrual Rates and Pension Cost by Sex

Because women on average live longer than men, women would typically receive pension benefits longer than otherwise equivalent men. The effect of this difference in life expectancy on pension accrual and the value of pension benefits is considered in this section. The ratios of the weighted average of the accrued benefits of women to that of men by age are shown in table 10.25 for all plans in the sample. At the most common vesting age, 10 years, the ratio is about 1.08, so that women's vested benefits are approximately 8% higher than men's. The ratio increases gradually to about 1.10 at age 60 and about 1.13 at 65. If otherwise identical men and women were to work until age 70, the average ratio would be 1.17. The ratios do not vary significantly by

Table 10.22 Weighted Average Accrual Rates for Percent-of-Earnings Plans with 10-Year Cliff Vesting, by Early and Normal Retirement Age, Starting Job at Age 41

Age	55/55 (N = 38)	55/60 (N = 63)	55/65 (N = 576)	60/60 (N = 169)	60/65 (N = 86)	62/62 (N = 27)	62/65 (N = 10)	65/65 (N = 56)
50	.618	.347	.209	.349	.127	.017	.135	.126
51	.106	.066	.040	.065	.026	.051	.021	.029
52	.123	.082	.046	.075	.029	.059	.024	.033
53	.141	.095	.052	.085	.035	.068	.027	.038
54	.160	.109	.060	.098	.041	.083	.030	.044
55	**.184**	**.125**	**.070**	.112	.047	.095	.034	.052
56	.006	.094	.069	.128	.055	.101	.037	.061
57	.002	.099	.065	.146	.064	.118	.042	.070
58	.0003	.107	.068	.167	.077	.137	.047	.085
59	−.004	.116	.071	.185	.088	.155	.053	.099
60	−.010	**.120**	.073	**.209**	**.103**	.179	.056	.116
61	−.016	.001	.075	−.007	.080	.198	.061	.123
62	−.022	−.004	.074	−.015	.081	**.223**	**.067**	.138
63	−.029	−.006	.075	−.023	.080	−.016	.035	.161
64	−.036	−.012	.075	−.031	.083	−.027	.034	.181
65	**−.043**	**−.019**	**.073**	**−.040**	**.084**	**−.038**	**.032**	**.204**
66	−.116	−.115	−.107	−.192	−.060	−.193	−.077	−.117
67	−.128	−.137	−.117	−.195	−.074	−.191	−.077	−.126
68	−.141	−.159	−.125	−.197	−.089	−.190	−.076	−.134
69	−.154	−.167	−.134	−.197	−.102	−.189	−.075	−.141
70	−.166	−.174	−.142	−.198	−.114	−.188	−.074	−.148

NOTE: Plans with early or normal retirement supplements are excluded.

Table 10.23   Weighted Average Accrual Rates for Percent-of-Earnings Plans with 10-Year Cliff Vesting, by Early and Normal Retirement Age, Starting Job at Age 51

Age	55/55 (N = 23)	55/60 (N = 23)	55/65 (N = 143)	60/60 (N = 60)	60/65 (N = 419)	62/62 (N = 52)	62/65 (N = 11)	65/65 (N = 425)
55	**.000**	**0**	**.001**	.0002	.000	.004	0	.000
56	.000	0	.001	.0002	.000	.004	0	.000
57	.000	0	.001	.0002	.000	.004	0	.000
58	.000	0	.001	.0002	.000	.003	0	.000
59	.000	0	.001	.0002	.000	.003	0	.000
60	**.923**	**.774**	**.613**	1.040	**.451**	**.644**	**.541**	**.449**
61	.041	.033	.081	.034	.056	.132	.091	.084
62	.036	.029	.081	.028	.059	**.169**	**.103**	.098
63	.028	.023	.082	.021	.063	.047	.077	.112
64	.022	.018	.084	.015	.065	.039	.079	.126
65	**.013**	**.012**	**.081**	**.007**	**.067**	**.030**	**.083**	**.145**
66	−.104	−.045	−.076	−.039	−.036	−.057	−.075	−.070
67	−.108	−.059	−.083	−.052	−.043	−.061	−.074	−.077
68	−.113	−.073	−.091	−.066	−.050	−.066	−.079	−.085
69	−.118	−.077	−.099	−.074	−.051	−.068	−.083	−.092
70	−.124	−.080	−.106	−.081	−.056	−.076	−.088	−.099

NOTE: Plans with early or normal retirement supplements are excluded.

Table 10.24   **Pension Accrual Rates for Percent-of-Earnings Plans with 10-Year Cliff Vesting, by Early and Normal Retirement Age and by Age of Initial Employment, for Selected Ages**

Starting Age and Age	Early-Normal Retirement							
	55/55	55/60	55/65	60/60	60/65	62/62	62/65	65/65
31:								
40	.24	.11	.07	.03	.05	.04	.05	.04
50	.14	.08	.05	.07	.03	.07	.02	.03
55	.26	.13	.10	.15	.08	.13	.04	.07
60	−.04	.14	.08	.27	.17	.24	.05	.12
62	−.06	−.09	.06	−.09	.12	.25	.07	.15
65	−.09	−.09	.04	−.12	.11	−.14	.01	.21
66	−.29	−.17	−.15	−.14	−.09	−.27	−.08	−.19
41:								
40	0	0	0	0	0	0	0	0
50	.62	.35	.21	.35	.13	.02	.14	.13
55	.18	.13	.07	.11	.05	.10	.03	.05
60	−.01	.12	.07	.21	.10	.18	.06	.12
62	−.02	−.00	.07	−.02	.08	.22	.07	.14
65	−.04	−.02	.07	−.04	.08	−.04	.03	.20
66	−.12	−.12	.11	−.19	−.06	−.19	−.08	−.12
51:								
40	0	0	0	0	0	0	0	0
50	0	0	0	0	0	0	0	0
55	0	0	0	0	0	0	0	0
60	.92	.77	.61	1.04	.45	.64	.54	.45
62	.04	.03	.08	.03	.06	.17	.10	.10
65	.02	.01	.08	.01	.07	.03	.08	.15
66	−.10	−.05	−.08	−.04	−.04	−.06	−.08	−.07

early and normal retirement age, and thus a breakdown by plan type is not presented.

10.6 Summary

The ratios of pension benefit accrual to wage earnings are presented for a wide range of pension plans. Typical plan provisions provide a strong incentive for retirement after the age of plan-normal retirement, and several plan types provide a strong incentive for retirement after the age of early retirement. A striking feature of the incentive effects of pension plans is their wide variation among plans. For example, while the average plan may provide reduced but still positive accrual after the age of early retirement, for a large proportion of plans the accrual rate after this age is very negative. It would not be unusual for the reduction in pension benefit accrual after the age of early retirement

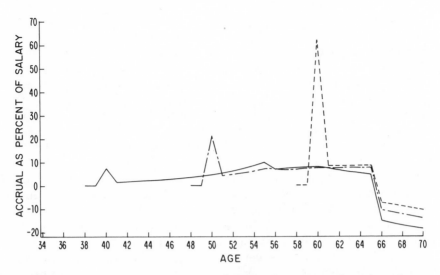

Fig. 10.11   Weighted average accrual rates for percent-of-earnings plans with 10-year cliff vesting, early retirement at 55, and normal retirement at 65, by age started job. (Note: Plans with early or normal retirement supplements are excluded.)

Table 10.25   **The Ratio of Accrued Pension Benefits of Women to That of Men, by Age, All Plans**

Age	Ratio	Age	Ratio
31	1	51	1.109
32	1	52	1.106
33	1	53	1.103
34	1	54	1.099
35	1.032	55	1.094
36	1.030	56	1.096
37	1.032	57	1.098
38	1.037	58	1.101
39	1.036	59	1.103
40	1.082	60	1.102
41	1.083	61	1.108
42	1.085	62	1.113
43	1.087	63	1.120
44	1.089	64	1.126
45	1.091	65	1.131
46	1.094	66	1.138
47	1.096	67	1.145
48	1.099	68	1.153
49	1.102	69	1.161
50	1.105	70	1.170

NOTE: There are 2342 plans. Starting age is 31.

to be equivalent to a 30% reduction in wage earnings. Thus even a relatively small proportion of plans with such benefit losses could have a substantial effect on aggregate labor force participation rates of older workers. The accrual rate at the age of vesting can range from as low as 2% of wage earnings in that year to as high as 100% of wage earnings, depending upon the plan type and on the age of initial employment. Thus for some employees, vesting could be a very important determinant of labor force participation decisions. Special early and normal retirement provisions may also add very substantially to accrued pension wealth at particular ages and may thus encourage workers to remain with a firm until these benefits are received. The accrual profiles under flat benefit plans seem very similar to the accruals under percent-of-earnings plans, if one assumes that the flat benefit is increased to keep pace with the rate of inflation. Given early and normal retirement ages, there is little difference in plan accrual profiles by industry or by occupation. Differences in pension benefits by industry depend more on the type of plan than on variations among plans with the same basic provisions. While the expected loss in pension benefits due to job change is apparently relatively small in many instances, it is rather large in others, and there is very wide variation among plans with the loss very high in some cases and, indeed, in other cases a gain may be had by changing jobs. In addition, accrued benefits at the age of retirement are typically very much lower with job change than if a person remains on the same job. Because women typically live longer than men, accrued pension benefits at any age are higher for women than for men, about 13% on average at age 65, for example. In short, the evidence suggests that the rapid increase in pension plan coverage over the past two or three decades may well have contributed very substantially to the reduction in the labor force participation of older workers during this period. The plans may also have an important effect on labor mobility.

Appendix

The source of discontinuities in age accrual profiles is clarified by considering a simple earnings-related defined benefit plan with cliff vesting at 10 years of service. Vested accrued benefits are clearly zero prior to the age at which the worker has 10 years of credited service in the plan. Let $R(a,t)$ denote the ratio of $I(a)$ to $W(a)$ for a worker age a with t years of tenure, where $I(a)$ is defined in (1) in the text. Then

$R(a,t)$ is zero for $t \leq 9$. If a person age a with 9 years of service works an additional year, the ratio of the increment to the wage, $W(a)$, is

(A1) $\qquad R(a,9) = \dfrac{B(a,t)A(55)\,(1\,+\,d)^{-10}\,(1\,+\,r)^{-[55-(a+1)]}}{W(a)}$.

In (A1), $B(a,t)$ is the retirement benefit available to the worker who terminates employment with the plan sponsor at age a after t years of service, but who delays receipt of pension benefits until the plan's normal retirement age. The normal and early retirement ages assumed for this stylized plan are 65 and 55, respectively. Terminating workers in this example are eligible for early retirement benefits. Our hypothetical plan reduces benefits by $d\%$ for each year that early retirement preceeds normal retirement. The benefit reduction rate, d, is assumed to be less than the actuarial fair rate.

The function $A(55)$ is the actuarial discount factor that transforms benefit flows initiating at age 55 into expected stocks of pension wealth at age 55. Expectations here are taken with respect to longevity. Thus $A(55)$ is the annuity value of a dollar's worth of pension benefits to be received each year until death, beginning at age 55. For simplicity assume that the probability of dying prior to age 55 is zero. Hence the present value at age a of $A(55)$ is $A(a) = A(55)\,(1\,+\,r)^{-(55-a)}$ for $a \leq 55$. If pension benefits are determined as a constant λ times the product of final year's earnings and service, and there is no offset for receipt of social security benefits, $B(a,t)$ is simply

(A2) $\qquad\qquad\qquad B(a,t) = \lambda W(a)t$

and

(A3) $\quad R(a,9) = \lambda(1\,+\,d)^{-10}\,(1\,+\,r)^{-[55-(a+1)]}\,A(55)10\,\dfrac{W(a\,+\,1)}{W(a)}$.

$R(a,t)$, for t increasing paripassus with age, is zero prior to t equals 9 and jumps at t equals 9 to the value given in (A3). Cliff vesting thus produces spikes in the accrual profiles such as that in figure 5.1 at 10 years of service. Between the age at cliff vesting and age 55 pension wealth, $Pw(a)$, is given by

(A4) $\qquad Pw(a) = \lambda W(a)(1\,+\,d)^{-10}\,(1\,+\,r)^{-(55-a)}A(55)t,$

and the increment to pension wealth $I(a)$ divided by the age $W(a)$ is given by

(A5) $\quad R(a,t) = \lambda(1\,+\,d)^{-10}\,(1\,+\,r)^{-[55-(a+1)]}$
$$A(55)t\left[\frac{W(a\,+\,1)}{W(a)}\frac{t\,+\,1}{t}\,-\,1\right].$$

Equations (A3) and (A5) suggest a drop in $R(a,t)$ as a increases to $a + 1$ concurrent with an increase in t from 9 to 10. Equation (A5) will be positive if the bracketed term exceeds zero. This will be the case if the percentage increase in the wage plus the percentage increase in years employed ($1/t$) is greater than zero. Assuming the term in brackets is positive and is roughly constant, $R(a,t)$ will increase exponentially due to the exponential decline in the discount factor, $(1 + r)^{-[55-(a+1)]}$, as a approaches 55.

If the value of d is considerably less than actuarially fair, a discontinuity in $R(a,t)$ occurs at the early retirement age, 55. At ages 55 and 56 we have

(A6) $$Pw(55) = \lambda W(55)(1 + d)^{-10} A(55)t$$

and

(A7) $$Pw(56) = \lambda W(56)(1 + d)^{-9} A(56)(t + 1).$$

Hence,

(A8) $$R(55,t) = \lambda(1 + d)^{-10}$$
$$(1 + r)A(55)t \left[\frac{W(56)}{W(55)} \frac{t + 1}{t} \frac{A(56)}{A(55)} \frac{(1 + d)}{(1 + r)} - 1 \right].$$

Assuming wage growth at 54 is close to that at 55 and $A(56)$ approximately equals $A(55)$, then $R(55,t)$ primarily differs from $R(54,t - 1)$ because the first term in the bracket in (7) is now multiplied by $(1 + d)$ while the second term, -1, is multiplied by $(1 + r)$. Since r exceeds d by assumption, $R(55,t)$ can easily be less than $R(54,t - 1)$. Indeed, this change in the functional form of $R(a,t)$ can produce sharp drops in accrual rates at the early retirement age for a host of pension plans and a range of realistic economic assumptions.

It is important to realize that the early retirement reduction, lower wages, and one less year of tenure yield lower benefits at 55 than at 56. The early retirement reduction reduces benefits at rate d. But if benefits were taken at 55 they could accrue interest at rate r. Thus by forgoing the early retirement option of receiving benefits at 55, one incurs a cost that depends on the difference $r - d$. If this loss is not offset by the increase due to wage growth and one year of additional tenure, there will be a drop in the benefit accrual rate between 55 and 56.

The same considerations pertain to benefit increments between 56 and 65. Recall that we have assumed a less than fair early retirement reduction so that benefits accrued before 55 are valued based on the assumption that benefits are received starting at the age that yields maximum pension wealth. The optimum time to receive benefits accrued between 55 and 56 is 56, between 56 and 57 is 57, and so forth. But to gain benefits from working another year, it is necessary to forgo the option of immediately taking accrued benefits at an advantageous reduction rate.

Between ages 56 and 65, $R(a,t)$ equals

$$(A9) \quad R(a,t) + \lambda(1 + d)^{-(65-a)}(1 + r) A(a)t \left[\frac{W(a + 1)}{W(a)} \frac{(t + 1)}{t} \frac{A(a + 1)}{A(a)} \frac{(1 + d)}{(1 + r)} \right].$$

In contrast to the $R(a,t)$ formula in (A5) that applies to the period between cliff vesting and early retirement, (A9) indicates that the actuarial reduction factor d, rather than the interest rate r, imparts an upward tilt in the $R(a,t)$ profile between early and normal retirement, as long as the term in brackets is positive. In (A9) as in (A5) and (A8) the accrual rate, $R(a,t)$, is an increasing function of the rate of nominal wage growth. Larger nominal interest rates reduce accrual rates at all ages, with a negative interaction with age prior to early retirement.

While the expression (A5) is unlikely to be negative, large differences between wage growth and the interest rate r can yield negative increments in pension wealth after the early retirement age. To a first approximation, the bracketed term in equation (A9) will be positive if $\Delta W/W + 1/t > r - d$, where $\Delta W/W$ is the percentage increase in wages and $1/t$ is the percentage increase in tenure. It is easy to see, however, that low wage growth and high interest rates will yield negative increments.

Pension accrual after normal retirement can be significantly negative. Assume that our hypothetical plan neither credits service after normal retirement nor provides an actuarial increase in benefits for postponing benefit receipt beyond the normal retirement age. In this case $R(a,t)$ after normal retirement is given by

$$(A10) \quad R(a,t) = \lambda t^* A(a) \left[\frac{A(a + 1)}{A(a)} - (1 + r) \right],$$

where t^* equals the worker's service prior to age 65. Note that for the following reasonable parameter values—$\lambda = .02$, $t^* = 30$, $A(a) = 15$, $r = .04$, and $A(a + 1) = 14$—$R(a,t) = -.96$, a quite substantial negative accrual ratio.

While the preceding formulas suggest the general shape of accrual rate profiles, there are few earnings-based plans with features as simple as the one considered here. In addition to more complicated rules for plan participation and vesting that often involve age as well as service requirements, there are a variety of methods of computing earnings bases, including career averages and averages of earnings, possibly highest earnings, over a specified period or number of years. Reduction rates for early retirement are often a specified function of age, if not length of service. Some plans allow no further accrual after a given number of years of service. Roughly 30% of defined benefit participants belong to plans that are integrated with social security, and the form of "integration" can have an important effect on the pattern of benefit accrual. Other plans, in particular those with social security offset formulas, provide supplemental benefits for early retirees prior to their receipt of social security benefits. In addition to these earnings-related plans, a significant number of plans covering over 40% of defined benefit participants calculate benefits independent of the participant's earnings. Finally, there are plans that specify minimum and maximum benefit levels.

Notes

1. Only plans with incomplete or inconsistent information were classified by the BLS as unusable.

2. Our calculations ignore service requirements for early retirement, since this inclusion could have considerably complicated our accrual computations. Excluding early retirement service requirements from the analysis is not likely to alter the results significantly. Virtually all workers covered by such requirements are enrolled in plans with early retirement service requirements of 15 years or less (Kotlikoff and Smith 1983).

References

Bulow, J. 1979. Analysis of pension funding under ERISA. NBER Working Paper no. 402.

Kotlikoff, Laurence J., and Smith, Daniel, eds. 1983. *Pensions in the American economy*. Chicago: University of Chicago Press.

Kotlikoff, Laurence J., and Wise, David A. 1984. Labor compensation and the structure of private pension plans: Evidence for contractual versus spot labor markets. Working Paper no. 1290.

Lazear, E. P. 1981. Severance pay, pensions, mobility, and the efficiency of work incentives. University of Chicago. Mimeographed.

————. 1983. Pensions as severance pay. In *Financial aspects of the United States pension system,* ed. Zvi Bodie and John B. Shoven. Chicago: University of Chicago Press.

Comment   Thomas A. Gustafson

This paper reports on extensive simulation exercises exploring the detailed structure of pension accrual profiles by age. It builds directly on work by the same authors presented in a paper entitled "Labor Compensation and the Structure of Private Pension Plans: Evidence for Contractual versus Spot Labor Markets" (Kotlikoff and Wise 1984). Both papers employ information on the structure of a large number of actual pension plans from the 1979 Level of Benefits survey prepared by the United States Department of Labor. In both papers, information on individual plans was weighted by the number of plan participants. Unfortunately, information on the wage profiles of plan participants, which would be desirable for calculating pension profiles, is not available because of privacy restrictions. The authors instead used wage profiles derived from the Retirement History Survey to represent workers in the plans under investigation.

The first paper found age profiles of pension accruals characterized by a number of "spikes" at key ages—the age of vesting, of eligibility for early retirement benefits, and of eligibility for normal retirement. The authors argue that these lumpy pension profiles are inconsistent with a spot market interpretation of the operation of labor markets, since no compensating troughs are observed in wage profiles.

Findings presented in the present paper are generally consistent with the first. The same sort of profiles are observed; the authors also present evidence on the rather substantial dispersal to be found around the average pattern. This paper extends the limited empirical analysis contained in the first paper to explore a number of additional dimensions of pension profiles.

First, the authors examine accrual ratios beyond the normal retirement age for the plans, and discover substantial discontinuities at the age of normal retirement and negative values in the post-normal-retirement-age range. Second, they examine differences in profiles across industries and occupations. They discover that most apparent differences result from the distribution across industries and occupations of plans with particular configurations of early and normal retirement ages, but that industry and occupation do not seem to matter much once account is taken of plan type.

Third, they examine early and normal retirement supplements, and find these features accentuate the "spikes" on the profiles at the ages they become available. Fourth, they examine the effect of offsets for

Thomas A. Gustafson is a staff economist with the Office of the Assistant Secretary for Planning and Evaluation, United States Department of Health and Human Services.

social security benefits. Offset provisions vary widely, but in general plans without offsets have higher accrual profiles and higher spikes at vesting. Fifth, they provide information on flat benefit plans; the prior analysis was limited to earnings-related plans. The profiles observed for these plans are very similar to those for earnings-related plans, given an assumption that the flat benefit increases in line with a rate of inflation of 6%.

Finally, the paper gives new evidence on the effect of a job change late in life, which can be dramatic, and on the effect of differences in life expectancies of men and women on overall pension benefits, which can result in differences of 10% or more in total lifetime benefits.

These results reflect an obviously extensive encounter with the data, and the authors are to be commended for their energy in this exercise. While the effort extends our knowledge beyond its precedessor and Lazear's earlier paper (1983), it cannot be described as a dramatic leap forward. The results are simulations based on data on real plans, but they rely on earnings profiles that are only hypothetically connected to the information on the plans. As mentioned above, nothing better was available, but the results cannot be seen as having the same reliability as would calculations involving actual microdata on individuals.

An additional drawback is that Kotlikoff and Wise are in fact looking at only a relatively small portion of pension plans. The level-of-benefits data are restricted to private plans with certain minimum size restrictions. The authors chose to analyze, however, only a subset of the plans in the data set; almost all the analysis in this paper treats only defined benefit plans with 10-year cliff vesting. In 1977, plans with this vesting schedule represented only about 28% of private defined benefit plans; these plans, however, included 65% of plan participants (see Kotlikoff and Smith 1983, p. 184).

Limiting the analysis to plans with cliff vesting serves to dramatize the size of the spike in the accrual profile at the age of vesting; plans with more gradual, "graded" vesting schedules, such as the "rule of 45" or the "40-5-10" rule, should have a much flatter accrual profile in the early years of service. The profiles with cliff vesting are thus most at variance with a spot labor market interpretation. Restricting the analysis to this group of plans, however, means the profiles are not necessarily indicative of the experience of many workers, and the reader should be cautioned to interpret the results presented as suggestive of a modal pattern, rather than necessarily an average, "normal," or universal pattern.

The analysis does not treat three major types of plans: (1) defined benefit plans with other than 10-year cliff vesting, (2) defined contribution plans, and (3) public plans. Especially considering the evidence presented by the authors about extent of variability around the average pattern, these restrictions are limiting. In particular, the authors' claim that they are looking at the whole universe of defined benefit pension plans is overstated.

I find the discussion of spot labor markets not particularly enlightening, mostly because in this context the spot market model is very much a straw man, a hollow foe whose defeat gives little surprise and also little indication of the mettle of the victor. Of course, the pension accrual profiles might be less interesting if one rejected this model in advance. It is the spot market model that demands attention to vesting, as opposed to some other measure of pension accruals. A 9-year veteran in a plan with 10-year cliff vesting may be thought of as having substantial expectations of pension benefits, even though they have not yet been given the legal status we call "vested." A less rigorous measure of expectations, however, would mean a smoother accrual profile, at least in the early years.

Finally, the results presented by Kotlikoff and Wise, and those by Lazear as well, refer only to pension accruals and ignore all other fringe benefits. Let me cautiously advance the hypothesis that other fringe benefits may exhibit age-related patterns that are of interest in this context. In particular, the cost of providing health benefits probably exhibits a rising profile with the age of the worker. (Of course, the extent to which the firm perceives this rise may depend on the bargain it makes with its health insurance carrier.) This profile may even rise steeply in the years following early retirement, just when we observe pension accruals falling off; in such a case, the sum of declining pension accruals and rising health benefits might be more nearly straight. This question seems to deserve further attention.

References

Kotlikoff, Laurence J., and Smith, Daniel E. 1983. *Pensions in the American Economy.* Chicago: University of Chicago Press.

Kotlikoff, Laurence J., and Wise, David A. 1984. "Labor Compensation and the Structure of Private Pension Plans: Evidence for Contractual Versus Spot Labor Markets." NBER Working Paper no. 1290.

Lazear, Edward P. 1983. "Pensions as Severance Pay." In Zvi Bodie and John B.Shoven, eds., *Financial Aspects on the United States Pension System.* Chicago: University of Chicago Press.

11   Pension Inequality

Edward P. Lazear and Sherwin Rosen

Much attention has been given to earnings inequality in recent years. Although most agree that the variable of interest is lifetime wealth rather than current earnings,[1] there has been relatively little study of differences in nonwage and salary components of earnings. Pension inequality is interesting for a number of reasons: First, pensions are a large fraction of total nonwage compensation. Second, there have been recent changes in laws that regulate sex-based differences in pension benefits. Third, private pensions have grown in importance over time and may become even more important in the future.

What follows is an attempt to determine whether pensions exacerbate compensation inequality across groups. There are two aspects to this issue. The first is that the probability of receiving a pension may not be random across groups. For example, in Lazear (1979), Retirement History Survey data revealed that 49% of the workers in the sample had pension plan coverage, but blacks were 6.6% less likely to be covered than whites. Similarly, female coverage was 8.6% less than males. These patterns are investigated in more detail in the CPS data below. The second aspect is how the size of pensions varies with sex and race of people who are eligible to receive them. This is more difficult to determine and is the main focus of this study.

Edward P. Lazear is professor of industrial relations, Graduate School of Business, University of Chicago, and research associate, National Bureau of Economic Research. Sherwin Rosen is Edwin A. and Betty L. Bergman Professor of Economics, University of Chicago, and research associate, National Bureau of Economic Research.

We thank Sylvester Scheiber for thoughtful comments on an earlier draft, Beth Asch and Richard Knudsen for expert research assistance, and the National Science Foundation for financial support.

341

There are two empirical tasks before us. The first is to determine the characteristics of the average retiree in each sex and race group. Especially important is the average tenure, age, and salary of the typical retiree because pension amounts in most plans depend on these variables. The second task is to estimate the pension that each group's typical retiree receives. This depends on the plan in which he is enrolled, so it is necessary to use some representative sample of plans.

The May 1979 Consumer Population Survey is used for the first task. This was chosen over the Retirement History Survey because of the emphasis in this study on male/female and black/white comparisons. The coverage of females in the Retirement History Survey is nonrepresentative, whereas the CPS has a better cross-section of the relevant population. For the second task, a data set that was constructed by Lazear (1983) was used. It is based on the Bankers' Trust *Corporate Pension Plan Study* (*1980*), covering about 200 plans.

11.1   Age, Tenure and Salary of the Typical Retiree

The 1979 CPS was used to impute the average age, tenure, and salary of the typical retiree in four race/sex categories. This task was less than straightforward because the relevant information is not reported in an appropriate form. Since the CPS is a cross-section, the date of retirement, and therefore age, tenure, and salary at the date of retirement, are not known for the group of individuals who are currently working. For the individuals who have already retired, neither tenure nor final salary on their career (or even last job) is reported. Thus, it is necessary to devise a method that estimates the requisite information from the cross-section.

The idea is to examine different cohorts and to infer from the distribution of individuals across retirement and employment-tenure classes what the retirement age and tenure must have been, using a variant of synthetic cohort analysis. The following example illustrates the basic ideas.

Suppose we are interested in the average level of tenure at retirement for some group and that only three age groups are relevant: No one retires before age 55, some retire at ages 55 and 56, and all are retired by age 57. The cross-section has workers and retirees at each age. So let us stratify the sample by age. None age 55 are retired, and their tenure on the current job is reported. Suppose that half have tenure of 20 years and half have tenure of 30 years. Although we cannot observe what happens to these individuals over the next year, we can examine the individuals who are currently 56 years old. In a steady state those individuals are identical to the current group of 55-year-olds, except that they are one year older. Suppose that half of the 56-year-olds are retired and of those who continue to work, three-fourths have tenure of 21 years, whereas only one-fourth have tenure of 31 years. That implies that three-fourths of those who retired before age 56 did so with 30 years of tenure and one-fourth did so with 20 years of tenure. Thus, $(\frac{1}{2})(\frac{3}{4}) = \frac{3}{8}$ of the population retire at age 55 with 30 years of tenure. Similarly, $(\frac{1}{2})(\frac{1}{4}) = \frac{1}{8}$ retire at age 55 with 20 years of tenure. Since all workers are retired by 57, it follows that $(\frac{1}{2})(\frac{3}{4}) = \frac{3}{8}$ of the labor force retire at age 56 with 21 years of tenure and that $(\frac{1}{2})(\frac{1}{4}) = \frac{1}{8}$ of the labor force retire at age 56 with 31 years of tenure. Given this information it is easy to calculate the expected level of tenure at retirement. In this case, it is

$$(\tfrac{3}{8})30 + (\tfrac{1}{8})20 + (\tfrac{3}{8})21 + (\tfrac{1}{8})31 = 25.5 \text{ years.}$$

The actual procedure is more complicated because there are many more age and tenure categories and because some workers take new jobs and others die. But the basic idea is the same. The procedure is applied to four groups: white males, white females, black males, and black females. The subset of the CPS sample analyzed consists of individuals who reported themselves either as retired or as currently working with valid information on job tenure, and who were from 55 to 76 years old.[2] The CPS reports whether individuals who are working are enrolled in a pension plan. We restricted the sample to those who were enrolled because there are large differences in employment status, tenure, and salary levels by pension enrollment.[3]

The next few pages begin with some definitions and describe the method used in more detail. The estimates are based on a counting algorithm and steady-state assumptions. Define marginal counts

$N(a,i)$: number of workers in the cross-section of age a who have i years of tenure.

$N(a,R)$: number age a who are retired.

and transition counts

$N_j(a,i)$: number of age a with tenure i who will have j years of tenure next year.

$N_R(a,i)$: number of age a with tenure i who retire during the year.

Ignoring unemployment, for transitions we have, for $i \geq 1$ either:

(1) $j = i + 1$: if the person remains on job

  (2) $j = 1$: if the person turns over and obtains a new job

(3) $j = R$: if the person retires between years.

Finally, define

$N_D(a,i)$: number aged a and tenure i who die before age $a + 1$.

The following accounting identities apply in a steady state:

$$N(a,i) = N_{i+1}(a,i) + N_1(a,i) + N_R(a,i) + N_D(a,i).$$

A person must go to one of the four mutually exclusive and exhaustive classifications. Further

$$N(a + 1, i + 1) = N_{i+1}(a,i).$$

Persons found with one more year of tenure in the following year must be those who transited to that state between years. And

$$N(a + 1, 1) = \sum_i N_1(a,i) + N_1(a,R).$$

People with one year of tenure are those who changed jobs or who came out of retirement. Similarly,

$$N(a + 1, R) = \sum_i N_R(a,i) + N_R(a,R).$$

Those observed retired in the next year either transited to that state during the year or were retired earlier and remained retired. Therefore

(1) $\quad N_R(a,i) = N(a,i) - N_{i+1}(a,i) - N_1(a,i) - N_D(a,i)$
$\qquad\qquad = N(a,i) - N(a + 1, i + 1) - N_1(a,i) - N_D(a,i).$

We seek to estimate $N_R(a,i)$. Both $N(a,i)$ and $N(a + 1, i + 1)$ are observed in the cross-section data. However, no data are available from a cross-section on transitions $N_1(.,.)$ or $N_D(.,.)$, so some assumptions are required to impute them.

Let $P(a,i)$ be the probability that a worker aged a with tenure i takes a new job and transits to state $i = 1$. Include R in the set $\{i\}$. Then

$$N_1(a,i) = P(a,i) N(a,i)$$

so

(2) $\qquad N(a + 1, 1) = \sum_i N_1(a,i) = \sum_i P(a,i)N(a,i).$

If there are A age groups and T tenure classes (2) represents $A - 1$ equations in $(A - 1)T$ unknown $P(a,i)$. The marginal counts $N(a,i)$ are not sufficient to estimate $P(a,i)$, and therefore $N_1(a,i)$, without additional restrictions on $P(a,i)$. We know from other studies (see Mincer and Jovanovic 1981) that P is decreasing in i and probably in a as well.

To make things simple and computationally tractable we assume that $P(a,i)$ takes the form

$$P(a,i) = (\alpha_0 + \alpha_1 a + \alpha_2 a^2 + \beta_1 i + \beta_2 i^2 + \delta ia)(1 - R) + R(\delta_0 + \delta_1 a),$$

where $R = 1$ if the person is retired and $R = 0$ if not.

Define $N(a) = \Sigma_{i=R} N(a,i)$ as the working population of age a and $N(a,R)$, as before, as those retired. Then, substituting for $P(a,i)$ in (2) and summing yields

$$
\begin{align}
(3) \quad N(a + 1, 1) = {} & \alpha_0 N(a) + \alpha_1[aN(a)] + \alpha_2[a^2N(a)] \\
& + \beta_1[\sum_i iN(a,i)] + \beta_2[\sum_i i^2N(a,i)] \\
& + \delta[a\sum_i iN(a,i)] + \delta_0 N(a,R) + \delta_1 aN(a,R).
\end{align}
$$

Treat (3) as a regression equation, in which the observed counts $N(a + 1, 1)$ are regressed on observed variables $N(a)$, $aN(a)$, . . ., etc. across age groups. There are eight unknown parameters in this regression, so if $A \geq 9$, this regression can be estimated.

In our data $A = 21$, so there are only 13 degrees of freedom. Therefore, the individual parameters $(\alpha, \beta, \lambda, \delta)$ are not estimated precisely. In addition some of the regressors are collinear. Nevertheless, we get unbiased estimates $\hat{P}(a,i)$. From these we obtain unbiased estimates of $N_1(a,i)$, from

$$\hat{N}_1(a,i) = \hat{P}(a,i)N(a,i).$$

A similar procedure works in general for estimates of $N_D(a,i)$. However, we find that the data are too thin to obtain meaningful results for the relationship between death probabilities conditional on both age and tenure. We therefore assume

$$\hat{N}_D(a,i) = P^*(a)N(a - 1, i)$$

where $P^*(a)$ is the 1979 age-specific death rate for this race-sex class. We know that there is a strong negative association between work and death so $\hat{N}_D(a,R)$ is likely to be biased from this procedure. The biases with respect to i are less clear-cut, though it is probable that $\hat{N}_D(a,i)$ for large i is upward biased, since people who are currently working and with long tenure are likely to be healthier than average.

From the identity above, $N_R(a,i)$ is estimated from

$$(4) \quad \hat{N}_R(a,i) = N(a,i) - N(a + 1, i + 1) - \hat{N}_1(a,i) - \hat{N}_D(a,i).$$

Now $\Sigma_i N_R(a,i)$ is the total number of people aged a who retire and $\Sigma_{ai}\Sigma N_R(a,i)$ is the total number who retire in the whole population at any age. Therefore,

$$(5) \quad n(a) = \Sigma_i N_R(a,i)/\Sigma\Sigma N_R(a,i)$$

is the probability of retiring at age a, given that death does not occur prior to retirement, and

$$(6) \qquad \Sigma_i \, an(a) = E(\text{age of retirement}) = Ea_R.$$

Similarly, $\Sigma_a \, N_R(a,i)$ is the number of people who retire after i years of tenure, so

$$(7) \qquad m(i) = \Sigma_a \, N_R(a,i)/\Sigma\Sigma \, N_R(a,i)$$

is the conditional probability of retiring at tenure i given that death occurs after retirement.

Therefore

$$(8) \qquad Ei_R = E(\text{tenure at retirement}) = \sum_i im(i).$$

Before turning to the estimates, some qualifications are in order.

1. If $\hat{N}_D$ is biased upward for larger i, then there is a downward bias in $m(i)$ for large i (and upward bias in $m(i)$ for small i). Therefore Ei_R is probably biased down on this account. However, this source of bias is likely to be small.

2. Even though the estimates of $N_R(a,i)$ are no doubt imprecise, the usual sampling theory suggests that $E(a)$ and $E(i)$ are better measures than any of their components, through the law of large numbers. Now if the pension formulas were linear in a and i, these means are sufficient statistics for our problem. However, these schemes are not linear. Therefore in predicting expected pensions and pension wealth from each plan, it would be preferable to take weighted averages across (a,i) pairs rather than taking the outcome for the average person. The preferred alternative is simply not feasible with these data.

3. The imputation procedure assumes no cohort effects. This is dictated by a cross-section since it is well known that cohort and age effects cannot be identified in a cross-section except through arbitrary assumptions. The formulas above make the strong steady state assumption that for $a < a'$ people who attain age a' at $(a' - a)$ periods in the future will behave "as if people age a' are behaving today (1979)."

We know that the age of retirement has shown a secular decline for males in the post–World War II period. Increasing wealth, changes in tax laws and in the social security system, as well as changes in family composition and yet other factors are all contributory causes. If these trends continue, then $E(a)$ is likely to be smaller in the future than our estimate: The average age of retirement for older cohorts in our sample was surely larger than our estimate. On the other hand, those issues are reversed for females, given the large increase in female labor force participation in recent decades. Since our estimates for females are conditioned on working, it is probable that cohort bias of this sort is far less important for women than for men.

The influence of cohort effects on expected tenure is less clear-cut. There are little data on secular changes in tenure on which to base an a priori judgment. If retirement continues to occur at younger ages this is likely to reduce tenure at retirement as well. However, the relation between age and tenure is noisy, so though there may be cohort bias in $E(i)$ qualitatively similar to that of $E(a)$, it is likely to be quantitatively smaller. Changing labor force behavior of women and conditioning on labor force participants again makes these considerations less important for women; if anything, the cohort bias for women tends to go in the opposite direction than for men.

4. This procedure is based on actual counts in the CPS tape for $N(a,i)$. If all cohorts were the same size, and if sample data reflected this exactly, then, on the usual synthetic cohort assumptions, everything works out correctly. However, some adjustments are necessary if either birth cohorts vary in size (which they do) or sample sizes vary randomly with age. The following approach, which is incorporated into the calculations, corrects the problem.

Define $N(a)$ as the total number of individuals in the sample of age a. We normalize everything in terms of $N(55)$. If this were a panel, then the difference between $N(55)$ and $N(56)$ reflects only deaths during the year. But in our synthetic panel, $N(56)$ may deviate from $N(55)$ because of real differences in cohort sizes or random sampling differences across age groups. However, death rates are known with accuracy, so an estimate of the corrected age 56 sample can be easily obtained. In fact, $P^*(a)$, defined above, does exactly that. Thus, as an initial condition set

$$\hat{N}(56) = N(55)[1 - P^*(55)].$$

Then the following recursion applies for $a > 56$

$$\hat{N}(a) = \hat{N}(a - 1)[1 - P^*(a - 1)].$$

The ratio of $N(a)/\hat{N}(a) = \lambda(a)$ reflects random sampling size or cohort size differences. To correct our estimates for these factors, it is necessary only to divide all $\hat{N}_R(a,i)$ by $\lambda(a)$. Then equations (5)–(8) follow as written.

This discussion points to another possible source of bias that we have ignored, nonretirement transitions out of the labor force. This is likely to lead to relatively small error for the aged population we study here because these transitions are relatively minor among older workers.

5. In the data actually used we identify 21 age classes, $a = 55, \ldots,$ 75, and 54 tenure classes, $i = 1, \ldots, 54$. Since the sample consists of some 1,600+ persons, many of the $N(a,i)$ cells are very small, and

many are empty. To deal with this problem we aggregated across tenure intervals and then interpolated tenure-specific totals by regression: In particular, define

$$x(a,I_j) = \sum_{i \, \epsilon I_j} \hat{N}_R(a,i).$$

After inspection of the raw cells, 11 such sums were defined for each age: $I_1 = (1)$, $I_2 = (2,6)$, $I_3 = (7,11)$, $I_4 = (12,16)$, $I_5 = (17,21)$, $I_6 = (22,26)$, $I_7 = (27,31)$, $I_8 = (32,36)$, $I_9 = (37,41)$, $I_{10} = (42,47)$, $I_{11} = (48,54)$. Define $\bar{I}_j$ as the midpoint in years of the jth I_j interval.

We fit the regression

$$(9) \quad x(a,I_j) = b_0 + b_1 a + b_2 a^2 + b_3 \bar{I}_j + b_4 \bar{I}_j^2 + b_5 \bar{I}_j a + b_6 B$$
$$+ \; b_7 F + b_8 D + b_9(aB) + b_{10}(aF) + b_{11}(D \cdot B) + b_{12}(D \cdot F)$$

to the aggregated data for purposes of smoothing and interpolation. The variables B for black, F for female, and D for $i = I_1$ are dummies. Then

$$N_R^*(a,i) = \hat{b}_0 + \hat{b}_1 a + \hat{b}_2 a^2 + \hat{b}_3 i + \hat{b}_4 i^2 + \hat{b}_5 ia$$

was used to calculate the distributions $n(a)$ and $m(i)$ used for our estimates of Ei_R and Ea_r above. Appendix A reports the regression in (9).

The estimates are contained in table 11.1.

Expected age of retirement of persons covered by private pensions is remarkably uniform across race and sex groups. Remember that these numbers are conditioned on labor force participants as well as pension eligibility. This explains the lack of appreciable differences between males and females. While older females are far less likely to participate in labor market activity than males, those that do participate show average retirement ages that are similar to those of men. In fact, Ea_R is slightly larger for women. Since estimated Ea_R is close to the early retirement age under social security, the somewhat larger value for women may reflect known smaller coverage and experience under

Table 11.1   Estimated Age, Tenure and Salary at Retirement

	$\hat{E}a_R$	$\hat{E}i_R$	ES
White:			
Male	62.1	22.0	$17,970
Female	63.2	21.8	11,414
Black:			
Male	63.0	15.3	13,194
Female	65.9	16.8	10,754

Thus the older individuals in the sample who were working found it in their interest not to retire because their wage prospects were evidently larger than their opportunity cost of leisure. People who continue to work are generally healthier than average and many have superior earnings prospects, so the observed wages of older-than-average workers in our sample are likely to be larger than the wage prospects available to workers of these ages who chose not to work. Therefore expected salary at age of retirement calculated above probably is too large for the average worker.

11.2 Pension Values of the Typical Retirees

Given the information in table 11.1, the pension of these typical retirees can be calculated from information on pension benefit formulas. The information used comes from a data set generated by Lazear (1983). A description follows.

The data for Lazear's analysis were constructed using the Bankers' Trust *Corporate Pension Plan Study (1980)*. The study consists of a detailed verbal description of the pension plans of over 200 of the nation's largest corporations. The data set applies to approximately 10 million workers, and this comprises about one-fourth of the entire covered population. The major empirical task was to convert the verbal descriptions into machine-readable data. This required setting up a coding system that was specific enough to capture all of the essential detail associated with each plan. It was then necessary to write a program which calculates the present value of pension benefits at each age of retirement.

Pension benefit formulas are of three different types. The two most common fall under the rubric of defined benefit plans, which specifies the pension flow as a fixed payment determined by some formula. The *pattern plan* awards the recipient a flat dollar amount per year worked prior to retirement. The *conventional plan* calculates the pension benefit flow from a formula which depends upon years of service and some average or final salary. In contrast to the defined benefit plans are defined contribution plans in which the employer (or employee) contributes a specified amount each year during work life to a pension fund. The flow of pension benefits that the worker receives upon retirement is a function of the market value of that fund. The defined contribution plan is much less frequently used than is either the pattern plan or conventional plan. Only defined benefit plans are used here.

Some plans do not permit the individual to receive early retirement benefits or only permit early retirement up to a given number of years before the normal date. This means that in order to perform the necessary comparisons, some plans had to be deleted because age or tenure values in table 11.1 violated restrictions of the plan. Less than 15% of plans were deleted for this reason.

Most plans have restrictions on the maximum amount which can be accrued, and many provide for minimum benefits. Additionally, a number reduce pension benefits by some fraction of the social security benefits to which some basic class is entitled. Moreover, a number of plans provide supplements for retirement before the social security eligibility age. Sometimes these supplements relate directly to social security payments; at other times they depend upon the individual's salary or benefit level. Other restrictions have to do with vesting requirements, with the maximum age at which the individual begins employment, and with the minimum number of years served before the basic accrual or particular supplements are applicable. The accrual rate, or flat dollar amount per year to which the individual is entitled, is often a nonlinear function of tenure and salary, and these kinks had to be programmed into the calculations.

This permits computation of the flow of retirement income in each of these plans, for each of the four typical workers. To get present values of the pension flows, a 10% discount factor was used. Finally, in performing the actuarial correction, it was necessary to choose a life table. The 1979 United States Vital Statistics tables were used. The choice of table turns out to be the least crucial part of the analysis. Values do not vary greatly from year to year, and discounting makes unimportant whatever small differences there are among tables.

Each of our four typical individuals was run through 172 of the plans for which qualification criteria were met. The expected present value of retirement benefits (in date of retirement dollars) was estimated for each of those individuals in each of the plans. Table 11.2 provides some summary statistics on the results of that simulation.

Table 11.2   **Pension Present Value for Typical Retiree (All Pensions)**
                  ($N = 172$)

Group	Mean	Expected Pension*	S.D.	Max	Med	Min
White males	$30,284	$18,412	$17,860	$142,111	$28,422	$862
White females	23,527	11,340	11,152	87,193	22,000	833
Black males	17,396	9,550	9,545	78,342	16,067	833
Black females	15,997	6,558	8,771	59,723	15,105	740

*Expected pension is defined as the raw probability (from table 11.6) times the mean pension.

11.3 Results

There are a number of interesting findings that come from this analysis. Let us turn first to the question that was posed at the outset, namely, does pension wealth exacerbate inequality? Recall that there are two aspects to the question. The first relates to the probability that a worker in a given demographic category has a pension; the second regards the expected pension value for pension plan participants. The first was investigated by using the CPS data to estimate a linear probability model. In table 11.6, the dependent variable is a dummy equal to one if the individual in question participates in a private pension plan. The sample consists of all working individuals between 55 and 76 years old with tenure reported.

A look at the coefficients in table 11.6 makes it appear as if blacks and females do not differ from white males in terms of their probabilities of participation in a pension plan. (Both coefficients are essentially zero.) Appearances are deceiving because earnings are held constant. Earnings have a strong positive association with pensions, and since blacks and females have lower earnings than white males, most of the difference can be accounted for by differences in earnings. While women and blacks who earn the same wages as white males are likely to enjoy the same pension participation status, women and blacks are unlikely to earn the same amount as white men.

The more important statistic for this analysis is the raw probability of participation in a pension plan. Those probabilities are reported in table 11.6 as well. White males have the highest probability of participating in a pension plan while other groups, especially black women, are substantially behind. These probabilities will play an important role in the subsequent discussion.

To examine the second question, namely, how do pensions vary among participants by race and sex, we call on the information in tables 11.2–11.5. First, compare the first and last columns of table 11.5.

The first column reports the ratio of pension value means from table 11.2 for the relevant group so that the first entry is 23,527/30,284. The fifth column reports the ratio of salary means from table 11.1 so the first entry is 11,414/17,970.

Table 11.3   **Pension Present Value for Typical Retiree Defined Benefit Pattern Plans ($N = 48$)**

Group	Mean	S.D.	Max	Med	Min
White males	$23,277	$6,822	$40,483	$23,724	$ 4,486
White females	22,318	6,502	39,105	22,459	4,333
Black males	15,067	4,280	26,612	15,000	13,750
Black females	15,110	4,285	26,817	15,105	3,110

Table 11.4   **Pension Present Value for Typical Retiree Defined Benefit Conventional Plans (N = 124)**

Group	Mean	S.D.	Max	Med	Min
White males	$32,991	$20,042	$142,111	$31,264	$862
White females	24,032	12,520	87,193	22,000	833
Black males	18,260	10,833	78,342	16,523	833
Black females	16,342	8,899	59,723	15,105	740

Table 11.5   **Ratios of Means**

	Pension Values and Final Salary				
Groups	All	Pattern	Conventional	Expected Pension (ALL)	Final Salary
White female/white male	.776	.958	.728	.615	.635
Black male/white male	.574	.647	.553	.518	.734
Black female/white female	.679	.677	.680	.578	.942
Black female/white male	.919	1.002	.894	.687	.815

NOTE: Black male pattern/white male conventional = .456. Black female pattern/white female conventional = .628.

First consider black males and white males. The second row of table 11.5 is relevant. Note that the ratio of the mean salary at retirement for these groups is .734 and that the ratio of pension benefits is .574. If workers were distributed randomly across the plans (which they are not), then the existence of pensions would tend to increase black/white male inequality. This is true for two reasons. First, as reported earlier, blacks are less likely to have pensions than whites. Second, given that black males do receive a pension, they receive a considerably smaller amount in pension benefits than whites. A measure that combines both aspects is the ratio of expected pension, defined as the ratio of the mean pension times the raw probabilities from table 11.6. That number is reported in the fourth column as .518 so pensions appear to exacerbate inequality. (Recall, however, that results for blacks are not robust to specification.) The magnitudes, although not astronomical, are not trivial either. For white males, the present value of pension wealth averages somewhat less than 2 years' income. For black males, the average value of pension wealth is somewhat less than 1 year of income.

Because of the significant salary differences, conventional plans, which base the pension on final salary, exacerbate the black/white male differences. Tables 11.3 and 11.4 split the sample of plans into pattern and conventional plans. The second column of table 11.5 reports the ratios of means given in table 11.3 and the third column reports the ratios of means from table 11.4.

Table 11.6   **Probability of Participation in a Private Pension Plan**

Variable	Coefficient	Standard Error
Constant	1.559	.121
Annual earnings (1000s)	.01856	.00098
Black	−.0019	.0298
Female	.0035	.0186
Age	−.0205	.0019

Raw probabilities of participation:

White males   = .608
White females = .482
Black males   = .549
Black females = .410

A comparison of column 3 with column 1 in table 11.5 reveals that the ratios in the third column are smaller for all groups that do not include black females, because salary levels are important for computation of conventional pension plans. Black males who have conventional plans are at even more of a disadvantage relative to white males in the same plans because their earnings are lower. Perhaps more important is that blacks and whites are unlikely to be found in similar proportions in the two plan types. Pattern plans are more typical for production workers, whereas the conventional plan is the norm for management and white-collar workers. To the extent that blacks are overrepresented among pattern plans, pension inequality is even more pronounced. At the extreme, if all black males had pattern plans and all white males had conventional plans, then the ratio of the pension value means would be .456, whereas salary ratios are .734.

The findings for black females and white females are even more striking. The salary column of table 11.5 reveals that the ratio of black to white female salary is .942, whereas the ratio of pension value is only .679. If all white females were in conventional plan occupations and all black females were in pattern plan occupations, the pension inequality would be even greater. That ratio would be .628 instead of .679. The reason for the difference is that conventional plans are generally more lucrative than pattern plans, except at very low salary levels. Similarly, the ratio of expected pension for these groups is .578, implying even greater inequality because black females are less likely to be enrolled in a pension plan at all. No matter how we measure it, pensions appear to increase black/white inequality relative to that estimated by salary measures.

The male/female comparisons are less clear-cut. Effects go in opposite directions. As reported above, female workers are less likely to be enrolled in a pension plan than male workers, but if they are enrolled, the white females do well relative to their male counterparts. The first row of table 11.5 contains the relevant information. The ratio of final salary of white females to white males is .635 whereas the ratio of pension values is .776. This implies an equalizing effect of pension benefits. Part of this results from the fact that defined benefit plans are not sex-specific, so that women, with longer life expectancies, do better than men. But this cannot account for the large difference between .776 and .635.

The reason why women do so well in pension benefits can best be understood by examining the distinction between pattern and conventional plans. Note that women are almost on par with men in terms of pension benefits received in pattern plans. This results from one factor: Pattern plans depend only on years of service, and in that respect, the women who are working at age 55 are quite similar to men. This large value of tenure maps into high pension flows in the pattern plan. (Because of the actuarial unfairness of the plan, it could actually have gone the other way. Since tenure levels are close to comparable, the longer life expectancy of females could have made their pattern plan pensions worth more than those of males.)

The equalizing effect of pensions is offset almost exactly by the fact that fewer women than men are enrolled in pension plans. From table 11.6, white men had a probability of receiving a pension of .608, whereas white women had a probability of .482. It is useful, therefore, to compare expected pensions. The ratio of expected pension for white females to white males is .615 from the last column of table 11.5. Thus, pensions leave white female/white male wealth inequality unaltered.

The same pattern is displayed for blacks. The black female's final salary is 81% that of the black male in this sample, and the mean black female's pension benefit is 92% of the mean black male's pension. But expected pension ratios tell the opposite story. Since black females are much less likely to be pension recipients, the ratio of expected pension benefits is .687. Thus, pensions increase male/female inequality substantially among blacks.

This conclusion is strengthened somewhat when it is recalled that these women are not a random sample of the overall population of women. Since a larger proportion of women will have dropped out of the labor force before reaching age 55, and since it is likely that those individuals have very small pension wealth, the numbers presented in the last paragraph tend to understate the disequalizing effect of pensions in the overall economy.

Other interesting findings are worthy of discussion. Most obvious is that there is much more variation in the benefits provided by conventional plans than in those provided by pattern plans. A comparison of tables 11.3 and 11.4 is instructive. For all four groups, the standard deviation is much larger for conventional plans. Similarly, with the exception of white males, medians are about the same across plan types, but the maximum and minimum values are much more extreme in the case of conventional plans.

Variance in pension benefits received in conventional plans depends on two factors. The first is that for a given salary, companies differ substantially more in their conventional pension formulas than in their pattern plan formulas. Second, a positive correlation between the firm's average salary and generosity of the pension formula contributes variance to benefits received. Although it is conceivable that the two types of variation will offset one another, it is unlikely. There is already some evidence of a positive correlation between average salary in the firm and the generosity of pension benefits (see Asch [1984] and the salary coefficients in table 11.6).

Before concluding, we should mention that another study addresses the same questions as we do but obtains somewhat different results. McCarthy and Turner (1984) find that blacks actually have higher pensions than whites do, both in terms of pension flow and pension wealth (see their table 1). They use the Survey of Private Pension Benefit Amounts, a data set that permits pairing of individuals with the actual pensions they receive. On the face of it, this data set is superior to those that we have used. But their findings leave some grounds for doubt on that score. In particular, it is difficult to believe that blacks have higher pensions than whites because even in the group of pension plan participants, the average final salary of a black male is only 63.5% of the white male (see our table 11.5). Since many pension plans depend on final salary, even if tenure at retirement did not differ between groups, the pension flow ratio would mirror the salary ratio. It is important to reconcile the two sets of results, but McCarthy and Turner are unable to make their data available to the public, so their results cannot be replicated.

11.4 Conclusion

The existence of pension plans appears to contribute to black/white inequality but leaves male/female inequality unchanged among whites. Even though females are less likely to receive pensions than males, those females who do receive pensions tend to receive relatively generous ones. Of course, the average pension that the typical retiring female receives is well below that received by the typical male retiree. But the difference is not as pronounced as male/female differences in salary. Among blacks, pensions exacerbate sex differences, mainly because black women are only about 75% as likely to receive pensions as black males.

Appendix
Regression Results

Var	Eq. (9)	Eq. (10)			
Dep. Var.	$= X(a,I_j)$	White Male Earnings	White Female Earnings	Black Male Earnings	Black Female Earnings
Constant	−12.80	66,077	13,777	28,493	214,280
	(8.59)	(61,992)	(40,979)	(121,344)	(351,051)
a (age)	.488	−1,199	−102	−404	−6,738
	(.262)	(2,028)	(1,377)	(3,900)	(11,913)
a^2(age^2)	−.0043	5.47	−.24	1.34	54.6
	(.0020)	(16.5)	(10.8)	(31)	(101)
$\bar{I}_j$ (tenure)	−.0570	279	305	441	327
	(.0484)	(104)	(77)	(261)	(262)
$\bar{I}_j^2$ (tenure^2)	−.00021	−1.82	−3.38	−8.17	−7.45
	(.00034)	(2.48)	(2.01)	(5.91)	(6.85)
$\bar{I}_j a$	.00092				
	(.00068)				
B	−2.96				
	(1.41)				
F	−1.69				
	(1.41)				
D	.556				
	(.445)				
aB	.038				
	(.021)				
aF	.024				
	(.021)				
$(D)(B)$	−.258				
	(.457)				
$(D)(F)$	−.613				
	(.457)				
df	911	937	509	65	42
R^2	.038	.077	.112	.074	.076
Mean of dependent variable:		18,855	10,397	13,857	10,206

Notes

1. E.g., see are Lillard (1977), Rosen (1977), Lazear (1979), and Lillard and Willis (1978).

2. We ignore those who retire earlier than 55 because it is likely that only a very small number of workers with pensions retire before age 55.

3. For example, not enrolled black women earn an average of $3,471 per year, whereas enrolled black women earn $10,206.

4. Note that although the earnings regressions are imprecise, the estimates derived from them and used in table 11.1 are close to the unconditional mean for each group.

References

Banker's Trust Company. 1980. *1980 study of corporate pension plans*. New York: Banker's Trust.

Lazear, Edward P. 1979. The narrowing of black-white wage differentials is illusory. *American Economic Review* 69:553–64.

———. 1983. Pensions as severance pay. In *Financial aspects of the United States pension system*, ed. Zvi Bodie and John Shoven. Chicago: University of Chicago Press.

Lillard, Lee A. 1977. Inequality: Earnings vs. human wealth. *American Economic Review* 67:42–53.

Lillard, Lee A., and Willis, Robert. 1978. Dynamic aspects of earnings mobility. *Econometrica* 46:985–1012.

McCarthy, David, and Turner, John A. 1984. Earnings comparisons and race-gender differences in private pension benefits. Washington: United States Department of Labor. Mimeographed.

Mincer, Jacob, and Jovanovic, Boyan. 1981. Labor mobility and wages. In *Studies in labor markets*, ed. Sherwin Rosen. Chicago: University of Chicago Press.

Rosen, Sherwin. 1977. Human capital: A survey of empirical research. In *Research in labor economics*, ed. R. Ehrenberg. Greenwich, CT: JAI Press.

Comment   Sylvester J. Schieber

The question that Lazear and Rosen address here is whether private sector pensions exacerbate compensation inequality across groups—specifically by race and gender. There are two aspects to consider. First, the probability of receiving a pension is not random across groups. The second aspect is conditional on receiving a pension and whether systematic variation exists in benefit amounts received based on race or gender. The authors focus on the latter.

Organizationally, Lazear and Rosen undertake their analysis in two stages. They first determine the average age, tenure, and salary char-

Sylvester J. Schieber is director of The Research and Information Center of the Wyatt Company.

acteristics at retirement for each race-gender group on the basis of the age, tenure, and salary characteristics estimated in the first stage. They then estimate the pension that each group prototype person would receive under 172 different pension plans. They use the results of this exercise to assess the distributional effects of pensions.

The first stage of their paper is an interesting exercise in adapting data to an analytical problem for which appropriate, straightforward data generally are not available. I refrain from commenting on the mechanics of this segment of the paper because I think the generated results are inappropriate for addressing the question of the role pensions play in distributing income. I concur with the view that pensions may exacerbate wage inequality, but they are more likely to do so on a coverage than a benefit structure basis. Lazear and Rosen did not address the pension coverage, participation, and benefit receipt issue, but it is well known that pension participation rates are significantly lower at the bottom of the earnings than at mid-or-upper earnings levels. To have ignored this aspect of the question is a general limitation that weakens the remaining analysis.

In the estimates of final average salary/age/tenure characteristics for each of the race-gender groups shown in Lazear and Rosen's table 11.1, the authors include pension plan participants and those not enrolled in pension plans. Their reported estimate found that blacks' tenure in their terminal job was less than half that of whites—11 years versus 23 years. They estimated that the terminal salaries varied significantly by race and gender. For example, white males' final salaries were estimated to be about two-thirds higher than those of both white women and black men. At the same time, while estimated black males' final salaries were roughly equal to those of white women, they were about twice those of black women.

My concern is that the authors' tenure and salary estimates tend to exaggerate differences that might exist across the groups studied. The classes of workers participating in pension plans are more homogeneous at or near retirement than the authors' analysis suggests. To illuminate this point, I have looked at the same 55–75-year-old workers from the May 1979 Current Population Survey that Lazear and Rosen used in their analysis. Consider, for example, the difference in the percentage of each relevant race-gender group working full-time by whether or not the group was participating in a pension plan. Table 11.C.1 shows that, across the four groups studied, pension participants consistently were more likely to be working full time. Also, there was only one-third the variation in the percentage of pension participants, compared to nonparticipants, working full time.

Though full-time employment status is not a precondition for participation in a pension plan, table 11.C.2 does indicate that a strong cor-

Table 11.C.1   **Pension Participation Status of 55 to 75 Year-Old Full-time Workers**

	Percent Working Full Time		
	All Workers	Pension Non Participants	Pension Participants
White Males	86.3%	76.4%	96.1%
White Females	66.7	53.9	83.3
Black Males	82.5	69.9	92.1
Black Females	55.1	37.2	84.0

SOURCE: May 1979 Current Population Survey

Table 11.C.2   **Pension Participation 55 to 75 Year Old Workers**

	Percent Participating in a Pension Plan	
	Part-time Workers	Full-time Workers
White Males	14.5%	56.0%
White Females	21.9	54.4
Black Males	25.9	63.5
Black Females	13.7	58.5

SOURCE: May 1979 Current Population Survey

Table 11.C.3   **Estimated Final Job Tenure and Median Attained Tenure of Workers Aged 55 to 75 by Pension Participation Status**

	EiR	Pension Nonparticipants*	Pension Participants*
White Males	23.1	11.1	19.5
White Females	22.9	6.3	13.8
Black Males	10.8	10.6	21.0
Black Females	10.6	7.2	16.2

*SOURCE: May 1979 Current Population Survey

relation exists between full-time employment and participation status. Table 11.C.2 also suggests that the prevalence of pension participation among blacks actually exceeds that for whites among full-time workers within the age cohorts considered here. In any event, it is clear that from a pension participation perspective, far more homogeneity exists across the four groups of full-time workers than from full- to part-time workers in any combination.

The incentives built into pension plans to discourage worker turnover also differentiate pension participants from nonparticipants. Comparison of group median tenures in table 11.C.3 indicates that among older pension participants blacks have attained longer tenures than whites and men longer tenures than women. This is a different result than that suggested by the Lazear-Rosen estimates also shown in the table 11.C.3. Analyzing pension benefit distributions based on tenures that do not reflect reasonable periods of participation under the plans biases the results. The low tenure estimates for blacks from the Lazear-Rosen model used here would have significantly reduced the estimated benefits for blacks and inflated the relative benefits estimated for white women.

The other crucial variable for determining pension benefits under most defined benefit plans is final salary. The estimated final salaries from the Lazear-Rosen model are compared in table 11.C.4 to estimated median earnings derived from the May 1979 CPS. Again the model exaggerates the group salary differences across the racial groups when the Lazear-Rosen estimates are compared with median earnings levels of pension participants from the May 1979 CPS. It is only when white males are compared to white females that the relative differences in the two sets of estimates are similar. To the extent the model systematically underestimates final salaries of blacks, it also would tend to exaggerate the authors' conclusion that "the existence of pension plans contributes to black/white inequality."

Pension plan design is regulated by the Internal Revenue Code that limits the ability of plans to discriminate among participants on the basis of salary. A pension benefit structure that provides relatively higher benefits to upper-income beneficiaries can only do so within the strict confines of the IRS integration regulations. The regulations recognize social security's redistributive nature and allow an employer to take partial advantage of the relatively higher benefits provided to lower-wage workers by social security in designing the pension benefit formula. But in no case is the progressive structure of social security to be fully offset by the pension benefit structure. The result is that the combined benefit structure, even for highly integrated plans, should still be somewhat progressive. Only 11% of the final pay plans and 23% of the career average plans included in the Bankers' Trust Survey were not integrated. The mere existence of integrated plans, and especially their prevalence included in the Lazear-Rosen analysis, suggests that social security should be included in further analytic efforts of the distributional issues addressed here.

Table 11.C.4   **Estimated Final Salary and Median Earnings of Workers Aged 55 to 75 by Pension Participation Status**

	ES	Pension Nonparticipants*	Pension Participants*
White Males	$17,830	$9,663	$16,300
White Females	10,680	4,816	9,524
Black Males	10,118	6,119	12,501
Black Females	5,109	3,284	8,564

*Source: Derived from the May 1979 Current Population Survey.

In their simulation of pattern plans the authors assume the same worker age, tenure, and final salary variations across the race-gender groups that they used for their simulations of conventional plans. A basic characteristic of pattern plans is that they provide almost no variation in benefit levels across groups of workers with equal tenure. For such a benefit structure to be acceptable to a participant population, there usually would have to be minimal variation in final salaries under the plan. Otherwise the plan would play an inconsistent role in maintaining the standard of living for workers retiring under the plan. Most pattern plans operate in unionized settings where the ability to discriminate on the basis of gender or race for purposes of setting salaries is quite limited. In addition what salary discrimination that previously might have existed has been obviated by the Civil Rights Act of 1964.

Furthermore, pattern plans often have only a tenure requirement as the criteria for retirement eligibility prior to the normal retirement age specified in the plan. For example, the "30 and out" provisions in the UAW plans permit retirement with unreduced benefits at any age for workers with 30 years of service. The prevalence of such criteria means that many workers retiring under "30 and out" plans tend to have the full tenure needed to fulfill this provision. This phenomenon is accentuated because many of these plans include portability provisions that grant a worker credit for tenure under similar plans with other employers. So, an auto worker shifting from one firm to another will get credit from the second employer's plan for service under the first.

The combination of limited salary variation and relatively consistent tenure patterns under pattern plans tends to suppress variation in benefits. A more careful specification of the characteristics of individuals participating under both conventional and pattern plans would likely result in different comparative results than those presented in the Lazear-Rosen analysis.

The analysis conducted here should be expanded and refined in several regards. First, any analysis of the distributional effects of retirement programs certainly should include social security. Second, much more attention should be paid to the distributive effects that might arise because some workers do not participate in pension plans. Third, a more precise specification of attained age, tenure, and final salary characteristics under the various types of plans is critical for such an analysis. Finally, I think the basic question posed here can only be adequately addressed with better data. Regrettably, such data exist at the Department of Labor but will probably never be made available for public use.

Contributors

B. Douglas Bernheim
Department of Economics
Stanford University
Stanford, CA 94305

Zvi Bodie
School of Management
Boston University
704 Commonwealth Avenue
Boston, MA 02115

Michael J. Boskin
Department of Economics
Stanford University
Stanford, CA 94305

Jeremy I. Bulow
Graduate School of Business
Stanford University
Stanford, CA 94305

Thomas A. Gustafson
Department of Health and Human
   Services
ASPE/ISP
Room 410E Humphrey Building
200 Independence Avenue S.W.
Washington, DC 20201

Alan L. Gustman
Department of Economics
Dartmouth College
Hanover, NH 03755

R. Glenn Hubbard
Department of Economics
Northwestern University
Andersen Hall, Room 234
2003 Sheridan Road
Evanston, IL 60201

Michael Hurd
Department of Economics
State University of New York at
   Stony Brook
Stony Brook, NY 11794

Laurence J. Kotlikoff
National Bureau of Economic
   Research
1050 Massachusetts Avenue
Cambridge, MA 02138

Edward P. Lazear
Graduate School of Business
University of Chicago
1101 East 58th Street
Chicago, IL 60637

Jay O. Light
Harvard Business School
Soldiers Field Road
Boston, MA 02163

Alan J. Marcus
School of Management
Boston University
704 Commonwealth Avenue
Boston, MA 02215

Robert C. Merton
Sloan School of Management
Massachusetts Institute of
   Technology
Cambridge, MA 02139

Olivia S. Mitchell
168 Ives—NYSSILR
Cornell University
Ithaca, NY 14853

Randall Mørck
School of Management
Boston University
704 Commonwealth Avenue
Boston, MA 02215

André F. Perold
Department of Finance
Harvard Business School
Boston, MA 02163

Sherwin Rosen
Department of Economics
University of Chicago
1126 East 59th Street
Chicago, IL 60637

Michael Rothschild
Department of Economics, D-008
University of California, San
   Diego
La Jolla, CA 92093

Sylvester J. Schieber
Director Research and Information
   Center
Wyatt Company
1990 K Street N.W.
Washington, DC 20006

Myron S. Scholes
Graduate School of Business
Stanford University
Stanford, CA 94305

William F. Sharpe
Graduate School of Business
Stanford University
Stanford, CA 94305

John B. Shoven
Department of Economics
Stanford University
Stanford, CA 94305

Avia Spivak
Department of Economics
University of Pennsylvania
Philadelphia, PA 19104

Lawrence Summers
Department of Economics
Harvard University
Cambridge, MA 02138

Robert A. Taggart, Jr.
School of Management
Boston University
704 Commonwealth Avenue
Boston, MA 02215

David A. Wise
JFK School of Government
Harvard University
79 Boylston Street
Cambridge, MA 02138

Author Index

367

Subject Index

372   Subject Index

113; economic well-being of, 114; financial status of, 1; income of, 6–8, 113, 116; leisure for, 121; older workers, 332; replacement rates, 115; retirement income, 6–8; savings and, 237; taxes and, 6; well-being of, 113. *See also* Age; Medicare; Social Security

Employee Retirement Income Security Act (ERISA), 2, 21, 49, 51; nondiscrimination provisions, 172; pension obligation and, 83

Equilibrium models, 108, 189

Equity, value of, 66, 108

ERISA. *See* Employee Retirement Income Security Act

Estates. *See* Bequests

European option, 50, 153

Event study approach, 98

Excess plan, 149, 167

Exercise price, 54, 56–57

Explicit contract model, 108

Exploitative strategy, 67

Factor prices, 213

Families, 203, 220, 222–25, 232, 270; annuitization through, 272; family deals, 214, 218; uncertainties and, 235. *See also* Intergenerational transfers

Family insurance solution, 216

FASB. *See* Financial Accounting Standards Board

Feldstein-Mørck equation, 92

Females. *See* Women

Financial Accounting Standards Board (FASB), 22, 78, 93; data, 23–24, 44; statement, 36

Financial slack effects. *See* Slack effects

Finite-period model, 77

Fixed benefit plans, 34

Fixed income securities, 17

Flat benefit plans, 34, 315

Floor levels, 156, 158–59, 161

Fortune 100 firms, 6, 52, 66

Funding levels: asset mix and, 44; bond ratings and, 31; profitability and, 30, 41; retirement level and, 46; risk and, 31; RONA and, 28; size and, 39. *See also* Overfunding; Underfunding

Graded vesting, 338

Graduated premium rate, 5

Greenwich Research Associates, 24, 37

Growth rate, 278

Growth variables, 92

Health care: benefits, 85; costs of, 6, 121. *See also* Medicare

Hedonic equation, 92

Hourly workers, 34

Households, 260; annuities and, 253; composition of, 123, 240; portfolio allocation, 184; sample selection, 245

Household work, 120

Housing, 238–39, 251–52; owner-occupied, 271

Human capital, 203

Implicit contracting, 84–85; model for, 108

Incentive effects, 1, 7, 10, 276, 283–340

Income, 213; of elderly, 6–8, 113, 116; generational transfer, 202, 208, 217, 270; required levels, 115; Social Security and, 199. *See also* Wealth

Indexation, 266; integration and, 167

Individual Retirement Account (IRA), 3, 17, 50, 203

Industry: accrual rates, 302

Inequality analysis, 341

Infinite-horizon model, 214

Inflation 82, 332; adjustments for, 24; illusion hypothesis, 100; impact of, 1; Modigliani-Cohn hypothesis, 100; price-level uncertainty, 167; rate of, 160, 273, 338; risks of, 46

Inheritance. *See* Bequests

Insurance: alternative arrangements, 227–32; bargaining, 217; environments for, 214; fair market value, 6; family insurance solution, 216; longevity, 8, 117; maturity date, 53; model of, 52–60; perfecting, 212; put options and, 3, 50; risk pooling, 212; value of, 66. *See also* Annuities; Pension Benefit Guaranty Corporation

Integrated plans, 7, 147–72; actuarial methods for, 167; aggregating benefits, 164; floor levels, 160; institutional tax and, 171; model of, 150; multiple employers, 165; optimal risk-bearing properties, 166; partial offset, 161; put option and, 154; risk-sharing, 171; skewed benefits and, 172; value to